For

Merylyn & Paul Hammond

with affection

Mark Perlman

15 February 2002

Editing Economics

'His editorship was courageous, liberal scholarship at its very best and his retirement from the role of editor should not, we believe, go unmarked by the profession, which is much in his debt'.

Letter from members of the American Economic Association, 9 June 1980.

Mark Perlman was the founding editor of the *Journal of Economic Literature* and responsible for issues from 1969 until 1980 when he retired. He has also written and edited a number of books and articles, concentrating on aspects of the labour market, population growth, health economics, the environment and the history of economics. His extraordinarily significant contribution to economics has been recognized by economists worldwide and in 2000 the History of Economics Society made him their Distinguished Fellow.

In this volume nineteen scholars have contributed chapters exploring the following themes:

I An evaluation of Mark Perlman's written contributions
 Kurt Dopfer

II Editing and intolerance in the profession
 Ingrid H. Rima and Paul A. Samuelson

III Economic, political and social systems
 Ewald Nowotny, Nicholas W. Balabkins, Charles McCann, Jr. and Ungsuh K. Park

IV History of economic theory
 Richard Swedburg and Arnold Heertje

V Economic theory
 Samuel C. Weston, Uwe Cantner, Horst Hanusch, John Komlos, Peter Salamon and Joseph E. Stiglitz

VI Applied economics
 Herbert Giersch, Hank Lim and James W. Dean

Hank Lim is Associate Professor of Economics and Statistics at the National University of Singapore. **Ungsuh K. Park** is President and CEO of Kohap Ltd., Korea. **G. C. Harcourt** is Emeritus Reader in the History of Economic Theory, Cambridge, Emeritus Fellow, Jesus College, Cambridge and Professor Emeritus, University of Adelaide.

Routledge Frontiers of Political Economy

Editing Economics

Essays in honour of Mark Perlman

Edited by
Hank Lim, Ungsuh K. Park
and G. C. Harcourt

London and New York

First published 2002
by Routledge
11 New Fetter Lane, London EC4P 4EE

Simultaneously published in the USA and Canada
by Routledge
29 West 35th Street, New York, NY 10001

Routledge is an imprint of the Taylor & Francis Group

Typeset in 10/12 AGaramond by
Newgen Imaging Systems (P) Ltd.
Printed and bound in Great Britain by
St Edmundsbury Press, Bury St Edmunds, Suffolk

British Library Cataloguing in Publication Data
A catalogue record for this book is available
from the British Library

Library of Congress Cataloging in Publication Data
Editing economics: essays in honour of Mark Perlman/[edited by] Hank Lim, Ungsuh
K. Park and G. C. Harcourt
      p. cm. — (Routledge frontiers of political economy; 37)
   Includes bibliographical references and index.
    1. Economics—History—20th century. I. Perlman, Mark, 1923-II. Lim, Hank. III. Park,
Ungsuh K. IV. Harcourt, Geoffrey Colin. V. Series.

HB87 .E35 2001
330—dc21   2001019669

ISBN 0–415–25677–1

Contents

Tables

Contributors

Nicholas W. Balabkins, Emeritus Professor of Economics, Lehigh University, Bethlehem, PA, USA.

Uwe Cantner, Professor of Economics, Friedrich-Schiller-Universität, Lehrstuhl für volkswirtschaftslehre/Mikroöknomik, Carl-Zeiβ-Str. 3, D-07743 Jena, Germany.

James W. Dean, Professor of Economics, Simon Fraser University, Burnaby, B.C., Canada and Kaiser Professor of International Business, Western Washington University, Bellingham, W.A., USA.

Kurt Dopfer, Professor of Economics, University of St. Gallen, Institute of Economics, St. Gallen, Switzerland.

Herbert Giersch, Professor of Economics, Kiel Institute of World Economics, D-24100 Kiel, Germany.

Horst Hanusch, Professor of Economics, Universität Augsburg, Augsburg, Germany.

G. C. Harcourt, Emeritus Reader in the History of Economic Theory, University of Cambridge; Emeritus Fellow, Jesus College, Cambridge, UK and Professor Emeritus, University of Adelaide, South Australia.

Arnold Heertje, Professor of History of Economic Thought, Faculty of Economics, University of Amsterdam, The Netherlands.

John Komlos, Professor of Economics and Chair of the Institute of Economic History, University of Munich, Germany.

Hank Lim, Associate Professor of Economics and Statistics, National University of Singapore, Singapore.

Charles R. McCann Jr., Research Associate, Department of Economics, University of Pittsburgh, USA.

Ewald Nowotny, University Professor, Wirtschaftsuniversität, Wien, Austria; Vice-President, European Investment Bank, Luxembourg.

Ungsuh K. Park, President, CEO, Kohap Ltd., Seoul, Korea.

Ingrid H. Rima, Professor of Economics, Temple University, USA and Distinguished Fulbright Professor of Economics, Peoples' Republic of China, 2000.

Peter Salamon, Professor of Mathematics, San Diego State University, USA.

Paul A. Samuelson, Institute Professor Emeritus, Massachusetts Institute of Technology, USA.

Joseph E. Stiglitz, Professor of Economics, Stanford University, USA.

Richard Swedberg, Professor of Sociology, Stockholm University, Sweden.

Samuel C. Weston, Professor of Economics, Department of Economics, University of Dallas, USA.

Preface

This volume, conceived originally by Hank Lim and Ungsuh K. Park and subsequently joined by Geoff Harcourt, has been several years in the making. We would like to thank the following for their help and support: first and foremost, Mark Perlman, not only for making the volume possible by being Mark Perlman, but also for much material help and advice, wise comments and for providing his bibliography; second, the contributors for their chapters and patience in what has been a long drawn out process; third, Routledge for their support of the project and agreement to publish the volume; fourth, Susan Cross for her efficient and cheerful expertise in putting the volume together to be sent to Routledge.

H. L., U. K. P., G. C. H.
September 2000

Acknowledgements

The editors' and the publishers' thanks are due to Springer-Verlag GmbH and Co KG for permission to reprint 'The participant observer in the formation of economic thought: Summa Oeconomiae Perlmanensis' by Kurt Dopfer which was published in the *Journal of Evolutionary Economics*, vol. 8, 1998, 139–156.

Introduction*

Hank Lim, Ungsuh K. Park and G. C. Harcourt

Mark Perlman is an original. He cannot be classified under any particular heading or regarded as belonging to any particular school. He reflects his upbringing and experiences, as we all do, but he has used these to mould a unique and attractive philosophy of life and economics. Mark is a down-to-earth realist, as is to be expected of someone who served in the Second World War, but he combines his healthy scepticism with noble ideals, most of all, the priority which he gives to teaching and his liberal, open-minded attitude to the work of people with whom he does not agree. His knowledge of our discipline, of philosophy, and of history and institutions, is encyclopaedic. Though he has not often practised high theory himself, his powerful conceptual grasp allows him to make balanced and informed judgements about its achievements and worth in other people's writings. This, and his unsurpassed knowledge of the issues in our discipline since its inception, made his appointment as the founding editor of the *Journal of Economic Literature* an inspired choice. The character of his *Selected Essays*, Perlman (1996), shows what substantial contributions his own writing in many areas are to modern economics. But we suspect that he would agree that even more, his teaching and his role as editor of the *Journal of Economic Literature*, and of the many volumes associated with his name, may be even more significant when the definitive history of the economics of the twentieth and twenty-first centuries is written.

Mark is a strong character with definite, explicit and articulate views. Any harshness is more than offset by his warmth, loyalty and affection for friends, colleagues and pupils (overlapping sets, of course). Excellent company, a generous host, in partnership in this, as in his intellectual contributions, with Naomi, he is rightly held in esteem and affection in equal measure by the profession.

Mark was born in 1927 in Madison, Wisconsin, the younger son of the distinguished labour historian, Selig Perlman who was teaching at the University of Wisconsin, and Eva Shaber. His mother died when he was six (his elder brother was ten). His father married her younger sister and they had two daughters. Mark was much influenced by his father who taught and discussed all manner of things with him, but he never went through a rebellion akin to that of another famous father and son relationship in economics, the Mills. Selig Perlman died when Mark was 35 years old. Selig Perlman's approach to economics and social science generally was that of an episodic institutionalism with which was allied scepticism, especially concerning deductive theory. Certainly Mark's own work and attitudes reflect those characteristics but they are by no means a carbon copy of his father's approach.

Mark went to school in Wisconsin in an environment which was not that friendly to an intelligent Jewish boy who was not good at games. Here is his response to his math(s) teacher who accused him of arrogance – of a very high order. 'Mrs Cowles: for a guy who's chosen last for every sports team and who hears those who have to carry him on their team groan, I tell you that my problem isn't arrogance; this is just not the word you're groping for' [Perlman 1996, n. 18: 32].

His tertiary education was interrupted by over three years of war service. He never expected to survive the war, for two reasons. First, following 'one intellectually splendid year at Cardiff, Wales, High School for Boys' in 1938–9 [Perlman 1996: 3], a year which he otherwise thoroughly enjoyed,[1] he became aware of the Nazi threat to Jews everywhere. Only when Pearl Harbour occurred and the US came into the war did Mark think that the Nazi threat might be overcome. For himself, the second reason why he thought he would not survive was his lack of ability to be a soldier, his 'size and physical ineptitude', as he put it [Perlman 1996: 2].

But he did survive and he tells a sad tale about Paul Douglas in relation to this. Perlman had obtained Baccalaureate and Master's degrees from Wisconsin by 1947 – he started in 1941 but there were the interruptions of the war years – and he was trying to decide whether to go to Chicago for doctorate work. He had lunch with Douglas who was going through a vicious stage of extreme cold-warism and anti-communism. He asked Mark whether he would be willing to fight the Russians. Mark sensibly said 'no', feeling he had done his bit against the Germans. To which Douglas responded bitterly: 'You're one of those Jewish intellectuals who talk but don't fight. Are you a communist like your father?' Perlman admits to replying aggressively, saying 'Look who is calling whom a communist. Professor Douglas, when you reviewed his *A Theory of the Labor Movement* in the late 1920s, you attacked him because he wasn't and you were' [Perlman 2000, n. 16: 81].

The result was that Mark did not go to Chicago for this stage of his education, despite a warm welcome from Milton Friedman at the same time. He went instead to Princeton for a year as an instructor. There, he sat in on courses by Jacob Viner, 'who in his aggressive way was very kind to [him]' [Perlman 1996: 3–4], and Frank Dunstone Graham. He also learnt much from conversations with Ainsley Cole and Harvey Leibenstein, 'one of the few authentic near-geniuses of [his] cohort', [Perlman 1996: 5].[2] In 1945 Perlman went to Columbia for his PhD and 'began [his] courtship of Naomi Waxman', [Perlman 1996: 6]. He survived George Stigler's attempt to plough him in the theory generals. (He and Stigler subsequently became good friends and it was on Stigler's recommendation to Milton Friedman that Mark became the founding editor of the *Journal of Economic Literature*.)[3]

His PhD dissertation was on Australian labour relations and the roles of the law and lawyers and judges in them. It resulted in his first book, *Judges in Industry: A Study in Labour Arbitration in Australia*, Perlman (1954), the start of a lasting association with Australia and the start also of one of Mark's many friendships, in this case with Mr Justice John Vincent Barry, 'the great intellectual friendship of [his] life', Perlman [1996: 8]. Barry was 'an indefatigable letter writer' and matched Mark 'letter for letter ... Marvellously organised and brilliant ... a wonderful challenger of most of [Mark's] conservative views ... From 1950 until his death in 1969, [Mark] participated in a weekly debate with the best-read man, ... the man with the most catholic knowledge and one of the most generous souls [Mark had] ever met', [Perlman 1996: 9].

Mark Perlman started his tenure-track teaching life first in Hawaii in 1951 for a year and then a three year assistant-professorship post at Cornell. In 1956 he moved to Johns Hopkins in Baltimore. The happiest academic years of his life were those which overlapped with Fritz Machlup and Simon Kuznets[4] who became his complementary mentors.

The Johns Hopkins Faculty disintegrated in 1960–1 and Mark moved to Pittsburgh for the rest of his academic life. He was chairman for about five years, starting in 1965 and resigning suddenly over a point of principle involving a junior dean's intervention into departmental autonomy. He was appointed University Professor of Economics in 1969. As Chairman and then University Professor he was a guiding star for the Faculty, with central emphasis on teaching (how as well as what) of both undergraduates and graduates. He himself taught a wide range of courses, from American history to history of economic thought, taking in demography, health economics and labour economics on the way.[5] He also brought the ideals of collegiate behaviour, particularly the importance of mixing with other disciplines preferably in a social setting: For example, well-hosted dinner parties where serious conversation was the main object but good food and wine were *not* neglected (an Oxbridge style emphasis as scholarship is born in food and drink at Oxbridge!)

The economists who most influenced him as he developed his attitude to theory and theorising were Frank Knight, J. M. Clark, Machlup and George Shackle. Shackle was the first person Mark invited to Pittsburgh when he became Chairman. He 'came to realise [that Shackle's] idea of uncertainty ... was infinitely better than the von Thünen-Knight variant' [Perlman 2000: 83]. They became great friends. Mark admired George as 'one of the best writers of prose in the profession' and for the breadth of his knowledge and his patience as a teacher, expositor and critic.

Over the years Mark Perlman has written or edited a remarkable number of books and articles. (We append a bibliography of his contributions at the end of this volume.) And, of course, he was the founding editor of the *Journal of Economic Literature*, responsible for issues of the journal from its inception in 1969 to 1980 when he retired, handing on the baton to Moses Abramovitz. Perhaps the best way to mark this extraordinarily significant contribution to the profession is to reprint here the letter which over thirty members of the American Economic Association from all round the world sent to Abramovitz when Mark retired:

June 9th, 1980

Dear Professor Abramovitz,

We, all members of the AEA, would like to place on record our appreciation of the splendid job that Mark Perlman did as Editor of the *Journal of Economic Literature* from its inception in 1969 until 1980. His choice of survey articles was relevant and imaginative; his choice of reviewers was such that interesting, fair and authoritative reviews usually were written. He endeavoured always to see that *all* sides of a question were considered and that *all* approaches received a fair hearing. He enthusiastically encouraged and where necessary, defended the writers of survey articles. Altogether, his editorship was courageous liberal scholarship at its very best and his retirement from the role of editor should not, we believe, go unmarked by the profession, which is much in his debt.

Yours sincerely,

G. C. Harcourt	University of Adelaide, Australia
L. Tarshis	Ontario Economic Council
Jon S. Cohen	University of Toronto
T. A. Wilson	University of Toronto
Paul A. Samuelson	Massachusetts Institute of Technology
Michio Morishima	London School of Economics
John Cornwall	Dalhousie University
A. M. Sinclair	Dalhousie University
Paul Huber	Dalhousie University
R. L. Comeau	Dalhousie University
Barry Lesser	Dalhousie University
Joan Robinson	Cambridge University
A. Asimakopulos	McGill University
James Tobin	Yale University
Edward Nell	New School, Graduate Faculty New York
D. E. Moggridge	University of Toronto
Robert M. Solow	Massachusetts Institute of Technology
B. Schefold	University of Frankfurt, West Germany
John Hicks	All Souls College, Oxford
Richard Fabrikant	University of Denver
Harry Bloch	University of Denver
Katherine B. Freeman	University of Denver
Martin J. Wyand	University of Denver
Gene Ellis	University of Denver
William E. Burford	University of Denver
Lawrence A. Boland	Simon Fraser University
Michael Meeropal	W New England College
Kenneth J. Arrow	Sanford University
A. B. Atkinson	London School of Economics
Amartya Sen	Oxford University
Werner Meiβner	University of Frankfurt, West Germany
Donald J. Harris	Stanford University
William Peterson	Cambridge University
F. H. Gruen	Australian National University
Aubrey Silberston	Imperial College, London
Moses Abramovitz	Stanford University

From Mark's writings it is clear that he is not altogether in sympathy with the characteristics of modern economics and university life. He misses the interplay of ideas between colleagues in different disciplines, especially when it is associated with hospitality such as those dinner parties he went to and presided over in his years as a university teacher. He also misses the willingness of people to 'muck in' by sharing the various tasks in a faculty or department rather than concentrating on filling up their curriculum vitae in order to accelerate promotion, or, in these harsh times, to try to ensure the receipt of tenure. It has to be said that Mark's generation belonged to a Golden Age of university teaching. Funds were relatively plentiful, teachers were relatively few because of the drop in the birth rate of the depression years, so that they came of age as teachers just as subsequent bulges in the population were moving through vastly expanding tertiary sectors. Nevertheless, there are constants of behaviour and attitude which should hold in good and bad times. Mark's example is witness *par excellence* to this truth.

As we noted, in his own work he chose to concentrate on important central issues – aspects of the labour market, population growth, health economics, the environment and, of course, but now alas, not regarded as either important or central, the history of the subject. It is good that his contributions are gathered together in those three recent volumes, Perlman (1966), Perlman and McCann (1998; 2000). Browsing through them will introduce coming generations to the writings and attitudes of one of the most significant figures of the profession in the postwar era. The history of thought volumes should make them think anew about the sheer stupidity of not being acquainted with the past of the subject, historically and in terms of the dominant figures in the subject. At the very least it may prevent the rediscovery of often inferior wheels that happens so much now, because of a training which suggests that the subject only started ten or so years ago (with which is associated a moving peg).

Mention should be made of his wife, Naomi, who worked with him in the design and administration of the *Journal of Economic Literature* – in particular, the classification system for all economic publications. Mark continues to be as energetic and interested as ever, writing, reading and commenting on the manuscripts of friends, again as ever interested in issues of and gossip in the profession. The History of Economics Society made him their (year 2000) Distinguished Fellow. At the session devoted to his work, each of the speakers wore a bow tie (his signature attire), a fitting index of the affection and respect in which he is held. The present volume is in his honour and we hope that for many more years he will continue to illuminate and inspire.

Nineteen scholars and friends of Mark have contributed chapters to this volume in his honour. Their essays are classified under six headings: I, An evaluation of Mark's written contributions based on an analysis of his selected essays in the 1996 volume; II, Editing and intolerance in the profession; III, Economic, social and political systems; IV, History of economic theory; V, Economic theory; VI, Applied economics.

Kurt Dopfer has provided great value to both the profession and the editors of this volume by his review article essay of Perlman (1996). He sets up an appropriate framework and takes us through the wide range of topics and issues that are contained in Perlman's scholarly, deeply thought through essays. We thus learn of Perlman's life, most significantly of his relationship with his father, the distinguished labour economist, Selig Perlman, and the effects of Second World War on Mark Perlman's social and intellectual development, of his views on editing and teaching, of his vast knowledge of past and present economists (which led him to rate Simon Kuznets as the greatest of them all in the twentieth century) and of his wide ranging interests in social matters, especially in health issues in developing countries.

The heading of Part II, Editing and intolerance in the profession, may seem at first sight to put together strange bedfellows. However, we hope that readers will agree that Ingrid Rima's experiences while editing the *Eastern Economic Journal* for twelve years and Paul Samuelson's account of religious intolerance in American academia, mainly in economics departments, have features in common, so that the pairing of these topics does make sense. Rima's essay is a fascinating and lively account of her life and times in the Eastern Economic Association (EEA) and as editor of the Association's journal from 1979 to 1991. She took Mark Perlman at the *Journal of Economic Literature* as her role model as editor. She saw her own role as that of providing outlets for the young, the unorthodox and the maverick, as well for HET scholars (even though they do not teach HET at MIT. Of course, some of the founder scholars there *are* HET itself). She describes in vivid passages the struggles which a new journal has to become financially viable and to publish papers which have not been submitted to it as journal of last resort. Rima's solution for the latter, perhaps both, was to attend as many conferences as those two fundamental scarce resources, time and money, allowed and commission the interesting and provocative papers she heard at the conferences. Browsing through the contents for the twelve years she was editor gives a good idea of the success of her noble endeavours.

In the early days she was blessed with the support of open-minded luminaries, those who often did their stint as President of the EEA before they received their Nobel Prizes, who believed in letting 1,000 (heterogeneous) flowers bloom. As the years went by and the professions narrowed this environment of tolerance gradually disappeared, until Rimas's time as editor ended too. Nevertheless, she left an indelible mark on the profession and the issues analysed, a contribution not unworthy of comparison with the performance of Mark Perlman's identical stretch of years at the *Journal of Economic Literature* and she pioneered 'blind referring', which now even the *AER* has adopted. One of the editors of this volume – GCH – must add a sceptical note, based on many years of editing different journals and much refereeing, that blindness is often only in the eyes of the beholder. A glance at the bibliographies of most submissions usually allows a shrewd guess as to who the unknown author really is. Be that as it may, Rima's value added over those twelve years was great and we are all in her debt, as we are, of course, to the value added of the twelve years of the person who inspired her to take on this role in the first place.

Mark Perlman has written perceptively about his Jewishness, about how the combination of living through the period of Hitler and of being a 'Jewish Faculty child ... in a semi-hostile Madison, Wisconsin', Perlman (1996: 1), created 'all-too-evident insecurities'. Knowing this helps us to make sense of his own interests and of the emphases and nuances in his writing and conversation. Knowing of Selig Perlman's legendary struggles with academic anti-Semitism in the still earlier First World War era, Paul Samuelson has written of a later age when the climate was *beginning* to change. He gives an absorbing account, drawing mostly on his own experiences and observations, of anti-Semitism (and religious and racial intolerance generally) in, mainly, economics departments in USA over the period 1920–45.

Looking back now at the turn of the century, the stories seem hardly credible, unless you happen to be the same age as, or even 20 or more years younger than, Samuelson himself. One especially astute remark, which strikes a chord even today, is that anti-Roman Catholicism has always been an allowable prejudice in academia, a disgraceful but true observation.

Samuelson is extremely fair in his discussion of even the worst offenders, finding countervailing stories of their kindness and often inconsistencies. As two of the people whom he mentions are Maynard Keynes and Samuelson's own patron, Joseph Schumpeter, it is inevitable that inconsistencies figure large. Thus, many of Keynes's intimate friends, colleagues and protégés were Jews and he was among the first to take practical steps to get Jewish students out of Hitler's Germany and Austria and to help them in their new homes; yet his reported remarks and often writings are classic examples of the thoughtless British anti-Semitism of his class and time. Samuelson provides numerous examples in mainly Ivy League departments which match or more than match Keynes's behaviour. With anti-Semitism emerging again in many parts of the world, possibly even in the USA itself, it is salutary to have on record these examples of a shameful past to remind us of the ever-present need for vigilance – and that anti-Roman Catholicism sentiments too should be purged immediately.

Part III, Economic, social and political systems, has three essays. The role of the welfare state (or its absence) in different economic systems, backed, or not backed, by different economic and social philosophies, is the important theme of Ewald Nowotny's essay, 'Communitarianism and welfare state dynamics'. He presents fairly Hayek's thesis concerning minimising or even eliminating the role of the state in a system of spontaneous order, in order to preserve individual freedom; but Nowotny clearly prefers the European model of an effective welfare state combined with government intervention generally. He argues that, over a wide range, there is no trade-off between efficiency and equity, that if anything, they are complements not substitutes, and that this may be illustrated by important periods of recent European history. He poses fairly Perlman's question: is it possible for globalisation and the welfare states of individual countries ultimately to remain compatible with each other, and if not, will it not be the latter than has to go? Nowotny remains an optimistic and fair-minded supporter of the justice and the (economic) virtues of the well-ordered welfare state.

The second essay is by Nicholas Balabkins who contributes a compelling essay on the price of totalitarianism. The essay is based partly but vividly on his personal experiences of living under both the Soviets and the Nazis during Second World War. Balabkins is well read in the writings of the great political philosophers, especially in the writings of Thomas Hobbes. He is trained in modern economics (he went to

Rutgers) but is sceptical of the value of mathematical techniques and analysis. His own approach is much more broad – he presents historical, sociological and institutional arguments for a viable society (or perhaps, an ultimately unviable one, as he explains persuasively why the Bolshevik revolutionary era, and especially its Stalinist phase, were eventually destined to fail). These arguments arise from his lifelong academic interest in which he has focused on the components of the social orders in Nazi Germany and the Soviet Union. He has been particularly concerned with the material damage inflicted by the Nazis' Hobbesian social order (1933–45) on its victims. Thus far, Germany has paid 100 billion Deutschmark ($75 billion) to redress those damages. He interprets these payments as part of the latent costs of the genocide of the former Third Reich and as a price for Germany's re-admission to the comity of the non-Hobbesian civil societies of the world.

Charles McCann contributes a thoughtful learned essay on the revival of communitarianism and of its critics past and present. He starts with the views of Jean-Jacques Rousseau and ends with those of Isaiah Berlin. On the way we take in Hegel, Hayek, Rawls and C. B. Macpherson, to name only a few of the highlights. His major theme is the age old one of the good society and role of the individual in it. Subsidiary themes are whether society can create or should precede the individual, or should only follow and be subject to individual rights, and what these writers have had to say on this. McCann himself favours the creation of institutions which allow the individual both choice *and* responsibility, which allow individuals to fulfil their potential and to be rewarded for doing so, rather than to be subjugated to some communal idea of the good and the just. This is, if you like, a true liberal's interpretation of the parable of the talents. We feel that this philosophy fittingly complements Mark Perlman's own, and that he will enjoy this wide-ranging essay with its clear accounts of the views of great thinkers from the past, combined with searching criticisms of their arguments and of the conceptual issues with which they all are grappling.

Ungsuh K. Park has written a reflective essay on the fundamental changes in the philosophical, political, sociological and economic attitudes of East Asia in (mainly) the postwar II period, and on their role in the present crisis. He draws on his own personal experience of living in and working through the changes themselves in his own society, as well as critically on the analyses of outside commentators. He highlights the role of the strong leader, the entrenched bureaucracies, the intensity of labour required in the medium period, the scapegoat role of the rest of the world, and the contradictions implicit in casting off the old ways and taking on the new. We have included his chapter in Part III, but its arguments and findings should also be borne in mind when reading James Dean's chapter on the same historical episode in the last Part of the volume.

History of thought and theory has always been one of Mark's real passions. His knowledge of past writers compares favourably with that of Schumpeter. The two essays in Part III are appropriately about a scholar who is a household name and one who is, undeservedly, much less well known. Richard Swedberg contributes a delightful essay on Knut Wicksell's sociological writings. He precedes his discussions of them by a masterly précis of Wicksell's life and character, showing what a good and courageous person his subject was, as well as being deeply intelligent (in office hours anyway), stubborn and idiosyncratic. As with many great thinkers, Wicksell was dogged by bouts of depression which, Swedberg argues, often affected his ability to work – yet his curriculum vitae, as we would say today, would certainly impress all but the most hard-nosed on tenure committees.

Swedberg emphasises the link between Wicksell's economics and his sociology, and his desire to bring the same high standards of scientific discourse to both. A theme running through all of Wicksell's writings is his fervent Malthusianism; this even had the unpleasant by-product of his extreme views on eugenics – not uncommon for his day and age, of course, but unpleasant reading just the same.

Swedberg cites examples of Wicksell's contributions to the sociology of his day (which, he tells us, was not at all like the modern discipline). He starts with Wicksell's famous 1880 speech on the link between drunkenness and poverty. Next, Swedberg documents Wicksell's Malthusianism and his friends' irritation with his continual reiteration of his central point. Swedberg points out that Wicksell established one important theoretical concept in this area, that of an optimum population.

Wicksell was a supporter of a (reformed) capitalism, but thought that the state should play a relatively small role in the running of society. Swedberg finally mentions Wicksell's concept of educational capital, which he developed by observing the loss to Swedish society through emigration not only of people but also of the broad education that had gone into them. Altogether Swedberg's essay confirms what a remarkable thinker and fine person Wicksell was – in the judgement of many people, the finest human being to grace our profession and one whose writings belong to its classics.

Arnold Heertje contributes an absorbing chapter on the development of the thought of the Dutch economist, J. J. Klant. Both Klant and Heertje were pupils of Peter Hennipman (1991–4), who Heertje tells us 'influenced Dutch economic thinking in a most sensible way through his teaching, his pupils and his writings'. Klant had much experience in policy-making and was extremely well read in the history of economics and the philosophy of science. His views, especially his later views, were based on these past experiences – a vast store and source of knowledge. He understood well the strengths and limitations of economic analysis, and the difficulties of giving policy advice based only on pure understanding and analysis, as opposed to a methodological understanding of the process, taking into account personal values and ideologies. This led him to argue that, because of its very nature, economists should be modest about their claims for their subject and the robustness and strength of their explanations and policy suggestions. Klant emerges as a person who was as thoughtful as he was knowledgeable, with interests and understanding that ideally complement those of Mark Perlman whom Heertje honours in his essay.

Part V has four essays on theoretical issues. We start with Samuel Weston's essay on the nature of capital, which is much influenced by the approaches of Schumpeter and Lachman, though his starting point (and, in his judgement, correct end point) are Adam Smith's writings on the topic. He couples his historical and analytical discussion with a discussion of the strengths and limitations of equilibrium as a tool in discussions of capital. He concludes that equilibrium is a straight jacket which has prevented advances in our understanding of the fundamental processes of accumulation, especially of those which characterise modern advanced societies. Weston has perhaps been less than generous to the writings of some writers (e.g. Joan Robinson, Nicholas Kaldor, Piero Sraffa) on similar themes, but his emphasis on the importance yet neglect of the contributions of Fetter and Lachmann is well taken. His essay is an appropriate tribute to Mark Perlman's own interest in and study of capital theory.

Uwe Cantner and Horst Hanusch praise Mark Perlman for his support for, and great influence on, the development of evolutionary economics, especially through some of the emerging journals and institutions devoted to it. Their chapter outlines the particular perceived limitations of neoclassical economics which have led to the emergence of evolutionary economics as, in some ways at least, an alternative approach to the analysis of the processes of change and development. They recognise that these modern developments are partly an attempt to overcome the basic dilemma and ultimately inescapable contradiction in Schumpeter's writings: that while he admired Walras and his system above all others as a theoretical achievement, he could never make a satisfactory link between its theoretical requirements and Schumpeter's 'vision' of the role of the innovating entrepreneur whose activity made the application of a static general equilibrium model impossible in an analysis of growth and development. By a careful and thorough survey of the literature on evolutionary economics, our essayists show how the moderns are trying to come to grip with this dilemma, aided by analytical tools which were not available to the pioneers. They are modest in their claims and point out explicitly the limitations of these developments. Nevertheless, an air of sturdy optimism pervades their essay which, no doubt, will gladden Mark's heart and the hearts of its readers too.

John Komlos and Peter Salamon write on a topic – distribution and growth – which is also dear to Mark's heart, though not, as they say, necessarily in a form of which he would approve. (The title of their essay is 'Growth and social welfare with interdependent utility functions'.) The emphasis on formal analysis and the lack of institutional detail would not be to his liking. But the issue – whether growth necessarily raises well-being when people are people, that is, envious human beings living in society and taking note of what happens to others – would find all in accord. Using a simple but seemingly robust model, our essayists show that an increase in economic growth, the fruits of which accrue to only one section of the community, may not raise overall well-being. Whether it does or not depends upon the initial distributions of well-being and on how envious (or altruistic) are the groups who miss out. This is a neat exercise in the implications of the interdependence of utility functions (Perlman might add, whatever they are).

The analysis suggests a need for more research into the characteristics of different groups in society – how envious/altruistic they are, for example – and into how growth might be achieved without the relative and, indeed, absolute worsening of the positions of certain groups in society. That is to say, we have clear, modest piece of theory on a defined issue which leads to sensible policy conclusions – exactly what Perlman always hopes our discipline will achieve.

Joe Stiglitz has made profound internal critiques of the foundations of modern microeconomics and of its application to understanding real world processes and providing the basis for sensible policy recommendations. After having made his very considerable presence felt in many areas of economic theory, Joe embarked on a new career of policy advice, initially to President Clinton and then as Senior Vice-President and Chief Economist of the World Bank.[6] His experiences in these new roles have led him to apply the findings from his and others' academic research to the issue of the role of the state in modern societies and the modern world. As befits his acute understanding of how markets work, not always in a beneficial way, he remains a strong and intelligent supporter of a crucial role for the state. Of course, he never commits the *non sequitur* that just because a 'market failure' has been identified, therefore the state should be called in and will do better. But he does discuss how the state and market may be combined in an intelligent manner as helpful complements in achieving the objectives of a decent, just and equitable society. He shows that it is not the size of the government which is the crucial issue but, rather, how well or badly the public sector achieves its legitimate aims.

His essay is full of insights and intuitions from economic theory, many of which arise from his own innovations, and common sense reflections on what form reforms should take in a rapidly changing world experiencing globalisation and ever closer links. He makes suggestions for future research and reflection, as well as providing intelligent answers and optimistic hope for those who, like Stiglitz himself and Mark Perlman, continue to see a crucial role for co-operation among citizens through the state, at both national and local levels, in the good society.

The last section is concerned with applied economics, taking as two case studies, the development of Germany in the post-war years and the recent East Asian crisis. Herbert Giersch provides a comprehensive essay on the distinct phases of German economic history and development since the end of Second World War. It is an absorbing blend of economic, political, cultural, sociological and historical factors. He explicitly believes that freedom from constraints and the use of the market, especially on the supply side, bring the best results. He illustrates this theme by the German experience in the 1950s and 1960s. He then discusses the reasons for the slow down in the late 1960s and 1970s, the recovery in the 1980s and the problems caused by unification in the 1990s. He remains an optimist, foreseeing a promising future, especially if classic economic principles continue to underlie the government's approach to policy. What he thinks of the prospects for the post-Kohl regime is unfortunately not included!

Hank Lim writes on the institutional developments in the Asia-Pacific region and especially on the emerging institutions which he sees as a response to growing regionalisation and protectionism in the rest of the world. The latest developments are in particular a response to the emergence of the European Union and changing attitudes in the USA following the end of the Cold War. Lim argues that the extraordinary rapid growth of what are now the APEC nations over the last thirty years or more owed much to the postwar movement towards freer trade and freer capital movements. The reversal of these trends could have adverse effects on the region. The institutions which are currently being developed are designed in part to be buffers against the damaging changes elsewhere.

James Dean vividly describes a recent 'memorable meal ... shared with Mark and Naomi Perlman,' at which Mark roamed far and wide over his extensive and tightly packed intellectual fields in response to what began as Dean's specific answers to questions on the East Asian crisis from a reporter of the *New York Times*. In his essay Dean provides a lucid, enthralling overview of the crisis and the conflicting analyses and often incoherence of the major economists who have addressed themselves to the problem. A central feature that emerges is that economists of all persuasions pay too little attention to the length of interrelated economic processes and too much attention to ultimate outcomes – if there are any. This lesson is now being painfully and slowly learnt as economists put their mind to the order of the sequences in proposed reforms, but the previous neglect of this by economists and policy makers alike has led to increasingly harsh hardships for those least able to protect themselves – so what is new? An ironical aspect is that amongst the chief perpetrators of these misfortunes are people in just those institutions – the IMF, the World Bank – that were set up in the optimistic and humane atmosphere at the end of Second World War to help avoid such catastrophes.

Dean draws attention to all the ingredients of the present circumstances – asset inflation and deflation (bubbles), too rapid deregulation of financial and other markets, moral hazard and asymmetric information, the extraordinary height of the recent growth rates of the economies now in crisis, the unpleasant racist overtones of Western commentators concerning crony capitalism; and so on. He shows that all points on the ideological spectrum in the debate still only see through a glass darkly but are starting to learn some humility in preparation for the time when they shall see clearly face to face. In this process they can only be grateful for the guidance of Dean himself and the wisdom and knowledge of his mentor (and ours), Mark Perlman.

Notes

* The editors are most grateful to the contributors to the volume and to Peter Kriesler and Mark Perlman for their comments on a draft of the introduction.
1 So did Selig Perlman, not least because his place in the sun was recognised by many other heavies, for example, Beatrice Webb, Harold Laski (who 'identified Perlman as his ' "prize target" ' but who was also his 'jolly' friend) and Maynard Keynes, Perlman [1999: 355].
2 See Perlman and Dean [1998] for his overall assessment of Leibenstein's life and works.
3 For Mark's considered views on Stigler see Perlman and McCann [1993].
4 Mark regarded Kuznets as the greatest economist of the 20th Century, see Perlman and Kapuria-Foreman [1995].
5 The contents of his history of thought courses are now in the public domain in Perlman and McCann [1998; 2000]. Ingrid Rima [2000] has written a superb account of the aims and contents of Perlman and McCann [1998].
6 He has now (April 2000) returned to academic life at Stanford.

References

Perlman, M. (1954) *Judges in Industry: A Study in Labour Arbitration in Australia*, Melbourne, London and New York: Melbourne University Press.
—— (1995) 'What makes my mind tick', *American Economist* 39 (2): 6–27.
—— (1996) *The Character of Economic Thought, Economic Characters, and Economic Institutions. Selected Essays by Mark Perlman*, Ann Arbor: University of Michigan Press.

Perlman, M. (1999) 'Perlman, Selig (9 Dec. 1888–14 Aug. 1959)' in Garraty, John A. and Mark C. Carnes (gen. eds) *American National Biography*, vol. 17, New York: Oxford University Press, 353–5.

—— (2000) 'Getting on and off the merry-go-round' in Roger E. Backhouse and Roger H. Middleton (eds) *Exemplary Economists, vol. 1, North America*, Cheltenham, Glos., UK and Northampton M.A., USA: Edward Elgar, 74–91.

Perlman, M. and James W. Dean (1998) 'Harvey Leibenstein as a pioneer of our time', *Economic Journal* 108: 132–52.

Perlman, M. and Vibha Kapuri-Foreman (1995) 'An economic historian's economist: researching Simon Kuznets', *Economic Journal* 105: 1524–47.

Perlman, M. and Charles R. McCann Jr (1993) 'On thinking about George Stigler', *Economic Journal* 104: 1–21.

—— (1998) *The Pillars of Economic Understanding: Ideas and Traditions. Volume 1*, Ann Arbor: University of Michigan Press.

—— (2000) *The Pillars of Economic Understanding: Factors and Markets. Volume II*, Ann Arbor: University of Michigan Press.

Rima, I. H. (2000) 'The pillars of economic understanding: a review essay', *Review of Political Economy* 12: 351–8.

Part I

An evaluation of Mark Perlman's written contributions

1 The participant observer in the formation of economic thought

Summa Oeconomiae Perlmanensis

*Kurt Dopfer**

The book[1] that is the subject of this essay is an extraordinary one indeed, and it provides the reviewer with the pleasurable task of presenting reasons why it can, should and must be recommended.

Mark Perlman offers us a 503-page collection of twenty-five previously published essays. In rough outline, the book comprises three parts (1) '*On Economic Literature and Literary Economics*' (pp. 35–59), (2) '*History of Economic Thought*' (pp. 63–380) and (3) '*Labor Problems and Institutions*' (pp. 383–503). The core of this work – 63 per cent of the text – is the second part, which is further subdivided into the broad categories of '*General Essays*', '*Essays in American Institutionalism*' and '*Essays in Biography*'. The general arrangement of Part 2 corresponds to an in-depth treatment of the analysis of economic problems, which Perlman uses to bring into focus these three facets: history of economic theory, comparative economic analysis, and contextual (e.g. biographic) analysis. This approach runs like an analytic fractal throughout the book.

The individual articles are well-written, providing a wealth of information one may use to fill gaps in a library devoted to such topics. One can compensate for possible duplication of effort by merely reaching into the bookcase (at $79.50) for the *Summa Oeconomiae Perlmanensis*. One could recommend the book on this basis alone.

The Character of Economic Thought then differs from similar efforts in that its contributions have unusual interdisciplinary depth, but still do not suffer from a lack of eclecticism. The individual portions do not combine to form a total picture, but they do form many original configurations which provide the reader with new relationships and interpretations. In fashioning this mosaic, Perlman uses the method of comparative analysis. While not quite new, this approach lets Perlman fulfill in a most exemplary manner the need for simultaneous differentiation and generalization of the material. If for no other reason, this characteristic alone should recommend it to the reader.

There is also, however, another reason for recommending the book, one having to do with historical perspective. The essays included were written over a span of forty years. While one could argue that the range of articles from which one can choose, other things being equal, is correspondingly greater given a longer time span (which gives a kind of selective advantage), the quality of Perlman's *oeuvre* does not require that kind of preselection. The distinctive perspective of this book is that, while its treatment of the 'history of economic thought' is wide ranging, its predominant emphasis is on its links to the present. One could contend that this is merely a comparative analysis of theories and not of history, since history by definition lies in the past. But what does 'past' mean? Perlman's opus is a *tour de force* which, by its unconventional treatment of the history of economic thought, forces us to reconsider the analytic perspective of this branch.

History of economic thought: the role of the participant observer reconsidered

Perlman's presentation prompts us to divide economic theories into those of economists who (1) died long ago, (2) died recently and (3) are still living. The sole criterion for distinguishing between the three is the manner of participation in the process of observation or analysis. Category (1) deals with economists whom we know only from statues and copper engravings. Metaphorically, these media reflect the great distance between ourselves and these economic thinkers. They lived 'in their time', in a completely different socioeconomic and technical-cultural environment, and it requires a special effort of imagination to comprehend their roles as human beings and as scientists. We can attempt to interpret the environment that gave rise to their theories, and in which they achieved their purpose; but in the true sense of the word, we cannot *understand* them: there is no *Verstehen* involved. The epistemological situation is similar to that of the ethnologists who explored the Tobrianders or other populations which, for them, were exotic: they approached this task with methods suitable for reducing a deficit in their understanding. The observer cannot 'participate', since here both space and time are remote and alien.

The *participant observer*, on the other hand, works with material that can be *genuinely understood* and this understanding presents itself as a possible *method for analysis*. The concept of the *participant observer* is borrowed from physics where it is mainly related to the phenomenon that, under certain experimental conditions, the observer influences the observation; methodological discussions sometimes refer to an analogous 'fuzziness' in the observation of economic phenomena. The economist who takes part in the 'experiment' of contemporary history of economic thought is, however, a participant observer in a far more radical and immediately insightful sense. He is not connected to the object of his perceptions on some subatomic level, but rather on the basis of multifarious and complex social interactions; it is not a matter only of relationships between forces, but rather between *ideas*. In his status as observer, the economist differs from the physicist in that the observation is not (primarily) defined by the experimental measurement equipment, but rather by *psycho-cognitive disposition*. The person is thus an observer in a genuine perceptual and cognitive sense, and the result of the observation depends significantly not only on the objective and instrumental equipment and method, but on the *subjectivity* of the cognitive apparatus of the observer. In this connection, it is important to recognize that the biography of the observer constitutes a significant determinant of the process of observation and of its results.

Autobiography: on the superego of a participant observer

We do not need to inquire as to Perlman's motivations for beginning his book with a detailed autobiography and why, again and again, autobiographical elements make their way into the analytic arguments. Suffice it to note that autobiography also makes an epistemological statement and that in the present case we also learn something about Mark Perlman – the participant observer. The first striking feature in his autobiography is the extraordinary relationship with his father:

> In my boyhood I must have spent a minimum of three hours each week in one-on-one sessions listening to him discussing the way as well as the substance of how he interpreted events. It was an overwhelming, if European-Jewish-style, intellectual relationship – a brilliant father and an admiring son; and neither ever forgot who was the father and who was the student.
>
> (p. 2)

The reader cannot fail to find this close relationship touching; it runs like a thread through the whole work. We can but assume that Sigmund Freud would derive unalloyed pleasure from so clear a confirmation of his thesis of the superego. Perlman further followed in the footsteps of his father in choosing economics as a scientific discipline, by the choice of his research area – as the history of economic thought of type (3) – and by his choice of specific research foci, on the analysis of the labor movement, labor unions, labor history, community values, labor arbitration and related organizational and institutional issues. The effect of a superego shows up most obviously in the countervailing forces which must be marshalled in order to eliminate effects perceived as disadvantageous. Perlman is surely aware that here we deal with a general phenomenon, as indicated in his reference to one of the greats in the history of economic thought:

> ... John Stuart Mill came to regard his father's domination of his mind with anger and repugnance. I was clearly far less prescient than the younger Mill, and all that I can truly say is that I was well into my late thirties before I even began to realize that, unlike his explanation of external events, my father's interpretation of personal events was not necessarily to be my own. Unlike John Stuart Mill, I was never strong enough in mind to be able to detach myself that completely from the impact of my father's influence.
>
> (p. 3)

Perlman's autobiography prompts the general consideration of what effects the existence or particular kind of superego has on the analysis of a participant observer in economics. In Freud's original concept, superego stands for the transmission of norms and rules by a father figure, which is the actual father in the first phase of the biography, and emerges as society later on. The father figure of the first phase appears as an intermediary who also conveys societal norms and rules. This formation of ego is a part of the process of socialization, but, in contrast to conscious learning, it occurs mostly subconsciously and is therefore possibly more firmly implanted in the deeper psycho-cognitive strata. An immediate and fascinating question would be the effect of the personal superego – let us call it α-superego – on the research work of a participant observer. Suffice it to note at this point that Perlman's biography provides valuable inductive building blocks for such a generalization.

More important for the present topic is the question of whether in one's intellectual life there does not also exist an intellectual superego – let us call it β-superego. It would be implausible to assume that the psychic mechanism of childhood does not also work in adult life if analogous conditions exist. A young person entering academia relives his childhood a second time, encountering superegos in the form of father figures as professors and established scientists. The imparted ideas exercise an authority much like the norms of childhood education. On this level, the participant observer runs through the formative years of an intellectual childhood, and his later creations are more or less noticeably affected by the superego formed in this early intellectual phase. The formation of the α-and β-superego can take place hand in hand, if the personal and the intellectual father figure happen to coincide. Consciously or unconsciously, the father–child relationship becomes a 'father–student' relationship.

The psycho-cognitive formation of the β-superego is not, however, primarily a matter of rules and norms of conduct as in the case of the α-superego, but rather one of *cognitive* content. Perlman's essays about his experience in university administration and as a journal editor do indicate that, as in ordinary life, such behavioral norms in academia indeed are effective. The more basic question is, however, whether scientific notions (such things as theories, for instance) establish themselves as superegos. Because of their inherent power of persuasion, ideas often exercise a 'natural' authority over those who hold them. However, an idea which affects a person as a superego, is independent of this kind of authority; it requires no support. Beyond their content, ideas derive their strength only from being the result of a specific psycho-cognitive process of formation. The concept of such an effective *formative-context* includes the 'visible colleges' – instructional and research institutions and universities – as well as the 'invisible colleges' – scientific paradigms, research programs, and theories.

The *historical entry* of an idea into a formative context has critical significance for its strength. Other things being equal, an idea A is only superior to an idea B because it appeared at the onset of a psycho-cognitive process of formation and was able, in the course of this process, to usurp the role of superego in the thinking of the person involved. In the present case, it played a role in the intellectual formation of the author that he attended the Universities of Wisconsin and Columbia and not, say, those of London or Vienna, and that early on he came into contact with the paradigm of American Institutionalism of the Veblen-Commons-Mitchell type and had less of a connection with neoclassical orthodoxy. In this connection, the author's remark may prove instructive that Mitchell entitled his usual lectures at Columbia University '*Formative* Types of Economic Thinking': 'Mitchell even came to a conclusion that economic theory as we teach it (a mass of abstract principles) was mostly the abstract idiosyncratic statements made by the *Fathers* of the Profession.' (p. 129, emphasis K. D.).

With an eye on an approach that purports to explain scientific progress, we can conclude from the above that scientists do not choose or test paradigms and research programs on the basis of an *a priori* rational calculus. Rather, this process and way of thinking are fundamentally contingent on the circumstances of where and when an individual was exposed to the intellectual force of a scientific idea, and which personalities assumed the role of father figures in the course of intellectual formation. Perlman largely eschews the treatment of methodological questions; the discussions of scientific paradigms and research programs that have had a renaissance in the last few years hardly come into focus in his work. The author's main inclination is to write a history of economic thought of type (3). However, as he does so, he implicitly suggests a reappraisal of the status of the *observer* – no small contribution to current methodological discussions.

Learning and Wanderjahre: on the dynamics of theory formation

Perlman wrote his dissertation on 'Australian Labor Relations' along the lines of his studies of labor relations and courses on judicial review of the legislative process (p. 6). This first work already contains the two characteristics of the author's theoretical creations: an interdisciplinary treatment and the identification of links between theory and factual evidence. The empirical part included not only a reading course on Australian history, but, above all, interviews of judges and legislators in order to determine the workings of the arbitration tribunals. His doctoral committee included George J. Stigler, but the candidate remembers the remark of a historian who said: 'Perlman, you write in the tradition of Adam Smith, but not as well,' and the help he got from a political scientist who replied: 'Yes, he also writes in the language of Shakespeare, but not nearly so well.' The quotation is an example of the wit and irony that suffuses the text.

The whole third part of the book is dedicated to '*Labor Problems and Institutions*' and, in Chapters 20 and 21 he presents the most important general and special theories of the American labor movement. The two chapters differ from others in their detailed discussion of aspects of causality, and especially of the link between economic-political desiderata and their possible consequences. A further part in Chapters 22–25 comprises historical or empirical analyses. Interestingly enough, the last article, on '*An Analytical Theory of Australian Labor Arbitration*' falls into the part entitled '*Labor History*' (pp. 419–503).

After his doctorate and a first teaching appointment at the University of Hawaii, the author spent three years at Cornell University, a period which brought him little inspiration in teaching, but which led to his second book, '*Theories of Labor Unionism*'. Perlman also utilized this experience creatively, in that he introduced Gierke's idea of the *Genossenschaft* (translated as 'fellowship' or 'brotherhood') into the discussion of his situation (pp. 11–12).

The author spent the following years at John Hopkins University, in a *Genossenschaft* that brought 'intellectual guidance' and 'personal-professional friendships' and made him a devotee of 'two quite different men, both historical luminaries: Fritz Machlup and Simon Kuznets' (p. 13). With Machlup, Perlman completed his formative studies on 'Austrian Economics', which left theoretical and also methodological traces: 'Machlup was a Hayekian, and like Hayek he had his own reservations about economic theory as "scientism"' (p. 13). Hayek's concepts are further discussed in a chapter on '*Hayek, Purposes of the Economic Market and Institutionalist Traditions*' where his notion that the primary purpose of the market is the exchange of information is counterposed to the ideas of institutionalists such as J. M. Clark, Ronald Coase and John R. Commons: 'Their resulting insights were similar; what differed were their philosophical foundations – Hayek's was Kantian; the others' were Hegelian'. (p. 254).

The influence of Kuznets was overwhelming and, as an economist of category (3) in Perlman's history of thought, he acquires truly herculean stature because he 'did measurably more to shape the world's destiny before and during World War II than any economist in history has ever done. Men like Smith, Malthus and Keynes did much to shape ideas; but Kuznets truly caused epochal history' (p. 14). In Chapter 17, '*An Economic Historian's Economist: Remembering Simon Kuznets*', coauthored with Vibha Kapuria-Foreman, the authors, following the aforementioned mode of analysis, first present the biographical stages of the 'paternalistic legacy' of Kuznets, and then proceed with an analysis of his contributions to economic growth, national income accounts, measurement of capital formation, and demographic economics. The latter area of research was to occupy Perlman again and again, and this established a link with the work of Harvey Leibenstein, a subject he treats in Chapter 19. This chapter too demonstrates the 'in-depth structure' of analysis, in that he begins with a section on '*The Legacy of his Training*' followed by one on '*His Taste for Economic Theorizing*' and '*His Taste for Observational Generalizing Close to the Level of Fact*' (pp. 361–80).

Johns Hopkins, however, also offered the author possibilities for empirical research. Perlman became a member of a team put together in 1953–60 to evaluate the reports of the US-Brazilian Agency the task of which was the furtherance of public health with special emphasis on preventive medical care. Perlman's activities within this project were not merely along the lines of his theoretical interests; in the course of his travels to Brazil he acquired abundant empirical insights. The results of this stay were numerous articles and the editing of three books in the area of health economics.

Schumpeterian vs institutional thinking

The special theoretical insight of the Brazilian adventure was that 'broader economic questions like when and how to invest in public health, particularly in disease prevention facilities' were more important than 'the popular question of how to improve health care delivery' (p. 15). His general theoretical conclusion was that economists had not treated the 'mechanism of economic growth' concretely enough and that 'from a macro standpoint almost anything could be considered *abstractly* as either a simple, fixed or variable factor' (p. 15, emphasis in original). Adopting a theoretical perspective in the tradition of institutional analysis, Perlman maintains

> that studying the economic process required a set of foci on several concrete
> factor markets: (1) *land and other natural resources*, (2) the availability of *water*

and power, (3) the cost of *transportation,* (4) the availability and spectrum of *labor skills,* (5) the sum of *capital* – that is, control of scale and production time, including technology, (6) *managerial talent,* and (7) access to effective *markets.*

(p. 15, emphasis in original)

It is useful to relate this classification scheme to the measuring stick of Schumpeter's concept of economic development – whereby we may remind ourselves that Perlman was a co-initiator and co-founder of the International Joseph A. Schumpeter Society. His scheme is reminiscent of Schumpeter's well-known classificatory attempt to relate economic development to the implementation of innovations in five major areas of the economy. Schumpeter clearly distinguished between the movement of economic resources and the behavior that causes these movements. The core of his theory of development is an assertion of causality of the type $x \rightarrow y$, where x denotes behavioral and y resource-related variables respectively. Schumpeter criticized the notion of regarding development as mere resource dynamics and, analogous to mechanical trajectories in physics, starting with a causality of the type $y_1 \rightarrow y_2$, with subscripts denoting different resource variables. In particular, he turned against classical economics, where, for example, Malthus and Ricardo drew his critical wrath because they viewed development merely as a long-run change in the relationship between the resource magnitudes of food demand, agricultural supply capacity and population.

In his research, Perlman dealt with demographic economics to which he made empirical as well as theoretical contributions (pp. 25–6, in bibl. pp. 507–18). He went beyond Ricardo in dealing not only with the dynamics of resources but also with the fertility conditions which give rise to them. Likewise he goes beyond Malthus in addressing the Schumpeterian type question of the 'natality among the educated and social leadership'; programs of fertility control 'if officially favored, might well work best in just that portion of the population from which future entrepreneurs would come' (p. 26).

This analysis is, however, at best a first approximation to that of Schumpeter. This is not to suggest that he is the measure of all things, and we need to remind ourselves that we are only asking whether Perlman's analysis follows along the lines of Schumpeter's – love it or leave it. Schumpeter worked with a type of linear causation and explicitly rejected the circular causation suggested by Veblen in explaining economic evolution; specifically, he accepted the notion of a *linear-cumulative causation,* but not of a *circular cumulative* one, which is at the heart of evolutionary institutional economics. Schumpeter thus also rejected the notion – widely implicit in Perlman's analysis – that one can explain economic development by showing how population dynamics work backwards towards economic behavior.

Schumpeter, moreover, not only excluded a reversal or circularity of the direction of causation, but also limited the unidirectional causality exclusively to economic variables. The causal connection is thus specified as $b(e) \rightarrow y$ and not as $b(n) \rightarrow y$, where b is behavior and (e) and (n) stand for 'economic' and 'non-economic', respectively. The core of Schumpeterian economics ultimately boils down to the question: What is the key variable $b(e)$? Methodologically, this stands for the non-classical causality concept of 'uncaused cause', of self-creation, self-movement, and spontaneity. Theoretically, it represents the creative and active economic actor who creates something new and changes the environment. In Perlman's classificatory scheme, category (6), 'managerial talent' must take on this role. However, this variable *reacts* only to changes in the conditions, as listed in the other categories, and is not creative by itself, as Schumpeter demands. Perlman's theoretical works on labor economics, labor unions, social climate, and labor arbitration likewise find a rather subordinate role in Schumpeter's research program. In their passivity, workers stand there on the same level as the consumer whom, contrary to his otherwise neoclassical inclinations, he did not at all regard as the 'sovereign' of a dynamic economic process.

Schumpeter is also important in conveying the image of the *creative-innovative* individual in his analysis of the *history of economic thought*. Perlman's essay '*On Schumpeter's History of Economic Analysis, 40 Years After*' (pp. 179–204) was originally written as an introduction to a reprint of Schumpeter's book of that name. This essay not only presents a comprehensive overview of the existing literature on this work, but, in the course of his own interpretation of Schumpeter's ideas, also indicates the core of an explanation of scientific progress in economics: at the beginning of the development of any economic approach, there is 'the hero's ability to build an original system' (p. 188). In line with this innovative contribution to the dynamics of theory formation, the inquirer gives out his 'grades'.

The notion of 'innovator' serves thus as a *principal paradigm for the explanation of scientific progress*, in which the 'creative destruction' of the status quo, the discontinuity of the intellectual process, and not the gradual movement in 'little steps', are held to the fore.

Beside this, it may be recognized that the observer's own *theoretical* stance may play a significant role in the historical analysis of theories. As a case in point, in '*History of Economic Analysis*' Schumpeter criticizes the classical labor theory of value not in the usual manner of neoclassical economics, noting the superiority of the marginality principle with its determinate intersection point equilibria; he rather objects to the way in which the classical surplus represents merely a difference between resource magnitudes – the dynamics of which remain unexplained, since an analysis of the entrepreneurial behavior that 'causes' them to move is absent.

Teoria Perlmanensis

Perlman's analytical perspective stretches very far and his theoretical competence allows him to develop a fascinating array of theoretical comparisons and interpretations. Yet, at the end, the cosmopolite and polymath of theory finds his home in American Institutionalism. Of its founding fathers, he writes: 'The principal underlying premise for all of them was that the study of economic relationships was of a "long run" nature, and each was contextually, that is time and space, bound' (p. 227). Perlman introduces his essay '*Understanding the "Old" American Institutionalism*' noting that

(t)he 'older' American Institutional Economics if often perceived and described … as monolithically mostly anti-abstract theory, but such is a silly judgment, and has too often been made by people who ought to know better. For the more serious, it is traditional to identify three kinds of 'old school' American Institutionalism: Veblenian, Mitchellian, and Commonsonian. Each of these is related, but it is an error to lump them.

(p. 227)

In the essay '*Orthodox and Heterodox Economics*', Perlman suggests several political, methodological, and theoretical differences between the two types. The standard of political comparison is the prototype of *laissez-faire* capitalism, as described in Mandeville's '*Fable of the Bees*'. The author devotes Chapter 5 to this fable, discussing the interpretations of Jacob Viner and Friedrich von Hayek, as well as its publishing history, reviewing five different interpretations of it from secondary sources, and then offering his own analysis 'of what Mandeville may have been up to' (pp. 87–120). In this chapter, the reader experiences in an exemplary way the advantages of Perlman's approach, in which biographic, historical and bibliographic elements are interwoven with theoretical comparisons and interpretative aspects. Of the above-mentioned Institutionalists, only Veblen attacked the fable-capitalism of Mandeville directly, while Mitchell 'was in no sense part of the conventional anti-market crusade' (p. 243). Commons believed (well in line with Schumpeter) in the power of monopolistic competition and Perlman remarks that 'the willingness of some to lump Commons with Brandeis as sharing a mutual distrust of big business is something for which I find virtually no evidence' (p. 243).

Given these gradations, commonalities and differences with the work of Hayek are discussed; these are featured in the earlier mentioned essay on '*Hayek, Purposes of the Economic Market, and Institutionalist Traditions*' (pp. 253–68) which, interestingly enough, figures in Section B of the second part, among '*Essays on American Institutionalism*'. Perlman contends that

(t)here has long been a purported conflict between economic theorists, particularly of the line from which Hayek stemmed, and 'empirically oriented socioeconomic' Institutionalists of which Wesley Clair Mitchell, John R. Commons and John Maurice Clark were exemplars.

(p. 254)

Reviewing Hayek's theorizing and the position of American Institutionalism, Perlman concludes that '(t)he tie is there, expressions of intellectual animosity to the contrary notwithstanding' (p. 254). Especially in the field of political economy, these are given by a different level of trust in Dr. Pangloss' optimism. In their methods, however, all proponents follow a common path with reference to the notion that economic phenomena can only be treated in context, as process, and beyond the notion of equilibrium.

Methodologically and theoretically, Wesley Clair Mitchell and John Rogers Commons represent the opposite poles of American Institutionalism. Mitchell studied with Veblen, but his mentor was James Lawrence Laughlin, who suggested that Mitchell test empirically the validity of Fisher's Quantity Theory of Money. Along the way, he analyzed variations in the data on output, employment levels, and prices in specific industries, and presented them in numerous statistical graphics. 'It is hard to overestimate Mitchell's impact. He gave material form to the soul of macroeconomic analysis. Ideas cast no shadows; numbers, when tied to ideas, do.' (p. 238).

Mitchell was variously reproached for his 'dogged fact-gathering'. But, as Perlman remarks, nothing could be further from the truth:

> For Mitchell institutional economics was the study of historical context as the basis for and background of the interpretation of economic ... phenomena. The study of historical context involved measurement of relevant variables or their proxies. Measurement, while quantitative, was never mechanical; the investigator always had to seek the significance, which Mitchell thought was a cultural phenomenon. To Mitchell most economic theories were simply a set of idiosyncratic explanations of economic events. As they were idiosyncratic they reflected essentially personally-imagined constructs, the relevance of which would ebb and flow even as they were made quantitatively more reliable.
>
> (p. 233)

Here one can recognize parallels with the German Historical school. Its influence on American Institutionalism is undeniable. In a review of Schmoller's *Grundrisse*, Veblen laments Schmoller's lack of understanding of institutional evolution. In what way does this criticism also apply to Mitchell's approach? While this issue remains unexplored, Perlman reminds us that Mitchell was a student of Veblen's and he a student of John Bates Clark. The latter, 'the Abraham of American economics' (p. 228), was brought up in Bismarck's Germany, from whence he appropriated his 'paternalistic plans for social welfare'. In 1885, Clark was one of the founders of the then 'anti-pure-laissez-faire American Economic Association'. He was

> fascinated with capitalists, a distasteful aggressive parvenu class, which had seemingly cynically rejected any obligation to exercise any traditional *noblesse oblige*, and, instead, openly avowed exercising its economic power with and its slavish emulation of the worst of eighteenth century English and French aristocratic consumptionism.
>
> (pp. 228–9)

Later, this was Veblen's great theme and, conversely, nothing could demonstrate more clearly the distance between Clark's work and that of Schumpeter.

Commons was the other pole of American Institutionalism. His work showed a similarly strong empirical flavor to that of Mitchell, but the emphasis of his analysis lay not on the descriptive statistics of regularities in resource relations, but rather in the social behavior that lies behind the economic quantities. The focus of this analysis is the process of *social bargaining*; from it, he expects an 'intellectual answer as to why the economy operates', and from the political agenda, a response as to which 'palliatives could be introduced to counter the excessive burdens the system put on labor' (p. 234). Commons thought

> that the leadership of capital and the leadership of labor would develop a capacity to govern industry wisely and each specific leadership would be able to educate and control the excesses of its own clientele. He favored 'voluntaristic industrial government' not 'government in industry', and he sought to lay out both the patterns which had emerged in his America and how he had discerned what those patterns were.
>
> (p. 235)

I think that here the difference between neoclassical and institutional economics finds clear expression: in the former, the variables 'capital' and 'labor' signify productive factors and resources, while in the latter, they reflect specific *social behavior*. The author follows, perhaps with some nonchalance, the self-estimate of the 'new' Institutionalists who present their work as 'a reconstruction and extension of what Commons described as his results' (p. 235). The reader is invited to compare the individualistic concepts of contracts and of transaction costs, with those of the above-mentioned 'collective bargaining' and 'voluntaristic industrial government' and to judge the extent to which the 'new' Institutional Economics follows the spirit of the 'old'.

In the tensions between resource appraisal and behavioral analysis, Veblen appears as an *integrator*. In his chapter on the 'old' Institutionalism, Perlman describes Veblen above all as a *homo politicus* and concludes that the simple elements of his scheme

> plus the imaginative use of pseudo-'scientific' rhetoric caught the eye of many, in and out of academia, who were puzzled and disgusted with the excesses which they associated with a pecuniary free enterprise system and, in practice, to comparative excesses in consumption. This social irresponsibility inspired many to form a Veblen cult.
>
> (p. 231)

This interpretation refers not to the turn of the present century but to that of the last one, and it poses the question whether Perlman does not hide his real target, since he never mentions the living proponents of the 'old' Institutionalism.

The praise and criticisms Perlman directs at the Institutionalists is interesting. They do generally well in empirical analysis, data collection, index calculations, tabular displays, and the general presentation of factual evidence. Remarkable, though fully justified, is his criticism of their *psychology of decision-making*. As far as Veblen was concerned, Perlman says

> ... it is apparent that he was not particularly aware of developments within the field of *Gestalt* psychology, to say nothing of the later developments that led to Watsonian behaviorism. Indeed, it is rather remarkable how little Veblen seemed to know about the contemporary developments in psychology which had occurred and were occurring in Baltimore and Harvard under Peirce and William James.
>
> (p. 244)

Similarly, Commons was interested in the 'evolution of group values' and defined Institutionalism as 'collective choice in control of individual choice'. Yet he was 'not *au courant* with developments in social psychology. If anything, he seems to have been relatively skeptical about the discipline of psychology offering very much to economics' (p. 244). Finally, Mitchell had 'recognized the importance of psychology in the decision-making process', but unfortunately confined himself to posing 'only very interesting and critical questions' (p. 250).

This is a criticism that may, however, be well extended to the proponents of an 'individualistic' line. Are they not the very ones who consider the *individual* as the theoretical reference point? Schumpeter, for instance, placed the individual agent at the very center of his theory, but he questioned the need for psychology. He introduced the concept of *Methodological Individualism*, yet worked out his theory with a hand-made image of humanity (even though he lived in the Vienna of Freud and Adler). Hayek gave a sharp profile to his politico-economic 'individualism', but explicitly denied the usefulness of psychology for economics. And, of course, ruling neoclassical theory operates with the atomistic concept of *homo oeconomicus*, which, in connection with the axiomatization of its behavioral assumptions, leads to the explicit rejection of any further psycho-cognitive foundations.

The unity of teaching and research

At least since the time of Wilhelm Humboldt, the relationship between teaching and research has played a central role in the discussion of the good university and the good teacher. Perlman does not refer to Humboldt's ideal, because non-American sources generally play the second fiddle (his acknowledgment of an American provincialism in connection with a discussion of Institutionalists appears genuine, as well as sympathetic). In addition, Humboldt belongs to Category (1), that of the long dead greats. Perlman's ideal is, however, in the spirit of Humboldt, and even if he does not use his sources, he reinvents him in his way.

For Perlman, learning is first of all a *thinking* process. While it is the task of a lecture 'to convey data and constructs', it is just as important 'to show why and where one applies both'. In this abductive sense, a lecture should 'reflect the organic nature of the lecturer's thinking process' (p. 11).

By its nature, this organic thinking process is played out within the *communicative* framework of a teacher–student relationship. This relationship is a dynamic one, insofar as in the course of their lives people change their roles, sometimes playing the part of teacher, sometimes that of student. Perlman's relation to other economists can be seen as a fascinating account of this dynamic multi-generational trajectory in that he sometimes looks up to his teachers and at other times lectures. We encounter Perlman as student in several chapters of the book where one should not fail to note that to him (as well) teachers are not limited to those met in colleges and universities, but above all include colleagues encountered in the course of his scientific career. Perlman dedicates a section of the book titled '*Essays in Biography*' (pp. 271–380) to these teachers among his colleagues; it takes up a quarter of the volume.

The chapters on Fritz Machlup, G. L. S. Shackle, George Stigler and Simon Kuznets stand out; therein, Perlman conducts his analysis with an 'upward glance', while simultaneously emancipating himself as participant observer, a role in which he carries out history of economic thought of type (3) and related comparative analysis. Machlup's *'Economic Semantics'* and Kuznets' *'Historical Economics'* mark the breadth of the analytic approach.

For Perlman – the active participant observer – this choice of teachers often is, explicitly or implicitly, a choice of economists who become possible candidates for the history of economic thought. The *'Essays in Biography'* often represent generalizing statements about the history of economic thought that form a conceptual framework for working out and integrating the individual biographic aspects into a broader discussion of the history. In an essay on G. L. S. Shackle, Perlman writes,

> (t)he body of economic knowledge as we know it, I propose, should be imagined as a tapestry, or, better yet, considering our propensity for wiping our feet on the past, as an oriental rug. It is a rug woven by different generations of thinkers and doers, each working within the framework of the facts and ideas of his or her time, and each hoping that from observation and/or excogitation some immutables could be distilled and put to permanent use.
>
> (p. 271)

Perlman adds a reflection on the utility of the history of economic thought which I would like to recommend as a guideline for any analysis that involves a participant observer of type (3): '… it can be argued that *a*, if not *the*, principal utilitarian-type reason for the study of the history of economic thought is to avoid a pattern of cyclical extremes of overconfidence and self-doubt about the subject' (p. 272, emphasis in original).

In further chapters, the author describes his own role as teacher. He does this in the role of practical educator as well as philosopher of education, whereby his statements indicate how little these two roles can be separated. In a subchapter, *'What Should an Economics Department Be?'*, Perlman recounts his experience as department chairman; he mentions that in his 'teaching department', those responsible for the communication 'from the top down' had their special duties: '… I assumed, really without thinking much about it, that professors should teach a lot. …Whatever creative research they wanted to undertake should generally be done after their teaching responsibilities had been met' (p. 18).

It is of particular interest to note the way in which the content of a subject is imparted within the framework of the 'organic nature of the lecturer's thinking process' and of the asymmetrical communication. The approach nearest to Perlman's own point of view may be found in the biographical chapter on Machlup, where he writes of his teacher that

> … one of his wonderful teaching skills was to misunderstand purposefully a student's language to lead the student to things the student had not realized were there – like Molière's M. Jourdain, many of Machlup's students found after

he had finished with them that their thinking was deeper than they had ever imagined.

(p. 359)

We may assume that this kind of consciousness-raising presupposes specific theoretical and conceptual premises. Conventional learning consists generally in the elimination of a knowledge deficit by means of an importation of new knowledge. An initial disequilibrium in the form of a knowledge deficit is successively diminished by imparting knowledge until an equilibrium (state of complete knowledge) is reached. In an evolutionary interpretation, learning means that (analogous to conventional wisdom) there are *asymmetries* of knowledge; but the transmitted information is not handed down with finality. It is rather *generated, mutates,* and *develops* in a process of communication.

The context of *communication* between teacher and student is thus characterized by a *global* knowledge deficit in concomitance with a *relative asymmetry* of knowledge between teacher and student. With regard to the principal (global) lack of knowledge, the relationship between teacher and student is egalitarian and, in a radical sense, they are group members with equal rights. A historical model that comes near to this kind of group is given by the intellectual 'circles' of the Vienna of the interwar years, which were significant also for the development of economic theories. One of the salient characteristics was that, over time, all members were equally teachers and students, and that the *teacher* was only distinguished by the *greater generation of new knowledge.* I believe that it is in this sense that we ought to interpret the author's notion of a *Genossenschaft* in which 'fitting-in' is the decisive criterion: if its members fit together intellectually, they can develop, as teachers and as students.

Editing and the two cultures of economics

Pittsburgh was a kind of home port for Perlman. He began at the University of Pittsburgh with an intensive reading course in demographic economics and concluded his career after 45 years, 'at 70 with no significant regrets' (p. 32). Pittsburgh was not only the communicative context for teaching and research, but it evidently also offered him the infrastructure on the basis of which he could apply his extensive editorial skills.

Reflections from the viewpoint of an editor appear in the book in many places, but in Chapter 3 (pp. 47–59) we find a coherent account of these aspects in an essay entitled '*On the Editing of American Economic Journals: Some Comments on Earlier Journals and the Lessons Suggested*'. Alongside the preceding chapter on '*Snow's Two Cultures Reconsidered: Why Study the Past?*' (pp. 35–46), it provides a fulminant ouverture to the subject of economics as a science and to the possibilities of its communication.

The first essay, based on Perlman's experience as founder and editor for many years of the *Journal of Economic Literature*, provides a synoptic history of the earlier economic journals of the English-speaking world. Beyond the biographic and historical presentations, we encounter, as so often, a comparative discussion of theories, including those of Marshall, Edgeworth, Clark, Böhm-Bawerk and Knight.

In a further section, the author puts forth several generalizations on the characteristics of the supply of and demand for professional journals. While perhaps meant ironically, it nonetheless illustrates the polarizing nature of Perlman's writing when he remarks that 'the older Austrians were right; the market is dominated by the subjective expectations of the consumer', yet also stresses that the supplier can shape the consumer's preference schedule by means of advertising and other forms of "education"' (p. 54). The 'supply' of the editor consists in offering 'their potential buyers (or society members) something to preserve hope that the journal will prove interesting enough to read' (p. 56). One could say, that the reader winds up in a market in intellectual futures. In this connection, the reviewer is grateful that Perlman twice quotes the remark of a popular novelist, since it reduces the risk of being overlooked: '... any rational author should be willing to trade 1000 readers at the time of publication, for 100 readers ten years later or ten readers 100 years later.'

The core problem for an editor is, of course, the question of what articles he chooses for publication and thus what discussions he wishes to propagate in his journal. This purpose is closely linked to the concept of how economics is to be conducted and ultimately touches on the general question of scientific understanding. The choice of an article, whether for publication or for a lecture, is based on the acceptance of specific ontological, epistemological and communicative premises.

In this book, the *ontological* status of economics comes into focus in various ways. The main issue can ultimately be reduced to the Hamlet-like question '*To know or not to know?*', as addressed notably in the work of Perlman's friend and teacher G. L. S. Shackle. Ontologically, the past differs fundamentally from the future, in that we know something about the former while we are basically ignorant with respect to the latter. Perlman traces the principal paradigms of economics back to differing conceptions of the symmetry of time, where the conventional theories of resource allocation and 'Shackle's uncertainty' form opposing poles: 'One lays the foundation for a belief that economics deals with the allocation of scarce resources; the other for the belief that economics has to handle the unknowable as well as the knowable' (p. 138). In Perlman's view, God punished economists not only with the original sin of finding solutions to the scarcity problem, but also with a second original sin in the form of Shackle's uncertainty (p. 121).

With this metaphor, we accept implicitly a paradigm in which nomothetic and time-symmetric elements, as well as those of context and process, stand arguably against each other as equal partners. In the text, we do not find clarification as to how that kind of fire and water may be combined. However, let it be remembered that the author, as a practicing institutional economist, has presented the contextual and process elements of economics as its paradigmatic core, and that, based on this premise, nomothetic-causal laws can only claim a local validity defined by a theoretically reflected global historicity of economic processes.

In the solution of the methodological problem, Perlman employs the artifice of distinguishing between 'systematization' and 'abstraction'. In line with Mitchell, the author declares that '... a systematic approach ... [is] more basic to scientific inquiry than an abstract approach' (p. 128).

Following the author's lead, we may conjecture that great problems of contemporary theory are not primarily of an ontological nature but rather of an epistemological one; and there again, these are not problems of a lack of consensus about individual cognition, but problems of *communication*. In the article on '*Two Cultures*', Perlman suggests that it is time to forget 'our ideological differences about what we think' and to move the questions of 'why and particularly how we think what we do' (p. 45) to the foreground. He views the present crisis in economics not so much as a 'battle of ideology' than as a 'battle of inter-cultural communication' (p. 45). His contributions to editing and teaching can be read as variations on the theme of communication. The author is in his element in his reviews of D. N. McCloskey's '*If you're so Smart: The Narrative of Economic Expertise*' and A. O. Hirschman's '*The Rhetoric of Reaction*' (Ch. 6, pp. 121–40), but the theme of language and communication also runs through the contributions on Shackle, Stigler, and Machlup, even if the actual topic follows different lines.

Inspired by the author's representation of the communication problem, two genres of theory discussion are crystallized. The one can be called *abstract-deductive*, the other *systematic-discursive*. The logico-deductive and empirico-deductive approaches of the mainstream can be subsumed under the abstract-deductive type of theory; method and language are directed to abstraction and rigor, and scientific progress consists in the solution of precisely defined 'puzzles'. The systematic-discursive type of theory discussion differs therefrom in its *discursive openness* with respect to the formulation of questions and the framework of accepted approaches to solutions. The approach is evolutionary in the sense described earlier, in that questions and answers, giving and taking, writing and reading, form part of an ongoing process of communication, and discussion of theory takes place as participation in a 'circle'. (Systematic-discursive theorizing is in line but not quite identical with Richard R. Nelson's 'appreciative theorizing'.)

The two genres of theory discussion have a dynamic of their own. In the abstract-deductive genre the participants of a discussion stand, to use a metaphor of Karl Popper, around a 'bucket' which they fill with theoretical and empirical results until it is full and a new bucket in the form of a new formulation of theoretical questions can be put in its place. The gradual degeneration of intellectual 'puzzles' is no small problem for the leading 'pure' theoreticians, and the complaint of econometricians – that the theory does not offer interesting tasks – is well known. In contradistinction, the *systematic-discursive* type of theory does *not exhaust itself* in its questions and answers, because its discursive impetus *generates them continuously and endogenously*. In methodological discussions, the abstract-deductive type is fully covered, whereas the alternative systematic-discursive one is still in a nascent state; this itself is perhaps an expression of the increasingly accepted *pluralism* of methods and ontologies. It may well be the greatest, albeit not necessarily intentional, merit of Perlman's work, that it makes so major a contribution to the understanding of the systematic-discursive mode of theory discussion.

At this juncture, we can return to the 'analytic fractal' mentioned at the beginning, which constitutes an instance of the systematic-discursive type of theory discussion. It unites contextual, biographic, historical, and comparative aspects of an analysis and, in their mutual dependence, these drive the discursive dynamics and production of scientific perceptions. In the framework of the systematic-discursive genre of discussion, the strict distinction between 'pure' discussion of theories and of their history fades away. The *history* of economic thought, especially of the participant type, becomes an essential part of the *theoretical* discourse. In any event, classical and early neoclassical economics would experience a reevaluation because the half-life of quotations more than three or four years old would be accepted and a kind of intertemporal theory discussion could be developed. The uncritical acceptance of the prevalence of the abstract-deductive mode of theory discussion creates a risk not only for Perlman but for other economists who move along heterodox lines, that their work falls between the two chairs of 'pure' theory discussion and a 'professional' discussion about their historical derivations.

We may assume that Perlman tried to become an editor in the spirit of the systematic-discursive mode of theory discussion. He quotes at length from a report he wrote on his departure as managing editor of the *Journal of Economic Literature* in which he presents two 'styles of editing':

> One puts a nominal emphasis on the process of editorial choice as a (competitive rationing) process; the editor receives the manuscripts (or ... commissions them), chooses appropriate referees, sends the manuscripts to the referees, and lets the referees make such suggestions as they think appropriate and carry the burden of the final selection process.
>
> The other ... is for the editor to judge the manuscripts. In this instance he uses referees to expose to critical review those manuscripts that the editor thinks interesting. The referee's opinion should be transmitted to the author but with the view that the referee was not always chosen for his impartial qualities. 'You might as well know what your worst critic will say when the manuscript comes to the light of day.' Then this editor works with the author to tighten up loose points, to illuminate or eliminate irrelevancies; but in the end to let the author's neck stick out. In the first instance the editor tries to be *hors de combat*; in the second he assumes that the readers want interesting material, even if a scrap is involved. In the former case, the process of refereeing should be optimally double blind; ... In the latter ... (i)t is important for the referee to know who the author is, since part of the mission is to present a provocative paper.
>
> (p. 57)

Perlman's work represents is not only a contribution to the intellectual positioning of present day economics and the profiling of institutional economics, but is also instructive from the perspective of scientific communication and its conditions.

Notes

I gratefully acknowledge comments by G. C. Harcourt, Uerich Witt and Lukas Hagen. It is a pleasure to intend my thanks to John Veemann who translated (most of) the German manuscript into English and to Charles McCann and Stephen Freedman for their additional comments. Do I have to emphasize that I deserve all the blame for remaining errors that the reader or Mark Perlman might detect?

1 Mark Perlman (1996) *The Character of Economic Thought, Economic Characters and Economic Institutions: Selected Essays.* University of Michigan Press, Ann Arbor, MI.

Part II

Editing and intolerance in the profession

2 Parallels and differences in editing academic journals; Mark Perlman as a pioneer and role model[1]

Ingrid H. Rima

Perlman's pace-setting editorship

High on the list of Mark Perlman's numerous contributions to 'the quality of life' of economists, in particular academic economists, is his founding and editing of *Journal of Economic Literature*. His twelve-year stewardship of this prestigious publication with its legacy of close to fifty issues, brought a major survey article to a readership that exceeded 23,000 with each printing. The topics, whether the product of Perlman's own perceptive mind, or the result of consultations with the *creme de la creme* among his professional colleagues, provided what was, in effect, a postgraduate course by mail with each successive issue.

No one can duplicate the star quality of publishing survey articles by such leading thinkers as Machlup, Tobin, Fellner, Krueger, Rawles, Harcourt, Mincer, Johnston, Burmeister, Furubotin, Ferber, Pejovich, Mikesell, Sharkle, Stern, Malkiel, Morgenstern, Frisch, Etzioni, Sen, *et al.* (to mention those whose names first come to mind) as the best 'way to learn the high points about areas which [we] had no time to study' (1996: 21).

Along with the more than 23,000 professional colleagues who were also regular *Journal of Economic Literature* readers, I owe Mark Perlman the profound debt of ministering to my ongoing education and, particularly for alerting me to the writings of such scholars as George Shackle, Geoff Harcourt, and Amitai Etzioni long before I was able to meet them personally. All belong to academic circles which (lamentably) relatively few American trained scholars find reason to seek out, for the latter's professional lives hew closely to the mainstream paradigm that is the bedrock of all but relatively few economics programs.

As a recipient of an economics PhD from the University of Pennsylvania, I am the product of a graduate program that is substantially neoclassical, although I had the good fortune to study with Simon Kuznets and to learn post-Keynesian economics first hand from Sidney Weintraub. Unfortunately, Kuznets moved on to Harvard, while Sidney, who influenced my thinking as few others have, was unable to substantially change the focus of either the economics discipline or his own economics department, despite his success as co-founder and co-editor of the *Journal of Post Keynesian Economics*. While there were (and still are) several other important American journals concerned with dissent in economics, in particular the *Journal of*

Economic Issues, Review of Social Economy and the *American Journal of Economics and Sociology*, they reflect the particular points of view of their own founding fathers and also are more concerned with criticism rather than with articulating alternatives to mainstream thinking. Thus, Perlman's commissioning of survey articles which included such non-neoclassical themes as uncertainty, the capital theory controversy, economic justice, and poverty, under the highly respected banner of the American Economic Association, remains an inestimably valuable contribution. While I have no way of knowing whether these surveys (and others like them) made many converts to new ways of thinking, it certainly educated many of us. Perlman's mind-opening surveys alerted me not only to the gaps in the graduate program of which I was a part at my own university, but also made me sufficiently critical of the narrow focus of the journals I subscribed to, the conferences I participated in, to lead me to become an eager and committed founding member of the Eastern Economic Association as an 'open' professional society that would be as intellectually hospitable to scholars whose perspectives and training were non-neoclassical as it was to the substantially larger number whose professional interests mirrored those of the main-stream tradition. Unlike its national counterpart, the American Economic Association, whose annual meetings were comprised largely of 'invited' papers and sessions planned and presented by already established scholars along with some of their protégées, the objective of the Eastern Economic Association was to be 'inclu-sive' in the sense of extending an open 'call for papers' to facilitate not only broad participation but also broad representation of alternative approaches to economics.

Founding a new regional association

The Eastern Economic Association came, so to speak, 'late to the ball'. By the time that the Eastern was incorporated in 1973 under laws of the Commonwealth of Pennsylvania from its original headquarters at Bloomsburg State College (now the University of Bloomsburg), regional associations had existed for decades in other parts of the country. The Western Economic Association, founded in 1922, was meeting regularly, though the first issue of the *Western Economic Journal* was delayed for some forty years. The Southern Economic Association was organized in 1927, and began quarterly publication of its journal in 1934. The Mid-Western Association had also long been in existence, though it remained without a journal.

Why the delay in establishing a separate economics association to serve the east-ern region of the country? The chief reason, it would seem, was that an overwhelm-ingly large portion of the membership of the American Economic Association (specifically forty-five per cent in 1973) was geographically located in the eleven eastern states and Washington DC. To all appearances, therefore, east coast econo-mists were well served by the national association.

Yet, in the minds of more than a few who chanced to come together at the December 1972 meeting of the American Economic Association in New York City, our needs and interests were less than well satisfied by the national association. Despite the new vistas offered by Mark Perlman's *Journal of Economic Literature*, what was especially felt to be needed were opportunities for publication, presentation, and discussion, particularly by younger and less well-established scholars, than those offered by the national association, which was more receptive to proposals from scholars whose credentials and approach reflected their mainstream connections. Indeed, our spirit of dissent was reminiscent of the rebellion of the younger generation of American economists, among them Richard T. Ely and Edwin R. A. Seligman who, in 1885, organized *The American Economic Association* with a view to breaking the dominance of orthodox doctrine.[2] There was thus ample historical precedence at the time the Eastern Economic Association was organized that what was needed in the economics profession was a new association that would hold conferences and establish a journal whose venue would be more reflective of the heterodox economic doctrines and social policy issues that were under-represented at the most prestigious PhD granting private universities of the eastern states. Yet, because the faculties of these institutions dominated the profession, their participation, support, and guidance was eagerly sought as the late Tej Saini, Professor of Economics at Bloomsburg State College, assumed responsibility for organizing the new association's first conference which was held in Albany New York, October 25–27, 1974.

Close to a thousand economists attended, and some 600 of them presented papers. Several luminaries, including MIT's Robert Solow and Paul Samuelson, Yale's James Tobin, and Laurence Klein of the University of Pennsylvania, were there. Theodore Schultz (Chicago), Daniel Fusfeld (University of Michigan), and Robert Heilbroner (The New School) who, tongue-in-cheek, referred to himself as part of the 'eastern dis-establishment', were also participants.[3] It was hoped that their simultaneous presence, given the broad spectrum of their differing beliefs, signaled support for the idea of an intellectual bridge of the sort the Eastern Economic Association undertook to help build. The conference was a huge success, and with this heady beginning, the expectation was that the Eastern Economic Association would become all and more than what its founding members hoped.

The next several conferences did not disappoint, especially when they convened in such major convention cities as New York City, Boston and Washington. Our intellectual benefactors, who included such different intellects as Paul Samuelson, Kenneth Galbraith, Joan Robinson and Harry Johnson, generously lent us the lustre of their star status in the profession by their presence at one or more of our annual conferences. Their relationship with the Association was never formalized with the *quid pro quo* of high office, though Harry Johnson succeeded Barbara Bergman (then a relatively unknown feminist) as the association's second president. However, it became the ongoing practice of the Association (perhaps to establish professional acceptability by the company we kept) to select its candidates for Association President and Vice President from the faculties of the most prestigious private institutions of higher learning in the east. In their turn, Laurence Klein and James Tobin became both Presidents-elect and, soon afterward, Nobel Laureates. Indeed, the saying that 'one becomes a Nobel Prize winner after first serving as President of the Eastern Economic Association' became something of an 'inner circle' joke. (I continue to hope on behalf of Will Baumol, who became our third President-elect, and who was, in every respect, a joy to work with.) Under the Association's bylaws, the Association's past President, current President, President elect, and Vice President, became the Executive Board, which appointed the journal's editor, its editorial board, and the association's secretary treasurer. Tej Saini, whose brainchild the Eastern was, became the Association's Secretary–Treasurer. He was an entrepreneur *par excellence* and a brilliant organizer without whose drive, energy and persuasiveness it is unlikely that the profession's most prestigious scholars would have been amenable to membership in the Eastern Economic Association.

Editorial responsibility was considerably more difficult to assign, and passed in short order from Louis Salkever (SUNY Albany) to Albert Smigel (PA Department of Commerce), and henceforth to Alan Abouchar (University of Toronto). Understandably, the journal's publication was behind schedule from its inception, while the expense of even sporadic printing ate up Association revenues more rapidly than increasingly expensive conferences and an inappropriate dues schedule could replenish them. My appointment in 1979 as Editor of the *Eastern Economic Journal* might thus have been ill-fated had it not been for the willingness of Temple University to finance outstanding printing bills, reduce my teaching load, and pay office expenses. The combination provided an incredible and enviable opportunity to move the Journal in the direction of the greater eclecticism that I and my fellow founding members envisioned!

I took on my own duties as editor of the *Eastern Economic Journal* ten years after Mark created *The Journal of Economic Literature*. Like Perlman, it was a responsibility I carried on for twelve years. Also, like Perlman, the experience 'gave me a kind of entree which was like a dream', and 'I enjoyed the job thoroughly'. While the opportunities for close contact with the 'greats' of our profession were far fewer for me than those which Mark enjoyed, I count among my close friends my associate editors, more than a hundred reviewers, and many whose first published papers appeared in the *Eastern Economic Journal*, and who have since gone on to establish themselves in the profession.

While my acquaintance with Mark at the time of my appointment as editor had not yet blossomed into the warm friendship I was later to enjoy (nor was I sophisticated enough to appreciate that there were different styles of editing) I did have on my shelf some forty issues of the *Journal of Economic Literature*. Thus, I had already come to appreciate the possibility of editing a journal which, unlike most already well-established economic journals, including both the *Southern* and the *Western* (now *Economic Inquiry*), would offer an hospitable outlet for articles that did not necessarily reflect the criteria of 'scientific economics' which had by the 1970s become substantially *de rigeur*. This was among the objectives for the establishment in 1974 of the Eastern Economic Association, and it is one which I pursued with all the energy, commitment and judgment I could muster. My efforts were considerably facilitated when after my initial five-year term, the Executive Board ceded to the Editor responsibility for appointing the members of the editorial board and two Associate Editors. These were carefully selected with a view to promoting the intellectual openness and eclecticism on which the Association was founded.

Factors shaping the demand and supply characteristics of the EEJ

To paraphrase Mark, 'it takes no great wit to realize that an editor has to be concerned with the demand for and the supply of his product' (Perlman 1996: 53).

Both on the demand side and the supply side the circumstances which shaped my editorial experience with the *Eastern Economic Journal* were not only fundamentally different from Mark's, but they were different in ways that, in retrospect, were harbingers of things yet to come in our profession and the academic journals they supported. First, as was implicit in the founding of the Association, the perceived need for a new journal stemmed not from the identification of new sub-disciplines whose needs were less than well satisfied by existing journals; nor was it dictated (as was the case with the Union for Radical Political Economics, URPE) by ideological considerations. It was instead dictated substantially by the needs of a young and rapidly growing professoriate peopled by large numbers of newly minted economics PhDs during the 1960s and for at least a decade afterward. Most brought with them the training in mathematical economics and econometrics that was, by then, considered the hallmark of scientific economics. Those who were inclined towards academic careers, especially if their graduate training had taken place in a reasonably well regarded doctoral program, found employment in the rapidly expanding economics and finance departments of academic institutions.

In an era of large undergraduate enrollments, many new PhDs were part of institutions that reinvented themselves as four-year colleges and universities while new community colleges and technical institutions mushroomed beside them. Their mission was to establish themselves not simply as teaching institutions, but also as 'research' institutions. The economics department of Temple University's School of Business, which generously supported me during the first five years of my editorship, is surely a case in point. It more than doubled the number of assistant (and a few associate) professors who were hired as tenure track appointees. Their futures were contingent on the publication of between four and seven articles in a time frame of three to six years in journals which, though they might not be 'high level' had, at a minimum, to be documented as 'refereed'. Clearly then the very growth of the economics profession brought with it a demand for journal space to accommodate the burgeoning number of new submissions by tenure track appointees. Their need, which my editorial board and I were technically able to fill, was to review and publish articles that conformed to the mainstream paradigm.

Their needs were of course only part of the demand for journal space, for even while the profession as a whole tilted increasingly towards abstraction and empiricism, so too did the number of economists who, complaining of the profession's *rigor mortis*, sought publication opportunities for articles relating to heterodox issues and approaches, and the history of economics. Though the latter were being served by specialized journals, the supply of publication opportunities remained limited, especially in view of the relentless tick of the tenure clock.

By the 1970s membership in the profession was disproportionately a young professoriate, employed by relatively small and recently established institutions. Since the focus of economic research, particularly early in one's career, is characteristically reflective of the degree-awarding institution and its history, it became apparent that economists whose intellectual roots were established in the public (and land grant) institutions that dominated in the West, mid-West, and South, were (and to some extent remain) substantially different from those cultivated at Eastern institutions which are (except for New York State) predominately private. Based on records relating to the 975 new PhDs in economics conferred in 1973 (the year of the new association's founding), the 'output' by region was 356 from mid-Western institutions, 282 from Eastern institutions, 192 from Western institutions, and 145 from Southern institutions.[4] While the Association was founded to accommodate more broadly the needs of east coast economists, my inference, given the rapid growth of undergraduate education in the east, was that the number of new PhDs whose job search ended with migration, would expand the Eastern Economic Association's prospective membership pool. This reality substantially added to the difficulty of closing the very large gap between the demand for and the supply of journal space. In particular, the Universities of Michigan and Wisconsin were a rich source of new eastern region talent. Much to my surprise (and delight) many new members with non-neoclassical interests came not only from the mid-west, but also from Canada and Europe, in particular, Germany, Italy and the UK. Thus, our membership became virtually international, and I soon became fond of saying that the Journal's 'natural market' extended clear across the Atlantic.

Developing an editorial style

My 'style of editing', if I may call it that, was to provide a 'double blind' review for every paper I received that was outside my several areas of expertise. Meeting with my fellow Journal editors at the annual Allied Social Sciences Association (ASSA) breakfast meeting, I learned that this practice was generally viewed as unnecessary, or worse, inappropriate. Yet, after my initial screening, those papers which were not rejected outright were sent to reviewers who, in addition to their technical expertise, also shared the author's paradigmatic perspective. I followed this procedure as though it were 'the one true religion', knowing instinctively that papers are often rejected because they are not coming from 'the right place', or even the 'right person'. The editor of a general journal, even one who is well versed in multiple fields, serves his/her readers and authors more effectively by also factoring into a publishing decision the expertise of outside reviewers who while they may have a 'clue' about the author and his/her affiliation, are less likely to glean information that is prejudicial when the author's identity is concealed. 'Double blind' reviewing was, I felt, especially in the years preceding the conscious raising efforts of CSWEP the Committee on the Status of Women in the Economics Profession, the proper thing to do. Indeed, I now note from a recent Report of the Editor of the *American Economic Review* (Orley Ashenfelter) that the American Economic Association Board voted to adopt double-blind refereeing (*Papers and Proceedings*, May 1998: 511). At least in this respect, the *Eastern Economic Journal* led the way.

Like Mark, I also appreciated the need to offer readers something provocative and interesting. I was truly envious that I could not duplicate his creative format for my readers. I not only lacked his wide professional contacts to commission the famous survey articles which he elevated almost into an art form but, given the goal of opening publication opportunities and mentoring young scholars, I necessarily began by waiting for submissions. With the Eastern's initial unreliable publishing record, most of the papers coming in turned out to have been previously rejected (appropriately) several times over. With nothing in the pipeline, I began an energetic 'outreach' by attending every conference for which I could spare time and money; it produced a sufficient number of issues to establish that we were indeed 'in business'.

My commitment to the 'Perlman view' that shaping the body of economic knowledge requires a 'balance' between technical analysis and historical knowledge of 'scientific economics' suggested the relevance of including an article relating to the history of economic thought as a regular feature of the journal. While my efforts to follow his lead and 'work both sides of the economics avenue of thought' (Perlman 1996: 45) garnered some applause, I was also reminded by the Executive Board that 'we don't teach HET at MIT'. While I nevertheless continued the feature, in keeping with the objective of printing a well balanced mix of papers, history of thought papers comprised only one in approximately eight published in each issue. Approximately half of the others were 'mainstream'.

My golden opportunity to suitably differentiate the Eastern's product did not present itself until 1985 when I first read McCloskey's *The Rhetoric of Economics*. We had not yet had an opportunity to meet, but when we did there was a particularly provocative exchange of ideas which I ultimately shared with the Journal's readers as 'A Conversation' with McCloskey on rhetoric. It proved to be an especially good choice for launching a new journal feature. Not only had the role of rhetoric in relation to economics already emerged as a 'hot' topic, but it also signaled more clearly the receptiveness of the Editorial Board of the *Eastern Economic Journal* to offer a venue sympathetic to proponents of unorthodox paradigms while also offering 'equal time' to the mainstream.

The 'Conversation' format was to become a vehicle for bringing the ideas of some of the profession's most provocative thinkers to our readers. Over the next six years each successive issue featured *A Conversation* as its lead. Among those who made time for interviews were Sir John Hicks, John Kenneth Galbraith, William Baumol, Jagdish Bhagwati, Amatai Etzioni, Dale Jorgenson and many others, including Joseph Pechman, whose conversation relating to the Tax Reform Act of 1986 was, sadly, published posthumously. I remember them all with great fondness and warm appreciation for their willingness to respond at length to my persistent questions. They made it possible for me to pioneer the conversation format as a vehicle for sharing economic knowledge. Of necessity, it is a less formal and largely non-technical format when compared with the Perlman survey articles which were their inspiration. The conversation format proved to be reader accessible and apparently lent itself so uniquely to reaffirming that economics is not necessarily a dismal science, that it has since been widely used by others.

From the beginning, the *Eastern Economic Journal* suffered a supply-side problem which Mark was fortunate to have escaped. While the American Economic Association enjoyed a surplus that enabled it to experiment with the *Journal of Economic Literature*, and later *Economic Perspectives*, the Eastern Economic Association was launched by a hundred or so life members who contributed the relatively small sum of about $125 in exchange for four issues per year. Journal printing and annual convention costs escalated beyond our apparent ability to generate revenues, even by fund raising and personal loans. The infant simply failed to grow up to fiscal soundness. So acute did the Association's financial problems become that in its efforts to achieve fiscal order, the Executive Board replaced Saini as the Association's financial officer. The result, unfortunately, was a protracted law suit which exacerbated the Association's financial problems and inevitably compromised timely publication of a journal whose carefully refereed papers now regularly filled 120 journal pages.

Most disturbing in terms of my editorship, now well into my second five-year term, was a substantial loss of support on the part of the Executive Board for the very objective of an eclectic journal. While earlier boards, led successively by Jim Tobin, Larry Klein, and Will Baumol, may not have shared the commitment of the Association's founders and its membership to establish an intellectually open organization and an eclectic journal, they were, nevertheless, willing, as I remember one of them expressing his sentiments, to 'let a thousand flowers bloom'. But the years passed, and as their successors came onto the scene, the disparity between the respective visions which the Editorial and Executive Boards had with respect to the Journal became increasingly wide. It also became clear that a short-term reconciliation was unlikely, because the profession had itself become increasingly characterized by paradigmatic dissent.

My fellow editorial board members and I were successful in persuading the Executive Board to approve an official Editorial Policy Statement. Following a lengthy and somewhat heated verbal exchange, the following was adopted: The *Eastern Economic Journal* is committed to free and open intellectual inquiry from diverse philosophical perspectives in all areas of theoretical and applied research related to economics (adopted by the Executive Board, April 1986, Philadelphia, Pennsylvania). Yet, it became increasingly difficult on both sides to politely set aside the differences of vision between the Executive and Editorial Boards about the content and the role of the *Journal*.

While we wait for the millennium, it is relevant to recognize that, as a profession, the economics discipline has now reached a stage in which the supply of new PhDs significantly exceeds the demand for them. This is partly the result of demographics, but it also reflects a clear rejection of our 'product' by a generation of undergraduates whose resistance to studying economics has reduced course enrollments so substantially that our graduate programs are becoming decimated for lack of a baccalaureate foundation, and are sought out largely by foreign-born students, if at all. The inevitable outcome is that a growing number of well qualified and sometimes well published younger faculty members confront terminal contracts instead of tenure. Analogously, many senior faculty who might reasonably have expected a ready reception at a more prestigious institution than the one at which they started 20 years ago, when the present glut of PhDs was not yet anticipated, are now substantially less likely to enjoy career openings that will utilize their talents more fully. In his paper 'On the Editing of American Economic Journals' Mark fully recognized the dismal prospect that the economics profession would find itself with a declining audience for its 'research' results, and likely experience a dearth of students in both its undergraduate and graduate divisions.

The minutes of the 110th annual meeting of the American Economic Association published in the *Papers and Proceedings* issue, May 1998, reflects an awareness that besides confronting a soft labor market for new economics PhDs (Siegfried and Stock, 1999) the Ad Hoc Committee on Journals (chaired by Thomas Schelling) had undertaken to survey the American Economic Association's membership about the 'usefulness' of its several journals in relation to their research interests and work (p. 503). This is essentially the signal that was sent a quarter of a century ago by the founders of the *Eastern Economic Journal* who believed in the relevance of greater product differentiation among journals. Did we fail in our mission?

Again I draw on Mark's wisdom in recognizing that the effectiveness of a journal's mission and the style of its transmission to its intended audience can only be known *ex post* (p. 51). The Association and its Journal undertook to become something of a conduit for the Perlman view that progress in economic science requires a broad spectrum approach in which technical analysis has its place, but is by no means sufficient. It also requires openness to an approach quite different from the formalism which has overtaken the profession since the 1960s. Even though the latter significantly defines its academic employment opportunities, the social concerns and dissenting attitudes that nurtured the institutionalist tradition and shaped Perlman's approach have retained their vitality and also achieved greater sophistication in their expression. As I peruse some recent issues of the Journal I once edited, as is to be expected over the ten years that have elapsed, more has changed than the color of its cover. Yet, despite an editorial shift closer to the mainstream, the journal remains both 'open' and eclectic. The mission undertaken by the *Eastern Economic Journal* as a relatively small regional journal to emulate the *Journal of Economic Literature* is itself a tribute to its founding editor, Mark Perlman. The social concerns and dissenting attitudes of the *Eastern Economic Journal* have now also nurtured several new journals and professional societies having essentially the same objectives that motivated the early days of the Eastern Economic Association. Indeed, I take pride in the fact that from amongst the members of the editorial board members with whom I worked so closely at the *Eastern Economic Journal*, two have recently become editors of other journals and are perpetuating its ideal of intellectual breadth and inclusiveness under a new masthead. While a thousand flowers are perhaps not yet blooming, the 'Perlman tradition' continues to flourish in contemporary economic journals, and, as this volume surely affirms, in many other venues as well.

Notes

1 My thanks to Professor Nicholas Balabkins of Lehigh University for his comments on an earlier draft. Of course, he bears no responsibility for the final product.

2 These American institutionalists were also the inspiration for the " 'Commons' tradition" at the University of Wisconsin. Selig Perlman (1888–1959), Mark's father and John Commons's disciple, was instrumental in defining the role of unions in American society. The origin of Mark's pioneering mindset is clearly in evidence.

3 The full program of the inaugural meeting of the Eastern Economic Association is available in the *Proceedings* volume published by the Association in 1974.

4 These numbers reflect the combined count published in the *AER* (63) May 1973 and *AJAE* (56) May 1974. The latter records the number of new PhDs that were in agricultural economics, which constituted twenty-four percent of the total.

References

Ashenfelter, O. (1988) 'Report of the editor', *American Economic Review, Papers and Proceedings*, 88(2).

Perlman, M. (1996) 'On editing of American economic journals: some comments on the earlier journals and the lessons suggested in the character of economic thought, economic characters and economic institutions', *Selected Essays of Mark Perlman*, Ann Arbor MI: The University of Michigan Press.

Perlman, M. 'Report of economics PhDs conferred', *American Economic Review*, 63, May 1973, and *American Journal of Agricultural Economics*, 56, May 1974.

Rima, I. (1991) 'Changing of the guard', *Eastern Economic Journal*, v. XVII, no. 4,

Saini, T. (1974) 'Editor's introduction', *Proceedings of the Inaugural Convention of the Eastern Economic Association*, Albany NY, October 25–27.

Siegfried, J. J. and Stock, W. A. (1999) 'The labor market for new PhD economists', *Journal of Economic Perspectives* 13(3): 115–34.

3   Pastiches from an earlier politically incorrect academic age

Paul A. Samuelson

Father and son teams are famous in economics: James and John Stuart Mill; John Neville and John Maynard Keynes; John Bates and John Maurice Clark. Therefore, to contribute for a Mark Perlman *Festschrift*, I select a topic that would have interested Selig Perlman, Mark's father and an acclaimed historian of the American Labor Movement in his own right.

Selig Perlman made his academic way at Wisconsin in the pre-World War I period when Jews were few in U.S. academic life. If scarcity makes for high price, those few ought to have enjoyed astronomical salaries. (Alvin Hansen told me that it was Perlman who first discovered him. While on sabbatical leave, Selig looked over the term papers in John R. Commons' Wisconsin graduate class. 'The one by Hansen is the only paper with real scholarly promise,' Perlman reported. The rest is history.)

Some careerists, after they have elbowed their way into Valhalla, wish to pull up the ladder behind them. Not Selig Perlman. By reputation, he was singularly zealous in speaking up for promising scholars who encountered theological bigotries: as we have seen, he even spoke up for a Danish-American farmboy, whose parents had independently migrated to America to escape the repressions against Baptists by the mid-nineteenth century established Danish Lutheran Church.

I am not an expert on anti-semitism and various racial prejudices. Nor can I claim personally to have particularly suffered the pains of bias. If anything the marketplace has imputed to me perhaps even more than my intrinsic worth. All the better then may be my qualifications to report on what the world was really like in the years from 1920 to 1945. Before then, we can be sure that Selig Perlman could have painted an infinitely worse portrait.

What my anecdotes lack in quantitative validation may be a bit atoned for by their authenticity. I was present at world centers of importance and confine myself largely to incidents and events of which my knowledge has been first hand. Although the present purpose pardons an unbalanced preoccupation with anti-semitism, strongly correlated with it factually will be found to be anti-Black, anti-female, anti-Catholic, anti-homosexual, anti-radical and even anti-class attitudes. No discrimination is intended here against the valid complaints of Hispanics, gypsies or Native Americans – it is just that their sample was very small in the academia of my early times, which is itself a testimony to something significant.

The good old days

Put bluntly, there were no tenured Jews in the Ivy League. None at all? Well, virtually none at all. And it was not all that different at the large state universities, particularly in the engineering faculties. Since almost no chemical companies would hire a Jew with a diploma in chemistry, graduates of the City College of New York (CCNY) sensibly opted to apply to law schools or schools of dentistry. Was the DNA of the Chosen People exceptionally biased in favor of tooth care and against care of the heart and kidney? Or was it more likely that Junior Phi Beta Kappa's from CCNY were largely unable to gain admission to medical schools?

In my older times, if you went to college at all, it was generally (a) to your father's college, or (b) to the university near to where you lived. That explains why, as a visiting lecturer, I would encounter a richer mixture of brilliant students at the University of Buffalo in 1940 than at State University of New York (Buffalo) in 1965: by 1965, the best and brightest in upstate New York often got drained off to Cornell or Harvard. That explains why in 1941 our crack MIT graduate school recruited much of the entering class from the University of Kansas and DePauw rather than as today so much more frequently from Princeton, Stanford and Harvard. This seems a case of *class* stratification giving way to meritocracy stratification.

I was lucky that the University of Chicago was near my home. It was a great age for the (Hutchins) Midway. The Rosenwald Foundation rightly ranked Chicago second only to Harvard *c.* 1935, with Columbia and Berkeley hot on their heels. What was Chicago's transient advantage? John D. Rockefeller's largesse as a Baptist? Yes, of course. But, also, I give importance to Chicago's monopoly advantage as a place that would hire some extraordinarily able Jews. That made their money go farther. Not that there was no anti-semitism at Chicago. There was some of that anywhere (and even in the CCNY faculty!). In the 1920s when Frank Knight, Jacob Viner and other Chicago economists decided to recruit Henry Schultz, protégé of H.L. Moore and an early econometrician, they were told: 'But President Max Mason does not like Jews.' 'Well, let him veto the appointment then. We think he's the best man for the post.' (I have this story from my Chicago classmate Jacob Mosak, who became Schultz's protégé and assistant. I may add that by general 1920–35 opinion, Jacob Viner had been Frank Taussig's prize student at Harvard and, as the world authority on both international trade and history of economics, he arguably deserved a Harvard chair more than most then sitting in those chairs.)

My next anecdote is exceptional because it represented something so rare. In my undergraduate time, a Chicago coach was reported to have said aloud (there is no other way to say something): 'There are getting to be too many Jews around here.' When this was reported to the venerable head-coach Amos Alonzo Stagg, Stagg called in the accused. 'Did you say that?' 'Yes, in a thoughtless moment I did say those words.' 'Well then, as of this hour, you are fired. Collect your pay and sweat garb and go.' Now what's unusual about that story? It is its rarity. In simple truth *most* non-Jews were not virulently anti-semitic at that time. Or even anti-semitic in any *significant sense*. (I exclude the racial slurs that peppered within-family conversations of your typical American family folk. 'You can't jew me down to a lower price.' etc., etc.)

Everywhere and at all times most humans are social cowards. We will not make waves just for an abstract principle. Even if you would not mind having proportionate Jewish representation in social or athletic clubs, you are not willing to go clubless on that account or join up with a largely Jewish group to make a point. Similar stratifications were observable within ethnic groups: successful Eastern European Jews becoming token members in exclusive clubs formed by wealthy German immigrants from an earlier age.

The Harvard of 1920–45 was not worse than other Ivy League schools. Since President Eliot's effort to make Harvard a great *university*, it had become distinctly better than Yale or Princeton. That is not saying much. Harvard presidents alternate between university and college leaders. A. Lawrence Lowell, as Eliot's successor, was a college person. I came to know him later – at Harvard's Society of Fellows, which he personally endowed with the last of his family fortune. Lowell denounced Sacco and Vanzetti because he believed them to be murderers, and therefore he said so publicly. He believed that the pushy 'new races' were pressing against the fine Yankee talent. And therefore he injudiciously announced that Harvard would apply a numerical quota on admissions. Better candid truth than under-the-table hypocrisy? This led to an unexpected public uproar. When he gave a speech to alumni in New York, apparently he explained the problem of uncouth immigrants with pushy manners. Besides, he is supposed to have validly pointed out that race-blind admissions at Harvard would vastly increase the number of New York Jews in the freshman class. One old-timer reported to me the following (so all this is hearsay and should be checked with the new history of Harvard that is in the making), that a number of wealthy listeners deemed this personally insulting and began to reconsider their charitable giving.

It is a matter of record that, for whatever reason, in 1923 Harvard introduced a new policy according to which *any* boy who finished in the highest *seven* of his high school class would be admitted to Harvard. In consequence, 1927 was a brilliant class that included Judge Charles Wyzanski, Professor Milton Katz of Marshall Plan and Ford Foundation fame and many others. A surviving member of 1927 believes that as many as twenty percent of his fellow freshmen were Jews. And pins on the map for subsequent Harvard students did become dispersed to include entrants from outside the Philadelphia–Portland axis. Not until 1935 did President Conant introduce Harvard's regional scholarships, which brought James Tobin all the way from Champaign-Urbana, Illinois, to Cambridge, Massachusetts.

Where were Yale and Princeton then? At Yale President Angell tried to be a university rather than college president. A call was sent out to Morris Cohen, CCNY's famous philosopher. In weighing it, Dr Cohen made a point of asking whether the philosophy department really wanted him. Since he asked, he is said to have been told: 'President Angell wants you. But we do not.' Yale's loss was CCNY's gain, and later Chicago's gain. Princeton's eating clubs, which operated much like private fraternities, effectively kept its undergraduate composition mainstream Protestant. Its graduate school stayed limited to the couple of hundred who could be housed in one gothic structure, where Oxbridge robes were *de rigueur* at meal times. So strong was Princeton's mathematics and physics that a Maxwell Demon passed a Richard

Feynman through the system's filter. Stars like Ansley Coale and Lionel McKenzie were relatively rare until Morgenstern-von Neumann mathematics attracted Shapleys, Nashes and Shubiks.

It used to be quipped: Anti-Catholicism is the anti-semitism of the academics. Less than the demographic quotas of brilliant Catholics were to be found in pre-World War II elite universities. Bias begets backlash. Cardinal O'Connell, the powerful archbishop of the Boston diocese, frowned on members of the flock who selected Harvard over Boston College. It was a wonder that Ambassador Joseph Kennedy, father of the Kennedy clan, went to Harvard back in the Teens. Alice Bourneuf, who was the one woman who got an A from the femmophobe Frank Taussig, was considered exceptional when she and her sister came to Radcliffe. After her time the two-sided barriers largely broke down.

In the 1930s Radcliffe and Harvard were not integrated at the undergraduate level. Edward Mason would lecture on Industrial Organization to 200 Harvard men at 9 am. Then from 11 am to 12 noon he would repeat that same lecture before eight Radcliffe women. When my fiancée would want to use Widener Library, she was supposed to wear hat and gloves and speak in hushed tones in the special ghetto space for females. In economics, graduate study was by then integrated. But not in delicate subjects like English. When I expressed surprise at this to Mr. Lowell, he expressed surprise at my surprise. 'Would you want your sister to be in the same Shakespeare class with men?' That, as the French say, gave one to think. (I by chance was at Cambridge University in 1948 the first day a woman received a Cambridge degree. It was the Queen Mother. I heard an old don mutter, 'Next they'll be riding their bikes in caps and gowns.') Joan Robinson, at Girton in the early 1920s, got a certificate, not a degree – even though Florence Brown Keynes and Mary Paley Marshall had received a Cambridge education back in the late 1870s. The great Alfred Marshall was a notorious femmophobe.

A proposal, around 1937, to admit a black undergraduate into Lowell House at Harvard gave rise to hot debate. (This was decades after Paul Robeson had starred in Ivy League football!) Finally, non-resident tutor Professor William Yandell Elliott, southern gentleman and lecturer in huge Freshman Government 1 caved in and said, 'All right, but don't expect me to sit next to him.' I tell this discreditable story only to make a point about the timing of the Great Change. Just ten years later, this same Elliott, as Chairman of the Government Department, went on hands and knees to Ralph Bunche hoping to fill a distinguished Harvard chair. Bunche by that time had bigger fish to fry elsewhere at the United Nations.

Repeating the same kind of anecdote N times does not proportionally multiply its importance or accuracy. However, to illustrate the positive correlation between one kind of bigotry and other kinds of bigotry here is a true account *within* economics itself. When I arrived at Harvard in 1935, Harold Hitchings Burbank had been department chairman since time immemorial. Burbank's incompetence as a scholar could not be exaggerated. I once thought to have caught him out with a publication: on the spine of a volume at old Phillips Bookstore across from Widener was written Burbank. But after incredulous auditing, it turned out to be an edited symposium where it was the other editors who had done the work. The easiest A I ever got was in Burbank's graduate Public Finance course. (Irreverent students called it a course, not *on* public finance but *against* public finance.) Class contents were a crib from the Princeton textbook of conservative Harley Lutz, which itself was a crib from Charles Bullock's reactionary Harvard lectures of 1901–33.

Burbank suffered fools gladly, but not Jews. On major departmental appointments, he could count on a near-majority of cronies. Where patronage appointments in the lower ranks were concerned, he was absolute king. Being myself royally supported by Social Science Research and Harvard Society of Fellows stipends, like William Tell I felt no need to cozy up to him. That did not stop Burbank from advising me: 'Samuelson, you are narrow. Keynes and Hawtrey are narrow. Don't take up economic theory until *after* you are fifty. This is what our great Allyn Young used to say.' Alas, I had already lost my heart, and aspired to become even more narrow; and furthermore Young died young, just before his rendezvous with greatness. Believing my male heredity to be (I write this in my ninth decade of life!) problematic, I was always a young man in a hurry.

Faced with a plethora of unsavory talent, H.H.B. solved his dilemma by confining the best of them to a ghetto of assistants in statistics and accounting under W. L. Crum and his satellite Edwin Frickey. Because Burbank had almost absolute pitch in his distaste for talent, such names as R. A. Gordon, Abram Bergson, Joe Bain and Lloyd Metzler made this a legion of honor. Metzler, a boy from Kansas with a German-sounding name, used to sing hymn duets with Marion Crawford – such as, 'Jesus Wants Me For a Sunbeam.' But as has been said, an anti-semite can smell out the last nine out of six Jews who have entered the room.

Burbank was catholic in his distastes. *Ceteris paribus*, he did not like foreigners. (As he discovered, they didn't speak accentless English.) He did not like radicals. Richard Murphy Goodwin, fresh from the farm country of Newcastle, Indiana, and Rhodes House, Oxford, drove him up the wall by asking: 'How little must I teach if I want a salary of only $1800 a year? I do like to paint.' When Senator Sinclair Weeks leaked an FBI report to Harvard concerning Goodwin's leftisms, that confirmed Burbank's distrust of dilettantes. (Neither Burbank nor Dick's friends knew that Goodwin did suffer from debilitating migraines. Painting may have been optimal decision making – at least up to Goodwin's post-Cambridge Indian Summer of scientific creativity late in life at Siena.) Under the Freedom of Information Act, Ken Galbraith learned that Burbie had reported to the FBI that Galbraith was as dangerous as President Franklin Delano Roosevelt. (I paraphrase from memory.)

I believe I have laid the background for the promised anecdote to come. (But before proceeding, one must face up to the complexity of real life. Yes, Burbie did have in him a sadistic streak which he took out on bullied graduate students: he did once call in Goodwin to say, 'Dick, I'd like to do to you what my father once did to me – tie you up to a wagon wheel and give you the whipping you deserve.' I learned this when sitting in the back of Gottfried Haberler's car on our way to Taconic, Connecticut, for Schumpeter's funeral in January 1950. On my right was Goodwin. On my left was Alfred Conrad, co-generator of Cliometrics with John Meyer. Alf chipped in: 'Say what you will about Burbie, he was the only one in the cold Harvard environment who asked me how my post-T.B. health was developing. One day he called me in to say: "I've got you figured, Alf, as a warm human being, and that's the kind of PhD thesis you ought to decide on." How could I then say that just yesterday I'd settled on a topic about matrices of Leontief input/output type!')

There is a different beast from every angle you view an elephant. My first run in with Burbie came on Registration Day 1935 when I refused to take the standard economic history course from the boring Edwin Gay. Yet, just yesterday, as I write, I read a charming memoir from Theodore Morgan of the University of Wisconsin. In 1938 when Ted was dithering between English (with two years of old English and one of Middle German as a graduate requirement) and economics, he reports, '… nice old Burbie … overweight and pleasant … talked to me with interest and kindness. … [and] let me sign up for the courses I fancied.' Also, as I have written elsewhere, our dear friend Jeanette Arnold (Whitmer) became Burbank's last departmental secretary. She worshipped the man we held in contempt. It was no strain on our friendship: by tacit agreement we never talked about H.H.B.

One summer day in 1937 or 1938, Russ Nixon our class radical and Radcliffe students' pin-up boy, told me about his tennis morning playing doubles with full professors Edward Chamberlin and Edward Mason and Instructor Paul Sweezy. Between sets, Nixon reported that Paul S. remarked, 'Wasn't that terrible what Burbie said as yesterday's departmental meeting was ending?' 'What was that?' Chamberlin asked. Paul filled him in: 'You'll remember that attendance was light and that encouraged me to move that we make Shigeto Tsuru a Teaching Fellow – a post he richly deserved. *Mirabile dictu*, we got a majority and the motion was carried. As we were breaking up, Burbie grumbled, "Next thing you know they'll be making Dean an instructor."' (Voice from the Greek chorus, me, PAS: Dean was one of two black graduate students, whose research under Abbott Payson Usher on location theory applied to economic history was deemed to be path-breaking.)

Ed Chamberlin, always logical, Russ reports as saying: 'Burbank wasn't wrong. If you appoint a Japanese, you can't refuse to appoint a colored man. Actually, the French do it right: if you're not trained in France, no chair for you.' Paul then replied: 'But if national residence is your test, then a Dean whose people have been in America for 300 years must surely qualify.' Chamberlin, always logical, replied: 'Yes to Dean. No to a foreigner.' (Greek chorus: Shigeto Tsuru was the only Harvard College graduate in the 1935 entering economics graduate class. His senior thesis, written in Adams House, won high honors. Later he was a bulwark for the MacArthur Occupation team, a primary bridge between Japanese and Western economics, Professor and President of Hitotsubashi University and a scholar whose collected papers filled more than thirteen volumes! He was also an authority on Marxian and on environmental economics.) To wind up this two-bigotry anecdote, at the next departmental meeting with a full complement attending, the provisional Tsuru appointment was rescinded and he had to settle for being Schumpeter's prize research assistant. As an honorable postscript to this tennis-court conversation, I can report that during World War II when Emile Despres was recruiting the famous team of pre-CIA Office of Strategic Services (OSS) economists, he felt duty bound to go to head honcho Mason and say, 'Ed, I've been recruiting many crack economists and a number of them turn out to be Jews. Is this a problem?' Mason replied: 'Pick the best you can. If ever it becomes a problem, let me worry about that.' The story ended there.

Summing up

There was once a time when many scholars honestly dismissed Jews as being incompetent – especially in Humanities departments. The early Binet I.Q. tests, culture bound, when applied to pre-World War I immigrants allegedly confirmed this thesis of racial inability. But by the time of my early days, attitudes were best understood as stemming from a contrary fear that ethnic-blind promotions might unleash an undesired avalanche. Few thought Einstein to be a dunce or a shallow master of physics. When Nazis in Hitler's Germany called Werner Heisenberg a 'White Jew' that was taken by him to be something of an honor.

Frisky Merriman, Master of Harvard's fashionable Eliot House, was a candid anti-semite. He never justified his position in terms of competence or incompetence. I am sure that, as a historian of the Spanish and Turkish Empires, he had never heard of Eli Heckscher's histories of Sweden or of Mercantilism. In 1940 I was an Instructor and Tutor in Harvard's Leverett House – known then as 'Moscow on the Charles.' Our Boston blue-blood Master, Kenneth Murdock, mischievously read to us members of the Senior Common Room the letter Merriman had written to all his 'cousins' serving as House Masters: 'What, oh what, are we going to do about this Jew problem? We are supposed to have a quota of twenty per cent [was he right in this?] but you have only to use your eyes to realize that they are more than forty per cent and growing.' It was *a* last gasp – but not *the* last gasp – of a decaying order.

Today Harvard, Princeton and Yale have presidents who, by Nazi calculus, are two-and-a-half Jewish and one-half Italian. This is not an equilibrium of maximal entropy, but one envisages well-born corpses rotating in their graves at the fact of it.

I have concentrated on MIT and the few Ivy League places I knew best. But one could write much about the great state universities and the smaller crack colleges. Wisconsin itself, Selig Perlman's academic base, once went through an intense bout of anti-semitism. Chancellor Dykstra, who left the University of Wisconsin to go to UCLA, confided in me that he had gone literally out of the frying pan only to end up in the fire. (On another bigotry front, a University of Virginia president for some odd reason came to me to ask my advice: 'What can I do about my overly conserva-tive economics department?' I, always a realist and pacifist, replied: 'Probably nothing. Why don't you work the other side of the street and try to develop the best conservative department outside of Cook County and indeed anywhere in the world?')

I have named names. This is all right. But I have failed to name names that I might have named. George Birkhoff of Harvard was America's first great mathe-matician. I saw a good deal of him in the years 1937–40. He was considered to be a strong anti-semite. That was not what he believed about himself. Being of a Napoleonic temperament, he genuinely believed that no one was quite as good as himself and he would have taken grave offense if anyone thought his Dutch-German name was Jewish. He ludicrously rationalized the peculiar composition of Harvard's math department in the 1920–45 period as being merely the consequence of their wanting to belong to a 'congenial' group. (In mathematics intrinsic ability is self-revealing. *Ergo* race bigotry becomes self-revealing.)

At a deeper level, G.B. believed that Jews were 'early bloomers' who tended to worm their way into prestigious posts while their deeper competitors were still maturing into genius. (Incidentally, George Birkhoff was an early bloomer – and also a late one. MIT's Norbert Wiener, who was Birkhoff's *bête noir*, was actually something of a *late* bloomer in his great researches even though he went to college as a boy in knickerbockers.)

By coincidence my teacher Joseph Schumpeter shared this view with Birkhoff. Alfred Conrad was Schumpeter's assistant when he died, and he relayed to Goodwin and me on our drive to the 1950 funeral a recent dialogue with Schumpeter.

Alf: Professor Schumpeter, what do you think of Nicky Kaldor?

Joe: Oh, these Asiatics. They are only early bloomers.

Alf: I am puzzled. Are you perhaps referring to Kaldor's Hungarian Magyar ancestry?

Joe: My dear Alfred. My figure of speech was to spare *your* sensibilities. It was my delicate way of referring to Kaldor's Mosaic ancestry.

The Greek chorus can report that in Kaldor's 78 years of life he was more prolific toward its end than early on; in my book, he deserved to split a Nobel Prize with Roy Harrod and Joan Robinson; any detectable foolishnesses in his work smacked of youth-like enthusiasms rather than senile dementias.

Final reflections

Maynard Keynes and Joseph Schumpeter were creatures of an earlier time. Can one be surprised that their diaries and letters to pals reflect the folkways and mores of Eton-Bloomsbury and Emperor Franz Joseph's Austria? Keynes's brilliant early discernment of a rottenness in Lenin-Stalin Russia becomes blemished by a Keynesian denunciation of Trotsky's Jewishness. This is from the pen of Richard Kahn's mentor, and from the pen that exaggerates the Old Testament virtues of Weimar's Melchior as elder statesman.

Elizabeth Schumpeter, widow, chucked into the Harvard archives *all* her husband's literary remains (including arguments with himself pro and con on marrying Elizabeth). Naturally a cottage industry of biographers sprang up. How should we weigh in the balance vulgar night thoughts against the fact that more refugees from Hitler were landed in U.S. professorial chairs by Schumpeter than probably by any other single person? When Schumpeter singled me out as a favorite protégé, did this betoken a belief that my candle would burn out quickly by virtue of defective DNA?

Things are often not quite what they seem. Mathematical polymath Edwin Bidwell Wilson, Willard Gibbs' sole protegé at Yale and my revered mentor, encouraged me to go to MIT, telling how he himself had never regretted leaving Yale for MIT early in the century. That carried weight with me: I was touched by his admiring solicitude. Years later Richard Swedberg, Schumpeter's best biographer, sent me an item he found in the Harvard archives of E. B. Wilson and Talcott Parsons.

It threw a new and different light on that Wilson-Samuelson 1940 correspondence. I paraphrase for brevity.

> Wilson to Parsons: I write to avoid misunderstanding. You left our Sociology Division meeting just after I had said: You must never appoint an able Jew to a temporary assignment. I fear you may have got the wrong impression that I am anti-semitic. That is not at all the case. I was merely warning that, since one will not be able to make him a tenured academic, his very ability will be the cause of embarrassment and heartburn later.

Pass-on-the-good-penny is a genuine problem in an imperfect, bigoted society.

Later ages will find it hard to identify the sheep and the goats of an earlier time but, with unearned self-confidence, they will not be deterred from making the effort.

Part III

Economic, political and social systems

4   Communitarianism and welfare state dynamics

A European perspective

Ewald Nowotny

The political economy of the welfare state

In his awe-inspiring volume of selected essays Mark Perlman (1996: 253) recalls that while in military service during World War II – 'like many of my generation' – he read both William Beveridge's *Full Employment in a Free Society* and Friedrich von Hayek's *The Road to Serfdom*. In this intellectual discussion Mark Perlman clearly was more impressed by Hayek's lines of argument. But he also clearly remained sceptical towards Libertarian positions. This was based both on methodological and on empirical considerations. Thus Perlman – 'expressions of intellectual animosity to the contrary notwithstanding' – stressed the existence of a tie between Hayekian theorising and American institutionalism (Perlman 1996: 254; Perlman 1986: 268) and at the same time elaborated the different philosophical foundations of these two approaches. This approach has to be seen as reflecting the broader intellectual background of the 'Post World War II Rise and Fall of Communitarianism'. This is because the underlying issue of this discussion always was (and is) the question of the role of society – or community – in socio-economic thinking and economic analysis.

It is in this tradition with regard to aspects of political economy that the concept of the welfare state may be seen as the dividing line between two philosophical views of human society, or community, each of which has a long tradition. On the one hand, we have the tradition of liberalistic individualism and on the other hand the tradition of 'community-oriented' approaches, which in a broader sense can be called the tradition of 'Communitarian Thought', as is the case in Charles McCann's contribution in this volume.

The most influential modern economist–philosopher of, especially economic, liberalism is still Hayek. Based on his view of society as a spontaneous, evolutionary phenomenon there is no room for state intervention except for securing the legal foundations of a market economy. Of particular importance for the appraisal of the functions of the public sector is the statement, that it is neither admissible nor feasible for the public sector to influence income distribution on the basis of so-called 'social justice' (see, especially Hayek 1991). For this Hayek offers the following reasons:

- The effort to establish social or distributive justice (meaning the reduction of the inequalities between individuals as far as their material well-being is concerned) leads to a reduction in 'liberty', which is defined as the absence of government intervention. For such an attempt means substituting a certain distributive state, at which government intervention is aiming, for a 'spontaneous order of society' (not motivated by specific goals).

- There is no general consensus of opinion on the relative importance of the different goals of public policy, especially as far as the distribution of wealth is concerned. Therefore, only individual preferences are relevant.[1]
- A 'spontaneous order', as is established by the market process, cannot be regarded as 'unjust', since no one is responsible for the outcome of this quasi natural order. 'Justice' has to be seen as a category of individual behaviour, in the sense of 'fairness', not as a social category.
- To accept the unlimited regulatory and interventionist power of government and parliament or, in particular, to accept the power of the majority to interfere in the market process that leads to a natural, spontaneous order, means committing a constructivistic error. A re-distribution of income (for example by progressive taxation), by which a burden is put on a minority, has to be seen as 'arbitrary discrimination'.

The line of thought which is basic for the concept of the welfare state can be termed 'community-oriented' and to some extent also the 'interventionist approach'. The schools of thought which are combined in the 'community-oriented approach'[2] are far more heterogeneous in their features and – in terms of economic policy – in the solutions they offer than the ideas of economic liberalism which have developed along a relatively consistent line since Adam Smith's time. Nevertheless, the following basic elements, which are common to all supporters of the modern community-oriented approach, may be identified:

1   In the tradition of the French Enlightenment, society is seen as more than a product of a natural process. Man is also capable of consciously deciding and planning his own fate and the development of society.
2   Liberty as one fundamental value of mankind goes beyond the mere absence of constraint. The concept also has to include the opportunity to live life with dignity. This positive definition of liberty then requires sufficient endowments for individuals. In other words, a certain degree of equality is a precondition for this more comprehensive kind of liberty.
3   Man is regarded as a social being opting for co-operation and aspiring to a secure livelihood, whereas the neo-classical image of man, drawn from utilitarian 'capitalistic ethics' (Max Weber), builds on profit-maximisation, which has to be seen basically as income maximisation. Besides liberty, values like solidarity and security play an important role. In this context it is seen as one purpose of the public sector to promote the economic and social security of the individual in particular, by going beyond charity. This contrasts with classical liberalism, which predicts that the economic process will lose its momentum as a direct result of increases in the degree of equality and security.

4   Contrasting the liberal concept of the 'invisible hand', the stated correspondence between individual profit-maximisation and social welfare in various areas can neither be expected nor can it be tested empirically, especially when issues of power and income distribution are addressed. It is therefore sometimes necessary to weigh the interests of the general public against the interests of the individual and to impose those of the former if necessary. Following a modern approach the interests of the general public are to be established via democratic ballots, a process in which each vote of a mature citizen is given the same weight. There are also, however, a number of fields where direct community action – and not organised state intervention – is possible. This is the approach of the 'Communitarian Movement' (Etzioni 1988, 1996). To some extent, this new Communitarianism combines the basic questions and perspectives of 'traditional' community-oriented approaches with an individualistic approach concerning morality and personal responsibility. This movement has had a substantial influence on European discussions concerning the welfare state, as, for instance, in Blair's Britain or with respect to the German Social Democrats.

5   The question of whether markets or other forms of running an economy should be employed is not one of principle, but a question which has to be answered according to the tasks which have to be tackled. Therefore, in cases where the market mechanism is not able to provide results which are socially adequate, the state has to intervene. In this context the economic function of the public sector has to be seen as being an instrument to reach socially desired goals. Basically, this proposition may be universally accepted – but interventionists see many more cases of market failure as compared to liberal economists, who tend to stress cases of government failure.

The basic principles presented – the idea of a clearly defined public or common interest and the use of the public sector as an instrument for its realisation – are implemented in quite different ways depending on history and the analytical approach towards the economy. The most important differences, however, arise when one tries to determine what the public interest is. Here, one can distinguish between authoritarian approaches, where determination is based on a supposed superior insight of a single person or a group, and democratic procedures. The decisive characteristics of the welfare state is the combination of the notion of 'public interest' and democratic decision-making.

The modern welfare state – some basic concepts

Based on the political concepts discussed above, two elements are crucial to the modern concept of the welfare state:[3]

- Provision of a more comprehensive kind of security relative to that offered by market processes, covering risks such as unemployment, illness etc.[4]
- Provision of social services based on legal claims rather than on mercy and charity.

Depending on the exact structure and scope of the welfare concept the following distinctions are made in the modern theory of the welfare state:

- The residual welfare state: public services in areas such as health care, pensions, family support etc. are regarded as a 'safety net' for the poor and therefore provision is subject to income testing.
- The institutional (universal) welfare state: in principle, public services in defined areas are granted to all members of society; differences in income are taken into account via taxation.

In the real world this distinction is somewhat incomplete. Just consider the various roles the state can play in the fields of employment, housing or education. However, Germany, Austria, Switzerland and the Scandinavian countries can basically be termed universal welfare states, whereas the USA is an example of a residual welfare state. Market-oriented Asian countries with their family-based Confucian tradition are generally sceptical towards the very concept of the welfare state. This may have aggravated the fall out from the recent crisis of some of the export-driven economies of this region.

Behind all these various developments there are different historical experiences, different intellectual and in part different religious traditions, but also efficiency and distributional objectives. Table 4.1 gives a first illustration of these structural

Table 4.1 Shares and structures of public expenditures (as per cent of GDP)

	Total public expenditure (all levels of government)	Social expenditures	
	1995	1980	1990
Canada	45.8	14	19
Australia	35.6	11	13
New Zealand	34.5[a]	15	19
UK	42.3[a]	21	24
US	34.3	14	15
Denmark	59.6	26	28
Finland	55.9	21	27
Norway	45.8	21	29
Sweden	63.8	33	33
Austria	48.6	23	25
France	51.6[a]	24	27
Germany	46.6	25	27
Italy	49.5	20	25
Netherlands	50.0	27	30
Japan	28.5	10	12

a 1994.

Sources: OECD, New orientations for social policy, Paris 1994, OECD in figures, Paris 1998, Eurostat.

differences which are of course also relevant when comparing taxes and social insurance contributions as a percentage of GDP (Table 4.2).

From the point of view of distributional policy, making services related to income means that more of the target group can be reached with a given budget. Apart from the difficulties of income testing, screening along differences in income can have a psychologically discriminating effect and therefore lead to a collapse in social solidarity. This, in turn, can eventually lead to a reduction of public interest in the quality and range of welfare state services ('services for the poor tend to become poor services'). A dramatic example of such a tendency is the decline of the quality of the state school system in Britain. The reversal of this decline is one of the main goals of Blair's 'New Labour'.

Looking at it from the point of view of efficiency, the residual welfare state will, generally speaking, be linked with a lower tax ratio, which, if the system is geared towards individual profit-maximisation according to traditional neo-classical theory, can lead – *ceteris paribus* – to greater overall efficiency. This is, of course, no longer valid if one takes into account various aspects of market failure, where problems of imperfect information are of special importance. This is related for instance to different non-insurable forms of uncertainty, for example, unemployment or inflation. There are also problem areas, where a more comprehensive approach, as opposed to a partial one, can make efficiency gains possible. This is relevant not only in cases of positive external effects (e.g. in education and health) but also for problems which arise in the areas of health insurance and old age pension with different – yet for the

Table 4.2 Structures of taxation, 1996 (as per cent of GDP)

Country	Taxes on income and profits	Social security contributions	Taxes on property	Taxes on goods and services	Other taxes	Shares of taxation[1] 1996
Australia	17.5	–	2.8	8.7	2.1	31.1
Belgium	17.5	14.9	1.2	12.4		46.0
Denmark	31.4	1.6	1.7	17.1	0.3	52.2
Germany	10.8	15.5	1.1	10.6	–	38.1
France	8.2	19.7	2.3	12.5	3.0	45.7
Italy	14.9	14.8	2.3	11.2	–	43.2
Japan	10.4	10.4	3.2	4.4	0.1	28.4
New Zealand	21.1	–	2.0	12.3	0.3	35.8
Netherlands	11.7	17.1	1.9	12.4	0.2	43.3
Austria	12.2	15.3	0.6	12.6	3.3	44.0
Sweden	21.3	15.5	2.0	11.8	1.4	52.0
Switzerland	13.1	13.0	2.4	6.2	–	34.7
US	13.5	7.0	3.1	4.9	–	28.5
United Kingdom	13.2	6.2	3.8	12.7	–	36.0
EU (15)[2]	14.7	12.2	1.8	13.0	0.6	42.4
OECD total[2]	13.4	9.8	1.9	12.0	0.6	37.7

1 Total tax and social security contributions revenue as per cent of GDP.
2 Unweighted average.

Source: OECD, revenue statistics, Paris 1998.

(private) insurer non-differentiable – risk groups (problems of 'adverse selection' and 'asymmetric information').

The specific forms of welfare state institutions will be defined not only by the abovementioned historical and social aspects but also by the development of the economic basis and economic demands of each specific society and country. Therefore, there are no fixed rules for a welfare state. There are, however, some general, closely connected functions of the public sector in the context of a modern welfare state.

Full Employment Policies. The labour market is not regarded as a 'market like all other markets'. This, of course, has been one of the main aspects of the scientific work of Mark Perlman. From the institutionalistic point of view special emphasis is given to the view, that the labour market is influenced by particular sociological and institutional conditions which stem from the unequal power positions of market participants as well as the fact that integration into the labour process has enormous sociological, psychological and economic importance for the individual. The free functioning of the price mechanism is therefore to be regarded as neither desirable for the labour market nor, according to Keynes's analyses, effective. Following an interventional approach the state must undertake the task to ensure a high level of employment. It is, of course, increasingly difficult for individual states to fulfil this demand in the context of internationally interwoven economies. However, open economies still have economically relevant leeway for more employment-oriented policies. It is possible to demonstrate empirically that welfare state-oriented governments take more advantage of this leeway than those which tend to be market-liberal (Rothschild 1986).

It can be the case that for the modern welfare state a conflict arises between long-term efficiency and welfare gains from greater international economic openness and the welfare losses stemming from reduced opportunities for national employment policy. The solution or alleviation of the problem can be seen in an 'internationalisation' of full employment policies through internationally co-ordinated economic policy measures, as are currently being discussed in the European Union (EU).

Redistributional Policies. The liberal position underestimates or ignores the empirically proven considerable inequality in the economic and social starting points of individuals as well as the phenomenon of the economic power of individual groups. If, on the one hand, the importance of economic power is underestimated and, on the other, intervention of the state is seen as a threat to liberty and productivity, this can only lead to the defence of particular group interests. From the point of view of the proponents of the welfare state it is legitimate in a democratic state to influence income distribution through the public sector if the order which results from free interaction of market forces is regarded as unjust by the majority of the people. 'The rational explanation for the support of government intervention by lower-income groups is the fact, that it is more likely that the interests of the poorer people are protected if matters are dealt with by public sector institutions rather than leaving them up to private markets' (Myrdal 1961: 29).

The proponents of the welfare state argue that social and economic reforms towards more equality do not only correspond with 'justice' but also enhance productivity. For the improvement in the working and living conditions of disadvantaged groups will lead, among other things, to a better performance at work, easier structural change and a higher rate of diffusion of technical progress. More equality and higher economic productivity are often complements and not substitutes as suggested by the liberal school of thought. Besides, it can be expected that a society will be politically and socially more stable and therefore foster economic development in the long run if it is not characterised by significant disparities in wealth and income. Taking the share of the public sector (including social security) of GDP as a rough indicator of the 'welfare state-intensity' of a country makes it possible to demonstrate – via international comparison – that against the predictions of supply side economists no inverse relation can be found between 'welfare intensity' and the growth of output and productivity (Muysken, Wagner, 1986). On the contrary it is a main point of the new endogenous growth theory, that measures that lessen income equality will have positive effects on the long-run growth performance of countries (see e.g. Bruno *et al.* 1996; Tanzi and Zee 1996).

There is also, however, another aspect with regard to the relationship between redistributional policy and economic development. This is the problem of the 'growth-dependence' of the welfare state. Phases of slump or stagnation will lead (not least because of automatic stabilisers) to a worsening of the budget situation. Especially under conditions of international competition, attention also has to be paid to the cost effects of social policy. In general, redistribution will be hard to realise whenever the applied measures lead to losses in real income for economically strong groups. If this constellation brings about a reduction in solidarity it can result in a greater instability and in a long-term dequalification of individual groups of society (problem of a 'two-thirds society'). As a consequence, the foundations of long-run growth can be affected negatively inducing vicious cumulative circles. Therefore, efforts are made in modern theory of the welfare state to combine social security with supply side measures, for example, raising the level of qualification and increasing flexibility, to develop the endogenous growth potential of the economy.

Social security: Going beyond the aspect of redistribution and social welfare, 'social security' is regarded as an immaterial good.[5] To a great extent the state has to take care of its production because the state can, unlike a private insurer, guarantee protection against inflation and regular adjustments of income. This is fundamental to satisfying the need for social security. 'Social security' as a comprehensive good, referring not only to the absolute but also to the relative social status, is not only of significance for lower-income groups. It has to be supplied throughout society. Looking at 'social security' in terms of the whole of society it exhibits the characteristics of a superior good. This is demonstrated by the fact of rising expenditures in the area of social security going hand in hand with increases in real income – a correlation which is not usually reckoned with by traditional social policy (compare Table 4.1).

The dynamics of the welfare state

At the end of the nineteenth century Adolf Wagner, a prominent member of the nowadays often-neglected institutionalist 'Historical School of Economics', predicted the evolution of the authoritarian 'administrative state' into an encompassing welfare state (compare Nowotny 1996: 116). This should have two effects: an increase in the share of government in GDP and a change in the structure of government expenditure. This means a decrease in the shares of military and administrative expenditures and an increase in the shares of public investments and social expenditures. Whereas the present economic theory discussion on the welfare state is almost exclusively concerned with allocative effects of the welfare state arrangements, it might be an interesting research strategy to take up again the more general view of an institutionalistic approach in the line of Adolf Wagner for a modern theory of the welfare state of today. In line with this approach, we analyse:

- effects of structural changes in the economy,
- productivity and cost effects,
- effects of changes of political structures.

Adolf Wagner himself put the main emphasis on changes in general demand structures, driven by income and population effects. On the one hand, many public goods are complementary to private goods with high income elasticity, which leads to increasing GDP-shares of public expenditures. The most striking example is of course the high impact, private and public transportation, and in a more general way communication, have had – and are having – on public expenditure. Even if some of these expenditures (highways, airports, etc.) can be taken over by the private sector in the form of private-public partnerships there remains a substantial demand for public sector financed infrastructure. An additional field of rapidly increasing importance is public involvement in basic research. These allocative effects of public investments may be subject to critical discussion in various detailed effects but are generally accepted and form part of many public policy programs (e.g. in the EU).

The other line of Wagner's proposition is much more disputed: this is the notion that many public goods experience the characteristics of 'superior' goods, that is, are subject to a high income-elasticity of demand. This holds true for education, for health services and also for 'security' as a general notion, both with regard to personal security vis-à-vis crime, etc., but also with regard to security concerning income support in old age, unemployment, sickness, etc. It is obvious that the single most important aspect is the influence of ageing populations on social expenditures. It has to be noted however that the increases in life-expectancy are not exogenous 'natural' phenomenon but are 'endogenous' effects related to the development of per capita incomes and to the volume and structure of welfare activities. A dramatic proof of these 'endogenous' characteristics is the decline of life-expectancy in the states of the former Soviet Union.

If one looks at empirical data it is a fact that the 'social infrastructure related' service sector has shown substantial increases in 'production' and employment shares. The controversial issue is, whether this obvious demand should be met by private or public production. In international comparisons we see two different approaches: in the Anglo-Saxon world these developments form one of the driving forces in the development of the private service sector. In continental European welfare states these developments have resulted in an increase in the public service sector. This is clearly demonstrated in Table 4.3, taking the United States and Sweden as examples of each approach: there are no great differences in the demand (measures as a percentage of private household expenditure) for health, education and pensions, but there are fundamental differences in the ways of providing and financing this demand.

Both approaches to providing social services have costs and benefits: the US approach obviously allows for a rapid expansion of sophisticated service sectors (compare Table 4.4), but leads to a very uneven social distribution of these services.

The 'European' approach enables a more general distribution (and thus also generally higher levels of health, education standards, etc.) but means higher shares in taxation. The most problematic constellation may be one, which is presently experienced in some European countries: insisting on public provision of 'social infrastructure', but being unable or unwilling to finance the corresponding expenditures, results in a situation where the substantial potential for employment-growth in these sectors cannot be exploited. 'Europe' is thus at cross-roads: either one has to be prepared to agree on high levels of public financing or one has to allow for higher shares of private production of 'social infrastructure'. The present combination of public production but insufficient public financing tends to be the worst of both worlds.

Up to now the dynamics of the welfare state were discussed with respect to their impact on real GPD. There are also, however, important impacts stemming from specific productivity- and price-effects. This is not of relevance for the transfer-aspects of the welfare state but it is an important aspect for the numerous service-sector activities,

Table 4.3 Public and private social protection spending

	As percent of GDP	
	Sweden	USA
Public social expenditure, 1990	33.1	14.6
Private education	0.1	2.5
Private health	1.1	8.2
Private pensions	1.8	3.0
Total	36.1	28.3
	As a per cent of private household expenditure, 1990	
Private health, education and pensions	2.7	18.8
Day care (child families)	1.7	10.4
Total	4.4	29.2
Taxes	36.8	10.4
Total + taxes	41.2	39.6

Sources: G. Esping-Andersen (1996: 19).

Table 4.4 Role and structure of the service sector, 1995 (contribution to employment as percent of total employment)

	Total service sector	Producers of government services	Community, social and personal services
Germany	59.1[c]	15.6	n.a.
Austria	59.6	18.6[a]	9.0
Netherlands	73.8[c]	12.1	17.2
France	69.5[c]	28.2	7.2
Sweden	71.0[c]	32.0	8.2
UK	70.6[c]	19.4	11.8[b]
US	73.3[c]	14.0[a]	17.7[a]

a 1994; b 1990; c 1996.

Source: OECD in figures, Paris 1998.

connected with the welfare state. In general, increasing the share of the public sector in GDP has to be seen not only as the result of different real growth rates of the private and the public sector of the economy but also as a result of the fact that there are – compared to the private sector of the economy – higher rates of 'price increases' in the public sector. A direct comparison is almost impossible because in general no direct prices are attached to public services. It is, however, feasible to gain information via the comparison of the cost developments in the two sectors (Pommerehne and Schneider 1982).

The basis of these considerations lies in the fact that the public sector has to be seen, to a great extent, as a 'service (producing) sector'. For this ('tertiary') sector, however, rates of increase in costs seem to be above average compared to the whole of the economy. This phenomenon, first analysed by William Baumol (1967), is described as 'tertiary cost behaviour'.

For the public sector this means: if the demand for public services grows, and the rate of growth is the same as or greater than the rate of growth of total demand, then its real share will at least remain constant and its nominal share will increase, as will the public sector's share of the total work force because of the below-average growth in productivity. The rise in the government activity rate should therefore be seen, in this respect, as a monetary (cost-) phenomenon and not (just) as a real one. This development, which was described as 'cost disease' of the service sector of the economy, can also be shown empirically, even though there are methodological difficulties in calculating price-increases for public services (Nowotny 1996). This means that this growing share of public consumption can for the most part be traced back to above-average cost increases, whereas the real shares have in fact dropped in many countries.

Allocative decisions in the context of the welfare state are political decisions. Adolf Wagner pointed out that the envisaged changes in the structures of public expenditures have not only 'economic', income-elasticity-related causes, discussed above, but are also due to changes in political structures. This relates especially to the effects of granting general voting rights in a modern democracy. This means that the demand-structures of the lower-income population will have a higher impact on the structure and volume of public expenditure and thus on the economy.

In modern public-choice economics this argument is turned around: Based on median-voters models and on 'Leviathan-models' of political processes the development of the welfare state is basically seen as a process of the exploitation of the rich minority by the poor majority (Atkinson 1987). There are, however, two developments that counteract this tendency. The first is a pressure on tax reduction, first via the political process and in some countries now contained also in constitutional provisions. It is, however, interesting to notice that these developments were able to gain momentum although – at least in the view of the interventionist position discussed above – they were in contradiction to the 'objective' economic and social interests of a majority of the voting population.

This leads to the basic question of how preferences are formed, both with respect to private and to public goods. This question is systematically avoided by neoclassical economists ('de gustibus non est dubidandum'). This then leads to a bias in modern public-choice theory which intensively deals with influences of the public sector and political agents on the private sector of the economy, but pays less attention to the influences of the private sector on public policy.

The role of special interest groups has been analysed mainly in the context of 'rent-seeking' activities. This is of course an interesting aspect and it can be shown that public policy will be more efficient in a structure characterised by large encompassing interest groups, such as, for example, nation-wide trade unions, than in structures characterised by a large number of small lobbies (see Olson 1982).

It is, however, important to see that the main effects of business-financed interest groups are not in creating, but in avoiding welfare-state activities. With the increasing role of privately owned – and thus basically business-oriented – mass-media and the increased difficulties in financing expensive election-campaigns the influence of lobbies representing business- and upper-class interests tends to grow. It is considered as somewhat 'unprofessional' to mention these 'brain-washing-effects' in economic analysis, but a profound discussion of modern developments of the welfare state cannot not ignore them.[6]

Welfare state and globalisation

A further powerful influence which tends to reverse the trends of 'Wagner's Law' can be seen in the effects of the increasing openness of modern economies. Although free flows of economic goods and factors of production may in the long run increase general economic welfare (given specific assumptions) this is not necessarily so for specific countries and specific groups. It is obvious that more mobile factors of production, such as capital, very high qualified and on the other hand poverty-driven labour, will profit from economic liberalisation, whereas the economic power of less mobile factors, like the 'regular work-force' in modern welfare states will decrease.

An immediate result of worldwide liberalisation is a tendency towards tax-competition and regulatory competition which has become a powerful limitation on welfare-state activities. Today, we still find substantial international differences, both with regard to levels and to structures of taxation (see Table 4.2). But welfare states here are faced with two problems: one is the increasing difficulty of adequate taxation of profits and other mobile forms of income. The other problem manifests itself in the fear (however theoretically or empirically unfounded) that increased wage-based taxes and social security contributions will have negative results on the demand for labour.

There are neo-classical models of the 'Tiebout-type' that try to show the welfare increasing effects of locational competition: If there are locations ('welfare states') with high levels of public services and high levels of taxation on the one hand and locations with low levels of public services and low taxes on the other hand, individuals are free to choose according to their preferences.

This model is already unrealistic for analysing the urban structures in the US, for which has been developed. It is absolutely misleading when applied in a world-wide context with low labour mobility and large income differentials (see Nowotny 1997). From the theoretical point of view one has to consider that Tiebout-type models of policy competition are based on the assumption that public expenditures are financed on the principle of benefit taxation. This excludes problems of free-rider-behaviour (e.g. big companies using the infrastructure and social stability of welfare states but using international tax havens) as well as aspects of income redistribution via ability-to-pay-oriented taxation.

A major challenge facing economic policy and theory today is therefore the question of whether and to what extent there is a trade-off between a modern welfare state and economic liberalisation and integration. In the context of the EU this discussion has led to several – but largely ineffective – attempts to harmonise basic social regulations ('European Social Charter') and taxes to prevent 'beggar my neighbour' policies that would eventually undermine the financial foundations of modern welfare states.

Also in this respect both the EU and the European welfare state are now at crossroads. If European integration and the Single European Market follow the neo-liberal tendencies discussed at the beginning of this chapter, and are seen as an instrument for deregulation and dismantling of the welfare state,[7] this will provoke increasing opposition to the EU's policies. This also holds for important new developments, especially EU's eastern enlargement. The alternative is not a uniform European welfare state. But it is a state of affairs where tax coordination prevents a permanent redistribution of the tax burden and where a combination of increased economic growth (especially in the poorer member countries) and of general and specific social standards avoids abrupt shocks in the labour markets. This is an environment where European integration, worldwide liberalisation and the welfare state could go together – a combination necessary to avoid bitter economic and political struggles that could destroy the progress made during the decades of the European welfare state.

A new global age?

To analyse the long-run perspectives of globalisation and the welfare state in a more general way it is advisable to follow Mark Perlman's approach to using economic history as a tool for economic analysis. Taking this approach many of the modern tendencies of globalisation – free trade, the 'Euro' as a currency without political governance, global capital flows – have a flavour of déjà-vu. And in fact many economists see – usually with an optimistic attitude – far reaching parallels between the fin-de-siècle of the twentieth, and the fin-de-siècle of the nineteenth century: After decades of turmoil and state-intervention the world is approaching an area of peace and prosperity, based on internationally open ('free') markets for goods, capital, services – and partly also for labour. This resembles the great liberal period of the gold standard and free trade, which abruptly ended in 1914. It is true that the GNP-shares of government expenditures now are much higher than compared to the nineteenth century. On the other hand, capital flows play a much higher role today and together with the technological revolution in communication this, again, leads to a constellation, where the 'laws of the markets' clearly tend to dominate over interventionist approaches such as the concept of the welfare state.

This 'return to the nineteenth century' is reflected in the OECD's recent concept of a 'New Global Age', based on a 'high performance vision' of the world economy for the year 2020. This vision explicitly recalls the 'wealth creating energy' of the 'market-oriented economic system' of the nineteenth century. Consequently, the proposals for the twenty-first century concentrate on higher flexibility (especially downward wage flexibility) of labour markets, more liberalisation and deregulation and a reduction of government social-policy interventions.

Does this mean that there is a worldwide consensus concerning a 'brave new world' that will, and should, end the welfare-state experiments of the twentieth century? To the astonishment of many Americans who do not share the knowledge and experience of intellectuals like Mark Perlman such a consensus does not exist in Europe. One can find proponents of the 'American way of capitalism' (as they see it) especially in Eastern Europe, but in Western Europe the intellectual and political discussion is dominated by critical voices.

These advocates for a 'European way' of economic and social politics have very different backgrounds, ranging from conservative, Christian, social-democratic to (politically) liberal. Thus, for example, the latest book of Marion Gräfin Dönhoff, editor of a highly influential and prestigious German magazine, is titled (translated) 'Civilise Capitalism'. Lord Dahrendorf, former Director of the London School of Economics and one of Europe's leading intellectuals recently warned against 'globalisation leading (again) to Social-Darwinism'. Also in the field of economic policy European Union officials are getting increasingly irritated by aggressive American positions with regard to WTO (World Trade Organisation) and World Climate agreements where Americans tend to consider European environmental and health concerns as just non-tariff trade barriers.

These different socio-economic attitudes reflect a different view concerning the lessons to be learned from the history of the liberal nineteenth century. In Europe the 'liberal era' is seen not only as one of 'wealth creating energy' but also as a period of increasing social disequilibrium. Together with the rising tide of nationalism this unresolved 'social question' led to the self-destruction of the liberal system of the nineteenth century. The welfare state was the democratic answer to the economic, social and political chaos resulting from the breakdown of economic liberalism – thus creating an alternative not only to pure ('free') capitalism but also to communist and other authoritarian approaches. Using the collapse of Communism as a strategy also to 'roll back' the welfare state would mean abandoning the countervailing institutions and influences necessary for a socially and politically acceptable working of market forces.

Does all this mean, that also in the age of globalisation, different – and perhaps conflicting – approaches to economic and social questions will remain, that there will be competition between an American, a European and an Asian way and what will be the effects of such competition? Looking at the large differences concerning GDP-share of public expenditure and taxes (Tables 4.1 and 4.2) it is obvious that there indeed is a wide variety of politically revealed preferences between the US, EU-Europe and other regions of the world. This variety basically reflects different perspectives with regard to welfare-state activities such as these which have been discussed in this paper. In practically all EU-Member countries discussions are under way concerning reforms of the welfare state, especially with regard to the challenges due to demographic changes. In some aspects this also may mean a reduction in welfare state activities. But in general the political discussion is centred on restructuring, not on reducing the European welfare state. This discussion is based on a broad political consensus as is demonstrated by election results all over Europe. This means that no long-run international convergence of government shares and structures is to be expected. This also means that contrary to the OECD's 'New Global Age' vision different socio-economic models will also exist in the future. The decisive question then arises, whether these different models can be expected to cooperate peacefully or not.

If, as has been argued in this paper, there is no trade-off between equity and efficiency, different models of society can also coexist in a globalised economy. Thus, basically it can be expected that European-type welfare states will also be able to prosper in a world of full economic liberalisation. Some caveats, however, are necessary – and in personal communications Mark Perlman very early raised doubts 'whether the welfare state is permanently compatible with free trade and open borders'.

One economically and politically sensitive aspect relates to the role of 'free' international money and capital markets. As has been demonstrated on several occasions (both in the nineteenth and in the twentieth century) these markets may not only reflect but may also create instability – with far reaching effects on other sectors of the economy. To a large extent this is a challenge for efficient international co-operation. There also remains, however, another political aspect.

International monetary authorities frequently point to the fact that today governments do not only need the confidence of their voters, but also the confidence of international capital markets (a former President of the Deutsche Bundesbank recently even reversed this 'order of confidence'). This means that the outcome of democratic elections may be overruled by 'the markets'. As the persons and interest groups representing these 'markets' tend to be biased against the welfare state this could result in a reduction of welfare-state activities, even if they may be beneficial to the long-run overall growth of the economy.

This external policy constraint – and the conflicts it may cause – will be the more severe the smaller and thus the more vulnerable is an economy. To overcome this constraint – and not to reap the relatively small welfare effects of lower transaction-costs – is the main argument for the creation of the European Monetary Union. Like the US, EMU-Europe will be a relatively closed economy with imports and exports amounting to about eight per cent of EMU-GDP. This does not mean that the Euro will be used as an economic or even political weapon. But EU and EMU can be seen as the economic and institutional foundations that enable Europe to co-operate in the world economy and at the same time preserve the type of welfare state that reflects the preferences of the people of Europe.

In a more general way it can be argued, that 'big' forms of national and supranational cooperation are necessary to provide an adequate 'umbrella' for different forms of 'macro'- and 'micro'-communitarism. This may be the main lesson economic history can teach us: to function, markets need institutions – both internally and externally. Mark Perlman has made us aware of how important this lesson is – and what a challenge it means for serious and fruitful economic research.

Notes

1 Compare Margaret Thatcher's famous dictum 'There is no such thing as society' (NZZ-Folio 3, March 1997: 11).
2 These approaches especially include the Historical and Institutionalist Schools of Economics and Keynesian and Post-Keynesian economics with regard to their economic policy aspects. In this paper 'Communitarianism' is thus seen in a broader perspective as compared to the new specific 'Communitarian Movement'. As will be discussed later, this movement is, of course, to been seen in the tradition of community-oriented approaches, but focuses less on the 'macro' and more on the 'micro' perspective of society.
3 See, for example, Wilson (1982); Rothschild (1982, 1992); Barr (1992); Nowotny (1996).
4 'The welfare state can be viewed as an insurance contract entered voluntarily by risk-averse individuals behind John Rawls' "Veil of Ignorance"' (M Barr 1992: 795).
5 For the role of 'security' as a basic human need see, for example, A. Maslov, *Motivation and Personality*, New York, 1970.
6 There are, for example, estimates, that in the US private lobbies (Medical Associations, insurance-lobbies) spend about $300 million to sabotage president Clinton's project to introduce – weak – forms of European style social security (*Newsweek*, 19.9.1994: 26). For a theoretical background see Potters, Sloof, Winden (1997: 1).
7 Compare Margaret Thatcher's quote: 'The EU has to be a project of deregulation.'

References

Atkinson, A. B. (1987) 'Economics of the welfare state,' *European Economic Review* 31(1/2): 177.

Barr, N. (1992) 'Economic theory and the welfare state: a survey and interpretation,' *Journal of Economic Literature* 30(2): 741.

Baumol, W. J. (1967) 'Macroeconomics of unbalanced growth: the anatomy of urban crisis,' *American Economic Review* 57: 415.

Bruno, M., Ravallion, M. and Squire, L. (1996) 'Equity and growth in developing countries: old and new perspectives on the policy issues,' World Bank working paper 1563, Washington.

Esping-Anderson, G. (1996) 'Welfare states at the end of the century: the impact of labour market, family and demographic change,' OECD-Working Party on Social Policy, Paris.

Etzioni, A. (1998) *The Moral Dimension, Towards a New Economics* New York.

—— (1996) *The New Golden Rule. Community and Morality in a Democratic Society* New York.

Hayek, F. A. v. Die Verfassung der Freiheit, 3. Aufl., Tübingen 1991.

—— The Fatal Conceit. London: Routledge 1988.

Myrdal, G. (1961) *Jenseits des Wohlfahrtsstaates* Stuttgart.

Nowotny, E. (1996) *Der öffentliche Sektor.* (3rd ed.) Springer, Berlin-Heidelberg.

—— (1997) 'Zur regionalen Dimension der Finanzverfassung der EU,' in St. Homburg, H.-W. Sinn, and E. Nowotny (ed.) *Finanzföderalismus in Europa,* Berlin 1997.

OECD (1997) *Towards a New Global Age – Challenges and Opportunities* Paris.

Olsen, M. (1982) *The Rise and Decline of Nations* New Haven-London.

Perlman, M. and Hayek, F. A. (1996) 'Purposes of the economic market and institutionalist traditions,' in M. Perlman (ed.) *The Character of Economic Thought, Economic Characters and Economic Institutions-Selected Essays.* University of Michigan Press: Ann Arbor, 253–68.

Perlman, M., (1986) 'Subjectivism and American institutionalism,' in I. Kirzner (ed.) *Subjectivism, Intellectibility and Economic Understanding: Essays in Honor of Ludwig M. Lachmann,* New York University Press, New York, 268–80.

Pommerehne, W. W. and Schneider, F. (1982) 'Unbalanced growth between public and private sectors: an empirical examination,' in R. H. Havemann (ed.) *Public Finance and Public Employment, International Institute of Public Finance* Detroit 309.

Potters, J., Sloof, R. and van Winden, F. (1997) 'Campaign expenditures, contributions and direct endorsements: the strategic use of information and money to influence voter Behavior', *European Journal of Political Economy* 13: 1.

Rothschild, K. W. (1986) ''Left' and 'Right' in Federal Europe,' *Kyklos* 39: 359.

—— (1982) 'Observations on the economics, politics and ethics of the welfare state,' *Zeitschrift für die gesamte Staatswissenschaft* 138(3): 565.

—— (1992) 'Wohlfahrtstaat: Inhalt, probleme, perspektiven,' in E. Nowotny (Hrsg.) *Sozialdemokratische Wirtschaftspolitik* Wien 93.

Sinn, H.-W. (1995) 'A theory of the welfare state,' *Scandinavian Journal of Economics* 97: 495–526.

Tanzi, V. and Howell H. Zee (1996) 'Fiscal policy and long-run growth,' IMF-Working Paper, October.

Wilson, Th & D. (1982) *The Political Economy of the Welfare State* London.

5   The inevitable price of totalitarianism

An economist's perspective

Nicholas W. Balabkins

Much ink has been spilled and endless debates triggered over the question of how nations can best organize their societal structures. How can they orchestrate steady improvement of material well-being? How can they assure a reasonably equitable distribution of the fruits of progress? How can they prevent the monopoly of political power by a few? And how can they best defend their citizens and property against local criminals or foreign invaders? Can a closed dictatorial society solve these age-old problems better than an open democracy? Or is it the other way around? This last question is still debated today. Thomas Hobbes, the English philosopher and political thinker posed his answer to these questions when he wrote *Leviathan or the Matter, Forme and Power of a Commonwealth Eclesiaticall and Civil* in 1651. In 1690, John Locke followed with his *Second Treatise of Government*. David Hume, Adam Smith and John Stuart Mill later articulated the system of natural liberty or 'laissez-faire'. In 1848, Karl Marx promised Europe's 'have-nots' a material paradise on this side of the grave, as Joseph A. Schumpeter put it, provided they eliminated their exploiters. At the end of the nineteenth century, Gustav Schmoller's *Verein für Socialpolitik* laid the foundations for the modern capitalist welfare state, that is still extant in industrially advanced countries today.

In this century, Lenin and Stalin tried to implement Marx's vision in Soviet Russia and Eastern Europe by liquidating all 'exploiters' or 'socially dangerous elements'. Hitler physically exterminated all racially unacceptable human beings from his 'Thousand Year Reich'.

It was my fate more than half a century ago to live under both of these totalitarian systems, communist and nazist. To this day, I believe that those who have not had such a visceral experience often do not quite grasp what these two types of tyranny are all about.

My long-time friend Professor Mark Perlman has heard many of my youthful stories. For his *Festschrift*, I am offering not a conventional essay in economics, but an attempt to show how my physiological empiricism laid the foundations for my later interest in intra-state reparations to the victims of the genocides in Nazi Germany and Soviet Russia.

For more than 350 years Thomas Hobbes has influenced political thinking through his concept of legitimate authority based on the tradition of the Anglo-Saxon social contract. Hobbes's despotic king exercises legitimate power as long as his rational subjects want him to. That means rational subjects would voluntarily surrender their rights and freedom to a despotic king.

Why did Hobbes create such a design for society? He was, of course, a child of his time and he knew the lawlessness, economic chaos, and social upheavals of England in the 1640s. He sought ways of preventing anarchy in the future. In addition, Hobbes was fascinated by Euclidian geometry, with its self-evident axioms and certainties. So he envisioned a societal structure of certainty, a Euclidian political philosophy. Such a society would be despotic, collectivist or authoritarian in today's parlance. Nazi Germany could qualify as a Hobbesian state, for Hitler came to power in 1933 by legitimate means.

In *Leviathan*, Hobbes posed three major ideas. He 'introduced empiricism as the method of discovering the sources of truth;' he noted 'that without a social contract every man feared every other man;' and he stressed that 'without an effective (meaning functioning) government the social contract would not be enforced' (Perlman 1996, 143). Or, in Perlman's words, 'a distaste for the Chaotic state of chronic struggle leads the parties to a willingness to settle for a system intended to bring peace'. (Perlman 1996, 493) Or, as Karl Pribram wrote (and Perlman quoted), 'the ideas of security as the basis for the Hobbesian social contract' is vital for understanding Hobbes (Perlman and McCann 1998, 39).

Hobbes' concept of the nature of man was not idealistic: all intellectual activities, he said, were reactions to outside stimuli and sensory impressions – not the product of spontaneous thought. And Hobbes stressed that man's desires for self-preservation and conquest create social tensions, which drive ungoverned masses to fight. He made strong pleas for a despotic government as a way to eliminate conflict and uncertainty. He recommended a collectivist society with absolute power, whose legitimacy rested on the voluntary surrender of power by its subjects. What is frequently overlooked is that such a voluntary contract is likely to become a covenant in which fear dominates the subjects (Perlman and McCann 1998, 43).

I was 14 years old, living in Stalinist Soviet Latvia in 1940–1, when I learned what fear was on a daily basis. I witnessed the consequences of denunciations of businessmen, officers, teachers and religious leaders by 'have-nots' to the dreaded NKVD. My father went into hiding, and with no income, my family subsisted on hidden bacon and potatoes. Stalinist Latvia taught me that people said what they did not mean and what they meant, they did not say. Life was a big lie. I was learning a life-long lesson in psychological empiricism.

This essay has four major themes. The *first* traces my teenage experiences with the Communist and Nazi despot in occupied Latvia during World War II. The *second* deals with my evolution as an economist in occupied West Germany where I witnessed the complete re-making of Nazi society by American and British military authorities. The *third* discusses how the current preoccupation of mainstream economists with mathematical formalism has failed to help the profession understand *Transition Economics* after the implosion of the Soviet Union and its former satellite states. The *fourth* theme shows that all major Hobbesian societies have long-term hidden costs that must be eventually be paid: the compensation for the material damages they have inflicted on its victims.

My teenage experiences with Communist and Nazi totalitarianism

My first encounter with a dictatorship occurred at the age of 8 in 1934, when Latvia became a dictatorship under Karlis Ulmanis. I lived for six years under his rule, up to the age of almost 14. No political parties were tolerated and he ruled by himself like a big boss. But private ownership of the means of production was permitted and markets functioned. There was a secret police organization, but nobody was ever killed. Ulmanis's political opponents were exiled to Sweden or left for the Soviet Union. I grew up in the prosperous home of a businessman, and I did not know what fear was.

As a teenager I witnessed the incorporation of Latvia into the Soviet Union. The Red Army occupied Latvia on June 17, 1940, and, by the end of July, Latvia had not fired a shot in resistance. Within three months, Latvia became a replica of the Soviet Union and Karlis Ulmanis's dictatorship became a Stalinist totalitarian society. The Communist party controlled everything and everyone, ably supported by the powerful and omnipresent secret police (the NKVD). Privately owned means of production were expropriated without compensation. My father's meat-packing plant was expropriated and an expropriation tax was levied against him to 'soak up' whatever funds he had. Since he could not pay the tax, the family's furniture, bedding, cups and forks were sold. We became pauperized, and were evicted from our own house. As a former employer of paid labor, my father became known as a 'blood sucker of the proletariat,' to use Karl Marx's phrase, and our family represented 'socially dangerous elements'. In the fall of 1996, 55 years later, the Latvian Archives of Riga sent me a copy of the list of people to be deported to Siberia on June 14, 1941. My entire family was slated for such transplantation to the Siberian Gulags while my father was to be arrested. But the communist police did not find us at home because we had been evicted from our own house. Some 15,000 other 'socially unacceptable elements' were not so lucky that night – they were forcibly transplanted to Siberia. Of course, in the Soviet Union these sweeping arrests and transplantations of undesirable elements had been the order of the day since the early 1920s (Shifrin 1980).

Millions of pages have been written on Stalin's role in the history of the Soviet Union (Courtois *et al.* 1998; Furet 1999). His appetite for power was equalled only by his indulgences in calculated paranoia, and his terror stigmatized not only individuals but entire nations, for any imaginable reason. In his book, *The Deportation of Nationalities* (1960) Robert Conquest detailed the process by which Stalin's secret police transplanted to Siberia some 1.6 million people simply because they were Chechens, Ingushi, Karachai, Balkars, Kalmyks, Volga Germans, Crimeans Tatars, or Meshketians. They were herded into box cars that took many weeks to make their trip to Siberia, with the result that mortality rates were as high as fifty per cent.

As a result of Lenin's Machiavellian monopolization of power, the Bolshevik repression of the 1920s, and Stalin's reign of terror in the 1930s, Russians felt as Boris Pasternak wrote in *Dr Zhivago*, that the onset of the Nazi-Soviet war on June 22, 1941 was like a liberation. It brought a sudden end to the show trials, the suppression of factual truth, the decimation of the officers corps of the Soviet armed forces, and the virtual annihilation of the old Bolsheviks. As German armies swept into the Soviet

Union, some three million Red Army soldiers voluntarily surrendered; they hoped that the Germans were likely to be better than Stalin's secret police (Fischer 1952).

The occupation of Latvia by the Germans was a change in totalitarian insignias, as the hammer and sickle were replaced by the Nazi swastika. For our family, the arrival of the German armed forces on June 26, 1941, in my home town of Daugavpils meant that the Soviets could not deport us to Siberia. Alas, within days of the onset of new occupation, I received the major shock of my youth: the occupation authorities, the dreaded Gestapo and their local hands, rounded up the entire Jewish population and within days all Jews had to wear a yellow star on their clothing. At the same time, Jews were forbidden to walk on sidewalks; they had to walk the cobblestones (Ezergailis 1996, 274).

Eventually, more than 90 per cent of all the Jews of my native city were killed. In Nazi-occupied Latvia, Soviet prisoners of war were systematically starved to death because they were 'Slav Untermenschen'. Thus, by the time I was fifteen, I had experienced the Latvian dictatorship of Ulmanis (1934–40), the Soviet occupation of Latvia (1940–1) and the Nazi occupation of Latvia (1941–4). I quickly grasped that in such totalitarian surroundings, people were saying what they did not mean. And what they meant, they did not say.

These experiences turned me into a practical youngster, who judged social ideas and ideologies by their consequences for individuals and their daily lives. Stalin's and Hilter's lawlessness helped me to understand instinctively the essence of John Locke's argument that every man has an unalienable right to own property (Perlman 1996, 143). No Marx, Lenin or Stalin could destroy it in the name of some ideology and kill its former owners. I also grasped that God, not Stalin or Hitler, gave man the right to liberty and life, and that, without property, life and liberty are virtually impossible. After the expropriation of my father's business, I felt free only in our family's un-expropriated summer cottage.

My university education in West Germany and the USA

In 1946, when I was 19, I was admitted to the University of Göttingen in the British zone of occupied Germany. Most German cities then were nothing but rubble, but Göttingen was untouched, an oasis in a defeated and destroyed country.

I discovered quickly that all my courses in economics were built upon a given societal structure – in German called *Sozialordnung* – based on privately owned means of production, a political system known as democracy, and a market system based on the interaction of demand and supply forces. The German economics literature usually took as its premise the capitalist welfare state, created in 1883, 1884 and 1889 by legislation.

Alas, my problem was that since 1934, I had lived *only* under different forms of dictatorships. After two years of muddling through my courses, I finally figured out the difference between 'neat' economic theory and the 'messy' reality of Latvian economic nationalism, Stalin's Soviet Union, Hitler's Third Reich, and the post-war military rule in the occupied three Western zones of Germany.

Yet for me, the concept of the social order, or societal structure, or the German *Sozialordnung*, or the Russian *obschchestvennyj ustav*, was ever present in my mind.

As a novice economist, I was trying to model the various social orders I had lived under into something analytical. How to explain the fact that Nazi Germany and the Soviet Union were totalitarian countries, yet the Third Reich had privately owned means of production, whereas in the Soviet Union all means of production were owned and operated by the government? All my attempts to model the concept of a social order came to nothing.

It was Walter Eucken's, *Die Grundlagen der Nationalökonomie* of 1947, that opened my eyes. It dealt with what he called the 'great antinomy', or contrast, between market-oriented economies and different types of centrally administered economies. This volume clarified for me the significance of the concept of a social order, or social space, within which economic activity takes place.

Later I discovered a short chapter in Joseph A. Schumpeter's *magnum opus* called 'Economics in the Totalitarian Countries'. He wrote that 'bolshevist economists are bound to discover in the end what Pareto and Barone realized half a century ago, namely, that there is an economic logic that has nothing specifically 'capitalist' about it (Schumpeter 1954, 1159).

Apart from my intellectual experiences at the university, I also witnessed the re-making of Nazi society into a Western-type society. From 1945–9, the British and American zones of occupation of Germany were nothing but a huge laboratory where military officers transformed the political, social, institutional, and economic dimensions of that society. With the unconditional surrender of the German Armed Forces in May of 1945, the Western Allies had first eliminated all traces of the racial aspects of the Nazi ideology and put Nazis behind bars under more than thirty automatic arrest categories. The Nazi party was banned, its property sequestered, and its police arm, the Gestapo, eliminated. The Western Allies also experimented with an 'industrial disarmament' policy for a few years in an effort to deprive Germany forever of the sinews of war. This endeavor called for a considerable across-the-board reduction of existing manufacturing capacity.

As a student of economics, I observed this process of industrial disarmament and wondered how the Americans could deliberately reduce German industrial production and hold down the standard of living in the heart of Europe? At that time, the average German lived on less than 1,500 calories a day. The Reichsmark bought virtually nothing, except the 1,500-calorie daily food ration, which was once described as being too much to die on and too little to live on. Yet, no matter how difficult the living conditions were, more than five million refugees from the Soviet occupied zone of Germany and the Eastern European countries poured into the Western occupied zones. They were a haven of security, compared to the Soviet-occupied territories.

By 1947, in Washington, D.C., the House and Senate were busy holding massive hearings on the European Recovery Program, later to be known as the Marshall Plan. It was a $20 billion program designed to restore the war-ravaged European countries and to unshackle the German economy from the strictures of the 'industrial disarmament' policy. For that to happen, Western occupied zones of Germany needed a new currency and the simultaneous elimination of wartime price and wage controls. It happened in June of 1948 and the German economic phoenix was born.

So, as a student at Göttingen, I witnessed how, on the ruins of the Third Reich, the Western Allies built a viable economy, a Western style democracy, and all the indispensable institutions to make it the envy of the world. Later, as a graduate student and professor of economics in the US, I would study in-depth how West Germany, under Chancellor Adenauer, created a *res nova* in international law by compensating the Jewish people for the collective and individual material damage inflicted on them by the authorities of the Third Reich from 1933–45.

After moving to the United States, I decided to obtain a PhD for I wanted to teach. I enrolled at Rutgers University, where the emphasis was on Keynesian theory and its relevance to the policy-makers' efforts to keep the US economy fully employed without triggering inflation. Since the early 1950s were the years of the decolonization of Europe's overseas empires, all graduate students were virtually force-fed various versions of the Harrod-Domar growth model. We took many other courses, but we were not trained to become mathematical economists, as was the case at a number of Ivy League universities, where Paul Samuelson's *Foundations of Economic Analysis* of 1947 became the bible for all young economists. After I took my PhD in September of 1956, I knew that my comparative advantage was not in the field of 'high' mathematical theory.

As a graduate student, I heard many older academic economists recall with horror the suffering of the American people during the Great Depression, and many voice their suspicions about the foundations of the US capitalist welfare state laid by the New Deal and by the Full Employment Act of 1946. Many were much taken by the spectacular Soviet growth rates after the end of World War II. At a safe distance from the Soviet Union, many still felt that 'socialism' had performed better than 'capitalism'. In 1949, Schumpeter provided normative support for the idea that capitalism had no future. In his presidential address to the American Economic Association, called 'The March into Socialism', he argued that the capitalist order tended to destroy itself in the course of time and centralist socialism was its heir apparent.

I was aware of these ideological preferences on the part of quite a few academic economists, including some of my instructors at Rutgers. Once I had my PhD, I could cope with the economic realities as I perceived them, regardless of the rapidly developing fads and 'prestige fields' in this country. I had no use for mathematical games that had little value to anyone other than math-oriented economists.

How mathematical formalism of the economics profession failed to prepare the economic profession for the challenges of the transition economics after the implosion of the Soviet Union in 1991

The Berlin Wall, erected in 1961 when I was in West Germany completing my research year in Kiel, was designed to stop the flood of refugees from East Germany. From then on, East German officials had orders to kill anyone trying to flee the East German 'worker's paradise'.

Returning home, I decided to teach a course in Soviet Economics at Lehigh University.

Being a Keynesian, I decided to use the inflationary gap analysis, developed by Keynes in his 1940 book, *How to Pay for the War*, as a point of reference. The focus of my attention was the inflationary gap in conditions of the Soviet 'investment war,' which started in 1929 with the First Five-Year Plan. Stalin's objective was to invest 40 per cent of the GNP into heavy industry each year and to avoid open inflation at the same time. Moscow suspended market forces and imposed price, wage and rent controls. Maximum prices of consumer goods were coupled either with formal rationing, or goods were sold on a first-come, first serve basis. Maximum wages were initially not coupled with labor conscription, but were so linked when excessive labor turnover occurred. All raw materials, half-fabricates and consumer goods were brought under the maximum price rule, and central allocations from Moscow. In 1938, the work-book, which tied every worker to his current job, was introduced.

The Five-Year Plan was actually an 'investment war,' to borrow Oscar Lange's apt phrase. The gamut of physical controls transformed the Soviet Union's economy into a typical war economy, as experienced in the United States during the two world wars. Such controls, in conditions of full employment, filled workers' pockets with rubles. But they could not buy what they wanted and in the amounts they wanted. Under this *repressed inflation*, earning an income did not automatically entitle workers to claim goods and services. Only rationing coupons did. With them, you could spend your rubles and pay constant, frozen prices. Without them, you could save your rubles or try to spend them in the non-controlled markets. In my course, I also discussed the different forms of repressed inflation and analyzed Soviet investment within the framework of Leontief's Input–Output method. I used a four-sector model to show students the interdependence among the various sectors with given technological coefficients. Later on, I would use a 10 sector model with computers. Other models revealed the failures of quantitative-output planning; they slowly unveiled the Soviet economy's monumental problems in coordination of demand and supply forces; they laid bare gross inefficiencies and wastefulness, and they showed the built-in disincentives for workers as well as managers. The annual plan-fulfillment mechanism revealed the enormous differences between the 'spirit' and the 'letter' of assigned targets.

Despite being a society so different from ours, the Soviet Union maintained a fully employed economy after 1929. Everybody had a job. Slackers were given concentration camp sentences. Thieves of government property, in well-advertised cases, were executed. Everybody had a room in a communal apartment, with shared kitchens and toilets, and everybody had free access to government medical care. A sense of egalitarianism prevailed, but envy still played a role. If somebody had 'more' possessions, he was usually denounced to the secret police as a 'Jew' or 'speculator'. It was a fully employed society with fear, Hobbesian fear, the only commodity in over supply.

My course used economic theory as a model or hypothesis. It also relied on sociology, designed to explain property relationships in the Soviet Union; on economic history, indispensable to reveal the 'spirit of the times' from the 1920s to 1990s; and finally, on statistical analysis, to gauge the quantitative aspects of Soviet economic performance.

When I taught my course, almost 1.5 billion people – in China, N. Korea, N. Vietnam, Eastern Europe and Cuba – lived under a Soviet-style economic system. The young minds of America needed to understand such non-market and non-democratic societies where full employment prevailed. These societies flouted the 'Opportunity cost principle' and paid virtually no attention to economic efficiency. They were the most wasteful economies on the globe! But they advertised full employment, free medical care, and free education for everybody.

Despite the failure everywhere of communist economies, economists worldwide became enamored of the so-called 'convergence' theory in the 1960s. Galbraith, who had never lived under a communist system, stated in 1966 that 'there are strong convergent tendencies as between industrial societies … despite their very different billing as capitalist or socialist or communist'.[1] In America, convergence was popularly treated as the inevitable corollary of industrialization. According to this view, industrialization displaces the predominance of ideology, and technology becomes the unifying force in the society. One social order changes so much that it becomes a near-replica of the former 'enemy'. In addition to Galbraith, such well-known American economists as C. Kerr, J. T. Dunlop, F. H. Harbison, and C. A. Myers subscribed to this thesis.[2]

Yet, some astute American analysts, such as Brzezinski, who knew the Soviet society intimately, rejected convergence as wishful thinking. I was very skeptical about convergence and in a public lecture on the 50th anniversary of the Bolshevik revolution, on November 17th, 1967, at the University of Missouri at St. Louis, I told the audience there would be no convergence by the year 2000. Why was I so negative? The reason was simple enough. I believed all societies were governed by four dimensions: ideological, political, institutional, and economic.

In the Soviet Union, Marxist ideology served as a substitute for religion and justified discrimination against all 'socially dangerous elements'. The Soviet secret police for decades used ideology to eliminate millions of 'enemies of the state'. Ideology was something no Soviet citizen could openly flaunt. And for this reason, people said what they did not mean, and what they meant they did not say. The lie became a way of life in all sectors of Soviet society. The Soviet one-party dictatorship ruled for seven decades unchallenged. Nominally, the communist party was the guardian of the Marxist ideology. The communist party shared its power with other power blocs, such as the military, the secret police, and the bureaucracy, but its political power was paramount.

Institutionally, the Soviet social order tolerated no privately-owned means of production, no independent judiciary, no independent labor unions, no bankruptcy laws. No matter how wasteful a factory was, it never went bankrupt. The administrative costs of this institutional inefficiency were monumental. Soviet society also failed to solve the basic economic problem of 'rationality', that is the coordination of demand and supply, the elimination of shortages and prevention of surpluses, and the provision of incentives. Central planners spelled out production targets for industries and plants, and allocated necessary inputs. But the imposition of price, wage, and rent controls made co-ordination difficult and caused shortages of all kinds.

Despite a number of attempted reforms, the Soviet social order remained basically intact. After Stalin's death, there was a dawn of more civility, more freedom of expression and more tolerance, but the secret police were as vigilant as ever, and denunciation remained the order of the day. The 'convergence' debate of the 1960s became a meaningless ripple, as the American and Soviet social orders continued to diverge during the Cold War. Meaningful convergence could take place only if all four components – ideological, political, institutional and economic – changed simultaneously, as it happened in a fragmented way after the implosion of the Soviet Union in 1991.

During the four decades of the Cold War, American academic economists paid little attention to developments in Communist societies. In the 1950s and 1960s, a methodological about-face took place in the preparation of young economists in this country and the rest of the world. Aspiring economists often obtained a Bachelor of Science in mathematics or physics first, and then went on to earn a Master of Science in computer science or statistics. Thereafter, the PhD degree was in econometrics (Coats 1997). The gurus of economics in the 1970s and 1980s were such well-known mathematical economists as Samuelson, Debreu, Arrow, and Solow, to mention only a few, all of whom have won Nobel prizes for economics. And even today, young economists strive to master sophisticated mathematical techniques and to acquire quantitative rather than verbal skills and institutional knowledge. Such quantification meant that only measurable entities' are studied (Coats 1997, 88). The mathematical economists are primarily concerned with the derivation of testable hypotheses. Today's mainstream economists use solely non-historical language (Coats 1997, 129) and try to transform economics into science or engineering.

The homogenized new economics have not helped solve pressing economic and social problems. Professor Wassily Leontief, the father of Input–Output analysis, sounded an early alarm-bell in his Presidential address to the American Economic Association at the end of 1970.

The creation of the *Journal of Economic Literature* in the late 1960s, under the able editorial guidance of Professor Mark Perlman, strove for 18 years to give the economics profession more breadth and depth. Alas, progress has been slow, and arcane math, marked by 'illegitimate' isolation of all non-economics variables from analysis, still rules supreme. All contiguous fields of economic theory enjoy low esteem and slight contempt, particularly area studies.

Academic economics at the very end of the twentieth century is elegant, and on paper looks 'scientific', but it is useless, for the most part, for economic policymaking purposes. This state of affairs induced the London-based *The Economist* to print a lead article with the astonishing title of 'The Puzzling Failure of Economics (*The Economist*, 1997, 11, 58).

The last two generations of economists have had virtually no training in law, social science, or economic history. They have done little to improve human welfare, as the Nobel Prize winner in economics, the late William Vickery admitted, and they were ill-prepared for the earth-shaking event of the early 1990s – the implosion of the Soviet Union in 1991.

After the Wassenaar Treaty of 1952, all future totalitarians will have to pay the long-term hidden costs of genocide

Mainstream economists have been puzzled by the collapse of communism in 1991. Mainstream economists have also ignored one unprecedented postwar event – West Germany's decision to pay voluntary reparations to the Jewish victims and survivors of the Nazi Holocaust.

After the unconditional surrender of Nazi Germany in 1945, members of the post-Hitler government were arrested by the Western Allies and tried for crimes against humanity in Nuremberg. The Nazi party was abolished and the Gestapo goons went to jails or internment camps. The Western Allies quickly revamped the Nazi social order and revealed to the German people and the entire world the full horror of the Nazi genocide.

Genocide can be conceived of as *intra-state war*. While the objective in an inter-state war is the defeat, not the extermination, of the adversary, genocide aims at the complete destruction of the enemy. In the Third Reich all Jews were declared to be such an enemy not fit to live among Aryans. Throughout the war, the Allies had warned the Germans that they would have to return all Jewish property seized, no matter how such sequestrations had been 'Aryanized' or legalized. Estimates of the value of looted Jewish property in prewar prices ranged from 12 to $32 billion (Robinson 1962, 163 Wyler 1966).

Also, during the war, various Jewish agencies, apart from the conventional restitution claims, insisted that 'the Jews had a collective claim against Germany based on *moral* justification rather than a legal one'.[4] Indemnification from the postwar German government would be demanded in the form of *individual* and *collective* compensation as well as *restitution* of the seized Jewish property. It was a truly revolutionary concept (Balabkins 1971, 84).

On May 14, 1948, Israel emerged as an independent state. In the fall of 1949, West German zones of occupation were transformed into an independent entity. Chancellor Adenauer was hardly eight weeks in office when he publicly ushered in his policy of restoring German relations with the Jews. He knew of the prevailing revulsion of all things German in the Western world and he was also aware that the West German economy lived by foreign trade. And how could one conduct international trade when nobody was willing to shake a German hand?

The *World Jewish Congress* paved the way for official contacts in December 1949, when it issued a five-point declaration demanding from the West German Parliament: (a) acceptance of moral and political responsibility for Nazi deeds toward Jews; (b) material indemnification; (c) legislation against anti-semitism; (d) re-education of German youth; and (e) a check upon nationalistic tendencies in the West German government.[5] In 1951, the Israeli government requested $1.5 billion from Germany and pleaded with the Western Allies for support. The American government said it could not impose on the German Federal Republic an obligation to pay reparations, but Jewish leaders demanded that the West German government assume a binding obligation to make collective reparation and accept the moral, political, and material responsibility for the deeds of the Third Reich. Chancellor Adenauer did that before the Bundestag on September 27, 1951, which made direct talks between the Germans and the Israelis possible.

The first encounter between the Germans and the Jewish-Israeli delegation took place on March 20, 1952, at Wassenaar, Holland. At the outset, the German delegation stated that the Federal Republic could pay only limited amounts.[6] In the end, the Germans agreed to pay DM 3.5 billion for the Israeli collective claim. The West German government committed itself to make payments in the form of various goods, as specified by Israel. The Jewish Claims Conference obtained 450 million marks. In addition the Bonn government committed itself to enact legislation for compensation of all Nazi victims, later to be known as individual compensation of various types.

In total, as of January 1, 1996, the Federal Republic of Germany has made public expenditures for various types of Nazi-inflicted damages to the amount of DM 100 billion. By the time these payments come to an end, the estimated total will be DM 123 billion.[7] I believe these payments can be interpreted as the costs of revamping the Nazi social order into a Western society with political democracy, market-driven welfare capitalism and privately owned means of production. They can also be conceived of as the cost of genocide of the intra-state war of the Third Reich.

Nothing comparable exists in any of the post-communist states in Eastern Europe or Eurasia. Of course, after de-Stalinization in 1956, the people in the Soviet Union were told the full extent of Stalinist purges, executions and exiles of socially danger-ous elements into Siberia. The Soviet government took small steps to compensate victims (Barry 1982). Yet, even with this new legislation the Soviet citizens were reluctant to sue the Soviet government. In 1994 Duma, the Russian legislative body, passed the decree 'On the Establishment of the Statute Governing the Procedure of Returning to Citizens Their Property Which was Illegally Confiscated, Extorted or Otherwise Disposed in Connection with Political Repressions, Reimbursing Its Value of Paying Cash Compensation'. This long-winded statute covers Stalin's vic-tims who are citizens of Russia, the ex-Soviet republics, foreign citizens, and people without citizenship. In the case of death of a rehabilitated person, the property or compensation for it shall be transferred in equal shares to his or her priority heirs-at-law. The confiscated property will be returned if it exists.[8] In the fall of 1994, the Finance Ministry earmarked 100 billion rubles to compensate persons who had been rehabilitated and had their property rights restored. At the then prevailing exchange rate of 5 rubles for 1 dollar, the sum came to $20,000,000,000 per annum.

Yet a closer look at the law on the rehabilitation of the victims of political repres-sions indicates the half-heartedness of the Russian legislators. Section 15 of the law states that the former victims are entitled to 180 rubles for each month spent in jail or camps, but, regardless of the length of time incarcerated, no one can receive more than 5,000 rubles. In 1997, at the exchange rate of 6 rubles for 1 dollar, the former victims would receive the paltry sum of $833.00 for a lifetime of incarceration! Given the difficult budgetary situation in Russia for the nine years, it seems that, apart from the law, the government intends to spend little on paying for the incredible blood-letting that the Soviet social order inflicted upon tens of millions of its citizens.

Germany paid for Nazi genocide whereas Russia does not

After almost half a century of the hostile 'East' facing a reluctantly hostile 'West' the 'East' admitted its defeat in 1991 by implosion. In the former Soviet empire and its Eastern European satellite countries people clamored for instant Western-style social order, hoping a market-driven economy, privately owned means of production, and democracy would produce well-being for the masses. And why not? It was generally expected that post-communist Russia could emulate what the West Germans were able to do. In America, the mainstream economists with their preoccupation with the development of testable hypotheses, were virtually lost with respect to what was happening in Russia and Central European countries (Angresano 1997).[31] They knew nothing about how to create privately owned means of production out of the state-owned means of production, which were formerly immune to bankruptcy and subject to quantitative-output planning, and they paid no attention to the stricture of the Western 'opportunity cost principle'. These economists were mathematicians, and econometricians, but they did not know how to quantify the prevailing or changing property relationships in the state or in the emerging private sectors. The post-implosion period in the former Soviet Union gave rise to a new field called Transition Economics and a score of new textbooks.[9]

Almost a decade has gone by and the halcyon days of 1989 in Central Europe and 1991 in Russia are definitely over. The former euphoric hopes of millions of Russians are gone for good. The reform of the former Soviet social order turned out to be a nightmare for a number of reasons. Unlike the defeated Third Reich, in 1991, when the Soviet Union imploded, it was still nominally one of the victors of World War II. The unconditional surrender of the Third Reich eliminated at once the entire Nazi political structure. In the former Soviet Union, by contrast, the Communist party did lose its monopoly power position, but is still very much alive and even kicking. Its former organizational network has remained in place and its former officials have obtained some of the party's wealth after the demise of the USSR.

After the implosion in 1991, nobody destroyed the secret police of the KGB, whereas the victorious Allies had eliminated the last vestiges of the Nazi Gestapo. Nobody eliminated the Red Army's General Staff, whereas in 1945 the Western Allies simply arrested all the generals of the German General Staff, and shot or hanged some of them. But above all, in post-communist Russia there was no massive 'debolshevization' of the Soviet bureaucracy, schools, universities, and the Red managers; nothing comparable to the postwar 'denazification' of the occupied Western zones of Germany. Without such a 'debolshevization' the former communists, KGB officials, camp guards, and false accusers of innocent people, are still in authority or live on pensions in peace and without any regrets for their past activities in the Soviet empire.

Another difference between Russia and Germany is that the Soviet Union, unlike the defeated Third Reich did not have privately owned means of production. In Nazi Germany, only the Jews, Gypsies, and active enemies of the Nazi regime were forbidden to own and operate businesses. In Russia, in contrast, after 1991, private ownership of the means of production had to be created from scratch.

After the demise of the Soviet Union, it was initially assumed that privatization laws passed by the Russian *Duma* would be an effective means of creating privately owned factories, mines, banks, insurance companies and land. The past nine years have shown how difficult this process is. Land reform is still to come. The entrenched bureaucracy is also dead set against privatization, and the process continues haphazardly. Russian reformers wanted to create a market-driven economy, but did not know how to do it (Handelman 1994; Brainerd 1998).

But the most significant difference between the defeated post-war Germany and the imploded Russia is that West Germany (called simply Germany since reunification in 1989) has paid DM 120 billion (close to $70 billion) to redress the material damages inflicted by the Nazi erected Hobbesian social order (1933–45) on its victims. These payments, begun in 1953, were the first necessary steps for Germany's re-admission to the comity of the non-Hobbesian civil societies of the world. They can be interpreted as essential costs of the transformation of the former Nazi society into a Western democracy, with free elections, an independent judiciary, unfettered mass media, and market-driven welfare capitalism. Thus, these payments can also be conceived of as part of the latent costs of the genocide of the former Third Reich. The former Soviet Union (now Russia) thus far has not made any comparable collective or individual payments to its surviving victims. The massive human sacrifice extracted by Soviet communism between 1918 and 1991 is virtually forgotten in America, although the English edition of St Courtois's book has moved the issue to the front burner today. Yet, sooner or later Russia will have to face and pay the hidden costs of its totalitarian past if it wants to be admitted to the community of non-Hobbesian states.

Notes

1 Galbraith, J. K., Article in the *New York Times*, 1966, November 29.
2 See their *Industrialism and Industrial Man*, Cambridge, MA., 1960, pp. 282–96.
3 Perlman, M. *The Character of Economic Thought, Economic Characters, and Economic Institutions*, Ann Arbor, Michigan The University of Michigan Press, 1996, see, in particular, Chapter 3 entitled 'On the Editing of American Economic Journals: Some Comments on the Earlier Journals and the Lessons Suggested' pp. 47–59.
4 The author of this claim was Israel's State Comptroller, Dr Siegfried Moses; see Balabkins, N. *West German Reparations to Israel*, New Brunswick, N.J., Rutgers University Press, 1971, p. 82.
5 Barou, N. *The Story Behind Reparations* (4 pages, typewritten manuscript). This sketch, written by Dr Barou after the Wassenaar negotiations were completed, is at the *Institute of Jewish Affairs*, London.
6 Abs, H. J., *Entscheidungen*, Frankfurt/M and Berlin, 1993, pp. 123–33. See also Abs, H. J., *Auslandsschuldenregelung und Wiedergutmachung*.
7 German Information Center, German Restitution for National Socialist Crimes, New York, January 1997, pp. 8–9.
8 FBIS-SOV, 'Victims of Repression to Receive Compensation,' in *Russia National Affairs*, August 22, 1994, p. 23.
9 A typical example is a text by Kennett, D. and Lieberman, M., *The Road to Capitalism. Economics Transformation in Eastern Europe and the former Soviet Union*, New York, The Dryden Press, 1990, pp. 367.

References

Angresano, J. *The Political Economy of Gunnar Myrdal. An Institutional Basis for the Transformation Problem*, Cheltenham, UK, Edward Elgar, 1997.
Balabkins, N. *West German Reparations to Israel*, New Brunswick, N. J. Rutgers University Press, 1971.
Barry, D. L. 'Compensation for Damages Caused by the Acts of Soviet Criminal Justice Organs,' in The 1981 Legislation, in *Review of Socialist Law*, vol. 4, 1982, pp. 331–40.

Brainerd, E., 'Winners and Losers in Russia's Economic Transition,' *The American Economic Review*, vol. 88(5), 1998, pp. 1094–114.

Cassidy, J., 'Department of Disputation. The Decline of Economics,' *The New Yorker*, December 1996.

Coats, A. W. *The Post-1945 Internationalization of Economics*, Durham, N.C., Duke University Press, 1997.

Courtois, S. *et al.* (eds) *Das Schwarzbuch des Kommunismus. Unterdrückung, Verbrechen und Terror*, München/Zürich, Piper, 1998.

Ezergailis, A. *The Holocaust in Latvia, 1941–1944*, Riga and Washington, D.C., The Historical Institute of Latvia and The United States Holocaust Memorial Museum, 1996.

Euken, W. *Die Grundlagen der Nationalökonomie*, Godesberg, 1947.

Fischer, G. *Soviet Opposition to Stalin. A Case Study in World War II*, Cambridge, MA., Harvard University Press, 1952.

Furet, F. *The Idea of Communism in the Twentieth Century*, The University of Chicago Press, 1999.

Handelman, St., 'The Russian Mafia,' in *Foreign Affairs*, vol. 73(2), 1994.

Perlman, M. *The Character of Economic Thought, Economic Characters, and Economic Institutions*, Ann Arbor, Michigan, The University of Michigan Press, 1996.

—— and McCann Jr., C. R. *The Pillars of Economic Understanding. Ideas and Traditions*, Ann Arbor, The University of Michigan Press, 1998.

Robinson, N., 'Spoilation and Remedial Action,' *Institute Anniversary Volume*, New York, Yivo Institute for Jewish Research, 1962.

Schumpeter, J. A. *History of Economic Analysis*, New York, Oxford University Press, 1954.

Shifrin, A. *Guide to Camps, Prisons, and Prisons for Mental Diseases of the USSR*, Switzerland, 1980. It lists 1976 concentration camps, 273 jails, and 85 jails for mentally-ill dissidents.

'Theoretical Assumptions and Nonobserved Facts' *The American Economic Review*, vol 61(1), March 1971, pp. 1–7.

The Leontièf, W. Economist, August 23, 1997, pp. 11 and 58.

Wyler, B., 'Reparations and not Handouts' *The Jerusalem Post* September 23, 1966.

6 Communitarianism and the individual

Charles R. McCann, Jr

Introduction

Political events since the 1980s pointed to a radical reappraisal of social and political attitudes towards the respective roles of the individual and the State. The elections of Margaret Thatcher's Conservative party in the United Kingdom and Ronald Reagan to the presidency of the United States signaled a fundamental change in the political dynamic.[1] The collapse of communism in Eastern Europe was taken as a significant event, not only in terms of the geopolitical reorganization that would inevitably follow, but more importantly in the realization that the western principles of individual liberty and the respect for individual rights had triumphed over the authoritarianism inherent in a collectivist view of society.

However, at the same time there emerged an intellectual counterrevolution of sorts. Political philosophers intent on rehabilitating collective approaches to decision-making began to argue a new justification for the promotion of a social ethic that would serve to advance their principal concerns of social welfare and social justice. The result was the beginning of a new interpretation of an old philosophy, communitarianism. With communism on the decline, a new communitarianism became ascendant.

Communitarianism has been used to identify both a philosophical social theory and a political movement. As a political *theory* the concept implies a social ontology, and so is more concerned with the *concept* of society than with the *nature* of society. It begins by acknowledging that individuals cannot be patterned as rational, deliberative agents, the agents, for example, postulated in neoclassical economic theory; they are not volitional utility-maximizers. Rather, they are (1) fallible, in the sense of being incapable of complete apprehension of their surroundings, and so prone to errors in judgment; (2) non-logical (non-rational), in the Paretian sense of behaviors influenced not by a logical process of reasoning but by custom, belief, and moral concern;[2] and (3) socially-defined, that is, incapable of acting outside of or being contemplated as prior to the social sphere of which they are part and through which their moral and ethical beliefs are fashioned. On this level, the individual cannot be said to have free will, because he is antecedent to and reactive upon his cultural frame, and so can be understood only with respect to the social institutions and collectives of civil society. These social institutions engender a sense of community and instill a sense of social welfare, as well as serve as a common set of identifiable ends. More importantly, because they are antecedent to the individual, social arrangements take on a real existence, and so extend beyond those comprising the social units.

As a political *movement* the term implies that the members of a society must be trained to reject their individualism and instead become *social* agents imbued with a *social* conscience. In pursuit of this end, the State must take a proactive stance and demand not just equality of opportunity but also equality of result. Uniformity is the State directive. Once again there is an understanding that institutions are real and have a meaning, existence, and direction independent of their constituents. Such a simplistic conception encompasses a tremendous variety of non-rationalist political philosophies and economic and social doctrines, from methodological individualism to the holistic societal forms of fascism, corporatism, communism, and socialism. Both the social theory and the practical political form of communitarian social design have served as the basis of, among other things, the welfare state and the eugenics movement, and more recently the push towards 'economic democracy'. The popular understanding of communitarianism and the concern for a common will incorporates a rhetoric that serves as grist for the politicians' mill; it is of tremendous political advantage for he who wishes to take on the mantle of national leader to espouse platitudes to the effect that the cultural environment shapes our being, and so we shall all be better off when society is restructured so as to provide a more 'nurturing' and 'caring' place. The idea of a 'communal village' in which each member is responsible for all derives from this political diatribe.

The new communitarian philosophy as social theory is much more complex than any pseudo-philosophic political movement, as it goes to the heart of the relation of the person to the society, including the very notion of self. This essay will examine the old and the new approaches to communitarian social theory to provide a survey of its main points. Specifically, the *new* communitarianism will be seen as a challenge to the liberal[3] vision of, among others, John Rawls. This critique will then be confronted with other (not necessarily complementary) expressions of the liberal position, which proceed from radically different interpretations of the nature of man in society.[4]

The philosophic basis of communitarian thought: Hegel as exemplar

Ideas of communitarianism can be found throughout western philosophy. Beginning with the *Republic* of Plato and the *Politics* of Aristotle, through the writings of St. Thomas Aquinas, to the *New View of Society* of Robert Owen, we find allusions to the need for the individual to submerge his identity to the betterment of the community or the State, if only for purposes of ensuring a just distribution of the social product. For the present, in discussing the notion of a communitarian ethic, an appropriate starting point may be the ruminations of the French philosopher Jean-Jacques Rousseau, who promoted the important concepts of the social compact and the general will. Rousseau's concept of society, as expressed in his 1762 *The Social Contract*, is one in which the individual members of the community surrender their individuality to the direction of the 'general' or societal will, and in so doing accept that they are but a part of the social whole. The 'clauses' of Rousseau's social contract 'may be reduced to one – the total alienation of each associate, together with all his rights, to the whole community' (Rousseau 1762: 191), suggesting the transformation of the person from individual to part of the whole, in accordance with the direction of the general will. Thus individual will and individual personality are replaced by 'common identity'. To do otherwise, namely, to allow the individual to retain certain (unspecified) rights and even to retain an aura of individuality, would lead only to the resurrection of the original state of anarchy, the very outcome for which the apparatus of the State was erected to avoid.[5]

While Rousseau's concept of the social compact can be very clearly understood as a *variant* of what has come to be identified as communitarianism – one need only consider Rousseau's direction: 'Each of us puts his person and all his power in common under the supreme direction of the general will, and, in our corporate capacity, we receive each member as an indivisible part of the whole' (Rousseau 1762: 191) – a more complete and extended definition of the philosophy is that offered by the German philosopher Georg Wilhelm Friedrich Hegel.[6] It was Hegel's presentation of the relation of the individual to the community and the State that lay at the heart of the German, and later the American, fascination with institutional approaches to the study and amelioration of what came to be known as 'social problems'. It was Hegel's organicist ontology that also influenced the writings of the leading economic theorist of the late nineteenth and early twentieth centuries, Alfred Marshall,[7] and also influenced the economic theory and policy proposals of the American Institutionalists.

In his 1821 *Philosophy of Right*, Hegel commented on the proper place of the individual within the broader context of the ethical system in which he functions. Individual interests are synonymous with the general interest of the larger, social collectives, these being (in order of increasing complexity) the family, the community, and the State. The essence of the individual is the essence of the whole. This identity implies that one need no longer focus on the separate interests of those comprising the whole – the separate individuals within the society – but rather the focus must be the general interest. To quote Hegel:

> Since the phases of the ethical system are the conception of freedom, they are the substance or universal essence of individuals. In relation to it, individuals are merely accidental. Whether the individual exists or not is a matter of indifference to the objective ethical order, which alone is steadfast. It is the power by which the life of individuals is ruled.
>
> (Hegel 1821: §145 add.)

This is not to imply that the individual has no interests of his own. Rather, he understands the importance of ethical obligation and finds 'liberation' in social duty, as 'he is freed from the dependence which he as subjective and particular felt towards moral permission and command' (Hegel 1821: §149). The interests of the individual become coincident with, and are seen by him to be advanced through reference to, the interests of the family and the community, and by extension to those of the State as the universal whole. The person in effect cannot identify himself and his interests as distinct from the State and its interests. He understands that the furtherance of the ends of the State, which are themselves rational and deliberate, must coincide with the furtherance of his own ends; he has by rational means come to identify his 'true' interests with those of the collective:

> Individuals in the civic community are private persons, who pursue their own interests. As these interests are occasioned by the universal, which appears as a means, they can be obtained only in so far as individuals in their desire, will, and conduct, conform to the universal, and become a link in the chain of the whole.
>
> (Hegel 1821: §187)

The general will is universal precisely because it subsumes individual, family, and community wills to the promotion of the rational direction of society. The general will exists only as an abstraction, possessing none of the limitations and socially retarding influences associated with individual desire, initiative, and enterprise (and, one should add, it denies the possibility of less-than-perfect knowledge and even unintended consequences).

Having identified the relationship between individual, family, community, and the State, Hegel then went on to define some of the duties and responsibilities of the civic community and the rationale underlying the importance of a social, as opposed to an individual, ethos. As in Plato's *Republic*, Hegel's community functions as an extended family, in which the interests of the one come to be seen as the interests of the whole, and vice versa. As defined by Hegel, the civic community has three important elements: (1) a reorientation of individual wants, such that each member of the community gains satisfaction through his own work and through his appreciation of the work and personal satisfaction of others; (2) a means to the administration of justice, where this is defined socially; and (3) a social provision for the maintenance by the community of its individual members, such that the interests of the members become identified with the interests of the whole (Hegel 1821: §188). The survival of the community takes precedence over any and all questions of the rights of the individual and even the family unit. *Social* utility is the primary concern; the community is ill-served if its members do not realize that the values of the community are paramount, and so, by seeing to the provision of the *social* welfare, they directly and indirectly promote their own *individual* welfare. Thus the community has an interest in actively interceding in the affairs of its members, compelling them if need be into compliance with community standards and social norms, both for the sake of their own well-being and for the preservation of the community. Hegel expressed it thus:

> The civic community, in its character as universal family, has the right and duty to supersede, if necessary, the will of the parents, and superintend the education of the young, at least in so far as their education bears upon their becoming members of the community.
>
> (Hegel 1821: §239)

Similarly, the community has the duty and right to take under its guardianship those who wantonly squander their subsistence and that of their family. In the place of this extravagance it substitutes their real end, which it seeks to promote along with the purpose of the community.

(Hegel 1821: §240)

The civic community takes upon itself the role of guarantor of individual outcomes, as decided through reference to the social whole. The State, as the ultimate social collective, is thus viewed as the ultimate guarantor of individual *and* social welfare. The idea of being 'a member of the State' is meaningless; '[t]he concrete state is the whole, articulated into its particular circles and the member of the state is the member of a circle or class' (Hegel 1821: §308, note). The State becomes in effect the realization of the general will. Further, the State 'insists that the interests of the family and civic community shall link themselves' (§260, add.). It is the *State*, not the individuals constituting it, that is rational; it is the *State*, not its members, to which may be ascribed a social consciousness:

> The state, which is the realized substantive will, having its reality in the particular self-consciousness raised to the plane of the universal, is absolutely rational. This substantive unity is its own motive and absolute end. In this end freedom attains its highest right. This end has the highest right over the individual, whose highest duty in turn is to be a member of the state.

(Hegel 1821: §258)

Hegel's philosophy of communitarianism followed the successes of the Cameralists[8] in establishing the general welfare principles of the Prussian State. Through this comprehensive economic, political, and social philosophy, Prussian writers such as Johann Heinrich Gottlieb von Justi and Veit Ludwig von Seckendorff proclaimed the State and civil society to be a single and comprehensible organic entity. Any distinction between society (culture) and the State could not even be contemplated. Every aspect of civil society – religion, family, institutions, economy and even art and science – had a corresponding dimension that could be identified with the furtherance of the general social order.

The philosophical basis of new communitarian thought: Sandel, MacIntyre, and the attack on Rawls[9]

Rawls and the liberal position

Modern political philosophers who define themselves as new communitarians typically begin their commentaries on the proper foundation of moral society with an attack on the contractarian theory of the State as put forth by John Rawls in his 1971 *A Theory of Justice*. This book is said to be *the* most significant statement of the liberal theory of social[10] justice.

As Rawls sees it, the provision of justice is the foundation of moral society; it 'is the first virtue of social institutions' (Rawls 1971: 3). The role of the State (or 'society') is to promote the *right*, defined with respect to the provision of social justice and fairness, principally as regards distribution. The extent to which this is achieved serves as the standard for the comparison of various alternative societal forms. Apart from providing the appropriate environment, the State must refrain from defining the social good (other than in identifying the least advantaged members of the society) or in interfering with the pursuit by its members of their own personal interests and the furtherance of their own self-defined ends. This, and the rational actor form the basis of his theory of social justice.

The abstraction of the social contract is the 'guiding idea' in Rawls' social theory, serving much the same purpose as did the abstract social contracts of Rousseau and Thomas Hobbes (in *Leviathan*).[11] Each in effect is stipulated as corresponding to the original 'state of nature'. The difference between the Rawlsian social contract and the forms of social contract suggested by eighteenth and nineteenth century political philosophers is that the Rawlsian contract is concerned solely with the establishment of parameters respecting social justice, and is not a preliminary to a theory of the foundation of the State:

> [T]he principles of justice for the basic structure of society are the object of the original agreement. They are the principles that free and rational persons concerned to further their own interests would accept in an initial position of equality as defining the fundamental terms of their association. These principles are to regulate all further agreements; they specify the kinds of social cooperation that can be entered into and the forms of government that can be established. This way of regarding the principles of justice I shall call justice as fairness.
>
> (Rawls 1971: 11).

As with all contractarian theories, the 'original position' is essential here to the establishment of the basic principles of social justice. Rawls suggests that a fair and just society can be established in the 'original state' by imagining that each member of the society is, at the time of the enunciation of the basic principles of justice that will serve as the basis of the society, completely impartial. He is ignorant of his own constitution, including his economic and social standing, intellectual and physical abilities, selfish desires, and the means at his disposal to their attainment; he is equally ignorant of the constitution of the other parties to the contract. This allows the parties to establish fair and equitable 'rules of the game'.

> The idea of the original position is to set up a fair procedure so that any principles agreed to will be just. The aim is to use the notion of pure procedural justice as a basis of theory. Somehow we must nullify the effects of specific contingencies which put men at odds and tempt them to exploit social and natural circumstances to their own advantage. Now in order to do this I assume that the parties are situated behind a veil of ignorance. They do not know how the various alternatives will affect their own particular case and they are obliged to evaluate principles solely on the basis of general considerations.
>
> (Rawls 1971: 136–7)

Behind the protection of the 'veil', each party agrees to abide by the principles of the social contract; as each is similarly situated, and no one has any informational advantage, none can advance any social purpose or principle which could serve to further his own ends. While self-interest is not extinguished, anything that can serve to create a bias in selection is ruled out, meaning that any decision as to the rules of social justice must be impartial. Rawls has through his use of the 'veil' effectively achieved a measure of universal equality in the initial state. Knowing nothing of their individual status, the members of the society must rely in their deliberations on the value of primary goods, these being those objects desired for their inherent goodness. Principal among these is justice. This criterion alone, according to Rawls, ensures that the principles of social justice agreed upon are fair and equitable, and fairly derived.

The point of the exercise is to establish a society along egalitarian lines, but without abandoning individualism (the single attribute making Rawls' society a liberal one). This means that Rawls must continue to accept the classical concept of rationality. In the 'original position', each person, despite a lack of knowledge of his own interests, nonetheless has a 'rational plan of life'. Rationality here means only that the person 'is thought to have a coherent set of preferences between the options open to him. He ranks these options according to how well they further his purposes; he follows the plan which will satisfy more of his desires rather than less, and which has the greater chance of being successfully executed' (Rawls 1971: 143). Rawls' man is, above all, risk-averse and, because he is uncertain as to his own preferences, he chooses to assess the meaning of social justice in terms of the certainty afforded by the knowledge of the social utility of primary goods. So, while being ignorant of his own ends, he can nonetheless still rank alternatives (again, 'according to how well they further his purposes'), but along a moral dimension; Rawls' rational actors 'must try to protect their liberties, widen their opportunities, and enlarge their means for promoting their aims whatever these are' (p. 143), doing so through the promotion of social justice. The only difference Rawls sees between his view of rationality and rational man and that of the modern social choice theory is that his man is not envious.[12] 'He is not downcast by the knowledge or perception that others have a larger index of primary social goods ..., and he does not believe that the existing inequalities are founded on injustice or are the result of letting chance work itself out for no compensating social purpose' (p. 143). In short, Rawls' man is engaged in a contest in which the only competition is himself, and the end is a personal best:

> They do not wish a high or a low score for their opponents, nor do they seek to maximize or minimize the difference between their successes and those of others. The idea of a game does not really apply, since the parties are not concerned to win but to get as many points as possible judged by their own system of ends.
> (Rawls 1971: 144–5)

From the original position derives Rawls' general conception of the principles of justice (originally two principles which he later combines into one):

> All social primary goods – liberty and opportunity, income and wealth, and the bases of self-respect – are to be distributed equally unless an unequal distribution of any or all of these goods is to the advantage of the least favored.
> (Rawls 1971: 303)

This notion – that a particular distribution is just only if, given a pattern of social and economic inequality, compensating benefits accrue to the least advantaged – is what Rawls terms the 'difference principle'. It is with this principle that he moves significantly from the Utilitarian position of maximizing the greatest happiness of the greatest number; in place of the Utilitarian calculus he substitutes the maximin principle, that is, the notion that social welfare is defined by the utility of the least-advantaged member.[13] The Utilitarian social welfare criterion of max $\Sigma_i U_i$ is replaced by the Rawlsian social welfare criterion of $\min(U_1, ..., U_n)$.[14]

The important point of Rawls' theory of social justice to be drawn here is that the parties in the 'original position' achieve an egalitarian social outcome because it is *rational* for them to do so. He needs no additional assumptions of community sympathy or social consciousness on the part of the parties, for self-interest alone is enough to generate the desired distributive outcome.[15]

Yet, Rawls does not deny the social nature of man. Indeed, the 'well-ordered society' is fundamentally a 'social union'. In the original position, each individual implicitly recognizes that society is 'a cooperative venture for mutual advantage, ... marked by a conflict as well as by an identity of interests' (Rawls 1971: 520). Rejecting the notion of a 'private society' – wherein each individual enters a social arrangement not through any kinship or fellow-feeling with others in the arrangement, but solely because it provides the best possibility for the achievement of his personal aims – Rawls opts for a view of association as inherently good in itself. His explanation takes the form of a Ricardian gains-from-trade argument: as '[t]he potentialities of each individual are greater than those he can hope to realize, ... everyone must select which of his abilities and possible interests he wishes to encourage ...'. This leads to cooperation and the formation of a social union, wherein 'each person can participate in the total sum of the realized natural assets of the others' (p. 523). This is derivative from the moral sense of justice that serves to instill feelings of sentiment:

> We are led to the notion of the community of humankind the members of which enjoy one another's excellences and individuality elicited by free institutions, and they recognize the good of each as an element in the complete activity the whole scheme of which is consented to and gives pleasure to all.
>
> (Rawls 1971: 523)

Thus while not *compelled* to engage in social relations, nonetheless, on the basis of a moral code of justice alone, the individuals form basic institutional arrangements and social unions, while surrendering neither the self nor their right to the good.

Sandel, MacIntyre, and the communitarian counterargument

The political philosopher Michael J. Sandel, whose 1982 book *Liberalism and the Limits of Justice* began in a sense the new communitarian movement, criticizes Rawls[16] primarily for his adherence to a liberal political ethic, through which central importance is given to individual rights. As the individual is necessarily, on Rawls' account, antecedent to any social order, Rawls must be seen as proceeding as if the individual is removed from the influences of his environment. Man as subject is relationally prior to purposes, so the right – defined to a large degree with respect to freedom of contract – is antecedent to the good. Sandel, on the other hand, feels that the emphasis should be placed on a broader conceptual teleological notion of the social good. Ends are constitutive, and so the good is a categorical imperative, not a contingent goal. In contrast to Rawls, and by extension all liberal philosophers who express an overarching concern with personal freedom and individual rights, Sandel wishes to make community the subject of human motivations. Good must become antecedent to right, and society antecedent to the individual.

Sandel considers the liberal notion of the individual (the 'unencumbered self') which Rawls accepts – as purposeful, rational, deliberative, and independent – to be at the core of what he perceives to be a perverse juxtaposition of right and good. The 'unencumbered self' as envisioned by Rawls (as interpreted by Sandel) can feel a communal spirit only in the sense that he is free to associate with whomever he desires. Rawls requires that the moral choices of the individual arise from personal preferences and not from social attachments or the pressure of socially-prescribed behavioral norms. Sandel criticizes Rawls for endowing the individual with a freedom of choice and for situating him relationally prior to his ends, thus ignoring the effects of the environment (in the guise of social collectives) in conditioning choice. Choice in Rawls takes precedence over what is chosen, and the individual is removed from identification with any perceived ends and, *ipso facto*, with any commitment to a larger conception of the social good. In short, a concern for basic individual liberties takes precedence over moral obligation and social virtue. As Sandel notes with respect to liberal social theory, nothing has any hold on the individual beyond the satisfaction of his own immediate wants, and there is nothing in his external relations which can serve as binding constraints on these desires:

> No commitment could grip me so deeply that I could not understand myself without it. No transformation of life purposes and plans could be so unsettling as to disrupt the contours of my identity. No project could be so essential that turning away from it would call into question the person I am. Given my independence from the values I have, I can always stand apart from them; my public identity as a moral person 'is not affected by changes over time' in my conception of the good.
>
> (Sandel 1982: 62)

By insisting on an entirely subjective self, given only to voluntary associations and so not bound to any social ends, Rawls (according to Sandel) denies that the individual can be in any way shaped or influenced by his social ties; the unencumbered self is by definition purposeful in *choosing* ends.[17] Where ties of cooperation and beneficence exist, they are made entirely for reasons of (ephemeral) mutual benefit, and not because of any commitment to ascribed associational ends, that is, they are not made through reference to any antecedent value structure. But Sandel believes more is required:

> What is denied to the unencumbered self is the possibility of membership in any community bound by moral ties antecedent to choice; he cannot belong to

any community where the self *itself* could be at stake. Such a community – call it constitutive as against merely cooperative – would engage the identity as well as the interests of the participants, and so implicate its members in a citizenship more thoroughgoing than the unencumbered self can know.

(Sandel 1984: 87)

Sandel thus argues that a theory of community must extend beyond an understanding of the social (communal) nature of the aims and value-structure of the individual members of the community. It is not enough, in other words, to accept that each member of a community (or at the very least a majority of the members) is governed by feelings of communitarian morality or shared sentiments.[18] A theory of community must, according to Sandel, accept as a first condition that each individual identifies himself with, and is only realized through, his community, that is, he perceives his *individual* identity in terms of the *social* (collective) identity. One cannot *choose* whether to belong, since the community identity itself defines choice. The concept of community becomes intimately tied to the very values of each individual comprising the society.

For them [the individual members of the community], community describes not just what they *have* as fellow citizens but also what they *are*, not a relationship they choose (as in a voluntary association) but an attachment they discover, not merely an attribute but a constituent of their identity.

(Sandel 1982: 150, emphasis added)

Yet while Rawls denies that social ties and constraints are antecedent to individual choice, Sandel suggests that Rawls' contract *must* presuppose a knowledge on the part of the individuals in the society of social structures, including institutions and other collective arrangements, and that each must be cognizant of both his individual desires and the means to their attainment, and of social ends. The 'encumbered self' is obligated to pursue ends not of his own choosing, but ends stipulated by culture and tradition. This is the crux of the argument.

In *After Virtue* Alasdair MacIntyre traces the evolution of moral doctrine from the ancient Greeks to the present. The basis of his argument is that a change in the Greek conception of virtue has resulted in a shift away from the notion of the importance of community and towards the notion of the centrality of the individual, the consequences of which have been most profound in the area of defining a social ethos. It is only through an understanding of the nature of this shift that philosophers can begin to appreciate the fundamental importance of community, and once again entertain questions of social justice and social equity. As a consequence, his interpretation of the communitarian argument is somewhat more extensive than that of Sandel.

MacIntyre limits his community to the family or the immediate society, as these groups tend to hold to a consistent set of moral beliefs. The State or the society in the large typically holds many, sometimes inconsistent, beliefs simultaneously; moral questions can never be subjected to rational solution, since there is no agreed-upon social hierarchy of values. The reason behind this lack of consensus is that contemporary society is 'emotivist' – moral questions are phrased in a rhetoric designed to give expression to personal standards and preferences. This makes it difficult to *define* moral conduct, for the language cannot facilitate the expression of concepts of social virtue. It is emotivism that MacIntyre challenges in his general criticism of liberalism. Specifically, he denies the emotivist (and liberal) claim that, while one may propose *rational* justifications for moral beliefs, it is not possible to entertain *real* ones. Emotivism in effect denies the existence of an objective standard of moral reference, but nonetheless proceeds as if moral *language* were on the same plane as objective principles of moral *conduct*.

Thus, to return to a vision of social obligation requires a rejection of emotivism and a realization that human beings are first and foremost social agents. This requires in turn an understanding of the critical place of virtue and a transcendent *telos*:

> unless there is a *telos* which transcends the limited goods of *practices* by constituting the good of a whole human life, the good of a human life conceived as a unity, it will *both* be the case that a certain subversive arbitrariness will invade the moral life *and* that we shall be unable to specify the context of certain virtues adequately.
> (MacIntyre 1984: 203; emphasis in original)

Of significance here are the three interrelated concepts of *practice* (which 'involves standards of excellence and obedience to rules as well as the achievement of goods' (MacIntyre 1984: 190)), *narrative unity* (a set of boundary conditions that serve to frame one's life story in terms of himself and his society (pp. 215–6)), and *tradition* (inheritances, including obligations and expectations, which one receives through social participation (p. 220)). Each of these elements is responsible for situating the individual within a social frame of reference, and for instilling in him group norms. Without an understanding of the way in which individuals are connected to social communities, there can be no understanding of or regard for moral virtue. It is the failure of liberalism to recognize and embrace the inherent sociality of the individual as exemplified in these concepts that MacIntyre sees as its central flaw.

Of central importance to MacIntyre's theory of society is the role of virtue in respect of distributive justice. This is what allows him to construct a communitarian vision on the basis of a premise held by liberal philosophers such as Smith.[19] Specifically, MacIntyre finds a major fault with Rawls in the inability of his (and all other) individualist theories to account for deserts; while very often arguments about justice are merely arguments about whether a given economic distribution is deserved, Rawls leaves the question of desert as secondary to justice. But in so doing, desert is removed from the equation altogether, since justice then rebounds to *expectation*, not justification for reward. In a social theory based on the centrality of the individual, there is no reason to expect agreement on such ideals to be forthcoming. Only in respect of the community, 'whose primary bond is a shared understanding both of the good for man and of the good of that community', does the notion of desert take on any significance and meaning (MacIntyre 1984: 250).

In addition, MacIntyre interprets Rawls as identifying virtues with sentiments, which are then taken to be the basis for obedience to social rules. Yet in so doing, Rawls (in line with David Hume) divorces virtue from any concept of the social good. Rules precede virtue ('since a virtue is now generally understood as a disposition or sentiment which will produce in us obedience to certain rules' (MacIntyre 1984: 244)), but as there is no basis upon which to secure agreement as to rules, there is no basis for agreement as to social virtues. Virtue – which MacIntyre sees as important 'in sustaining those traditions which provide both practices and individual lives with their necessary historical content' (p. 223) – becomes instrumental, bearing no relation to the social good. From the communitarian standpoint, the problem lies in the unit of analysis. With the individual as subject, man is independent of his social and moral relationships. With the community at the center, there is formed a bond, 'a shared understanding both of the good for man and of the good of that community', so that 'individuals identify their primary interests with reference to those goods' (p. 250).

So we see that, for MacIntyre, while the idea of community is crucial to the ideal of the social good, moral virtue is central to the concept of community: 'a community which envisages its life as directed toward a shared good which provides that community with its common tasks will need to articulate its moral life in terms *both* of the virtues *and* of law' (MacIntyre 1984:169; emphasis in original). Without a clear understanding of the place of virtue in defining social morality, it is not possible to view the individual as situated in society, or to entertain any concept of the good.

Remarks

In sum, communitarians base their attacks on individualist theories of justice, such as those of Rawls, on the ontological foundations of those theories: for the communitarian, the community or society in which the individual functions, not the individual himself, determines in large measure his constitution. They do not deny that 'individuals matter'. Rather, they stress that it is the social setting that identifies the individual and induces feelings of community and self. Ends define conduct; they are not themselves the objects of choice. As subject, the community is the basis of individual identity; as object, the individual is bound to the motives of the community. Thus, the community is not a mere voluntary association, but is a constitutive force defining individual purpose and existence. As Sandel phrases it:

> To imagine a person incapable of constitutive attachments such as these is not to conceive an ideally free and relational agent, but to imagine a person wholly without character, without moral depth. For, to have character is to know that I move in a history I neither summon nor command, which carries consequences nonetheless for my choices and conduct.
>
> (Sandel 1984: 90)

Communitarian concerns in an individualist frame: Hayek, Macpherson, and Berlin

The new communitarian philosophers tend to concentrate their attacks on individualism on the ethical philosophy of Rawls and, on occasion, Robert Nozick. This is not difficult to understand, for Rawls is taken as having revived interest in the theory of the liberal political State, and Nozick's *Anarchy, State and Utopia* (1974) is regarded as an important work in the literature on individualism.[20] But in so narrowing their attack, the modern critics ignore (or dismiss too cavalierly) three other important advocates of the liberal position, these being the Austrian economist Friedrich A. von Hayek, the political philosopher Crawford Brough Macpherson, and the social philosopher Sir Isaiah Berlin.[21] It is to these defenses, then, that we now turn.

Hayek and spontaneous order

Hayek's 1948 *Individualism and Economic Order*, a collection of previously-published essays, established him as a foremost critic of collectivist and communitarian approaches to social choice and social order.[22] Here, he set forth the distinction between *rules* and *orders*, a distinction that is important in demonstrating the difference between the liberal and the communitarian philosophies. Rules are abstract principles that serve to *guide* individual behavior, but which otherwise promote no specified end; orders are government (or otherwise organizational) edicts designed to *compel* behavior to a preordained end. Rules frame individual action by maintaining 'spheres of responsibility'; orders coerce in an effort to promote an outcome. It is this frame to responsible action provided by rules that is most important, as it promotes sociality and community (i.e., leads to the creation of social order). The concern of the liberal philosopher is 'to find a set of institutions by which man could be induced, by his own choice and from the motives which determined his ordinary conduct, to contribute as much as possible to the needs of all others' (Hayek 1948: 12–13). For Hayek, then, individualism 'is primarily a *theory* of society, an attempt to understand the forces which determine the social life of man' (p. 6; emphasis in original). The relation of the individual to society is in fact fundamental to Hayek's social philosophy: 'there is no other way toward an understanding of social phenomena but through our understanding of individual actions directed toward other people and guided by their expected behavior' (p. 6).

As much as it is the antithesis of communitarianism, individualism is also the antithesis of Cartesian rationalism and Benthamite Utilitarianism, both examples of what Hayek calls 'false' individualism. It is false individualism which provides the justification for conceiving social institutions as the result of deliberate design, 'the product of an exaggerated belief in the powers of individual reason and of a consequent contempt for anything which has not been consciously designed by it or is not fully intelligible to it' (Hayek 1948: 8). 'True' individualism – the individualism of Edmund Burke, John Locke, and Adam Smith – by contrast 'is a product of an acute consciousness of the limitations of the individual mind which induces an attitude of humility toward the impersonal and anonymous social processes by which individuals help to create things greater than they know' (p.8). The 'rational man', the individual condemned by the communitarians, is in reality *not* the subject of 'true' individualism. For the 'true' individualist philosopher, man is a social agent, and acts within the confines of the community. It is the Cartesian rational actor, the foil of the communitarians, who actually, in the end, pursues the very ambitions which the communitarian decries, but ironically arrives at the very constitution of society – the regimented State – toward which the communitarian philosophy leads.

In the second volume of his *Law, Legislation, and Liberty – The Mirage of Social Justice* (1976) – Hayek extends his defense of spontaneous order in a confrontation with communitarians *qua* collectivists. It is not true that there is a 'public' or 'social' interest that can be defined as the sum of individual interests, since to be so one would have to acknowledge the existence of both identifiable and mutually-reinforcing individual ends, and there through to a prescribed social end. The State or society is not an organic whole capable of defining ends. The purpose of the State is in 'the securing of conditions in which the individuals and smaller groups will have favourable opportunities of mutually providing for their respective needs' (Hayek 1976: 2). The State, in other words, must not employ resources to the attainment of particular group ends; it must reserve concern solely to the purpose of providing 'the conditions for the preservation of a spontaneous order which enables the individuals to provide for their needs in manners not known to authority' (p. 2).

Hayek laments the fact that teleological explanations of social order have taken hold of the imagination, including the peculiar notion of 'social justice'. This notion, and the related notion of 'distributive justice', are merely descriptive of 'organized efforts to enforce the rules of just individual conduct', and are employed 'to evaluate the effects of the existing institutions of society' (Hayek 1976: 63). They are attempts at conflating real concerns for justice with some notion of the granting to certain classes in society their 'just deserts'. Justice is an inherently *individual* notion, in that it applies solely in respect of adherence to the rules governing individual conduct. Fairness and equality have meaning only in so far as justice is applied consistently and equitably. Thus for Hayek, the concept of 'social justice' is vacuous, for it implies not fair and equitable treatment for all, but rather a demand for a social order designed to guarantee a specific pattern of economic distribution. Only *individuals* are capable of acting purposefully. The process by which, for example, wealth is created and distributed cannot, in a market economy, be interpreted as being purposive, and so the market cannot be castigated as being unjust; it is a process, not a constructed order, and so it can have no specific purpose nor can it act in pursuit of any end.[23]

This obsession with a consequence such as distributive justice Hayek maintains has been, and continues to be, the rationale of those who advocate collectivist and other coercive political arrangements. The argument reduces to an exercise in *post hoc, ergo propter hoc* reasoning: If the distribution of the product is unequal, it must by that fact be unfair and unjust. Since chance alone cannot have played any significant role, it follows that someone or something must have caused this injustice. Since no one person can be identified as culpable, society is objectified as the villain, and so a resolution to the 'unfair' outcome requires actions that alter the pattern of behavior of society. This of course, as should be clear, suggests that the social order is purposive, which Hayek denies. In his denial, he is led also to reject the very notion of social justice as in any way relevant to (let alone descriptive of) social arrangements that lack any teleological identification. Only where there is a design or a prescribed end can there be a prescribed code guiding individuals to its attainment. Social justice

> can be given a meaning only in a directed or 'command' economy (such as an army) in which the individuals are ordered what to do; and any particular conception of 'social justice' could be realized only in such a centrally directed system. It presupposes that people are guided by specific directions and not by rules of just individual conduct. Indeed, no system of rules of just individual conduct, and therefore no free action of the individuals, could produce results satisfying any principle of distributive justice.
>
> (Hayek 1976: 69)

Acceptance of the credibility of the notion of 'social justice' implies rejection of the notions of individual freedom and unplanned, undirected, spontaneous social order: the basis of reward shifts from individual initiative and freedom of contract to group assessments and pattern distribution, which of necessity require a coercive bureaucratic machinery designed to direct individual initiative to the maintenance of social ends. The result is the end of human action and the beginning of social design.

In reference to Rawls, while Hayek is unhappy with his use of the concept of 'social justice', he nonetheless expresses high regard for the road taken to its advancement.[24] In particular, he accepts the idea of a 'veil of ignorance' behind which the social contract is initiated, since it is entered into without regard to or even knowledge of prescribed social ends. In establishing the basic rule framework, one of the first conditions is 'that only such rules as can be applied equally to all should be enforced' (Hayek 1976: 97). But this is Rawls' own rationale, and Hayek in fact expresses his justification in very Rawlsian terms: 'Man has developed rules of conduct not because he knows but because he does not know what all the consequences of a particular action will be' (pp. 20–21). Once established, rules of law and society are binding on all, and must 'be obeyed irrespective of the known effects of the particular action' (p. 21).

To summarize, Hayek views the individual as a creature of society, and recognizes the critical importance of social relationships in molding feelings of community and belonging, as well as instilling a moral vision. But he rejects any notion of society as prior to the individual, or as having any power over the ability of individuals to engage freely in what can be defined as market activity. Justice in this respect applies to the correctness of *actions*, not the appearance of *consequences*, and so *social* outcomes have no meaning. Where the State attempts to promote social ends instead of restricting its functions to the delimiting of the sphere of action, it interferes with individual freedom and the result is coercion and tyranny.

Macpherson and 'Participatory Democracy'

In contrast to Hayek, Macpherson[25] concludes that the philosophy of liberalism is inconsistent with the concept of the free market; the market society and the self-situated individual are (in his view) antithetical to the goal of a democratic society.

As with any liberal theorist, Macpherson places the individual at the center of his social theory. What he rejects is the concept of the 'possessive' self, a concept central to the classical liberal (Hobbes, Locke) ideals of individualism.

For Macpherson, the classical concept of individualism – 'possessive individualism' – identifies man as distinct from any social commitment or fellow-feeling; man is 'seen neither as a moral whole, nor as part of a larger social whole' (Macpherson 1962: 3). 'Possessive individualism' has three defining characteristics: (1) the individual is essentially an 'absolute natural proprietor of his own capacities, owing nothing to society for them', with the implication that, since the ownership right is paramount, '[f]reedom is therefore possession'; (2) since social interaction is defined with respect to possessions, the 'market relation' is 'the fundamental relation of society'; and (3) since 'even life and liberty are considered as possessions, rather than as social rights with correlative duties', it must be true that political arrangements emerge as 'device[s] for the protection of property' (Macpherson 1973: 199).

Here lies the problem, for it becomes impossible to extend the qualities of this form of asocial individualism to society as a whole. The 'possessive' individual has no social base – he is committed only to self – yet he must seek and maintain social attachments in fulfilment of his interests. In consequence, '[s]ociety becomes a lot of free equal individuals related to each other as proprietors of their own capacities and of what they have acquired by their exercise', and to secure these acquisitions they require a political organization. But this political structure itself is motivated solely by the preservation of self-interest; for the 'possessive' individual, the political organization 'becomes a calculated device for the protection of this property and for the maintenance of an orderly relation of exchange' (Macpherson 1962: 3). Thus, does Macpherson find a dilemma:

> modern liberal-democratic theory ... must continue to use the assumptions of possessive individualism, at a time when the structure of market society no longer provides the necessary conditions for deducing a valid theory of political obligation from those assumptions.
>
> (Macpherson 1962: 275).

The *assumption* of the self-interested individual in pursuit of self-defined ends is legitimate; what is illegitimate is defining freedom as possession, 'as freedom from any but market relations with others' (Macpherson 1973: 194). It is the social institution of the *market* and the relations it engenders which must be replaced, for it is here that possession and similar concepts invaded the classical liberal moral philosophy. The result was a corruption of liberal morality, as it degenerated into a means for the perpetuation of class division.

Macpherson later extends the argument. Liberal democracy can mean either 'the democracy of a capitalist market society', or 'a society striving to ensure that all its members are equally free to realize their capabilities' (Macpherson 1977: 1). It cannot pursue both goals, since they are mutually incompatible. The former implies exploitation, while the latter promotes 'equal effective freedom of all to use and develop their capacities' (p. 1). Macpherson clearly believes the latter is the more appropriate goal, and is the only means to the realization of a liberal democratic vision. He thus proposes the abandonment of the fundamental principles of market society, and suggests replacing them with the concept of an 'equal right to self-development' (p. 2).

To realize his vision, Macpherson offers a model of 'participatory democracy'. Within this framework, first, individuals view themselves as having a sense of community, of developing their capacities not for their own benefit, but 'in conjunction with others, in some relation of community' (Macpherson 1977: 99). Secondly, there is at the same time a reduction in social and economic inequality which serves to strengthen social cohesion. Macpherson hopes to achieve these aims through greater political participation (an extension of individual initiative), but also by restricting economic opportunity through the placing of limitations on economic growth and the spread of corporate capitalism (p. 106). He thus proposes to generate equality and promote individual liberty by in effect replacing economic opportunity with the more socialized opportunity of political participation.

In summary, Macpherson maintains an individualist *ethic*, but within the confines of an instrumentalist collectivism designed, as he envisions it, to further individual potential. Social institutions are necessary contrivances that confer community privileges to all their individual members. This leads him to view property in the Aristotelian manner, distinguishing *ownership* from *use*. So, while extolling the virtues of individualism, Macpherson finds he can as well advocate social control of property. He in effect redirects the individual right, from the pursuit of individual ends to the pursuit of social or community ends.

Berlin and 'Communitarian Individualism'

Finally, Berlin offers an approach consistent with aspects of both communitarianism and individualism, but with serious reservations about each.[26] He embraces the liberal ideal of individuals making free choices among alternatives, but criticizes the very notion of rationality as leading to a denial of individuality.

Berlin sees in certain individualist approaches (including, but not limited to, Utilitarianism) an erroneous application of the principles of science to the study of human society (Hayek's 'false individualism'). The rationalism of science offered a method for the objective, unclouded analysis of all aspects of human endeavor. To be rational came to mean being capable of understanding the necessity of the laws of nature and, by extension, of man. This belief became a defining characteristic of *homo economicus* and *homo politicus*, as it represented rational solutions as timeless and universal: 'rational men, in all ages and countries, must always demand the same unaltering satisfactions of the same unaltering basic needs' (Berlin 1958: 27). The only problem remaining 'is to find the right means for their attainment' (Berlin 1980: 87).

Yet Berlin perceives in this search for ultimate truths a disturbing possibility, albeit one which began rather benignly. Once we accept the idea that 'rational self-direction' is the only escape from the passions and the prevailing mythologies, which we are told govern the actions of the unenlightened – once we discover for ourselves that the world is as it must be – it is inevitable that we wish to point others to the correct path, even if we must first 'educate' them to the rightness of the position in promoting the realization of their own 'true' natures and their own 'true' ends. The result must be a universal harmony of interests.

> If the universe is governed by reason, then there will be no need for coercion; a correctly planned life for all will coincide with full freedom – the freedom of rational self-direction – for all. This will be so if, and only if, the plan is the true plan – the one unique pattern which alone fulfils the claims of reason. Its laws will be the rules which reason prescribes: they will only seem irksome to those whose reason is dormant, who do not understand the true 'needs' of their own 'real' selves. So long as each player recognizes and plays the part set him by reason – the faculty that understands his true nature and discerns his true ends – there can be no conflict. Each man will be a liberated, self-directed actor in the cosmic drama.
>
> (Berlin 1958: 32)

But, notes Berlin, the reality is something different, namely, the subordination of individual freedom, autonomy, and will to the one true, objective, rational end. As the solution is a 'rational' one, it must clearly also be demonstrably the 'best', that is, the one which maximizes social welfare. To achieve the maximum social welfare, society must be prepared to take actions in furtherance of the rational end. The means are unimportant; it is the *result* which we must seek.

To counter this (unacceptable) reality, Berlin proposes (as did Hayek) that rights be given primacy, and that rules be established that serve as boundaries to individuals as well as barriers to the governmental abuse of authority. These guarantees are necessary to ensure to individuals the fundamental freedom of choice, allowing them to select freely from alternatives the consequences of which are unknown. It is in this context that Berlin (as Hayek), while rejecting rationalism, nonetheless recognizes the importance of rational inquiry in the process of selection from among alternatives. Every choice involves, to some extent, not only a gain but also a loss, so we must in choosing be conscious of the intricacies of choice. It is this unknowability as to prospective gain coupled with the creativity of imagination that is in a sense vital to the essence of individuality.[27] It is the principle of free choice that is central to liberty.

Holding the free individual, then, in the center of his social universe, Berlin embraces also the communitarian ideal of society as (to some extent) antecedent to the individual, in that culture influences individual choice. Yet, at the same time he denies the existence of any such thing as a common culture or an organic social unity. The individual cannot be defined with respect to any *single* moral community, membership in which serves to forge a social identity. Instead, he must be seen as having many different loyalties, which at times may conflict. While communitarians view this conflict as problematic, Berlin views it as an asset that gives rise to a pluralistic morality.

It is in his handling of these conflicting loyalties that Berlin embraces the notion of collective individuality. For Berlin, the definition of a national community is not one identified with the State or for that matter any politically structured entity. It is rather with the notion of cultural inheritances. It is these inheritances which serve to form the individual's sense of morality. Berlinian nationalism is thus defined with respect to (1) 'terms of common territory, customs, laws, memories, beliefs, language, artistic and religious expression, social institutions, ways of life, to which some add heredity, kinship, racial characteristics'; (2) a social organicism, meaning 'a special awareness, which need not be fully conscious, of the unique relationship that binds individual human beings into the indissoluble and unanalysable organic whole'; and (3) a realization that rules of moral and social behavior are to be followed 'not because they lead to virtue or happiness or justice or liberty, or are ordained by God or church or prince or parliament or some other universally acknowledged authority, or are good or right in themselves, ... [but] rather they are to be followed because these values are those of *my* group' (Berlin 1980: 341–3; emphasis in original).

Thus does Berlin at once reject Hegelian organic communitarianism, and also those individualist approaches that seek to explain social integration as the result of voluntary associations of freely acting agents. Social units are pluralistic in nature, not defined with respect to any single ideal; individuals do not coalesce into such units through choice, but through awareness of a common cultural legacy.

Conclusion

The 'older' communitarianism provided the basis for countless utopian social movements – including the New Lanark (Scotland) and New Harmony (Indiana, US) communes of Owen, and the Paris Commune of 1871 – as well as the rationale for national social experiments – the Prussian and later the German social welfare State, and the American social security and welfare systems. It also, by placing the interests of the society (the State) prior to those of the individual, formed the intellectual foundations of a host of political collectivities that retarded human development by severely restricting individual liberty in the promotion of the interests of the whole.

The 'new' communitarianism is not less utopian, but begins by redefining certain political directions. 'Socialism', for example, becomes 'economic democracy', a movement which is said to promote the universal aim of 'social justice'. The principles of the new communitarianism may be seen as negatively-defined: if liberalism can be shown to be flawed in its premises or to lead to inconsistent or even socially undesirable outcomes (again, defined with respect to the Ideal of an egalitarian society where consequences, and not freedom to act, are the criteria for justice), then some other basis for a just social order must be found.

For communitarians old and new, the community has a real existence; its value is in promoting a sense of social obligation, which in turn defines the self. Thus they tend to deny the very notion of 'free will' or 'freedom to choose', since values are socially determined and not subject to individual choice. In its place they posit a society as antecedent to the individual – the First Cause is an innate need for social belonging and social order.

For liberals *qua* individualists, the First Cause is the purposive individual. The community emerges as the result of spontaneous human action, as individuals form social bonds for mutual benefit, or in fulfilment of an inherent sociality. They reject what they perceive as the teleological notion of communitarianism and the rationalist individualism that underlies Utilitarianism thought in favor of a less rigidly defined notion of social order as resulting from undirected actions.[28] If anything, directed action serves a negative purpose, preventing individuals from achieving an effective and 'just' social order. Yet, a denial of social priority is not a denial of social awareness, or of a sympathetic feeling developed through a sense of belonging to a community. Quite the contrary, individualists (as we have seen) take seriously the social nature of man, and incorporate his feelings of community, sympathy, and belonging into the elements they perceive as making him human. They accept the three communitarian qualities of human beings as fallible, non-logical, and socially defined, but cannot accept that society precedes and is in some sense independent of the individual. They, thus, reject the communitarian teleology and the notion that the individual is somehow derivative of a real and independently existent social order. They also escape the consequences of such an order.

Acknowledgement

I wish to thank Geoff Harcourt, Mark Perlman, and two anonymous referees for comments on earlier drafts.

Notes

1 One may note also the 1975 election of Malcolm Fraser and the Liberal-National Party coalition in Australia, as the policies pursued were in many ways similar to those of Reagan and Thatcher.
2 The notion of non-logical behaviors was put forth by the Italian sociologist Vilfredo Pareto in his 1896–97 *Cours d'économie politique* and his 1906 *Manuale di economia politica*. In his 1903 *Les systèmes socialistes* he used the concept to analyze various socialist approaches to political organization.
3 The term 'liberal' as used here refers to a political philosophy that places emphasis on the rights of the individual. It is thus not to be confused with the American popular definition under which the State is viewed as a social provider. The American popular usage of the term suggests the ends of a communal society, and so is in effect an extension of communitarian doctrine.
4 An efficient, if partisan, overview of the debate can be found in Stephen Mulhall and Adam Swift (1992). See also the excellent introduction to the subject by Will Kymlicka (1990).
5 On this see especially Rousseau 1762: 191.
6 In suggesting that Rousseau and Hegel offer variants of communitarianism, I do not wish to claim that all modern communitarians follow their lead. The general will is as much a communitarian artifice as is majoritarianism (the acceptance of dominant social values as indicative of the good), which itself is not accepted by some modern writers on the subject, to wit Michael Sandel (whose views we shall discuss below).
7 On the notion of an organicist ontology and the extent to which the Hegelian notion was held by Marshall, see Geoffrey M. Hodgson (1993). Hodgson denies that Marshall believed in the organicist ontology, while still maintaining an organicist view of the economy and society. See also Peter Groenewegen (1990) for an account of the influence of Hegel's *Philosophy of History* on Marshall's economics.

8 An excellent introduction to the philosophy of the Cameralists is Albion Small (1909).

9 Others who have written on the philosophical bases of communitarianism include Charles Taylor and Michael Walzer. This framework is also evident in the so-called 'feminist' approaches to economic and political theory.

10 It is important to highlight the reference to *social* justice, for Rawls does not pretend to advance a *general* theory of justice.

11 This is important, for the contract is not to be conceived of in the sense of a historical reality; it is rather an analytical tool that allows Rawls to construct his system. It serves much as a First Principle.

12 Rawls later (p. 144) points out that his rational man is also not vain, affectionate, or rancorous. Rawls himself does not mention in this context that he also rejects the expected utility model that supports much of modern social choice theory.

13 Actually, Rawls focuses on the utility of the least-advantaged *group*, and so his theory tends to deviate from other individualist social theories.

14 In the Utilitarian social welfare function, the indifference curves are convex to the origin; in the Rawlsian social welfare function, the curves are orthogonal.

15 Cf. Adam Smith's use of the concept of the 'impartial spectator' in his *Theory of Moral Sentiments*.

16 His criticism extends to Immanuel Kant, and to others who accept Kant's notion of the 'transcendent subject'.

17 This is a profoundly Kantian idea. As Kant observed, 'I can never be constrained by others *to have an end*: only I myself can *make* something my end' (1797, p. 146, emphasis added).

18 Thus it would appear as though Sandel would have an even more difficult time with Adam Smith's liberalism, as stated in his *Theory of Moral Sentiments*.

19 MacIntyre maintains that Smith was a Stoic who equated virtue with rule-following and 'self-command', a virtue 'which enables us to control our passions when they distract us from what virtue requires' (MacIntyre 1984: 235). But note that Smith also wrote: 'The wise and virtuous man is at all times willing that his own private interest should be sacrificed to the public interest of his own particular order or society' (Smith 1790, Part VI, Sec. ii, Ch.3, p. 235).

20 Despite basing their theories on the premise of individualism, Nozick and Rawls approach the subject from opposite ends. Rawls holds that individual talents may be seen as common assets, while Nozick regards the rewards of labor as belonging to the individual. There are other differences of course, but an elaboration would involve a more detailed and extensive survey. Rawls has been singled out because he is viewed as the villain in the communitarian counterattack on liberalism.

21 Will Kymlicka (1988) also presents a cogent refutation of the communitarian counterattack to liberalism.

22 His 1944 *The Road to Serfdom* proclaimed the dangers for individual liberty of a collectivist approach to economic relations, especially centralized economic planning.

23 Steve Fleetwood (1995) concludes that, in his later writings, Hayek was a Critical Realist.

24 Hayek writes: 'I have no basic quarrel with an author who, before he proceeds to that problem [of social justice], acknowledges that the task of selecting specific systems or distributions of desired things as just must be "abandoned as mistaken in principle, and it is, in any case, not capable of a definite answer. Rather the principles of justice define the crucial constraints which institutions and joint activities must satisfy if persons engaging in them are to have no complaints against them. If these constraints are satisfied, the resulting distribution, whatever it is, may be accepted as just (or at least not unjust)." This is more or less what I have been trying to argue in this chapter' (Hayek 1976: 100). Hayek later (1988) criticizes the Rawlsian notion of justice as retarding the process of social and economic evolution.

25 Macpherson's political philosophy has been compactly summarized by Peter Lindsay (1996).

26 John Gray refers to Berlin's view as 'agnostic liberalism', which he defines as 'a stoical and tragic liberalism of unavoidable conflict and inseparable loss among inherently rivalrous values' (Gray 1996: 1). Gray also identifies Berlin's philosophy as 'communitarian individualism' (ibid., p. 103).

27 One sees this clearly in the work of G. L. S. Shackle, especially (1972; 1979).

28 Mandeville and Smith are the classic statements.

References

Aristotle. (1988) *The Politics*. Edited by Stephen Everson. Cambridge: Cambridge University Press.

Berlin, I. (1958) *Two Concepts of Liberty*, Oxford: Clarendon Press.

—— (1980) *Against the Current: Essays in the History of Ideas*, New York: Viking Press.

Fleetwood, S. (1995) *Hayek's Political Economy*, London: Routledge.

Gray, J. (1995) *Liberalism*, (2nd edn). Minneapolis: University of Minnesota Press.

—— (1996) *Isaiah Berlin*, Princeton: Princeton University Press.

Groenewegen, P. (1990) 'Marshall and Hegel', *Economie Appliquée*, tome XLIII, no.1, pp. 63–84.

Hayek, F. A. von (1948) *Individualism and Economic Order*, Chicago: University of Chicago Press.

—— (1976) *Law, Legislation, and Liberty*, Vol.II: *The Mirage of Social Justice*, Chicago: University of Chicago Press.

—— (1988) *The Fatal Conceit*, London: Routledge.

Hegel, G. W. F. (1821 [1996]) *Philosophy of Right*, trans. S. W. Dyde, New York: Prometheus Books.

Hodgson, G. M. (1993) *Economics and Evolution: Bringing Life Back into Economics*, Oxford: Polity Press.

Hume, D. (1739/40 [1984]) *A Treatise of Human Nature*, Harmondsworth: Penguin Books.

Kant, I. (1787 [1934]) *Critique of Pure Reason*. (2nd edn) trans. J. M. D. Meiklejohn, London: Everyman's Library.

—— (1797 [1996]) *The Metaphysics of Morals*, (ed.) Mary Gregor. Cambridge: Cambridge University Press.

Kymlicka, W. (1988) 'Liberalism and Communitarianism', *Canadian Journal of Philosophy*, 18(2): 181–204.

—— (1990) *Contemporary Political Philosophy: An Introduction*, Oxford: Clarendon Press.

Lindsay, P. (1996) *Creative Individualism: The Democratic View of C. B. Macpherson*, Albany: SUNY Press.

MacIntyre, A. (1984) *After Virtue* (2nd edn). Notre Dame: University of Notre Dame Press.

Macpherson, C. B. (1962) *The Political Theory of Possessive Individualism: Hobbes to Locke*, Oxford: Clarendon Press.

—— (1973) *Democratic Theory: Essays in Retrieval*, Oxford: Clarendon Press.

—— (1977) *The Life and Times of Liberal Democracy*, Oxford: Oxford University Press.

Mandeville, B. de. (1725–29). *The Fable of the Bees; or Private Vices, Publick Benefits*, London: J. Tonson.

Mulhall, S. and Swift, A. (1992) *Liberals and Communitarians*, Cambridge, MA: Basil Blackwell.

Owen, R. (1991) *A New View of Society and Other Writings*, Harmondsworth: Penguin Books.

Pareto, V. (1896–7) *Cours d'économie politique*, Lausanne: Librairie de l'Université.

—— (1903) *Les systèmes socialistes*, Paris: Giard et Briéne.

—— (1906 [1971]) *Manuale di economia politica*. Translated by Ann S, Schwier and Alfred N, Page as *Manual of Political Economy*, New York: Augustus M. Kelley.

Pareto, V. (1916 [1935]) *Trattato di sociologia generale*. Translated by Arthur Livingstone as *The Mind and Society*, New York: Harcourt Brace.

Perlman, M. (1997) 'Economics and Social Conscience: The Harcourt Case', in P. Arestis, G. Palma and M. Sawyer (eds) *Capital Controversy, Post-Keynesian Economics, and the History of Economics*, London: Routledge.

Plato (1987) *The Republic*, Translated and Introduced by Desmond Lee. Harmondsworth: Penguin Books.

Rawls, J. (1971) *A Theory of Justice*, Cambridge, MA: Belknap/Harvard University Press.

Rousseau, J.-J.- (1762 [1973]) 'The Social Contract', in J.-J. Rousseau, *The Social Contract and the Discourses*, trans. G. D. H. Cole, revised by J. H. Brumfitt and John C. Hall. New York: Everyman's Library.

Sandel, M. (1982) *Liberalism and the Limits of Justice*, Cambridge: Cambridge University Press.

—— (1984) 'The procedural republic and the unencumbered self', *Political Theory* 12(1): 81–96.

Shackle, G. L. S. (1972) *Epistemics and Economics: A Critique of Economic Doctrine*. Cambridge: Cambridge University Press.

—— (1979) *Imagination and the Nature of Choice*. Edinburgh: Edinburgh University Press.

Small, A. (1909 [1962]) *The Cameralists*, New York: Burt Franklin.

Smith, A. (1790 [1976]) *The Theory of Moral Sentiments*. 6th edn (eds.) D. D. Raphael, and A. L. Macfie, Indianapolis: Liberty Press.

—— (1776 [1937]) *Wealth of Nations*. (ed.) Edwin Cannan. New York: Modern Library.

Walzer, M. (1983) *Spheres of Justice: A Defense of Pluralism and Equality*, New York: Basic Books.

7 East Asian economic crisis and the communitarian development model

Ungsuh K. Park

Introduction

The rapid economic growth of East Asian countries during the last four decades, which was followed by a near-simultaneous and massive economic crisis, supplies an entirely new dimension to the economic development literature. The rapid industrialization processes of those countries combined with the open and export-oriented strategies, which directed the priority investment targets from labor-intensive to capital- and technology-intensive industries over time. This aspect of the so-called East Asian development model is fairly well understood by economists. But the similarity in development strategy provides no explanation of the near-simultaneity of the crises of 1997. Obviously the role of excessively volatile international capital movements is important in explaining the crisis but there is nothing unique in their role for East Asia. International funds invest profusely when they enter and withdraw in a panic when they exit wherever they go. The simultaneity of the East Asian crises is the inevitable result of the unique interdependence of the growth processes that depended heavily on the partial relocations of industries between these countries and the somewhat mysterious East Asian development model that depended heavily on the interactions between strong governments and cooperative people. The latter is called the social contract in the East Asian communitarian societies. This chapter attempts to define the social contract of East Asian communitarian societies and expose the latent weaknesses of their development model which is supposed to reflect another equally mysterious concept: the Asian value.

The communitarian society

There have been many non-economic attempts to explain the East Asian societies which collectively delivered economic growth faster than any where, any time in human history. 'Soft authoritarianism' is the phrase Chalmers Johnson coined, with a great many followers, in his attempt to explain the rapid growth of Northeast Asian from the viewpoint of political power dynamics (Chalmers 1982). Just as Meiji Japan did over hundred years ago, Chang, Kaishek's Taiwan, and Park, Chunghee's Korea also succeeded in launching their economies from the rut of thousand-years old poverty into rapid industrialization. The dynamic initiatives of strong leaders and strong governments proved so successful that emphasizing some sort of authoritarian rule of the governments, soft or otherwise, became an inevitable part of the explanation of East Asian success. In all these countries the concentration of power in the central governments, which committed themselves to economic development as the national priority, was the leading cause which led the communities out of the vicious cycle of poverty.

However, we also know of many authoritarian governments which failed to deliver rapid economic growth. Invariably, in all these failed cases, the governments were not only strong but also publicly committed to the pursuit of economic development as the nation's highest priority. Indeed, they tried hard, as economic development was conducive to maintaining their hold on power. Some communist governments tried too hard to usher in economic growth and failed miserably, but not because they did not know all the tricks of massive investment and resource mobilizations. Authoritarianism, soft or hard, at the beginning of any economic growth program is a *sine qua non* but it is not a sufficient condition to explain the East Asian experience.

Religion was the next champion chosen to explain the East Asian miracle single-handedly. Ever since Max Weber started to ask the unfortunate question, unfortunate from the East Asian point of view, concerning the role of protestantism and catholicism in explaining the differential economic growth performances of Western European countries during the period of the first industrial revolution, many socio-political economists have tried to explain the East Asian miracle by Confucianism and its role in these societies. Lucien Pye (1988) and Peter Berger (1988) may be quoted as the leading figures in such attempts.

To the eyes of non-Asian observers it may be surprising to observe the highly cooperative and well-disciplined work forces successfully executing massive industrial and construction projects, highly motivated in a voluntary participatory spirit under unimaginably harsh conditions in sizzling deserts and on suffocating tropical sites. Such attitudes, many suspected, cannot be taught, but must come from people who were born with exceptional tolerance or from traditional religion which made such tolerance a common practice, for example, as in the cases of slave cultures such as ancient Egypt. Nothing less than the promise of total redemption in the new life can entice so many workers to endure such hardships for so long.

The submissive attitudes of East Asian workers did indeed help rapid growth and might have some relationship with the Confucian tradition which emphasizes the importance of harmonious social order by defining desirable relationships between children and parents, man and wife, teachers and pupils, friends and the sovereign and subjects. However, the influence of Confucian ethics have long ceased to play the central role in the East Asian value system which affects the minds and behavior of most of its citizens. It no longer has such a large impact on workers on sites who are required to submit themselves to such hardship. The incentive had to be something far more tangible, powerful and relevant in the contemporary world of exceptional material prosperity.

George Lodge (1987) and Ezra Vogel (1988) proposed, as an alternative explanation, East Asian communitarianism. East Asian countries, and for that matter many other countries, for example, Germany, are seen as communitarian societies. They are a kind of living organism, a community, which is bound together by a certain common destiny and moves toward a certain goal. Its members are inexorably interlinked to one another, yet each individual's role is to achieve personal as well as community goals. This is an intriguing explanation, which we now try to elaborate.

In a broad sense, the communitarian societies contrast with associative societies which are also bound together by common purposes. An associative society is what the German sociologist, Ferdinand Tonnies (1963) described as Geselschaft in contrast to Gemeinschaft, which is our community. In the former case the members are contracted into it for certain purposes hence teleological: but in the latter members are born into it and so share some geographical or cultural common origin. In the latter case members bear certain responsibilities in fulfilling the community's needs and goals, so that it is a deontological society.

The purpose of an associative society is to bring the people together whereas in a community blood relations bring the people together. Lodge and Vogel also distinguish communitarian society from individualistic society. In the former, members realize their potential in the context of fulfilling community objectives: in the latter association is but a necessary evil to which only limited power is parsimoniously delegated in order to perform those functions needed to achieve a limited number of goals. Even that minimal delegation of power can always be withdrawn or be reduced from the association or states by collective action or simply by individual dissociation. Lodge (1987) says that 'it is extremely difficult to say the word individualism in Japanese without implying negative connotations'. In a communitarian society decisions are generally made by consensus whereas in an individualistic society major decisions concerning resource allocations are made through competition. Competition takes care of individual needs and total social needs are expected to be achieved through fulfillment of individual needs by the invisible hand. In a communitarian society the needs of the community are set first and individual members endeavor to achieve those common goals jointly. By doing so members' needs are fulfilled by rules which currently prevail. A rule, in most cases, is equal or, at least, fair distribution.

Equality, which is a binding condition, is equality in result, as opposed to equal opportunities as in Western societies. The society should plan for total needs as well as individual needs and that is a paramount responsibility given to the state when members relinquished, by birth, the right to oppose to the state. There are, of course, in these communitarian societies working hierarchies that assign roles to the individuals in the society. But the highest in the totempo, for instance the scholars and mandarins, are supposed to follow a stoic style of life and keep a strict distance from material gains. Whereas the class which conducts commerce and manufacturing, and pursues riches as a profession, is accorded the lowest status in the East Asian communitarian hierarchy.

In communitarian societies rights and duties of members are always regarded as necessary balances in the relationship with the community. Individual property rights are honoured but not sanctified and when the community is in great need, the society has the moral right to infringe individual property rights in order to mobilize the necessary resources within the community to satisfy that need. However, that privilege so accorded to the leaders of the community or the state has somehow to be restrained and held accountable.

This was the role given to Confucian ethics in East Asia, in order to provide the necessary countervailing control on the leaders of the community or the sovereigns of the states. In this sense East Asian communitarianism was moral communitarianism. The communities in East Asia did share a comprehensive religion, and philosophical and moral doctrines within each community. In this sense East Asian communitarianism was similar to the concepts of the Western communitarianists such as MacIntyre (1981) Sandel (1982) and Waltzer (1983).

To these scholars, a communitarian society should be united around a shared conception of 'good' as opposed to evil, and that conception should include, among other things, individual moral characters and moral practices. In that way the basic glue that holds together the members of a communitarian society would be the prevailing comprehensive doctrine. That shows how hard it is, for an insider in East Asian society, to explain our societies by the post World-War II western model of liberal communitarianism. We have already seen that in the modern East Asian communities, the moral characters and practices of individuals do not reflect the old Confucian doctrine.

John Rawls (1993) is another scholar who strongly challenged the moral doctrine in liberal communitarian society. He proposed a model society justly and liberally constituted. In this society the glue that holds the members together is basically made from civic friendship, mutual respect and an effective sense of justice. In the description of his model society he uses all the characteristics of communitarian society described above but refuses to call it a communitarian society. Instead, he calls it a cooperative society. In his model society, no single, oppressive doctrine, which can so easily come out of what we called above the prevailing comprehensive doctrine, should exist. Communities that are ruled by shared common moral values can easily be exploited by patriarchal autarchs. In fact in East Asian communities, we have experienced many abuses of these shared common doctrines by political dictators.

We have now a nasty dilemma. Obviously, it is impossible to label the present East Asian societies as some form of the Western liberal communitarian varieties of Sandel and MacIntyre. Furthermore, while communities do demonstrate the shared conception of moral values of communitarian societies, which were so easily exploited by modern dynamic, oppressive political leaders, they also demonstrate civic friendship or kinship in a wider sense, mutual respect and practical and effective sense of justice which are the central cohesive attributes of Rawlsian cooperative society. What are they then? Are East Asian societies communitarian societies as described by the Western moral communitarians or a kind of Rawlsian civic cooperative? Obviously neither model by itself explains the East Asian model well.

What makes East Asian communitarianism different from Western liberal communitarianism is that the East Asian model is a reality, not a theoretical concept. As such, its character must and did change under the bombardment and avalanche of various new cultural and material influences from the days of invasion by Western imperialism[1] and now from the new experiences of recent success in economic growth. The Confucian systems or the Buddhist philosophy, which worked so well as the prevailing moral doctrines, were fundamentally challenged by western doctrines of ethics and theology. Moreover, the old doctrines also proved to be defenseless against the onslaught of military invasion by economically superior external powers. With the collapse of nations, states, or at the least their sovereigns, the old doctrines relinquished the position of central state doctrine around which a new independence would have been moulded, and a new nation and order could have been built.

As the old state with the old doctrine of Confucianism and the communitarian hierarchical society proved to be totally irrelevant in providing security and freedom to the members of the community and failed to protect their lives and properties, new values replaced the old disgraced values. These new values were stark and raw reactions to the new reality where only powerful military forces backed by powerful industrial economies prevailed. Bukuk-Kangbyung in Korean or Hukoku-Kyohei in Japanese, implying literarily rich nation and strong army[2], became the central cohesive doctrine which bonded the members together in the new East Asian communitarian societies. This new doctrine almost totally lacked moral connotations to and dissociated the post World-War II East Asia from the western liberal schools. However, it is important to note the new East Asian societies still carry distinctive marks of communitarianism.

Aged parents are still revered and supported by many children almost by instinct. When disillusioned members discard their parents, the rest of the community scorns them but cannot forcefully dissuade them to abandon that 'bad' behavior. Just as 'good' is hard to define, so the 'bad' became equally hard to define.[3] As a result more and more ugly public behavior is tolerated in East Asia in the name of liberal democracy. Although the viscosity is somewhat lost in the old glue, the old values still survive as the 'functional' criteria to determine 'good' or 'bad'. The state is still loved and cared about, and the value of loyalty is not questioned. But East Asians now do have problems in defining the object: 'loyalty to whom', or 'to what'.

We can be almost certain that any casual survey on the street will get answers which are not expressions of loyalty to Park, Chunghee, Soeharto, not even Lee, Kwan Yue. It is loyalty to the concept of a state which is expected to serve the role of maintaining and preserving national security, and protecting its citizens from external oppression by building a strong industrial economy as effectively as possible. The old regime proved ineffective in providing these goals at the turn of the twentieth century, yet ironically this failure intensified loyalty to the modern states. Any state, whether it is democratic or not, which fails in these primary tasks will have to be dismantled and reorganized, even by military coups d'etat as we have seen repeatedly in East Asia. The state is now loved and cared for as the source of peace, liberty, and prosperity.

East Asian communitarian citizens have discovered that their state is but an instrument to achieve a common community objective. We know very well that this state instrumentalism is one of the central attributes of Western societies, which are based on individualism. In these societies, states are created and tolerated as a device to achieve these common goals of the society for the achievement of which separate individual efforts are inherently less efficient. In old communitarian societies the state was a transcendental institution and process. The division of roles between states and its members was predetermined and permitted only limited alteration. However, in the new East Asian communitarian societies the states can fail, be reorganized, cherished, strengthened and expected to provide protection for members. The state is an instrument here, but it is not the same kind of instrument as the state in Western societies. In East Asia states are not expected to be as small as possible and are not an object of toleration. Rather, loyalty to the state is genuine and natural. The members can choose among alternative styles of governments either to deliver common goals more efficiently or to achieve more comfortable middle class living. In East Asia members of communitarian societies do contract and terminate the contract made between them to achieve the objectives of the communities concerned. The rapid economic development of many East Asian societies is the result of this social contract and the recent dramatic failure of East Asian economies is another result of this same contract and its implementations.

The social contract of East Asian communitarian societies

The contracting parties to this contract are basically the strong leader and the people. The leader should possess a quality, which is more than simple aggressive driving style. He should be able to present an attractive future profile of the nation and persuade the people to follow him in achieving the goal of prosperity. The goal may not be realistic in fact, but the persuasion must be convincing enough to extract voluntary participation from the members of the community in the process of economic development – a process which will demand substantial personal sacrifice in hard work sometimes as long as twelve hours a day, seven days a week, with only a few days rest in a year. A contract between this charismatic leader and the people of the community is therefore accepted.

The vision and goals proposed by the leader and accepted by the people demand managers who translate them into strategies and policies. This role of management is taken on by the bureaucracy which consists of the best available talents in the community who are selected through a series of eliminating tests starting from primary school days.[4] The bureaucracy is selected purely on merit, and is completely open to all the members of the community. This vertical social mobility has always been a unique feature of East Asian communities, even in the feudal and dynastic periods when an aristocracy has always coexisted with and been supplemented by the new meritocracy, which was recruited from the entire population. This 'East Asian dream' of success through study of classic literature was open to not only intellectual stars but to people with high level military talents. From those two channels of social success came the word Yangban in Korean which directly translates as two classes, literary and military classes, but implies aristocracy. In East Asian communitarian societies, the ruling class was the meritocratic aristocracy. Blue blood helped one's career only by so much. Aristocrats normally coexisted with new meritocrats who were selected in series of contests open to everybody in the community except those from the lowest slave and serf classes. In modern East Asian societies even these last restrictions have completely disappeared.

The bureaucracy translated the vision and goals into overall and sectoral strategies, plans, and policies and the bureaucrats actually selected the people, organizations and corporations who were to implement the plans and achieve the policy targets.

Furthermore, the same bureaucrats decided how to raise the necessary financial capital, acquire the necessary technologies and mobilize the required land on which to build industrial plants. This is the reason why many commentators believe that the East Asian corporate sector is a creation of the government or at least is profusely assisted by the government to grow from a set of small local companies to internationally renowned transnational corporations. The decision of who to assist to expand in what industry during the planning period to achieve the production capacity target was the prerogative of the bureaucrats. Furthermore, bureaucrats assessed the performance records, and the achievement of targets by the private sector, just as in the planned socialist economies.

They decided whether to increase government assistance or terminate it, to reinforce some projects and penalize others, or even to alter the targets of the plan. Assistance ranged from pecuniary subsidies, tax exemptions, privileged finance at low interest costs, market protection from competition both in and out of the country, and subsidies on the costs of various imports of raw materials. They had the power to literally make or break private sector corporations. This enormous power to fundamentally change the composition of the private sector is derived from the powerful leader who in turn received far-reaching and extensive authority from the people. The huge probability of bureaucratic corruption from this concentration of power is controlled only by the accountability which the bureaucrats held to the strong leader. The bureaucrats are held accountable only to the leader, and not to the people directly. This peculiar arrangement for accountability proved to be the source of extremely difficult problems to solve after the strong leader disappeared.

Strong leaders can be removed physically from the leadership position by many causes such as natural death, assassinations, democratic revolutions and sometimes even by voluntary abdication. Once the strong leader is removed, the bureaucracy which was held accountable only to that leader invariably transmuted itself into a sort of self-protecting organism which needed to defend itself from chastisement and witch-hunting which arose from past mismanagements and excesses committed during the leadership of the removed dictator. They were usually quite numerous. Under the new circumstance, the powerful bureaucrats need to protect themselves individually by exercising the power of denial and by collectively engaging in shamelessly impudent and virulent turf fighting. The East Asian bureaucracies, which were so honest, dynamic, devoted, and efficient, and played the most important role in the economic development, but after the removal of the strong leader, no democratically elected leaders ever succeeded to completely harness this monstrous organism. The East Asian post-authoritarian bureaucracy became somewhat like a slave prostitute who offers loyalty and support only to a lasting power. A democratically elected leader with a fixed term to serve is hardly a lasting power and political reprisals by successive elected governments on the policy failures of the previous governments, and with it the persons associated with that 'failed policies', make it very hard for bureaucrats to enthusiastically support any newly elected leaders.

To make the situation worse, many of the policies of newly elected governments are aimed at cleansing, downsizing, and restructuring the overblown bureaucracy itself. The new leaders must implement reform policies which were diametrically opposed to the welfare and stability of the bureaucracy collectively and bureaucrats individually. In other words, like the reformist politicians of the Soviet Union during the last days of that regime, who had to rely on the support of communist party apparatchik, democratically elected East Asian leaders had to rely on the bureaucratic supports to destroy the old bureaucracy.[5] The post authoritarian bureaucracy made itself the most troublesome obstacle in the economic development efforts of many East Asian societies. Transforming this entrenched and corrupt bureaucracy into an instrument more conducive to economic development is, in fact, the most critical task the East Asian communities have to achieve in the process of democratization of their old political systems, which have become so outdated and detrimental to their overall performance.

Another instrumentality of economic development in this contract between the strong leader and the people is the corporate sector. The central task of economic development is economic growth; which in essence, implies creating greater wealth by producing more goods and services. The expansion in production and supplies can only be achieved by increased investment and in the modern market economies nearly all national investment is done by private corporations.

The private corporate sector, therefore, is, in large measure, where the ultimate economic growth took place in East Asia. The bureaucrats can determine who produces what and where and where to finance, and on what terms and conditions the necessary technology is acquired. But ultimately the success of any investment project depended on the ability to recruit the best manpower, train them in skills and devotion, and supply them with the best equipment at the most competitive cost. It is further necessary to come up with internationally acceptable product qualities produced at internationally competitive costs, and marketed in and out of the country so as to successfully open the purses of consumers, and to maintain consumer loyalty long enough to recoup the original cost of the investment. That is the role of the corporate sector.

The East Asian corporations were so successful that the firms which started to manufacture silk dresses and dress shirts have now become household names in most of the markets of the world, from Johannesburg, Moscow, Anchorage, San Tiago to Sydney. They are now known as producers of electronics, computers, automobiles, as well as of textiles. This phenomenal growth, however, was possible only by violating the key commandment of corporate management in the capitalist market system; that is, to maximize profit.

East Asian Corporations and profit non-maximization

One of the most awkward legacies in the modern East Asian market economy from the Confucian society is societal disdain and disregard for corporate profits and contempt for the profession which pursues mainly material gains or profits. Just as with the case of 'individualism', it is virtually impossible to describe the pursuit of profit without some derogatory implication in East Asian cultures and languages. The social totempo starts with the scholastic, military, and bureaucratic classes at the top, followed by farmers who engage in creating 'primary' and 'genuine' value with hard toil and perspiration, which is followed in turn by manufacturers and artisans who create some genuine values with equally hard toil and perspiration. But these goods are regarded not as important as food, as necessities of life. Then comes the meanest and lowest class of merchants, only slightly higher than slaves and untouchables. The merchant class is regarded as a sort of social parasite which contributes little to creating genuine values and generally engages in perspiration-free activities of arbitraging between price differentials over time and place. As such, the normal activities of merchants should, by necessity, include some dishonesty on the price differentials and margins, or at least exaggerations of personal sacrifices and understatement of personal gains. This dishonest profession, therefore, by nature is totally unsuitable for the members of genteel classes and proud farmers.

In a modern market economy, the social status of the corporate leaders and major shareholders rose considerably but not by enough to match the economic power they enjoy. However, as the size and not the profit of the corporation grows, the prestige accorded to corporate leaders rises commensurately. This is evidenced by the fact that the successive presidents of Korean governments invited only the heads of the ten largest corporate groups of Korea to occasional presidential luncheons and they were seated according to the size of the annual sales of their corporations. This has been done so regularly, and for so long that nobody now even raises eyebrows at this peculiarly humorous Korean practice.[6] Newspapers regularly report the list of ten or thirty largest corporations according to their annual sales, total assets and total bank liabilities but hardly ever by their profits. The Fortunes 500 corporation list did not help either. The Korean Supervisory Board of Banking regularly produces the list of the thirty largest corporate groups of Korea to exhibit excessive concentration of bank lending to these companies. But becoming a member of this list turned into a sign of social prestige. Cross loan guarantees among sister companies within corporate groups actually turned into the most desired mortgages by the lending banks. Naturally, smaller groups did their best to qualify for the list of thirty largest groups.

This disdain and disregard for profit comes from another important source in the East Asian communitarian societies. Under the social contract of these societies which was instrumental for the rapid economic success, the primary role of the private corporate sector was to deliver rapid growth in investment and output. Unlike the modern corporations in mature market economies of the industrial world, patriotic East Asian corporations defined their success criteria as (1) survival and (2) expansion. Only by continuous survival were the corporations able to retain employment, purchase primary and secondary input materials from suppliers, who, in turn, maintain their own large employments, engage in production activities, distribute the products through large networks of sales and distribution agents who also retain their large employments, and pay taxes to governments which not only provides the peace and security that is so vital in maintaining normal business but also retained nearly a quarter of the work force in the economy.[7] Corporate survival, therefore, is an act of patriotism and the fulfillment of the social contract in East Asian communities.

The second success criteria are the expansion of the corporation. The dreadful social contract which extracts so much hardship from the members was tolerated by its members in order to escape from poverty. The autarchic and disciplinary model of rapid economic growth can only be tolerated because there are no other attractive alternatives. The voluntary and seemingly enthusiastic participation by members in the hard and disciplined life with restricted personal freedom comes from the realization that the quicker is the achievement of common goals, the shorter will be the hardship the members have to tolerate. It was like holding one's breath to achieve a goal and impatience naturally grows as time goes by.[8] The reward for this voluntary submission to hardship was simply prosperity, a consequence which can be achieved only by continuous investment and sustained growth at an extremely rapid rate. Corporate expansion therefore is an even more important goal in the East Asian corporate management. The public wanted it, corporate shareholders and founders wanted it, and the government rewarded rapid growth with various decorations of national honour as well as substantial material reinforcements by arranging the take over of other dwindling companies at government arranged low-cost financing. That financing, in turn, improved the cash flow situation of the rapidly growing corporate group. In other words, if one is short of cash, invest more, produce more, and export more, then your cash flow problem will be resolved, and your empire will grow. Corporate expansion was a corporate as well as a national goal. This was the case until the middle of the 1980s.

One cannot miss the built-in paradox in corporate managements which pursues survival and expansion on patriotic grounds and leaves maximization of profits and shareholder values as matters of secondary importance. East Asian corporations must keep on borrowing; borrowing on a massive scale as the corporations grow in size, making their financial structure over-leveraged and vulnerably brittle under relatively modest liquidity squeezes. Over-borrowing by the East Asian corporations was done with perfectly sound minds and intentions even with patriotic pride for most of them any way. However, it took a crisis for them to wake up to the built-in paradox in their communitarian management model.

In the 1990s the East Asian corporate groups became too large, with their annual sales surpassing their government budgets, and government arranged cash supplementation was terminated as that became politically very unpopular. The local banks became too weak and too small due to the peculiar government policy of financial sector repression. The continuous corporate expansion hit the wall domestically and many of them sought new opportunities overseas. Unfortunately, the old criteria of corporate success, namely 'continuous expansion' was applied in a new international management environment, but the international environment was very intolerant of the cardinal sins of East Asian management, that is, the disdain and disregard for profits, and shareholder values.

Objectives of the social contract

With these four constituents, namely a strong leader, cooperative people, powerful bureaucracy, and fast growing corporations, the social contract was consummated to achieve (1) prosperity (2) for all of the members of the community in a highly egalitarian distribution of income and wealth (3) in the shortest possible time period.

East Asian states took the road to industrialization by inducing huge local and foreign investment in manufacturing industries of mature products which have large markets all around the world. They adopted the export-oriented strategy. This required world class capacities of most modern production facilities financed by massive external borrowing and backed by the world's highest domestic saving ratios and fine quality work force who were totally devoted to the economic development objectives. The ever expanding production capacity of these states often created severe over-supply situations in corresponding industries of the world, and forced many of the older production capacities of the old industrial countries to shut down, thereby creating enormous resistance and political frictions from existing industrial countries. While the East Asians made lot of enemies in the industrial world, they also helped the world's total productivity to rise by forcing capacity adjustment among inefficient plants, and they earned many friends in the international financial world for whom the emerging market was a sweet darling until the time of crisis.

The prosperity, however, must be distributed under their social contract strictly in accordance with egalitarian rules. The harsh personal scarifices required by political freedom and working conditions of the general public was justified only as this egalitarian condition became the most important part of the deal. As a result the fast economic growth did not generate any distortions in income distribution during and after the fast growth period.[9] Instead, the rapid rise in real wages, frequently much faster than the rise in productivity, became a serious problem in most of East Asian economies.

The third objective which qualified their contract is high speed. As the personal sacrifices are intense, the time to hold breath had to be short. The attempt to achieve continuously rapid, in fact sometimes absurdly rapid, growth rates by East Asians can be explained by this contractual stipulation. Paradise is promised to be delivered within an acceptable period of time, not after death as in religion, nor in an unspecified time in the future as in communist society, but in the shortest possible period at 'almost any cost'. That last phrase is symptomatic of many East Asian policies and even some personal behavior. Perfectly decent gentlemen are after discovered committing excesses and violating rules, if the issue at hand is to protect the interest of the organization, or the country to which they belong. It was done with absolutely no moral compunction because the act is intended to achieve community objectives. Speed limit violations in excessive borrowing are one such excess. It is doubly remarkable when we consider that only half a century ago, at the time of Myrdal's *Asian Drama*, the East Asians were noted for their lack of speed and non-cooperative behavior. The power which turned them into such a hard working, well disciplined work force cannot be explained without the help of this social contract which included an impatient achievement of the goals and termination clauses.

Potential flaws in the social contract

Among the many flaws of this social contract of the East Asian communitarian model, we now discuss the three most important flaws which took the form of either serious indifference or erroneous assumptions. In the end some of them contributed to the functional paralysis of their communitarian systems.

The first and most fundamental flaw is the apathy towards any other higher value than material wellbeing. This apathy is particularly serious for the commonly and universally accepted values such as virtues and decency. The whole community is mesmerized by the sudden material glut and that 'success' is directly related to pursuing the ideal of 'economic' supremacy pronounced by the strong leader to be the ultimate national goal. The old Confucian model which provided only poverty and feeble nation states unable to defend the lives and properties of their citizens was gladly thrown away in the economically successful East Asian communitarian societies. Of course, most of them did not even realize that what they thought they had discarded still haunted their lives visibly and invisibly. Unfortunately, only the restrictive and confining parts of the Confucian system were abandoned in earnest by the newly rich East Asians who discovered the pleasure of material indulgence.

'Market competition' became the prime rule of order in creating more wealth, and the communitarian social order, which required all the members to participate and divide the fruits equally, was shattered. The newly realized attraction of social Darwinism, the survival of the fittest, started to change the behavior of the people from the grass roots as economic success continued. Massive social dislocations of the people from rural to urban societies and from agrarian to industrial societies also reinforced the atmosphere of limitless competition and winner-takes-all rules. The separation of individuals from the community accelerated and the community as the 'provider of economic needs' started to take on a new meaning. The East Asians, in short, started to slowly transform their once dynamic and harmonious society congealed around common goals into a society of jungle rules.

It is possible to argue that there is nothing wrong in this new model of free competition. After all the entire Western civilization and economic prosperity are built on this premise of free competition. Why cannot the East Asians learn this valuable new way and create a new and efficient society grounded on the solid base of material prosperity?

This argument does not hold well in East Asia. When an old communitarian contract is terminated, the members choose to destroy those parts of the system which are most cumbersome to them. Consider trade union violence in Korea. Old communitarian protection of life-time employment is still regarded as the sacred rights of individuals. Trade union activists call that the 'right for survival' as if individual survival is equal to adherence to one job in one company for life. They did not abandon the reliance on the paternalistic role of state in the communitarian tradition. What they abandoned was simply the duty to be cooperative and responsible. The rest of the community abounds with all sorts of interest groups, such as oriental medicine doctors' union, owners of restaurants which were built illegally on the banks of reservoirs from which municipal water supply is drawn. They all call their monopoly, legal or illegal, survival right. Economic rents, which are compensation for an exclusive monopoly possession of a certain good or opportunity, hence a source of inefficiency to the society, are called survival rights and the communitarian citizens are mistakenly tolerant of these absurd claims for economic rents. Under this distorted view of individual rights and free competition, the kind of market efficiency of Western style competition society will not emerge. Instead only ugly turf fights proliferate in the name of free competition and the community turns into a society of 'Bellium omnia contra omnes' – hostility of all to all. The community slowly degenerates into a motley collection of greedy interest groups. In the name of power diffusion and democracy each will aggressively seek state protection of their exclusive interests, whether industry organizations, trade unions or even cultural organizations.

The paternalistic role of the state, allocating porks and rents to members of the community, is still guarded carefully by the bureaucracy which needs to protect itself by tightening up the power of rent allocations. The state lost some political authority through the diffusion of power but the bureaucrats still effectively maintained economic authority. In the absence of any consensual moral authority, the members sought to satisfy their unlimited greed only by ugly confrontation, in the name of competition. Shamelessness and temerity are no longer regarded as avoidable sins, but desirable qualities of survival to be taught to babies from early days of life. Civility and propriety became useless encumbrances needlessly surviving from the now completely discredited Confucianism. East Asians discredited their Asian value long ago because of economic development along with political democratization. It is not the economic crisis which discredited Asian values. The crisis actually highlighted the error of abandoning the wrong parts of Asian values by Asian themselves.

The second fundamental flaw in the East Asian social contract is that an enormous amount of decision-making was delegated upward. That concentration of power included not only administrative power but much of legislative and judicial power as well. The bureaucrats were empowered by the leader to exercise highly concentrated power in most actual contexts. After the leader is gone, the bureaucrats, selected by examination and accountable only to the strong leader, degenerated into a self-saving, self-protecting organism which became the main source of corruption and inefficiency in East Asia. The bureaucracy, furthermore, tried and succeeded in perpetuating their control by continuous introduction of highly ingenious institutional and systemic devices that made the private sector's economic activities progressively more difficult but were disguised as an act of deregulation. The title of a new proposal is clearly deregulating a certain regulatory activity. The purpose is same and the new rule thus proclaimed deregulates. But all the laws and regulations leave, without exception, a substantial part of the regulations unspecified, to be determined by various executive orders. The typical case of such deceiving deregulation either increases the area of executive orders or overly specifies the conditions of deregulations in detail so that it will take a lengthy bureaucratic time to verify whether a certain activity falls into one of those specified cases or not. That actually makes private activities much harder.[10]

We have discussed enough of this phenomenon before and need not repeat it here again. Basically, in a materially prosperous society which is used to a high material standard of living, the privilege to extract attractive wealth is not voluntarily relinquished. The moral chastisement in this modern prosperous society is too weak to do the job. Judicial chastisement is frequently hampered by very lenient laws which, needless to say, are made by the bureaucrats themselves and by a highly cooperative and friendly judicial branch responding to the wishes of an administrative branch which supplied the culprits in first place.

To supplement the systemic inadequacy arising from the human weakness which never voluntarily relinquishes privileges of material gains, graft and resource misallocations on national scales, men have invented various forms and devices to create effective checks and balances and countervailing institutions so as to hold the government and its branches accountable. We call that democracy. Just as political revolutions required bloodshed to achieve democracy, it would be too optimistic to expect that the East Asians can resolve the question of their powerful and inefficient bureaucracies without serious costs. Even the present economic crisis did not shake up the bureaucracy of East Asia in substantial ways.

The third fundamental flaw in the East Asian social contract which gave birth to rapid growth, lies in a very Asian view of the world and the foreign countries. Partly from the thousand-years old seclusion from the Western world, and partly from the sufferings through domination by imperialistic powers, East Asians started their economic growth with a clear goal of economically and militarily catching up with the powerful west. The west became the world, or the outside to the minds of East Asians. That world out there represented a danger to avoid and a vast opportunity to exploit, like our traditional view of nature which was regarded as limitless and invincible until only thirty years ago. The world out there, therefore, meant a benchmark or a target to catch up with in the shortest possible time. As in the old view of nature, the world is there to be used and controlled. It provided many of the vital ingredients with which to achieve the East Asian goals, namely capital, technology and markets. Just as reforestation was a recent concept, helping the world economy to prosper is an alien concept to many Asians even at a highly mature stage of economic development, as in the case of Japan.

The world is a source of foreign exchange, especially US dollars, which should be earned by any means and once they came into one's possession, they should never be parted with. If this threatens to cause domestic inflation, then lend them to the foreigners by all means, but never squander them for the purchase of luxury goods. Once earned, accumulate them in foreign exchange reserves for rainy days, for everyday in East Asia is a rainy day, the leaders warn. There is the threat of communists from the North or West. If there is not a visible source of threat, then invent one and convince the members of the community that there is always a powerful conspiracy against your own country. A modern form of mercantilism is invented and practiced. All those Northeast Asian countries succeeded in accumulating the world's highest levels of foreign exchange reserves, bettered only by the country which mints the dollars, except the somewhat schizophrenic Korea which seems never to have quite understood the objectives of her macroeconomic policies at various moments and the Southeast Asian countries. The latter have not had long enough time to accumulate reserves and moreover much of their foreign exchange was owned and controlled by members who did not particularly associate themselves with the community to which they belonged, due to continuous discrimination against and persecution of them.

The East Asian financial crisis unfortunately, partly vindicated the wisdom of Northeast Asian mercantilism, which worships dollar reserves as a savior. Those who were successful in amassing huge dollar reserves weathered the crisis much better than those with low reserves. The irony is that mercantilism became the dominant wisdom, and the financial world is prepared to refinance only those countries with successful records of earning and accumulating dollars. According to Northeast Asian mercantilistic minds the old imperialist west changed only the weapons of their invasion for economic annexation of East Asia, and they succeeded brilliantly in the expedition. Earn dollars, that is your ultimate defensive deterrent of economic aggression. So goes the newly invigorated conspiracy theory. Quite naturally East Asians created many enemies and unfriendly forces all around the world. *The Economist* advised that 'When the bell rings for rescue, let it ring for a while'.

As the East Asian economies grew to share four per cent[11] of total world GDP, the mother world like mother nature proved to be not only limited in size to our surprise, but also very sick because of joint and mutual exploitation with the West during the past half a century. But the perception of the world as the plentiful source is still the prevailing thought in Southeast Asia and China. The perception of the world as a target to catch up with is still the dominant view in Taiwan, Korea, Hong Kong and Singapore, and the cult of dollar reserve accumulation at the expense of the rest of the world is still the prevailing religion of Japan, Taiwan and China. The economic crises proselytized nearly everybody to this religion of the dollar-reserve cult.

The termination of the contract

History is never kind to old models, old orders and old contracts. The East Asian social contract in the communitarian context succeeded in achieving a quick escape from endemic poverty but the old model was ill-equipped to attract the continuous support from the members of the community who now are quite comfortable in their daily lives. Furthermore, the old contract was consummated under a special circumstance based on unusual and harmful perceptions and assumptions. It became obvious that the contract must be terminated and the question became how and when rather than whether to terminate or not.

Ezra Vogel (1996) lists four main changes to mark the end of one era in this region. They are respectively the end of the days of cheap labour, accumulation of sizable financial assets by the members of the society, growth of non-manufacturing sector such as services and finance, and the emergence of a highly vocal public. In terms of industrial compositions, labor-intensive industries have been replaced by technology and capital-intensive industries to justify high wages which are an inevitable result of successful economic growth. Domestically available financial capital started to introduce a bidding war for goods of limited supply such as real estate and the production costs rose even more rapidly. With newly available financial strength, corporations started to spread their operations to the low cost production sites of the world, hence creating Asian transnational corporations. Manufacturing which was the basis of export-oriented growth now became but one of the several alternative ways to absorb high wage manpower which became increasingly numerous due to industrial restructuring and emigration. The economic structure started to become deeper. Finally, the middle class which contains most of the community became materially comfortable and politically assertive. No longer are unilateral directives from the government taken by the public without resistance.

This new assertiveness by the members of the community inevitably grew in tandem with political democratization. Self-control by the members for the sake of greater community objectives is not visible any more and the public reacted unnecessarily violently to any attempted controls from the government or from corporation management. This unnecessarily strong reaction to a request for a normal dose of self-control needed in any civil society slowly transformed itself into a kind of socio-pathological problem where mothers raised their children to become overly aggressive. Consumption behavior became overly conspicuous seeking mainly demonstration effects with no real purpose. Violations of social norms became an act of petty heroism, and students and labour unions used unnecessary violence for many issues which could have been resolved peacefully.

For further economic growth, all the East Asian societies need a new paradigm to replace the old social contract. The self-sacrifice by members in the rapidly growing days has vanished under the temperamental and impatient demand for the termination of the old contract. The new paradigm requires a new ideal to put the people back to the work, off the streets. And this can only be consummated strictly by voluntary participation because the majority of the people are now quite comfortably well-off and assertively outspoken. Indeed for most of them any further economic growth is quite unnecessary if it can be achieved only through long hours of grueling work. Unlike the elite of the community who still dream about catching up with the strongest of the world, many people on the street became quite immune to the threats of foreign aggression from any directions.

The society is now divided into two forces. One attempts to prolong the old order sometimes for the noble purpose of continuous growth, or sometimes for the selfish purpose of preserving the old source of personal power and wealth. The other attempts to terminate the old contract as soon as possible and destroy the base of power of the old elite who benefited so much from the old contract. When these two groups resort to violence to achieve their purposes, most members of the community find it difficult to associate with either of them. When the middle part of the society becomes disoriented, the extremists take over and the community enters into wasteful and vicious power contests.

The casting vote is held by the powerful bureaucrats. But we have seen that this group has no desire to either promote the liberal market competition for that will diminish their power of regulation or to support the old conservative forces for that, while instinctively conducive to their own survival, is far too dangerous an act to publicly commit for fear of political reprisal. The bureaucracy opts to keep neutral as long as it can. It will also be too dangerous to initiate any reform activities, for that will alienate the individual bureaucrat from the bureaucratic organization. It waits, and waits in inaction with a cynical smile on its lips until the community eventually collapses in a hard crash landing.

A crash landing it was that Korea, Thailand and Indonesia went through. In Singapore a strong leader routinely revised the content of the social contract to maintain social cohesion and continuous growth. In Hong Kong with the return of the island to China, the existing social contract became formally illegal and the community was drawn into another totally new contract which has only begun its experiment now. In Taiwan the overwhelming crisis ahead of the nation preempted any attempt to demand a termination of the old contract. Malaysia, where the strong leader declined the necessary revision of the social contract and wished to revise only macroeconomic and industrial policies, is facing a great difficulty.

In Japan the powerful and efficient bureaucracy played the role of strong leader for nearly half a century. But even the hard landing of the bubble burst in the early 1990s did not bring out any demand for rewriting the social contract. The people are not happy with existing power-sharing arrangements but nobody publicly demands termination of the old contract and old system. This enigma of Japanese society seems to be the combined result of a successful scare campaign by the elite of the community, and the simple fact that the present model succeeded in achieving the economic development of which all the Japanese people can be proud of irrespective of personal hardships. They seem to be reluctant to change the horse while it is dashing.

Notes

1 Japan in this case behaved exactly as the Western imperial countries and she did not consider it necessary or even desirable to distinguish herself from the former as her national goals enunciated an expansionistic behavior, only in an augmented manner.
2 Lucien Pye traced this concept to the old Asian feudal days but it became far more relevant in the twentieth century for the survival of nation states in the East Asia.
3 The US congress seems to be confused about the definition of 'misdemeanor' which was prescribed in the US constitution as one of the causes of impeachment of public officers. The East Asians have similar difficulties in defining legally punishable misdemeanors by some of their members.
4 Some commentators insist that the elimination process starts from kindergarten days in the case of Japan.
5 At the beginning days of Kim, Youngsam in Korea, the Korean bureaucrats were accused of Bok-ji-bu-dong, which translates into English as 'Lying flat on the floor with belly down'. This sabotage of reform policies was endemic and lasted until the new government finally took on the corrupt old ways.
6 It was Park Chunghee who started this practice to encourage the corporate leaders who, Park regarded correctly, as the men at the front line in the endeavor to create a strong and prosperous nation.
7 According to records of imperial cabinet meeting of Japan, there was a decision made in the meeting in August 1906, just two years before the formal annexation of Korea, to prohibit all Koreans and Taiwanese from incorporating any modern form of companies. This was to grant a monopoly privilege of incorporation of large or small corporations to Japanese citizens only. State protection in East Asia extends to cover the right to incorporate and grow into large scale modern corporations for its citizens after their independence.
8 In fact many idealistic students and intellectuals did not consider material wellbeing important enough to forego personal and political freedom and vetoed and sabotaged the social contract even from the beginning. Even as the economic success continued to vindicate the legitimacy of limited and temporary dictatorship, this veto group's reaction grew even stronger because the economic success made the need for material wellbeing even less important compared to when they were absolutely poor. Herein lies the explanation for the extraordinarily violent demonstrations by Korean students against their development model of strong leadership.

9 Gini Coefficients

	1975–88*	*Designated years*
Korea	0.36	0.34(1988)
Malaysia	0.48	0.48(1989)
Thailand	0.47	0.52(1992)
Indonesia	0.31	0.36(1996)
Philippines	0.45	0.45(1994)

*: Average of that period.
Source: ADB, Key Indicator of Developing Asian and Pacific Countries 1995, 1996, 1997

10 As a member of the Board of Deregulation, Ministry of Industry and Resources, I was confronted by many such cases. There was one regulation of the Korean government, which required full time employment of a qualified quarantine specialist for companies which import raw hide to ensure proper inspection of any imported goods. A survey revealed that the average work time of these qualified quarantine specialists is only two hours per week for there is not enough work to justify a specialist on full time employment. To raise the efficiency of their employment raw hide importers jointly petitioned to relax that employment requirement substantially. The ministry officers in charge of this case came back with a proposal that would let only two companies jointly hire one specialist but the distance between warehouses of these two companies should not be more than 500 metres. That is the typical work-augmenting attitude of bureaucracy. In this case the ministry was able to only propose their alternative. Imagine how they would react if they have the rights to rule, which they have in most of the cases.

11 According to WEFA and Asian Development Bank, total GDP of World was 28,376 billion dollar and that of East Asia (5 nations) was 1.135 billion dollar in 1997.

References

Berger, P. L. and Hsiao, H. M. (eds) (1988) *In Search of an East Asian Development Model*, New Brunswick: New Jersey.

Johnson, C. (1982) *MITI and Japanese Miracle: The Growth of Industrial Policy 1925–1975*, Stanford, Ca.: Stanford University Press.

Lodge, G. C. and Vogel, E. F. (eds) (1987) *Ideology and National Competitiveness – An Analysis of Nine Countries*, Massachusetts: Harvard Business School Press.

—— (eds)(1987) *Ideology and National Competitiveness – An Analysis of Nine Countries*, Massachusetts: Harvard Business School Press.

MacIntyre, A. (1981) *After Virtue*, Nortre Dame: University of Nortre Dame Press.

Michal, S. J. (1982) *Liberalism and the Limits of Justice*, Cambridge, Mass.: Cambridge University Press.

Myrdal, G. (1968) *Asian Drama*, Twentieth Century Fund Press.

Pye, L. (1988) 'The New Asian Capitalism: A Political Portrait', in Berger, (1988).

Rawls, J. (1993) *Political Liberalism*, New York: Columbia University Press.

Tonnies, F. (1963) *Community and Association*, trans. C. P. Loomis, New York: Harper and Row.

Vogel, E. F. (1993) *The Four Little Dragons: The spread of Industrialization in East Asia*, Massachusetts: Harvard University Press.

Waltzer, M. (1983) *Sphere of Justice*, New York: Basic Books.

Part IV
History of economic theory

8   Knut Wicksell as a classic and as a social thinker

Richard Swedberg

The general argument of this paper is that there is much more to Knut Wicksell as a thinker than is currently realized.[1] In articles and books Wicksell is exclusively portrayed as an economic theorist (who also wrote some political and social pamphlets; these are only mentioned and never read). Like many of the great economists, however, Wicksell was not only an excellent economic theoretician but also had much to say about the *social* aspects of the economy. He also – again, like some of the great economists – made contributions to other social sciences as well as to economics. Furthermore, there is the fact that the lines between Wicksell's writings in theoretical economics and his social and political pamphlets (which, again, are often mentioned but never read[2]) are considerably less sharp than is usually thought. What Wicksell had to say about the social and political dimensions of some topic often found its way into his theoretical economic writings and vice versa. And, finally, there is to my mind a kind of general quality to Wicksell's writings – to all of his writings – which he shares with the classics – it is that when he writes on a topic, he nearly always has something to teach us today. The reason for this is difficult to pinpoint, even though the result is there for anyone to experience. Perhaps one of Wicksell's colleagues was right when he said that Wicksell simply 'dug a little deeper than anybody else in almost every problem' (Ohlin [1926] 1994: 25). In any case, there is a wonderful freshness to Wicksell's work, a freshness that can only be experienced by reading it in the original.

Some background facts about Wicksell's life and work

For several reasons it may be useful to start out by saying something about Wicksell's life and work. This will help to supply a context for Wicksell's analysis of society and the social dimension of the economy. Two things that characterize Wicksell need to be emphasised immediately so that the reader will be aware of them throughout this section of the paper. The first is that Wicksell, from early manhood on, was extremely interested in understanding and analyzing *all of society* – not only the economy! – in as stringent and objective manner as possible. The second is a fact of a very different order that nonetheless is important and deserves to be highlighted. It is that Wicksell, also from early on, showed a degree of personal courage in standing up for his opinions that is truly outstanding. Often alone against a crowd of angry people, and deserted by his closest friends as well as his family, Wicksell would nonetheless speak out; – and face the consequences. Wicksell did not only have a good character, but something that is even more rare, namely a good character in combination with a high level of moral courage. As Schumpeter (1954: 862) put it, 'No finer intellect and no higher character have ever graced our field'.

Knut Wicksell – as we can read in Torsten Gårdlund's superb biography – was born in Stockholm on December 20, 1851 (Gårdlund 1956). His father, John Wicksell, was a self-made man who owned a grocery store and a bit of real estate; his mother, Christina Catharina Wicksell (born Glassel), came from a family of merchants and artisans. The lifestyle of the Wicksells can be described as frugal and lower middle class. The conversation in the home is reputed to have been extremely quickwitted and highspirited, and it was to leave a clear imprint on all the children. What appears to have been a happy and healthy childhood for Knut Wicksell came, however, to an early end with the death of his mother in 1858 and of his father in 1866. The children were cared for by a relative, who seems to have done a good job in raising the children. But much of the early happiness was gone.

All of the Wicksell children received small inheritances, which lasted them for some years; and Knut Wicksell would later in his life propagate the idea that everybody in society should get an inheritance in early adulthood. In 1869 Wicksell moved to Uppsala, to attend the university; he remained there for more than a decade. He was primarily interested in the natural sciences and had secret hopes of one day becoming a professor of mathematics, a field in which he early excelled. Already in 1872 he had his master's degree, but it then took more than a decade before he received his next degree (a so-called fil. lic., in 1885). One reason for the long delay was that Wicksell gradually came to realize that it would be very hard for him to make a contribution to mathematics, since so much had already been accomplished in this field. Another reason was that Wicksell had a tendency to depression, and during these periods he was unable to work. All his life he would struggle against what the ancients called 'acedia', which made him silently despair and despise himself (see Zetterberg [1967] 1997).

But there was also a third reason why Wicksell hesitated about becoming a mathematician, and this was that he was passionately interested in what was going on in society. It is true that when Wicksell first arrived in Uppsala, he was more interested in religion than in social questions. After a few years, however, he went through a personal crisis and became a fervent atheist. Similarly to the literary and artistic avantgarde of his days, he became extremely critical of his parents' generation and the society it had created. Just as August Strindberg – the key figure in the famous 'generation of the 80s' in Sweden (and also a distant friend of Wicksell's) – did, he now began to question the church, the army, the rich, and all the other pillars of society (see Gårdlund 1954; 1956: 106).

Wicksell also became a feminist, under the impact of the ideas of Henrik Ibsen and Björnstierne Björnson, and began to read people such as John Stuart Mill, Herbert Spencer and Charles Darwin. While Wicksell had earlier believed in Church and Religion, he now transferred all of his allegiance to Reason and Science, and became a free thinker who fought prejudices wherever they could be found. Man lived in Society, and it was necessary to understand its laws in order to perfect Society. John Stuart Mill impressed Wicksell and his friends very much, and they especially admired Mill's emphasis on Rationality and Liberty. Wicksell's closest friend, Hjalmar Öhrvall, translated Mill's *On Liberty* into Swedish, and Wicksell would later say that this particular work became 'the basic text and codex' for the generation of the 1880s (Wicksell 1917: 359).

Wicksell as a young man was deeply influenced by John Stuart Mill – but it was another author who would have an even greater impact on him. This was George Drysdale, the author of a hefty volume entitled *The Elements of Social Science* (1854; Swedish translation in 1878). Few people today have heard of this book, let alone read it; but in the second half of the nineteenth century it was a true bestseller, appearing in thirty-five editions in England between 1854 and 1905. The basic thrust of Drysdale's work was that the growth of population was the main cause of all evils in society, especially poverty and prostitution. Wicksell became convinced that Drysdale was totally correct, and from then until his death he was a fervent Malthusian.

Commentators have often pointed out that Wicksell embraced Malthusianism with the same kind of enthusiasm that believers display towards religion, and that Drysdale's ideas became something of an *Ersatz* for Wicksell's lost faith. Implicit in this argument is also the notion that Wicksell's Malthusianism was as 'dogmatic' and intellectually 'unreasonable' as religion itself. This, however, is to misrepresent Wicksell's attitude to Drysdale's ideas. Malthusianism was a religion to Wicksell, mainly in the sense that it presented a coherent picture of society and gave a reason why there existed so much unhappiness in the world. But Malthusianism – it is important to notice this – also allowed Wicksell to take the leap from having mere opinions about society to being able to analyze what was going on in a logical and analytical manner. Malthusianism, in other words, provided Wicksell with a secular *Weltanschauung*, a scientifically coloured theodicy – and a rough form of social science.

That Drysdale's book helped Wicksell to order his ideas and to analyze a number of social phenomena with a certain rigor, is clear from Wicksell's first appearance as a public speaker. This took place in 1880 in Uppsala and was to become a *cause celèbre*. The topic that Wicksell chose was drunkenness. He argued that people drank because they were unhappy and poor, and that they were poor mainly because of overpopulation. It would therefore be a good idea, Wicksell continued, to limit the growth of the population through some form of birth control. All of official Uppsala, including the President of Uppsala University, were utterly scandalized by Wicksell's advocacy of birth control, and tried to silence him as well as to ostracize him. Wicksell, however, would not budge; he calmly argued back and marshalled more evidence in favor of his thesis. It was under the impact of Wicksell's 1880 speech, it should be noted, that Uppsala University chose its current motto, 'It Is Good to Think Freely, but It Is Better to Think Correctly'. More liberal proposals, such as 'Through Truth to Freedom' and 'Do Not Fear to Know', were rejected.

During the 1880s Wicksell gradually came to realize that he did not want to become a mathematician but rather some kind of social scientist. In an autobiographical sketch from 1891 he said, for example, that 'ever since [the late 1870s] I have mainly devoted myself to economic, statistical and sociological studies' – while his mathematical studies were not even mentioned (Wicksell 1995 [1891]: 159). The decision to become a social scientist was not an easy one to make because there existed no obvious career for someone like Wicksell, who had a general interest in society as well as an interest in reforming it. The first chair in sociology in Sweden, for example, was not created until 1902;[3] and the type of sociology that Wicksell knew of – the writings of Comte, Spencer, and kindred spirits – probably did not appeal to him since it was somewhat crude and amateurish.[4] As a result, Wicksell decided to take the only route open to someone like himself, which was to become a public speaker and writer. For some years in the 1880s, this is also how Wicksell supported himself.

Nonetheless – and the point deserves to be emphasised – if there had existed a sophisticated type of sociology in Wicksell's days (which also indicated how to change things), it is a reasonable bet that Wicksell would have opted for this type of social science rather than for economics. It should also be pointed out that if we look at the subjects that Wicksell lectured on in the 1880s, these turn out not to include economic topics but rather the kind of topics that nineteenth century sociologists liked to discuss. According to statistics supplied by Torsten Gårdlund for the years 1886–7, for example, Wicksell gave public lectures on the following topics: marriage (10), population questions (10), prostitution (4), socialism (3), spiritualism (2), free thinking (2), euthanasia (1), impressions from England (1), and religion (1).[5] Indeed, it was not till Wicksell began to get money from a private foundation to study economics, that 'the dismal science' began to seriously compete with his sociological activities.

Even when he was paid to study economics, Wicksell was not attracted enough by what he found in Mill, Ricardo and company to seriously consider becoming an economist. At the end of 1885, for example, he studied theoretical and mathematical economics on his own in the British Museum – but without the kind of enthusiasm that people usually show when they have found their true vocation. It was not until some years later, more precisely in the spring of 1889, when Wicksell stumbled over a work by Böhm–Bawerk on the nature of capital rent, that he became so excited ('a revelation') that he began to think seriously about becoming an economist. The fact that Wicksell around this time also found a woman with whom he wanted to share his life (but not marry – that was against his principles) also made him more willing to 'compromise' and settle for a conventional career as an academic economist.

During the 1890s Wicksell worked extremely hard to create a career for himself in economics. He did not succeed until a decade later when he finally secured an appointment at Lund University. It was also during the 1890s that Wicksell obtained a PhD in economics (1895) and wrote the only three monographs in economics that he was ever to author: *Value, Capital and Rent* (1893), *Research in the Theory of Finance* (1895) and *Interest and Prices* (1898). Still, it is clear that Wicksell had more ambitions in the 1890s than just to become a professional economist, and during this period he wrote a number of pamphlets on various topics, such as taxation, marriage and population. Wicksell also continued to give public lectures, albeit at a slower rate than in the 1880s; and several times he succeeded in totally enraging his audience. It was in the 1890s, for example, that he began to argue that Sweden should disarm and become part of Russia – hardly a popular idea in a country which by tradition feared the Russians more than any other nation.

Wicksell worked as a professor of economics at the University of Lund from 1901 to 1917, when he retired and moved back to Stockholm. During these years Wicksell published a huge number of articles in the leading economics journal in Sweden, *Ekonomisk tidskrift*, and put together his lectures on economics in book form (2 vols. 1st ed. 1901, 1906; 2nd ed. 1911, 1915). He also took part in the public discussion of economic topics by producing a never-ending stream of articles in the daily press. Wicksell also found time to continue with his non-economic activities, from public lecturing to writing on various social and political topics. That Wicksell was seen as something of a sociologist by his contemporaries is clear from the way that Wicksell is described in a biographical lexicon that appeared around this time in Sweden. The opening line of the article on Wicksell starts: '*Wicksell, Johan Gustaf Knut*, economist and sociologist' (*Svenskt biografiskt handlexikon* 1906: 720).

The social and sociological topics that Wicksell worked on, while a professor at Lund, included population, political representation and unfair taxation. More spectacular than all of his writings during this time, however, was his public behavior, especially on two occasions. At one of these, in May 1905 in Lund, he single-handedly challenged and enraged a huge party of nationalistic Swedes who had come together to celebrate a national poet, Esaias Tégner. On the second occasion, in November 1908, Wicksell deliberately set out to test the limits on public speech in order to produce more liberal legislation. He did this by making a couple of rather crude sexual jokes about the Bible, for which he was sentenced to two months in jail in 1909. These two months, it may be added, Wicksell spent by revising a Malthusian pamphlet on population, by working on his lectures, and by helping a friend to translate Adam Smith into Swedish.

During the last decade of his life – from 1917 to 1926, in Stockholm – Wicksell continued to do some writing on economic and social topics. Often, however, he seems to have been depressed, and his old problems with acedia seem to have resurfaced. At times, however, the old spirit was rekindled, and it was perhaps during one of these occasions that he produced the second edition of the pamphlet on population that he had written in Ystad Jail (Wicksell 1926). Knut Wicksell died on May 3, 1926, at the age of 74. He left behind a wealth of ideas, on economic as well as non-economic topics – and also a legacy of outstanding moral courage.

Glimpses of Wicksell the social scientist: sociological and social-economic observations

What has just been said should hopefully be enough to convince the reader that Wicksell was not only an economist but also a sociologist and that throughout his life he displayed great personal courage in standing up for his opinions. In this part of the paper I shall give some examples of Wicksell's sociology and also show how his social thinking was integrated at times into his theoretical economics. This means, among other things, that Wicksell's work in economics is both broader than is usually thought and that it contains some contributions which have been overlooked.

Before presenting the examples I have chosen, the reader is again reminded that when Wicksell is referred to as a sociologist, the word 'sociology' is used in its nineteenth century sense, which is quite different from the meaning it has today.[6]

Wicksell's Uppsala speech in 1880

The speech through which Wicksell made his entry into the political scene in Sweden is still worth reading for its fine arguments and social observations. Its full title is *Some Words about the Most Important Reason and Cure of Social Ills, with Special Emphasis on Drunkenness*, and it is around 100 pages long. Wicksell begins by quoting a fellow Swede, Benjamin Höijer: 'Search for the truth, and if this search takes you to hell, you should knock on the door!' (Wicksell 1880: 3). He then delivers his main message: people who drink are unhappy; and this unhappiness makes liquor have a dangerous and enchanting power over their lives ('*trollmakt*'; Wicksell 1880: 11).

The main cause for people's unhappiness, Wicksell continues, is poverty; and he gives a harrowing description of what a poor person's lodgings were like during this time.[7] Being poor, Wicksell adds, usually means lacking a *home*, and it is especially the lack of a home that drives a person to excessive drinking. Wicksell's emphasis on the importance of a home for the average person testifies to his powers as a social thinker (and adds to our understanding of the tragedy of today's 'homeless' people):

> But what the poor person in our country lacks more than anything else is *a home* – a home where he can have a nice time and where he can withdraw, once work is done, and at least enjoy some part of the good of life, in the company of his family. It is the lack of a home, I am convinced, that more than anything else drives people to the bars.
>
> (Wicksell 1880: 7–8, emphasis in original)

Wicksell gives a considerably broader definition of poverty than is commonly done today, and this allows him to include categories of people under this heading who would otherwise be excluded. 'With poverty', he says, 'I do not only mean living in rags (that would be to restrict the concept too much); but poor, as I see it, is each and everyone who does not own what he necessarily needs and also lacks a reasonable chance of getting it' (Wicksell 1880: 6). One of the groups who were poor in Wicksell's sense were the students – and the reader may recall that Wicksell himself had been a student for many years, when he gave this speech, and that many students as well. Wicksell describes in a vivid manner the emotional and sexual misery of the Swedish students. The average (male) student was old enough to live with a woman and to create a home, but he lacked the means to do so. As a result, Wicksell says, the student had to either resign himself to celibacy or make unhappy visits to prostitutes.

Population

Anyone who reads Wicksell's writings on social topics quickly notices that he was a fervent Malthusian and that population growth is usually singled out as the ultimate reason why something has gone wrong in society. In his 1880 speech in Uppsala, for example, Wicksell argued that 'we are poor because we are too many', and he then went on to show how such phenomena as prostitution, cannibalism and war could all be understood as manifestations of overpopulation (Wicksell 1880: 26).

An argument that is fresh when one encounters it for the first time in Wicksell's writings, however, soon loses its charm when it is repeated over and over again. Wicksell would make an interesting comment and say something like 'in nine out of ten cases the woman question is due to economic causes', but before the sentence was over, he would then add something like 'which [also] means that in nine out of ten cases it has to do with the population question' (Wicksell 1895–6: 1).

Wicksell's constant repetition that the population question constitutes 'the most important social question' and that every social problem ultimately depends on over-population naturally annoyed his contemporaries. Eli Heckscher, the well-known economic historian, dryly pointed out in his obituary on Wicksell that the latter's work on population 'hardly contained any novelty from a theoretical viewpoint' (Heckscher 1926). And the economist and sociologist Gustaf Steffen, who was also a friend of Wicksell's, complained that Wicksell was much too crude in his handling of the population question: 'Wicksell's contribution to the doctrine of population seems to me less successful [than his work in economics]. In my opinion, he is ... too little of a psychologist and a sociologist to get a good handle on the population question' (Steffen 1911).

My own opinion on Wicksell and Malthusianism is that Wicksell tended to be dogmatic and obstinate whenever population questions were discussed – but that he also has something valuable to say on the topic.[8] I would argue that Wicksell made both a few distinct, scholarly contributions to our understanding of population questions and that his more general, Malthusian viewpoint, while often dogmatic and repetitive, now and then could – and still can – result in an interesting perspective on things. If Wicksell had lived today, he might have pointed out that while people are very quick to notice that accepting refugees into one's country means an increased pressure on the economic system, they do not seem to notice that this also happens when the native population brings children into the world. The fact that the more children are born in a country, the less refugees it can accept, is an observation that is not considered relevant in today's Western societies. If Wicksell had been alive today, he might also have argued that one way of bringing down unemployment would be for people to have less children; and that a good way to improve the environment would be to prevent the world population from growing. All of these Malthusian (or 'Wicksellian') opinions are to my mind well worth discussing. I would also support Wicksell's more general observation that arguments in favor of population growth tend to be nationalistic in spirit, and that they are typically based on instinct, not on reason.

Regardless of whether there is some element of truth in the Malthusian position as such, it should be emphasized that Wicksell made at least one scientific contribution to the study of population and that was his notion of an *optimum of population*.[9] While it is often said that a country has too many people, Wicksell noted, a more relevant question is whether one can establish a point where an increase in the number of people would lead to a decrease in the level of average well-being. Exactly how such an optimum was to be established was, however, never resolved in a satisfactory manner by Wicksell.

It is also possible that another contribution, of a more sociological character, can be found in Wicksell's writings on population. The reader may recall Wicksell's argument in his speech from 1880 that the average student suffered deeply from not being able to live with a woman in a home of their own. In the little pamphlet on population that Wicksell wrote while he was in Ystad Jail in 1909, he also makes the observation, based on statistics, that married men live considerably longer than unmarried men (and widowers), while this is much less the case for women. This finding, as any sociologist knows, directly parallels Durkheim's important discovery in *Suicide* (1897) that marriage is an institution that benefits the male very much, but less so (if at all) the female.

The role of the state in the economy

But Wicksell's sociologizing type of analysis was not only aimed at non-economic topics, it also extended to the economy itself. It is important to note this because it means that Wicksell made contributions to economics other than to its theoretical branch. To some extent, this has been known for some time; and people such as James Buchanan, Gordon Tullock and Dennis Mueller have all noted Wicksell's contribution to public choice. Some of the material that interests the public choice scholars is touched on here as well, but I mostly concentrate on those parts of Wicksell's writings which fall into what could rather be called economic sociology. The difference between public choice and economic sociology, it can be added, is that while the former attempts to explain politics with the help of the analytical tools of mainstream economics, the latter attempts to explain economic phenomena by introducing a social perspective into the analysis of interests.

Wicksell wrote quite a bit on the role of the state in the economy, and his general stance was no doubt influenced by his positive attitude towards capitalism. If one gives too much economic power to the state, he notes in one of his early pamphlets, it will cease being 'polite' to the citizens (Wicksell 1892). The very idea of a socialist society, governed by an all powerful state, Wicksell found morally repulsive – just as he did not like the particular type of capitalist society that he saw around himself. His ideal, he said, was a different type of capitalism – one where 'all workers are capitalists' and 'the capitalist are workers' (Wicksell 1893: 192). Exactly what this type of capitalist system would look like, Wicksell does not say; but it would probably have been one in which each member of society was guaranteed some private property at the outset of adult life; where it was possible to build up a great fortune over a lifetime – but also where inheritance laws were such that one could not pass on a major fortune to one's children (e.g. Wicksell 1901; 1913: 32–5).

It is also clear that one can find a fully developed fiscal sociology in Wicksell's writings on taxation. Not only do we find a discussion in these writings of the two famous principles of taxation – '*the benefit principle*' ('*intresseprincipen*') and '*the ability-to-pay principle*' ('*bärkraftsprincipen*'); but they also contain attempts to see how the two principles will operate in different historical and institutional settings (e.g. Wicksell 1992 [1896]; 1898). Inheritance taxes, Wicksell suggests, should not be used by the state for normal expenses but only to create new capital. In his empirical analysis of the Swedish tax system, Wicksell also suggests a third principle of taxation, which is thoroughly sociological in nature. This is that *the distribution of taxes in society mirrors its distribution of political power* (Wicksell 1898).[10] This principle can also be formulated in the following way: the more political power you have, the less taxes you are likely to pay (or, alternatively, the more you will succeed in making other people pay for your expenses). It was also clear from the historical record of Sweden, Wicksell pointed out, that whoever held political power would try avoid paying taxes. In his own days, he added, the common people – who had next to no political power (since they lacked the requisite income to vote) – had to carry a disproportionate part of the tax burden, mainly in the form of indirect taxes on consumption. Wicksell also noted that the Swedish peasants, historically, had a certain amount of political power, and that this had helped them to withstand the demands from the rulers for ever more taxes.

'Educational Capital' and the role of collective emotions in the economy

One concept that Wicksell invented – and which has been neglected in the economics literature – is that of 'educational capital' ('*uppfostringskapital*'). This concept is interesting for a number of reasons, one of which is that it straddles the economy and the social. Wicksell formulated this concept well before he became an economist but he kept using it also when he was a professional economist. The place where Wicksell discusses this concept in the most detailed manner – and also the first time that it appears in his writings – is in 1882, in a pamphlet entitled *On Emigration* (1882: 23–9). Another time when Wicksell used the concept of educational capital was in 1910, when he worked for a state-appointed commission on emigration (Wicksell 1910: 101).

The basic idea behind the concept of educational capital is that when you bring someone up, you have to invest quite a bit of 'education and care' in that person. And if he or she then leaves the country – as so many Swedes in Wicksell's days left for the United States – this educational capital is lost for the native country and brought to the new country. The closest one gets to a definition of educational capital in Wicksell's work is the following statement: 'The education and care which are spent on those who grow up, is to be regarded as a kind of capital, which has been advanced and which people then have to pay back one day by taking care of the next generation' (Wicksell 1882: 24). In his pamphlet from 1882 Wicksell attempts to translate the educational capital that the average emigrant Swede brought to the United States into exact figures, and he does this by calculating three items: (1) clothes, shoes and food (paid for by the parents); (2) formal education (paid for by the state and the parishes); and (3) 'attention and care' (to a large extent paid for through the [unpaid] labor of the mother; Wicksell 1882: 25–6).

The average educational capital spent on a 15 year-old person towards the end of the nineteenth century in Sweden, Wicksell says, was around 1,000 Swedish Crowns; and to better understand this figure he adds that the annual wage in these days of a rural male worker was around 400 Swedish Crowns and of a female rural worker around 225 Swedish Crowns. Wicksell's efforts to translate educational capital into an exact sum must not, however, be interpreted as a sign that Wicksell had an 'econ-omistic' or non-sociological concept of educational capital. It is clear from his writ-ings that many items, which are hard to measure and express in money terms, nonetheless were seen by Wicksell as integral parts of that 'care and education' which constitutes the core of educational capital. In his 1910 article on emigration, for example, Wicksell makes no attempt to put a price on all the items that make up educational capital. He also mentions that quite a bit of 'tenderness' usually gets invested in the individual.[11]

Speaking about tenderness in economic matters naturally leads to another topic, where Wicksell tended to unite economic and social analysis, namely when he ana-lyzed *collective emotions in the economy*. To some extent, it should be noticed, Wicksell – like many other economists – had a tendency to turn sociological facts into psychological facts, and instead of mapping out a specific social structure and show its effects on the economy, he tended to vaguely speculate on the role of psychological factors in the economy. Nonetheless, Wicksell's occasional mentioning of the role that collective emotions play in the economy represents a fascinating topic in its own right.

In his well-known essay 'The Enigma of Business Cycles' Wicksell notes, for example, that among the factors which affect the unfolding of the business cycle is 'the internal structure of the economy viewed from a material and a psychological stand point' (Wicksell 1907: 256). Another factor that needs to be taken into account in order to understand the business cycle is 'the mood in the market' – which can be either 'pessimism' or 'optimism' (Wicksell 1907: 256). Similarly, in a minor article on unemployment Wicksell argues that one reason why not enough jobs are being created is that in situations where capital has been invested in an unwise way, production will typically turn 'onto the wrong track' – with 'resignation' among the capitalists as a result (Wicksell 1922). Also consumers can experience a similar 'resignation', according to Wicksell, namely when they realize that circum-stances are such that their level of consumption has to be lowered (Wicksell 1925: 210, 217). In a situation with falling prices, it is furthermore common that merchants try extra hard to sell to consumers, out of 'fear' that prices will fall even further (Wicksell 1925: 218).

Concluding remarks on Wicksell as a sociologist

Many more examples of sociological or sociologizing analyses can be found in Wicksell's work, especially if we include his unpublished manuscripts (for a brief presentation of these, see Jonung 1988). One topic that immediately comes to mind is Wicksell's discussion of marriage. There is also the fact that some of Wicksell's economic-theoretical ideas can probably be given a social interpretation as well, including his famous theory of the natural rate of interest. As Erik Dahmén (1991 [1986]: 134–5) has suggested, one could, for example, try to analyze the kind of dynamics that follows from the fact that different groups in an economy have different profit expectations. My purpose in this chapter, however, has rather been to indicate the need for a new reading of Wicksell's work than to be comprehensive, and I shall therefore stop at this point. The same is true for my statement about Wicksell's moral courage at the outset of the paper; this is also a topic that deserves much more attention than I have been able to give it here.

Before ending, however, one question remains to be tackled, and that is the following: If Wicksell indeed was a sociologist (albeit in the nineteenth century sense of the word), why did he never step forward and state that he was not only an economist but also a sociologist? As far as I know, it can be added, Wicksell *never* referred to himself anywhere in his writings as a 'sociologist'. The main reason for this, in my opinion, is that the kind of sociology that existed in Wicksell's days did not live up to his standards as to what science (including social science) ought to be like.[12] Wicksell firmly believed that there exist 'general laws which govern and direct human action', but he was not aware of any way in which it was possible to explore the laws that govern the non-economic parts of society in a reliable and truly scientific manner (Wicksell 1954 [1893]: 30). To simply pile facts upon facts or to just classify things, rather than analyze their causes, as the economists in the Historical School often did, was according to Wicksell (1954 [1893]: 30–1; 1958 [1904]) simply not enough.

Wicksell's scientific ideal – in economics as well as in social science more generally – was to produce a *mixture of* empirical analysis and analytical thinking or, more precisely, to produce an analytical explanation and ordering of empirical material (e.g. Wicksell 1954 [1904]; Henriksson 1991). Wicksell was not, in other words, one of those economists who prefer abstract theory to empirical facts and who are not very interested in what happens in reality. Indeed, at one of his last public appearances, Wicksell made such a forceful plea for economics to become more empirical that some of his fellow theorists became quite uneasy. Bertil Ohlin describes the scene in the following manner in his obituary of Wicksell:

> I remember the speech on the future of economics which he gave on his seventieth birthday [in 1920] at a dinner arranged by the Political Economy Club in Stockholm. It was pathetic to hear him express his envy of those who now started economic studies with all the advantages of having at their disposal a growing mass of factual material about what was actually happening. Himself an economist who had learnt from all schools of economic thought, except the German Historical School, his advice turned out to be: *Study history, study the actual development of economic life!*
>
> (Ohlin [1926] 1994: 25)

Knut Wicksell, I have argued in this brief essay, was not only a brilliant economic theoretician but also had many other talents. He was, for example, a gifted amateur sociologist and a writer with a fine eye for the social-economic structure of society. His economic writings, it should be added, are much closer to his social and political writings than is commonly thought. In all that Wicksell wrote, there is furthermore that wonderful freshness of thought and originality that is the true mark of a classic.

Notes

1 For information and suggestions I thank Torsten Gårdlund, Jan Hoem, Eric Nicander (of the Wicksell Archive at Lund University), and Hans Zetterberg. For financial assistance, I thank Humanistiskt-Samhällsvetenskapliga Forskningsrådet (HSFR) in Stockholm, Sweden.

2 That these pamphlets are not read by non-Swedes is easily explained: until recently none has been available in translation (for an exception, see Wicksell 1997). The reason why contemporary Swedes do not read them can to some extent be explained by the fact that these pamphlets are only available in libraries since they have never been reprinted. Erik Lindahl reports that in the early 1950s there were plans to publish 'a volume with the suggested title *A Radical View of Society* [*Radikal samhällssyn*], which was to contain a limited sample of Wicksell's lectures and essays, on the population question and on economic and political questions' – but the volume never materialized (cf. Lindahl 1951: 197). The fact that Wicksell's social and political pamphlets have never been reprinted testifies to a neglect in Sweden of the work of Wicksell which is deplorable.

3 The first professorship in sociology in Sweden – actually in 'economics and sociology' ('*nationalekonomi och sociologi*') – was held by Gustaf Steffen (1864–1929), a friend of Wicksell. See, for example, Wisselgren 1997.

4 'Authors like Comte and Spencer were being translated into Swedish in the 1870s and 1880s. Comte was introduced into Sweden by Anton Nyström, who was a good friend of Wicksell's. Nyström founded the Positivist Society (Positivistiska samfundet) in 1879 and like Wicksell was a fervent Malthusian.

5 Gårdlund 1956: 88–9.

6 During the nineteenth century, sociology was explicitly normative; it covered an enormous area; and it was in general infused by the kind of spirit that is typical of non-professional and non-academic writers.

7 'A few years ago I went to visit a shoemaker, who lived in the outskirts of the town [Uppsala], not far from myself. When I opened the door to his lodgings, thick white smoke immediately rushed out and the air that hit my face was so chokingly unhealthy that for quite some time I tried to catch my breath. When I finally had gathered enough courage to enter, I found myself in front of a room, which was not much larger than my own student room, but which was literally full of people. In the middle of the room master himself and a helper sat working, and around him were all of his many children who were not in school. Finally, at the stove were his wife and a few other women who were busy working on a large sugar dough, of which they were going to make Danish candy to sell; and I can assure my listeners that the strong smell of burnt sugar, in combination with an equally strong smell of wet leather, especially when united with the necessary smell from so many people, combined into something to which my nose was not accustomed. I thus hastened to do what I had come for, as quickly as possible, but the memory that I brought along with me, when I left, will not so easily be forgotten. And yet, what I had seen was no extraordinary or unusual misery – just even, ordinary poverty' – Wicksell 1880: 9.

8 A special mention should be made of Wicksell's opinions on eugenics, which exemplify the fact that also a morally highstanding person like Wicksell could make grave moral errors. On March 21 in 1887 Wicksell gave a talk on euthanesia in which he advocated that mentally ill people and especially mentally ill children be killed. These ideas, it could be said, were typical of the days; and many honorable intellectuals and politicians agreed with Wicksell. Nonetheless, several people around Wicksell also protested against his ideas, including the people who later funded him at the Lorénian Foundation. See Wicksell's article, 'Om evtanasi (On Euthanesia)', *Socialdemokraten* March 23, 1887; see also Gårdlund 1956: 88, 117–18. A close reading of Wicksell's works shows that these ideas on eugenics stayed with him till his death. In 1912, for example, he published an article – in one of Sweden's largest and most respectable newspapers – which was entitled 'Racial Hygiene and the Two

Children-System' (*Dagens Nyheter*, January 25, 1912). Finally, the very last word of one of his very last writings is 'racial degeneration' ('rasförsämringen'; see Wicksell 1926: 61).

9 The first mention of the concept of an optimum population is to be found in Wicksell's work from the early 1890s, more precisely in *Value, Capital and Rent* (1893). It then reappears in various writings, for example, in Wicksell's 1910 pamphlet on population. See Wicksell [1893] 1954: 166; 1926: 49–52. Wicksell himself felt that he had made one, and only one, contribution to the study of population, and that was his idea of an optimum. See Wicksell's letter in response to Steffen's critique of his work on population, published as Manuscript Nr. 107 in Part II of Wicksell's unpublished manuscripts. For discussions of Wicksell's idea of the optimum, see, for example, Fong [1976] 1994. For a critique of Wicksell's position, see, for example, Friedman 1981.

10 'Skatternas fördelning en spegelbild af den politiska maktställningen' – Wicksell 1898: 3.

11 Wicksell also used the term 'intelligence capital' in his writings. In *Socialiststaten* he thus refers to 'the intelligence capital that is slumbering in the people'. See Wicksell 1913: 35.

12 Wicksell, as far as I know, never read anything by Max Weber or Emile Durkheim. It is somewhat surprising that while Wicksell knew the German economic scene very well and even published in *Archiv für Sozialwissenschaft und Sozialpolitik*, he never once refers to Max Weber. I have seen references in Wicksell's work to Robert Liefmann (Weber's student), Alfred Weber (Max Weber's brother) and Joseph Schumpeter (co-editor with Weber at the *Archiv*) – but never to Max Weber himself.

References

Dahmén, E. 1991 [1986] 'Schumpeterian Dynamics', pp. 126–35 in Bo Carlsson and Rolf G. H. Henriksson (eds) *Development Blocks and Industrial Transformation*, Stockholm: Almqvist & Wicksell International.

Fong, M. S. [1976] 1994. 'Knut Wicksell's "The Two Population Questions"', pp. 184–95 in Vol. 1 of John Cunningham Wood (ed.), *Knut Wicksell: Critical Assessments*, London: Routledge.

Friedman, D. (1981) 'What Does "Optimum Population" Mean?', *Research in Population Economics* 3: 273–87.

Gårdlund, T. (1954) 'Wicksell och åttiotalet', *Svenska Dagbladet* December 12.

—— (1956) *Knut Wicksell, Rebell i Det Nya Riket*, Stockholm: Bonniers.

Heckscher, E. (1926) 'Knut Wicksell död', *Dagens Nyheter* May 4.

Henriksson, Rolf G. H. (1991) 'The Facts on Wicksell on the Facts: Wicksell and Economic History', *Research in Economic History* 6: 33–50.

Jonung, L. (1988) 'Knut Wicksell's Unpublished Manuscripts: A First Glance', *European Economic Review* 32: 503–11.

Lindahl, E. (1951) 'Till hundraårsminnet av Knut Wicksells födelse', *Ekonomisk tidskrift* 51: 197–243.

Ohlin, B. [1926] (1994) 'Knut Wicksell (1851–1926)', pp. 20–8 in Vol. 1 of John Cunningham Wood (ed.), *Knut Wicksell: Critical Assessments*, London: Routledge.

Schumpeter, J. A. (1954) *History of Economic Analysis*, London: George Allen & Unwin.

Steffen, G. (1911) 'Professor Knut Wicksell 60 år', *Aftontidningen* December 19.

Svenskt biografiskt handlexikon (1906) 'Wicksell, Johan Gustaf Knut', pp. 720–1 in Vol. 2.

Wicksell, K. (1880) *Några ord om samhällsolyckornas viktigaste orsak och botemedel med särskildt afseende på dryckenskapen (Some Words about the Most Important Reason and Cure of Social Ills, with Special Emphasis on Drunkenness)*, Stockholm: Författarens förlag.

Wicksell, K. (1882) *Om utvandringen, dess betydelse och orsaker (On Emigration: Its Meaning and Causes)*, Stockholm: Bonniers Förlag.

146   *Richard Swedberg*

—— (1892) 'Den modärna arbetarerörelsen (The Modern Labor Movement)', *Eskilstuna–Kuriren* July 14–August 18.

—— (1893) 'Socialism eller individualism', *Fritänkaren* 5: 191–2.

Wicksell, K. (1895–6) 'Kvinnofrågan och statistiken (The Woman Question and Statistics)'. Manuscript # 68, pp. 1–13 in Part II of Torun Hedlund-Nyström and Lars Jonung (eds), *Knut Wicksells opublicerade manuscript*, unpublished manuscript; copy at Lund University Library.

—— (1898) *Den politiska rösträtten och skatterna (The Political Franchise and Taxation)*, Stockholm: Folkupplysningsföretagets förlag.

—— (1901) 'Om arfskatten (Concerning the Inheritance Tax)', *Ekonomisk tidskrift* 3: 75–119.

—— (1907) 'Krisernas gåta (The Enigma of Business Cycles)', *Statsøkonomisk tidsskrift (Norway)*: 255–84.

—— (1910) 'Professor Dr Knut Wicksell', pp. 99–131 in *Uttalanden i Emigrationsfrågan.* Stockholm: Kungliga Boktryckeriet.

—— (1913) *Socialiststaten och nutidssamhället. Några socialekonomiska betraktelser (The Socialist State and Contemporary Society: Some Observations on Social Economy)*, Verdandis småskrifter. Stockholm: Bonniers förlag.

—— (1917) 'Review of the Translation of John Stuart Mill, *On Liberty* by Hjalmar Öhrvall', *Forum* 4: 358–60.

—— (1922) 'Arbetslösheten, dess orsaker och botemedel (Unemployment: Its Causes and Cure)', *Arbetet* March 1.

—— (1925) 'Valutaspörsmålet i de skandinaviska länderna (The Monetary Problem of the Scandinavian Countries)', *Ekonomisk tidskrift* 27: 205–22.

—— (1926) *Läran om befolkningen (The Theory of Population)*. (2nd ed.) Verdandis Småskrifter. Stockholm: Albert Bonniers Förlag.

—— (1954) [1893] *Value, Capital and Rent*, trans. S. H. Frowen, London: George Allen & Unwin.

—— (1958) [1904] 'Ends and Means in Economics', pp. 51–66 in Erik Lindahl (ed.), *Selected Papers on Economic Theory*, London: George Allen & Unwin.

—— (1992) [1896] *Finanztheoretische Untersuchungen*, Reprint. Bristol: Thoemmes Press.

—— (1995) [1891] 'En sjelfbiografi, med porträtt (An Autobiography, with A Portrait)' in Hitishi Hashimoto, 'Biografiska och självbiografiska arbeten av Knut Wicksell samt 4 privatbrev', *KSU Economic and Business Review (Japan)* 22: 127–208.

—— (1997) (ed. Bo Sandelin) *Selected Essays in Economics*, Vol. 1. London: Routledge.

Wisselgren, P. (1997) 'Sociologin som inte blev av. Gustaf Steffen och tidig svensk socialvetenskap', pp. 75–116 in Lars Hansen et al (eds), *Sociologi i tiden*. Stockholm: Daidalos.

Zetterberg, H. [1967] 1997. *Sociological Endeavour: Selected Writings*, Stockholm: City University Press.

9 On Klant's methodology and the natural order in Adam Smith

Arnold Heertje

Mark Perlman has always shown a strong interest in the history and analysis of economic thought and in the methodology of economics (Perlman 1996). Therefore, it seems appropriate to devote this essay, meant to express my esteem for him, to the penetrating thought of the Dutch methodologist Joop Klant. It appears to be the more fitting as Mark reviewed Klant's work not too long ago and considered it to be 'an unusually wise and beautifully written book' (Perlman 1995: 227).

The Dutch economist J. J. Klant (1920–94) belongs to the ranks of methodologists who have a thorough knowledge of both the history of economic thought and the philosophy of science. Together with Blaug (1980) he was one of the few who not only adhered to Popper's ideas but also applied them to economics. In particular, he analysed whether economic theories can be falsified.[1] The negative outcome of his careful analysis led him to conclude that economists should be modest and that economic theories are not objective. His concept of natural order that can be traced back to John Locke and Adam Smith, illustrates his point of view. This essay is devoted to the development of his thinking on major methodological issues. It also presents a critical appraisal of his opinions.

Pieter Hennipman

Klant may be considered a pupil of Pieter Hennipman (1911–94), whose major contributions to economic theory, more particularly, welfare theory and the history of economic thought, became available to an international audience only after his death (Hennipman 1995). Those who have studied his debate with Mishan in the eighties and Blaug in the nineties will be impressed by his enormous knowledge of the literature, his careful analysis and the wisdom of his judgement. Although Hennipman is far less known in the world of economists than Tinbergen, there is little doubt that since 1938 he influenced Dutch economic thinking in a most subtle way through his teaching, his pupils and his writings. Among his pupils are J. S. Cramer, M. M. G. Fase, H. S. Houthakker, J. Pen, H. Theil, D. J. Wolfson and the present author. Klant defended his thesis *Rules of the Game for Economists*, with Hennipman as his supervisor, in 1972.

Hennipman always defended the Austrian subjectivistic approach to economics. He interpreted welfare in the subjectivistic sense of satisfaction of wants in so far as it depended on the allocation of scarce resources. He also brought to the fore the formal character of welfare, in the sense that the level of welfare is influenced by each component of the satisfaction of wants that is considered by consumers to belong to their satisfaction. Thus, economics is concerned with the economic aspect of social phenomena. The preservation of nature and the concern for the environment are within the realm of welfare in the broad sense and these themes are not outside the scope of economics. According to Hennipman, no norms for economic policy can be derived from economic theory, and welfare economics is part of economic theory. It follows that the Pareto optimum is an analytical device, not a value judgement. His methodology draws a sharp line between analytical statements and policy prescription based on value judgements, which cannot be derived from economic analysis.

Klant as an economist

Klant came relatively late to the methodology of economics and the history of economic thought, after a career in the financial world and a teaching position on monetary theory and banking at the University of Amsterdam. After he took his doctorate he became Professor of History and Philosophy of Economics at the University of Amsterdam. His book on the *Nature of Economic Thought* (1994) is the mature product of his prolonged thinking and research on the history of economic thought and methodology. Klant had a deep knowledge of the ideas put forward by economic thinkers and their relationship to historical backgrounds and personal circumstances. In his view there has always been a close connection between the existing economic order and economic theory. Throughout the world economics is not practised in the same way (Klant 1994: 21). Although economists in principle present theories as vehicles of analysis, on the basis of his study of the works of the major economists, he made the observation that economists not only want to explain, but also to change the world. In his own words, there is not a single great economist whose social and political ideas have remained unknown (Klant 1994: 18). By considering what economists as writers of pamphlets, books and articles, really do, by studying their actual behaviour, he found it more and more useless to discuss how economists should arrive at scientific conclusions and, instead concentrated on what they do. Ultimately, he also defends methodology as a social metascience that examines what economists as economists do (Klant 1994: 72). There is in this sense a close relationship between his analysis of the history of economic thought and his conception of methodology. As he puts it: 'Economists write history' (Klant 1994: 22), with Adam Smith as their master.

Klant looks at economics as a science, a philosophy and an art. Klant does not deal with the question in what sense economics is a science. For his purpose it makes little difference whether it is right or not to call economics a science (Klant 1994: 24). Klant notes the tendency of economists to compare economics with physics. Testing with a certain degree of confidence requires the stability of events in the domain under research. In physics the discovery of universal numerical constants like the constant of gravitation, the speed of light and the Planck constant is in this respect of great help. Compared with physics the major drawbacks of economics as a science are that it has no universal numerical constants and that insufficient supplementary hypotheses are available to reconstruct concrete events and situations theoretically. Without these drawbacks it would be possible to make specific economic models that are not interpretations but faithful reflections or *instances* of a basic theory. In fact, the economic researcher is confronted with these drawbacks and therefore faces a dilemma in the case of negative results of tests. If he concludes from the rejection of the specific model that it must be changed, he may still assume that the basic theory is true. If he concludes that the basic theory must be changed, he assumes that he has chosen the correct interpretation of an untrue theory (Klant 1994: 36). The recent development in physics, whereby the possibility of quarks being composed of particles is indicated in experiments, indicates that falsification of a specific model of the basic theory also seems to falsify the so-called standard model. Still, the problem of testing in economics does not differ fundamentally from that in physics, as in both cases a complex of hypotheses has to be tested. The difference is a matter of degree. However, the difference is important as in economics the great number of assumptions of interpretative specific models causes instability in the domain of economic research such that a clear choice of theory and model on the basis of tests becomes impossible (Klant 1994: 3).

Klant's discussion of economics as a philosophy concentrates on Popper's criterion of falsifiability as a logical property to distinguish between empirical science and metaphysical statements. Klant goes on with a thorough discussion of value laden-ness. It is here that Klant introduces the idea of *a natural order*. According to Klant every science has its natural order, which is not derived but postulated. In the natural sciences the hard core refers to ideas about the world as it is seen. In the social sciences they are concerned with a world that is not only seen but also *made*. The theory is not value-free as the core becomes an ideal: a picture of the world as it should be (Klant 1994: 49).

This vision is apparent in a passage in Adam Smith's *Theory of Moral Sentiments*: 'Human society, when we contemplate it in a certain abstract and philosophical light, appears like a great, an immense machine, whose regular and harmonious movements produce a thousand agreeable effects' (Smith 1759: 493; 1976a: 316). The natural order created by God is looked at as a beautiful machine. Adam Smith equates the desirable social order with the existing order of nature.

From his study of the history of economic thought Klant derives the observation that in economics the inclination to see in the world not only a state of affairs but also a goal, has always come clearly to the fore. The natural order of the economists was in many cases not only an attempt to represent what is in existence but also what had to be brought about. Although objectivity is an ideal, the fact of the matter is that theory is value-laden, due to the ideas about the way in which life must be lived creeping into the theory. In this sense, according to Klant, 'economics is in part an expression of how we want to live life' (1994: 51). This does not take away the obligation of immanent and empirical criticism. The ideal of the empirical scientific method still applies to the economist.

Just like every science, economics may also be regarded as an art in the sense of a result of creativity in 'which expression is given to a form of experience undergone' (Klant 1994: 58). Here, Klant is inclined to subscribe to the ideas of McCloskey, and as economics is based on the art of interpretation, it does not describe laws but tells plausible tales (McCloskey 1986: 65; 1994). In Klant's view a theory is not derived from facts, but consists of bold ideas through which facts, which are facts in the light of theories, are trapped. The economist is a historian who tells stories about today and tomorrow and he provides us with ideas on goals to be pursued and concrete knowledge about the past. According to Klant, economics is science, philosophy, art and history. I should add here, that this vision is based on the actual writings of economists over centuries and on their actual behaviour. Klant does not distinguish between good and bad economics or between good and bad economists. He just takes economists for granted and the yardstick for his judgement is what economists do. Still, he selected quite a number of economists from a vast set, which implies some kind of judgement as to relevance and quality. Let us now turn in more detail to his thoughts on methodology.

Economic methodology

In his *The Rules of the Game*, published in Dutch in 1972, Klant started out as a normative methodologist who, along the lines of logical positivism, looked for the criteria to be met by a system of knowledge in order for it to be an empirical science (Klant 1984). Against this background, Klant saw in Popper's work an attempt to save logical positivism. In view of the impossibility of confirming basic theories on the basis of empirical data, the idea is to restrict testing to the falsifiability of statements derived from theories (Popper 1959; 1963). In order to have empirical content, hypotheses have to be able to produce an anomaly.

Klant compares the logical properties of economic theories with those of physics. Falsifiability is, in Klant's interpretation of Popper's philosophy, a logical property of a theory that enables the scientific community to distinguish empirical science from both metaphysics and logical statements derived from a set of axioms. Klant illustrates that general, basic economic theories contain insufficient restrictions to warrant falsifiability. The *ceteris paribus* clause serves as a stand-in for the necessity otherwise of postulating the stability of parameters. The assumption of stability is implied in specific economic theories or models, which are restricted in time and space and contain numerical parameters. From these specific models, conditional predictions can be derived that are falsifiable. However, falsification of a specific theory does not lead to the falsifiability of basic theories, as it is always possible to refer to an *a priori* unspecified content of the *ceteris paribus* clause. The refutation of a specific interpretation of a basic theory does not refute the theory as an open structure (Papandreou 1958: 135). Only if it were feasible to put all possible interpretations of a theory to a test, could a basic economic theory be falsified in principle. The econometrician chooses from the set of interpretations, and although his choice never represents the basic theory, exactly, it is always a variant not excluded by the basic economic theory. In other words, by referring to changes in coefficients thought to be constant, all empirical results can be brought into line with the general theory. In the special case that the basic theory does not postulate stable relations, then the parameters of the theory are in fact variables which again make the theory unfalsifiable. Klant calls this the 'parameter paradox', which refutes Samuelson's claim of the falsifiability of his meaningful theorems (Samuelson 1947). The theorems, in fact, are not testable and only a rational discussion of their plausibility is possible. A recent example of such a discussion is Cohen's contribution on Samuelson's revealed preference theory (Cohen 1995). A strict application of Popper's normative methodology[2] would imply that economics is not an empirical science, falsification, not being possible. Klant does not want to draw this far-reaching and logical conclusion. According to Klant Popper's view cannot be other than a long-term metatheory. 'It represents an ideal' (Klant 1994: 38).[3] In his neo-Popperian view, economists are scientists because they *attempt* to construct falsifiable theories. In other words Klant is not a strict follower of Popper, but in his methodology highly inspired by Popper. I, therefore, follow Klant's own practice and regard him as a neo-Popperian.

In his *The Rules of the Game* Klant did not go as far as to conclude that economics cannot be value-free, but in his later work, his conclusion is very explicit: 'Social sciences are not value-free' (Klant 1994: 129). Many questions in social sciences are such that one cannot decide whether an answer is true or untrue, and this opens the door to extra-scientific values and makes these sciences value-loaded. With regard to economics, Klant gives the example of welfare theory, which in his view describes an idealized social decision-making system and therefore a potential ideal. 'If welfare theory is applied, it functions as an ideal' (Klant 1994: 130).

In reality, economists as scientists do not behave in a value-free manner, and therefore economic theories are not objective. Methodology taken in the descriptive sense of what economists really do allows Klant to declare 'political economy' to be far from value-free. Here again the actual role of Adam Smith is in the forefront of his thinking.

Klant started out as a normative and ended up as a descriptive methodologist. The shift of emphasis in Klant's thinking from normative methodology to positive history mainly goes back to Kuhn's *Structure of Scientific Revolutions* (Kuhn 1970). But just like Lakatos, he remains in the 'Popperian camp'.[4] His main message is that, logically, economists should be modest. As economists we know little, are not able to know much, and therefore we have little to offer to policy makers. The logical reasons for modesty should have a bearing on the psychological behaviour of the members of the profession.

One would expect economists to feel very uncertain, to express their doubts about their views and statements and to be very reluctant to give advice to policy makers. Klant, however, points out that the opposite is true. Economists tend to defend with great vigour hypotheses and theories which in a strict sense do not belong to empirical science. Almost without reservation or qualification these theories are made the basis of economic policy. In Klant's view economic theories start out as instruments of explanation and end up as vehicles of change.[5]

Adam Smith and the natural order

Klant's detailed exposition on the natural order starts with the question: 'Do economic theories propound laws which describe how events occur, or do they contain rules showing how we must behave?' (De Marchi 1988: 87; Klant 1994: 101). Although Klant acknowledges that economists start out as researchers trying to explain the world around them and bothering about the truth, they often represent themselves also as designers of a blueprint for changing the world. 'Adam Smith had left no doubt about the latter' (Klant 1994: 101). In his view they have in mind some interpretation of a natural order, made up of moral laws by which man should behave and society must be ordered (Klant 1994: 103). Klant's idea of a natural order goes back, in particular to John Locke (Hutchison 1988: 61–2). Locke described natural law both in a normative and positive sense. In a book on the emergence of political economy, written in Dutch, Klant refers to Locke's comparison of physical laws and natural laws. In both cases a natural order can be detected, according to which society and nature are ruled (Klant 1988: 79).

Despite these observations by Locke, the claim can be made that the idea of a natural order is most prominent in Adam Smith. To grasp this let us quote in full a passage from the *Wealth of Nations*, which is complementary to the previous quotation from *The Theory of Moral Sentiments*. 'Every man, as long as he does not violate the laws of justice, is left perfectly free to pursue his own interest his own way, and to bring both his industry and capital into competition with those of any other man, or order of men. The sovereign is completely discharged from a duty, in the attempting to perform which he must always be exposed to innumerable delusions, and for the proper performance of which no human wisdom or knowledge could ever be sufficient; the duty of super-intending the industry of private people, and of directing it towards the employments most suitable to the interest of the society.' (Smith 1776: 289; 1976b: 687.) For Adam Smith the natural order is the culmination of both the working of the social system as a beautiful and perfect machine and as the best of all possible worlds. Still, Smith is referring to *possible* human behaviour and in this sense to an ideal.

Klant's idea of a natural order always being present in the writings of the great economists, as a reflection of the natural order being part of economics as a science, can also be detected in modern writers like Walras and Schumpeter. Walras wanted to see the world organized according to his pure theory, because the perfect market mechanism produces a maximum of utility for each individual. The interest of Walras in the theory of exchange value and the idea of a general market equilibrium is motivated by the search for a rigorous demonstration of the superiority of free competition (Ingrao and Israel 1990) along the lines of Adam Smith. In Schumpeter's writings, even on innovation and democracy, methodological individualism plays an important role. Schumpter did present it as a fundamental hypothesis, which may be justified by logical analysis and empirical tests. But if testing is deficient in economics, method-ological individualism may then contribute to justification of the theory, which makes it part of the natural order *à la* Adam Smith. The implied natural order provokes economists to make value judgements, for example, that if politicians serve their own interest, they also serve the public interest best. We are left with a mixture of theoret-ical non-falsifiable statements, views, beliefs and attempts to change the world.

Critical observations

Klant's evolution from a normative to a descriptive methodologist coincides with his insight that Popper, instead of being a defender of logical-positivism, encouraged a breach by emphasizing the importance of the historical process of scientific development, theorizing, criticism and empirical testing. Looked at from this angle, one already encounters in Popper's work the seeds of both a normative and a descriptive methodology. For a long time a complex of hypotheses which is maintained and is no longer being tested, is called a paradigm by Kuhn and a hard core by Lakatos. In his valedictory lecture of 1986 Klant defines methodology as a form of research into the behaviour of the producers of ideas, and at the same time expresses his belief that patterns designed for physics by authors like Kuhn and Lakatos have, in fact obscured 'insight into what economists do' (Klant 1986: 6 and 10). Economists are concerned with a domain in which very great complexity and very rapid historical change exist, so that general economic theories cannot be made falsifiable by partial equilibrium analysis. A further complication is that 'history cannot be written in advance: knowledge changes, and its changes are not predictable, since it is logically impossible to foresee when a presently accepted hypothesis will be refuted, still less when a still unimagined conjecture might replace it'.[6] Klant still has one leg on the neo-Popperian side of the fence – in the sense that falsifiability as a logical property is a long-term ideal – but near the end of his life he puts much more weight on the leg that is on the other side of the fence, as he takes economists for what they are. Realists criticize economists not for what they do, but for what they *pretend* to do. This attitude is also evident in his book on *The Nature of Economic Thought* (Klant 1994), although he does not explicitly refer to a school of methodologists, called 'realists' or 'pluralists'.[7] In a certain sense methodological pluralism is also a form of descriptive methodology.

One cannot avoid feeling a certain tension between Klant as a normative and as a descriptive methodologist. In the normative setting he cares for the questions of whether economics is a science and whether economic theories are objective, but within the descriptive framework these questions leave him rather cold. Although he started to look for the proper rules of the game, in his later work, he more and more took for granted the conversation of economists in terms of theories, political views and methods of testing as a public game, meant for the economists themselves to enjoy. The game was also meant for society to enjoy, as long as solutions to problems are proposed and suggestions for change made. The rules of the game are among the features of the game itself, but are no longer studied and judged in a prescriptive sense. This subtle change in attitude comes even more to the fore in the value-judgement conflict, centred around his discussions of the natural order.

I cannot deny that Klant's opinion as a description of what is going on in economics seems to be justified. The choice with regard to economic policy from a set of non-falsifiable theoretical statements may be influenced by value judgements intended to change the world.[8] The preference for a public-choice theory, based on methodological individualism, may be determined by the wish to teach civil servants a lesson and to change or influence their behaviour, but it is in my view, going too far to look at these events as inevitable necessities. Economic theory structured by the rules of logic is still value-free, and the choice between, for example, two theories of monopolistic price formation may be influenced by a more or less hidden intention to change or influence the world in view of a natural order, but it is not a logical necessity.

The choice may also be based on the intention to explain economic phenomena in the best way, even if the fact that we are now aware of the possibility of failure of collective action is not the result of empirical criticism (De Marchi and Blaug 1991: 55). Certainly there is reason 'to explicate the values by self-examination and by unmasking others' (Klant 1994: 131), but it is an *a priori* to assume that there are always extra-scientific values involved. There is always room for full-fledged scientific integrity. Adam Smith would have been the first to recognize this. Klant's example of welfare theory is an interesting case to note. As has been illustrated by Hennipman in his very convincing papers, in which he dealt with the views of Mishan and Blaug, welfare theory belongs to positive and not to normative economics, and the Pareto-optimum and the Pareto-criterion are from a logical point of view, analytical devices, not normative criteria (Hennipman 1982; 1984; 1992; 1995). The Pareto-optimum in theory functions as a frame of reference for comparing actual allocations of resources with a Pareto-optimal allocation under different institutional settings. This may also be called an application of welfare theory, but there is no logical necessity to interpret Pareto-optimality as an ideal in a normative sense: it is simply an analytical yardstick for making comparisons. This consideration does not exclude the possiblity of promoting Pareto-optimality to a norm within the framework of economic policy. It is then an ideal chosen by the policymakers and becomes part of their natural order. Although in this sense Klant's observation that welfare theory is a potential ideal is not untrue, it is at the same time too suggestive. It may be used as a building block for political decision-making, but such an application is not part of positive economics. Those applications have to be distinguished from welfare economics as a theoretical structure.

What is true for welfare economics, is true for economics in general. Our discipline, in fact, is very careless in passing the frontier between purely theoretical analysis and normative statements, but this behaviour by no means springs from the rules of logic. In my view it remains of great importance both for the development of economics as a science and as a subject to be taught to distinguish value judgements from analytical statements. It can and therefore should be done.

Conclusion

Klant's contribution to the understanding of economic theory in general and to economic methodology, in particular, deserves the attention of the profession, based as it is on his thorough knowledge of philosophy and the history of economic thought and, above all, on his vast experience with the actual doings of economists in the monetary sphere and the domain of economic policy.

It is significant that his methodological approach does help to unmask hidden value judgements, implicit beliefs and ideological assumptions. It is understandable that his reading of so many utterances of economists in both the theoretical and practical sphere has made him rather cynical as to the capacity of economists to adhere to the rules of the game they have set themselves. Time and again, the pretensions of economists are at the centre of his critical attitude. It comes as no surprise that value judgements in what at first sight appears to be objective economic reasoning do in fact play a role and determine in a vague manner the mix of economic analysis and policy recommendations. In this respect the writings of the father of economics, Adam Smith, is really a case in point. Still, it would be going a bridge too far to conclude from the non-falsifiable character of economics that by logical necessity our discipline is not value-free. The introduction of value judgements may be an observable feature of the actual behaviour of economists both in speech and in writing, but this behaviour does not interfere with the logical neutrality of economic theory. Game theory, welfare economics, the theory of rational expectations, and so many other components of modern economic theory, are no less free from value judgements than quantum mechanics or chaos theory.[9]

In comparison with Mark Blaug, Klant is much more sceptical as to the question whether economists are able to practise what they preach. While for Klant the wrongdoing is a natural and hardly avoidable feature of economists, for Blaug it is just wrongdoing. Blaug still adheres to Popper's original question: What facts may lead us to reject a research program? A program that cannot take care of this question falls short in his view of a discussion at a scientific level. Klant's knowledge of the history of economic thought has driven him beyond Blaug by accepting like Caldwell (1982; 1994) that the rejection of research **programs** that do not meet the falsification criteria of acceptability has to be avoided.

Our criticism of Klant's methodology does not in the least diminish the theoretical importance and practical relevance of his appeal for modesty on the part of economists, whether they are working as theorists or advisers. In this sense Klant's view counteracts the plea by Hausman and McPherson (1996) to introduce moral reflection in economic theory.

Notes

1 Other methodologists who introduced Popper's ideas into economics often in a more critical sense are Hutchison (1938; 1977), Boland (1982), Caldwell (1982; 1994) and Hands (1988).
2 Compare Blaug, 'His [i.e. Popper's] methodology is thus plainly a normative one', Kuhn versus Lakatos or Paradigms versus research **programmes** in the history of economics, in *Method and Appraisal in Economics*, edited by S. J. Latsis, Cambridge 1990, p. 152.
3 A critical analysis of Popper's methodology is also to be found in Boland, *The Foundations of Economic Method*, London 1982, p. 170.
4 Blaug, p. 155.
5 A very positive judgement of Klant's work is made by Pheby, *Methodology and Economics*, 1988, p. 34.
6 B. J. Loasby, *The Mind and Method of the Economist*, Aldershot 1989, p. 28.
7 See B. J. Caldwell, *Beyond Positivism*, London 1982, revised edition, London 1994, pp. 245–52.
8 See for a discussion of these issues, H. Katouzian, *Ideology and Method of Economics*, London 1980, pp. 135–56; also V. J. Tarascio, Value Judgements in Economic Science, in *The Methodology of Economic Thought*, edited by W. J. Samuels, New Brunswick 1980, pp. 166–70.
9 See also P. J. O'Sullivan, *Economic Methodology and Freedom to Choose*, London 1987, pp. 126–7.

References

Blaug, M. (1980) *The Methodology of Economics*, Cambridge: Cambridge University Press.

Boland, L. A. (1982) *The Foundations of Economic Method*, London: Allen & Unwin.

Caldwell, B. J. (1982 and 1994) *Beyond Positivism*, London: Routledge.

Cohen, J. (1995) 'Samuelson's operationalist-descriptivist thesis,' *Journal of Economic Methodology* 2(1): 53–78.

De Marchi, N. (ed.) (1988) *The Popperian Legacy in Economics*, Cambridge: Cambridge University Press.

De Marchi, N. and Blaug, M. (eds) (1991) *Appraising Economics Theories*, Aldershot: Edward Elgar.

Hands, D. W. (1988) 'Adhocness in economics and the Popperian tradition,' in N. De Marchi, (ed.) *The Popperian Legacy in Economics*, Cambridge: Cambridge University Press.

Hausman, O. M. and McPherson, M. S. (1996) *Economic Analysis and Moral Philosophy*, Cambridge: Cambridge University Press.

Hennipman, P. (1982) 'Welfare economics in an impasse? Some observations on Mishan's vision,' *De Economist* 130: 457–63.

—— (1984) 'Normative or positive; Mishan's half-way house,' *De Economist* 132: 86–99.

—— (1992) 'The reasoning of a great methodologist: Mark Blaug on the nature of Paretian welfare economics,' *De Economist* 140: 413–45.

—— (1995) *Welfare Economics and the Theory of Economic Policy*, (ed.) Walker, D. Heertje, A. and van den Doel, J. Aldershot: Edward Elgar.

Hutchison, T. W. (1978) *On Revolution and Progress in Economic Knowledge*, Cambridge: Cambridge University Press.

Hutchison, T. W. (1988) *Before Adam Smith*, Oxford: Basil Blackwell.

Ingrao, B. and Israel, G. (1990) *The Invisible Hand*, Cambridge, Mass: The MITT Press.

Katouzian, H. (1980) *Ideology and Method of Economics*, London: MacMillan

Klant, J. J. (1984) *The Rules of the Game*, Cambridge: Cambrige University Press.

—— (1986) *What is Methodology?*, Amsterdam: Wigman Press.

—— (1988) *Het ontstaan van de staathuishoudkunde*, Leiden: Stenfert Kroese.

—— (1994) *The Nature of Economic Thought*, Aldershot: Edward Elgar.

Kuhn, T. S. (1970) *The Structure of Scientific Revolutions*, 2nd ed. Chicago: The University of Chicago Press.

Lakatos, I. (1970) *Falsification and the Methodology of Scientific Research Programmes*, in I. Lakatos and Musgrave, A. (eds) Cambridge: Cambridge University Press.

Latsis, S. J. (ed.) (1976) *Method and Appraisal in Economics*, Cambridge: Cambridge University Press.

Loasby, B. J. (1989) *The Mind and Method of the Economist*, Aldershot: Manchester University Press.

McCloskey, D. N. (1986) 'Economics as a Historical Science,' in W. V. Parker (ed.) *Economic History and the Modern Economist*, Oxford.

—— (1994) 'How economists persuade,' *Journal of Economic Methodology* 2: 15–32.

Papandreou, A. G. (1958) *Economics as a Science*, Chicago: J.B. Lippincott.

Perlman, M. (1995) 'Review of Klant's Book,' *The European Journal of the History of Economic Thought*, 227–9.

—— (1996) *The Character of Economic Thought, Economic Characters, and Economic Institutions*, Ann Arbor: The University of Michigan Press.

Pheby, J. (1988) *Methodology and Economics*, London: MacMillan.

Popper, K. R. (1959) *The Logic of Scientific Discovery*, London: Hutchinson.

Popper, K. R. (1963) *Conjectures and Reputations*, London: Routledge and Keagan.
—— (1972) *Objective Knowledge*, Oxford: Clarendon Press.
Samuels, W. J. (ed.) (1980) *The Methodology of Economic Thought*, New Brunswick: Transaction Books.
Samuelson, P. A. (1947) *Foundations of Economic Analysis*, Harvard: Harvard University Press.
Smith, A. (1759, 1976a) *The Theory of Moral Sentiments*, (ed.) Raphael, D. D. and Macfie, A. M. Oxford: Clarendon Press.
Smith, A (1776, 1976b). *An Inquire into the Nature and Causes of the Wealth of Nations*, volume 2, (ed.) Campbell, R. H. and Skinner, A. S. Oxford: Clarendon Press.
O'Sullivan, P. J. (1987) *Economic Methodology and Freedom to Choose*, London: Allen & Unwin.

Part V
Economic theory

10 Has capital theory been the victim of the quest for generality and rigor?

Samuel C. Weston

There is a tendency in the history of economic thought to exalt abstract theorists and to undervalue empiricists. This is understandable and probably inevitable. It would be relatively easy to explain Ricardo's economics to Plato. It would be almost impossible to discuss meaningfully with him much of the work of Malthus, Schmoller, or Kuznets. The more abstract and general economic theory becomes, the more universal is its potential audience. Empirical work is necessarily concerned with particular places and times. The greater the distance from the events being studied, the smaller will be the number of people having the interest or necessary knowledge to appreciate it. Adam Smith is remembered much more for his logical arguments than for his digression on silver or his account of the discouragement of agriculture in Europe after the fall of Rome.

While this tendency is understandable, it is potentially dangerous if it encourages economists to write for the ages, at the expense of having anything to say to their own time and place. The price of excess generality is vapidity.

There has been more than a tendency in the twentieth century for economists to value theoretical rigor. In practice this has meant translating economic ideas into the language of mathematics. The use of math in economics is unavoidable, if for no other reason than that given by Jevons (1871: 3–4). If economists are thinking about quantitative relations they are thinking mathematically, regardless of the symbols they use to express this. The question, therefore, is not whether to use mathematics. But one can raise questions about priorities. If an idea does not lend itself to mathematical interpretation should the idea be dropped from economics? Is the discipline to be defined by its tools, rather than its substantive notions?

No doubt it is desirable that one be correct in one's reasoning. But attaining certainty that one is correct is not costless. William James (1963: 204) described two rules that guide the seeker of knowledge: (1) we must know the truth, and (2) we must avoid error. These two mandates can conflict. The way to avoid all error is to believe nothing. The modern emphasis on theoretical rigor in economics suggests an approach to knowledge seeking that is dominated by the fear of being mistaken.[1]

After a promising beginning in *The Wealth of Nations*, there has been very little significant progress in capital theory.[2,3] After a great deal of largely fruitless struggle from the 1880s to the 1950s, both the concept of capital and capital theory appear to be on the verge of extinction. It is not as if we learned that capital is not important.

We may have learned that much that is significant about capital does not lend itself to mathematical expression.

Much of the difficulty has been with the concept of capital. Capital is a multi-faceted concept that points in several theoretical directions. Unlike many economic concepts, capital is not solidly grounded in common speech. Economists have been less hindered by traditional usage than in the case of most terms. Quite a bit of ink has been used trying to establish what exactly capital is. In the twentieth century this struggle became largely reduced to an effort to find an essence that can be represented as a scalar magnitude. The concept of capital seems to have been sacrificed to serve the require-ments of the production function. In mainstream microeconomics today capital is merely a generic input with a positive but usually diminishing marginal product.

In the first part of this essay I discuss the problem of defining capital in econom-ics. The first section of this part looks at the historical origins of the business con-cept. The second section of this part is a description of Adam Smith's capital theory. The third section examines seven strands of thought that are suggested by Smith's treatment of capital. The second part provides an interpretive summary of the three rounds of capital debates. As much of the quest for generality and rigor has taken the form of equilibrium analysis, the third part addresses the question of why economic equilibria are so important. This is followed by some concluding remarks.

Why has it been so difficult to define capital?

It is difficult, perhaps impossible, to define 'money' clearly and precisely. This has not presented an insurmountable problem to economists because virtually everyone has a concept of money, based on common experience, prior to studying economics.[4] When a sophomore says there is a guns-butter trade-off because a nation has only a limited amount of money, the economist understands why the student says this. Communication can thus proceed. One cannot, on the other hand, presume that 'capital' is a part of the normal working laic vocabulary.

Böhm-Bawerk (1959: 32), in his attempt to define capital, presented some explicit guidelines for settling terminological disputes. These were: (1) A usage must be log-ically sound. It must not contradict itself. (2) 'Terminological prodigality' cannot be tolerated. One does not want to waste a valuable term on a concept that already has a name, while other important concepts 'languish in nameless bastardy'. (3) The concept must be scientifically important and productive. (4) If there are no demands for change because of self-contradiction or lack of appropriateness, the oldest and most widespread usage from popular language should be used. This fourth point was echoed by Alfred Marshall (1920: 43) who thought that economics must 'endeavour to conform itself to the familiar terms of everyday life.'

The business concept

In the case of capital the closest we can come to established usage in popular language is the business understanding. In Medieval Latin (*c.* 1100–1300 A.D.) 'capital' was an adjective referring to the principal of a loan, as distinct from the interest or 'usury'. During this period, the term was transformed into a noun meaning an interest-bearing sum of money. In the fifteenth century St Bernardine of Sienna used the term 'capital' to indicate the productive character of a sum of money used by a merchant in trade (O'Brien 1920: 181). From a businessman's standpoint it is not especially important whether a net yield is coming from a money loan, a piece of land, a retail outlet, or a manufacturing operation. Hence the term was generalized to include all of a person's revenue producing assets, or in the words of Joseph Schumpeter (1954: 322–3), 'actual money, or claims to money, or some goods evaluated in money.' This generalization was conceptually helped along by the development of modern accounting practices, which enabled a collection of diverse assets to be expressed as single quantity.[5] This convenience created an ambiguity, which was to have repercussions in later capital discussions. Does capital refer to a sum of value or a collection of objects?[6] From a technical standpoint the objects are more important, but when it is necessary to quantify the collection of objects their heterogeneity leads to this being expressed as a sum of value.

Schumpeter (1954: 323) said, 'What a mass of confused, futile, and downright silly controversies it would have saved us, if economists had the sense to stick to those monetary and accounting meanings of the term instead of trying to "deepen" them!' J. B. Clark (1907: 352), in defending his 'pure' capital against the criticisms of Böhm-Bawerk, claimed to be using the business concept.

> if the view of capital expressed in my work deserves to be cast out of theoretical thought, it deserves to be cast out of practical thought as well; for all that this part of the theory aims to do is to put into explicit terms the idea of capital which has possession of business men's minds.

Should economists simply have stuck with the business concept? This may not be so easy. One thing to notice is that the business concept is not a thing or collection of things so much as it is a way of regarding these things. The things are regarded differently in different contexts. Capital might be thought of *financially* in order to arrive at a price when buying or selling a business. The sum of value also helps in the evaluation of the degree of success of an activity, for example, by allowing the calculation of a rate of return. Capital may also be viewed *technically*, for example when an entrepreneur conceives of a detailed plan to produce something in hopes of making a profit. In this context it may be necessary to think about numbers and types of machines, buildings, raw materials and so on. Capital and capitalism are intimately related to property rights. An entrepreneur's plans are merely daydreams unless there is a way to bring the various capital goods under his control, so that he might determine how they are to be used. Related, but not restricted to this *legal* dimension is the fact that regarding things as capital is a *conventional* way of thinking. The business concept of capital developed historically along with accounting practice. Using the rate of return to evaluate the performance of an endeavor is a convention that organizes diverse individuals with different personal objectives. Both capital values and the technical arrangements of capital goods are often elements of a *strategic* way of thinking.

Economists are not generally thinking *as* businessmen, but *about* them. One approach to capital theory would be to think about how businessmen think about

capital. This is vaguely suggested by Clark's remark above although he did not follow this approach. Given the many dimensions to how businessmen might think
about capital, such an approach could lead in several directions. Both Israel Kirzner
(1966) and Ludwig Lachmann (1978) have written books stressing the importance
of plans in capital theory.[7]

The other approach, which has been much more prominent, has been to disregard
the fact that capital is a way of regarding certain objects, and to focus on the objects
themselves. The most common use of capital in the twentieth century has been as an
argument in a production function. While the formally represented mathematical
production function is a relatively recent development, one could safely assume that
the older writers had in mind an implicit quantitative relationship along the lines of
'more capital, more output'. But what does 'more capital' mean?

One should note that, at least up to a point, this is no more a problem than asking
what does 'more labor' mean? It is probably true that we are more comfortable with
abstract concepts when they seem to represent stylized facts. To use the concept of
homogeneous labor, measured, say, in man-hours, raises few eyebrows. Homogeneous
labor stands in for presumably observable unskilled labor. But of course even unskilled
labor is not a homogeneously employed generic input. It is fairly obvious, for instance
watching the employees at McDonalds while waiting for one's lunch, that labor is generally employed in teams. That is to say, that labor operates in a structure of complementary skills.[8] Even the most unskilled laborer quickly picks up some specialized skills,
such as answering the telephone, digging, sweeping, or toting things, through on-the-
job training. These skills are virtually always used in combination with other skills, such
as carpentry, repair, salesmanship and so on, as part of a larger strategic plan. Skills and
abilities differentiate individual persons, with regard to their potential contributions to
a business plan, just as surely as do the designs of machines, though perhaps most people are more flexible in their range of possible uses than most machines.

The struggles in twentieth century capital theory have largely been concerned
with giving an unambiguous meaning to the phrase 'more capital'. The lesson, which
may or may not have been learned, is that this cannot be done without reducing capital to an imaginary beneficent entity. Capital theory is thus reduced to hypothesiz-
ing about what would be the case were some such entity to exist.

Adam Smith's capital theory

It can be argued that Turgot[9] deserves credit for *inventing* capital theory, but it was
Smith's version of similar ideas that gained wide circulation in economics. Smith was
in Schumpeter's sense[10] the *innovator*, which is to say the one who made it happen.
The Wealth of Nations was so influential in the area of capital theory that at least one
disciple said, 'The theory of capital is new, and entirely of Adam Smith's creation'.[11]
It is because of the widespread and profound impact of Smith's ideas that he should
be regarded as the source of capital theory.

According to Smith, capital is one of the two pillars (the other being exchange)
that are needed to support the division of labor. Division of labor makes labor more
productive, hence causing a nation to be more prosperous. The role of capital in

making a nation richer is articulated in Book II of *The Wealth*. Capital is defined as that part of a person's 'stock' that is reserved for the purpose of earning further revenue. Capital is divided into two major parts. 'Circulating' capital consists of goods purchased for resale, goods meant to maintain productive labor, raw materials and money for trade purposes. 'Fixed' capital refers to factories and equipment, farm animals, and improvements in the land (Smith 1937: 262–3).

There are three reasons why the division of labor requires a prior accumulation of capital, and why a growing nation needs an increasing capital. Specializing in a particular task implies sacrificing the time spent attending directly to one's own needs. The means of subsistence are obtained by exchanging the fruits of one's labor for the fruits of other people's labor. However, there is a gap between the application of labor and the emergence and sale of the product. Capital is needed to sustain workers during this interval.

A second reason why capital must exist for division of labor to proceed is the increased productivity of specialized labor. Since a given number of specialized workers can produce more than the same number of unspecialized workers, the former need more materials per capita upon which to work. These materials must be amassed beforehand if the workers are not to be idle.

Finally, division of labor tends to lead to the introduction of machinery. Specialization leads to familiarity with the job, which leads to analysis and improvement. One sort of improvement is labor-saving equipment. The construction of such equipment must be performed in advance of it becoming productive. Since resources are used in the making of a piece of machinery, this requires a prior accumulation of capital (Smith 1937: 259–61).

Capital is the result of parsimonious lifestyles. Smith distinguishes between 'productive' and 'unproductive' labor. Productive labor adds value to a thing that it works on, while unproductive labor does not. Agricultural and manufacturing workers are productive, while menial servants are not. Wealth used to support servants merely evaporates. People with profligate lifestyles, i.e., rich idle landlords, tend to use more of their wealth in the support of unproductive laborers, hence they destroy or at least do not accumulate capital (Smith 1937: 314–22).

Some important capital-related ideas found in or suggested by Smith

Smith's 'capital theory *per se*' could be summarized in two lines. Capital aids prosperity by supporting the division of labor. Capital is accumulated through parsimonious behavior. The phrase 'capital theory' has come to refer to a broader cluster of ideas, or what we might call 'theories involving capital'. A number of these are suggested by ideas found in *The Wealth of Nations*.

It is possible to improve the yield of an activity by applying additional resources transferred from some other activity[12]

According to Smith (1937: 260) improved yield results from further dividing labor, and the ability to do this is in proportion to the amount of capital that has been accumulated. Modern economists may not think of it in these terms. In fact they may think of capital's contribution exclusively in terms of the productive powers of machinery; but Smith's idea is consistent with capital having a positive marginal product. That the marginal product of capital is positive is the one fundamental idea about capital to survive even the most abstract treatments. In Book IV, Chapter IX, Smith (1937: 650) criticizes both the 'mercantile' and the 'agricultural' systems for trying to 'draw towards a particular species of industry a greater share of the capital of society than what would naturally go to it'. Smith's complaint is that this causes the capital to support a less advantageous industry at the expense of a more advantageous industry. Thus Smith implicitly recognized that there is an opportunity cost to using capital for some particular purpose. This proposition is also fundamental and is in most theories involving capital. The creation of new capital regardless of its particular intended purpose requires the sacrifice of consumption. None of these ideas have been especially controversial. The question is whether they are the only things about capital worth considering.

Capital is required to support the division of labor

George Stigler (1976: 1209) judged the division of labor to be one of Smith's ideas that didn't work.[13] This seems a bit extreme. Like many things, division of labor has disappeared from modern micro theory, if we take intermediate and advanced textbooks as evidence. Yet it is hard to believe that this is not part of economists' thinking. It is of course hazardous to presume to know what other people think. My understanding of the process of economic education is that intermediate microeconomic students receive the tools and concepts that allow them, along with additional doses of math, to understand the abstract general equilibrium models of the advanced courses. The point of the general equilibrium models is to show how a society of specialists can be coordinated through a system of market-generated prices. The name 'Invisible Hand Theorem' applied to the claim that competitive equilibria are Pareto optimal may do violence to Smith's ideas. Nonetheless this does imply that general equilibrium analysts do still see themselves working in the field that Smith cleared. More to the point, without division of labor general equilibrium models makes no sense. What would the people be exchanging?

The idea that there are benefits in specializing to one's comparative advantage and exchanging is alive and well in international trade theory. This is a refinement and extension of division of labor.

One expression of Smith's idea that was influential well into the twentieth century was Böhm-Bawerk's 'Austrian capital theory'. Early in the *Positive Theory of Capital* Böhm-Bawerk (1889: 18–19) calls attention to the benefits of 'roundabout' production. A person can try to catch fish with his bare hands; or he can devote some time to constructing a fishing rod, a net, or a boat. The latter options require spending some time on activities that will not directly yield any fish to eat. When they are completed they will help the person to be a more effective fish-catcher. Thus spending time making a boat is a roundabout way of catching a fish. The more roundabout the method, the more goods will exist, such as partially completed boats or nets, that are removed in time from being able directly to serve human wants.[14]

That more roundabout production processes were more productive, and that more roundabout processes required more capital, viewed as objects removed in time from serving consumer purposes, led to the idea that the 'period of production' could be used to indicate the capital intensity of a process. This is what many people think of as 'Austrian capital theory'. Knut Wicksell followed Böhm-Bawerk in using the average period of production in *Value, Capital and Rent* (1893), but he gave it up for the forward-looking 'period of investment' in his *Lectures* (1934 [1901–6]). The period of investment was used and defended as late as 1941 by Friedrich Hayek in *The Pure Theory of Capital*. By the 1960s the idea of using time as a proxy for capital intensity was called 'an inspired simplification that did not work' (Solow 1964: 11).

While the average period of production may have been a new way of representing the ideas, Böhm-Bawerk's approach to capital did not diverge significantly from Smith. Roundaboutness results from division of labor. In Smith's pin factory, where ten persons perform specialized operations such as drawing wire, straightening it, cutting it, etc., each specialized task produces a quantity of intermediate goods. The more subdivided the jobs become, the more 'goods in the pipeline' that will accompany the production of a finished good. Smith's pin factory could easily be used to illustrate Böhm-Bawerk's roundaboutness. This should not be surprising as Böhm-Bawerk (1959: 23) himself insisted that his capital concept 'did not represent so much of an alteration as a more precise formulation of Smith's concept of social capital.'

Capital is an intertemporal link

In Smith's theory capital must be gathered in advance. If workers are to have adequate means of subsistence, tools, and raw materials, someone must have accumulated them before hand. Thus, decisions made in the past restrict present possibilities, just as present decisions will constrain the future.

Crucial to capital being a constraint is the notion of rigidity. Objects do not serve all purposes equally well, and they generally cannot be transmogrified costlessly into other objects. Hence decisions to commit resources to particular activities impose a structure on capital. Schumpeter (1954: 633) notes that the most fundamental capital structure can be found in Smith's distinction between the part of stock meant for consumption and the part intended to generate further revenues.

A capital-related example of past decisions imposing a constraint on present possibilities is the Wages Fund. In the caricature version of this idea[15] the average wage was determined by the ratio of labor demand to labor supply, where the former was given by the size of the wages fund, and the latter by the population. In the mid-nineteenth century a controversy arose concerning the possibility that labor unions could improve wages for all workers. The conventional wisdom putatively backed by the English classical economists was that they could not, because the total amount available for wages was pre-determined by past savings. Since the wages fund was at any moment fixed by past decisions, any particular group getting a larger share did so at expense of other workers. John Stuart Mill's 'Recantation'[16] in which he admitted that the wages fund was somewhat flexible within limits, by undercutting the prestige of classical economics, helped open the door for better microeconomic wage theories.

The newer theories, such as that of J. B. Clark (1899) argued that capital acts to 'synchronize' production and consumption, so that workers are paid out of current output, not accumulated capital. This is a paradigmatic example of the mischief that can occur when economists confuse their models with reality. The apparent synchronization of production and consumption is something that can only occur in equilibrium. Any disequilibrating change will disrupt it. This point was made decisively by Frank Taussig (1896: 17–20) in his attempt to salvage what was right about the wages fund. Even if workers are paid out of current output, the level and composition of current output depends on decisions made in the past. It would be impossible, for example, for capitalists to suddenly double real wages. The composition of output would have to be changed from luxury consumption and capital goods to more workers' consumption goods. This would require a different composition of fixed and variable capital, which could take several years to change. Paper available today depends on wood pulp that was made perhaps a week ago. The wood pulp may depend on trees that were harvested and shipped months earlier. The harvesting and shipping of trees depends on decisions to plant trees that might have been made years ago.[17]

Workers appear to be paid out of current output in Clark's model because all maintenance and planning necessary to maintain the current situation is assumed to take place automatically. Production and consumption are synchronized, but this is only a logical implication of his 'pure' capital, which is permanent by definition. If capitalists are permitted the freedom to make decisions concerning the maintenance or composition of capital, their choices can disrupt the apparent synchronization. The wages fund was a bad *theory* of wages. This does not imply that capital is not a *constraint* on real wages.

The notion of capital as a structure becomes considerably more complicated with the realization that the capability of an object to serve different purposes varies considerably from object to object and purpose to purpose. Ludwig Lachmann tries to express this idea with the term 'multiple specificity'. Drawing on Carl Menger's (1871: 58–63, 84–7) discussion, Lachmann asserts that, 'complementarity is of the essence of capital use,' and that 'heterogeneous capital resources do not lend themselves to combination in any arbitrary fashion'. Multiple specificity communicates the idea that capital goods do not generally work together in the manner expressed by rigid coefficients, but neither can the situation be characterized by Clark/Knight perfect malleability (Lachmann 1947: 199).

Different capital goods can be used in combination with other capital goods for various purposes with varying degrees of success. Rather than this information being given as data, it is an important function of the entrepreneur to discover combinations that produce desirable results. Entrepreneurs' decisions result in capital combinations that, connected through market interactions (including financial asset markets), form the structure of capital for a society. According to Lachmann, 'The Theory of Capital is, in the last resort, the morphology of forms which this pattern assumes in a changing world' (1956: 3–4).

In Lachmann's picture of the world, entrepreneurs make plans in which capital goods are intended to be used in complementary ways to produce desired outcomes.

Owing to inevitable unforeseen contingencies, the plans rarely turn out as envisaged. Responding to this, entrepreneurs reshuffle their capital goods, always working within the restrictions imposed by multiple specificity. Lachmann (1956: 37) thinks that the 'most egregious error' of equilibrium capital theories is that they necessarily neglect the malinvestment that is inevitable and significant in an uncertain world. It is not satisfactory to assume that non-optimal combinations have been weeded out by competition, because to Lachmann (1947: 10) 'the regrouping of existing capital resources in response to unforeseen change' is the most important topic in capital theory. This allows us to explain the fact that in older cities we see "merchants" palaces turned into hotels, the former stables now garages, and the old warehouses which have become modern workshops' (Lachmann 1956: 38).

Capital helps to explain the distribution of income

In Book I, Chapter VI, Smith resolves the price of a good into payments – wages, rent, and profit – to the factors of production. This serves as the basis for a scheme, the triad (sometimes a tetrad) of productive factors that is still often used as a framework for distribution theory. There are various ways that capital enters this scheme. The wages fund was one way that capital was used historically as part of a theoretical explanation of wages. In conventional microeconomic wage theory capital is significant as a determinant of the marginal productivity of labor. Capital also plays a role in explaining interest.

Economists have not yet arrived at a single unified theory to explain interest. Probably the leading idea, especially as translated by Irving Fisher (1930), is Böhm-Bawerk's claim that interest is fundamentally due to positive time preference. But J. B. Clark's (1899) argument that interest is due to the productivity of capital is also prominent, and these have never been reconciled. Moreover, it is not obvious how these microeconomic theories fit into the Keynesian monetary explanation widely used in macroeconomics.

Further complication arises from the relationship between interest and profit. In Book I, Chapter VI of *The Wealth* the price of a good is resolved into wages, rents, and profits. In Book I, Chapter VII, the natural price of a good is defined as a price sufficient to bring a good to market, which is to say a price that covers the wages, rents, and profits, where these are understood to be at their 'average or ordinary' levels. The reason that 'the quantity of every commodity brought to market naturally suits itself to the effectual demand' (the amount demanded at the natural price), is that deviations of the actual price from the market price cause wages, rents, and/or profits to vary from their normal rates. These variances will cause resources to be brought into or out of the production of the good in question, thus adjusting the amounts brought to market. So Smith seems clearly to have in mind a distinction between 'economic' and 'normal' profit, since his story hinges on this. In Chapter IX of Book I Smith connects profit to interest, writing, ... as the usual market rate of interest varies in any country, we may be assured that the ordinary profits of stock must vary with it ...'. In modern terms this could be read as saying that the rate of accounting profit varies with the interest rate.

The idea that the cost of an action is the value of the best opportunity sacrificed when that action is taken is a logical implication of a forward-looking subjective notion of value. Most modern Neoclassical economists view interest as a cost, rather than as part of profit, even if it is received in the form of a residual after contractually obligated costs have been paid. Schools of thought that have rejected the notion that value is subjective, such as the Marxian and post-Keynesian schools, have tended to ignore the distinction between economic and normal profit.

If one is willing to allow the concept of human capital into the discussion, then interest also can help explain wage differences. In Book I, Chapter X, Smith tries to account for different wages (and rates of profit) in different employments. He starts with an arbitrage argument. The sum of advantages and disadvantages in every employment should be equal or tending toward equality, at least in a world of perfect mobility and liberty. In equilibrium, wages should be higher or lower depending on what is needed to compensate for the other disadvantages or advantages of a particular employment. The second case Smith discusses is 'the easiness and cheapness, or the difficulty and expense of learning the business.' This is the principle that Smith uses to explain the difference in wages between skilled and unskilled labor. It serves nicely as a platform upon which can be built a theory that explains wage differences in terms of a normal rate of return on varying investments in human capital.

Capital is a social relationship

Smith's resolution of the natural price of a good into three parts – wages, rents, and profits – corresponded to the social classes in the Britain of his day. Wages are paid to a laboring lower class, profits go to a capitalist middle class, and rents belong to the land-owning nobility. When David Ricardo (1951: 5) asserted that determining the laws that regulate the distribution of the produce of the earth among the classes was the principal problem of political economy, it was a natural step to try to solve this by looking for an explanation of these factor payments. This framework is still followed in today's 'functional' approach to distribution, though it has lost much of its class significance in journeying across the Atlantic.

Karl Marx, in trying to explain the totality of historical social change, dared a much broader project than most economists have done.[18] Each Marxian epoch is based on a mode of production. The correspondence between control of a factor of production and social class has special significance to Marx in defining each particular epoch, and thus also in understanding the processes that cause each epoch to self-destruct and give way to the next (Marx 1977: 389).

Superficially Marx's capital is very similar to Smith's. It consists of 'raw materials, instruments of labor, and means of subsistence of all kinds' (Marx 1977: 256). However, Marx's capital has another dimension. It is a social relationship (Marx 1977: 256; 1894: 195). It is the means by which capitalists are able to extract surplus value from workers.

For specifically capitalist exploitation to occur certain conditions must exist. Labor must be a commodity for sale on the market. The laborer must be in a position where he is obliged to offer his labor for sale (Marx 1867: 165). The laborer's efforts must be under the control of the capitalist. The product of the laborer must legally be the property of the capitalist (Marx 1867: 180). Since in a capitalist system labor is a commodity just like sugar (Marx 1977: 249), the market or exchange-value of labor will tend to equal its cost of production. The cost of producing labor is equal to the cost of subsistence, plus the cost of training, plus the cost of maintaining a family so that worn out workers can be replaced (Marx 1977: 255). The capitalist gives the exchange-value of labor to the laborer. He receives the use-value of the labor. The worker might be able to create a product equal to the cost of production of labor in half a day. Everything he makes during the rest of the day is surplus value. It is the property of the capitalist (Marx 1977: 258; 1867: 181–92). Why does the worker continue to produce profit for the capitalist after he has created his own subsistence?

The power of the capitalist to insist that workers remain on the job beyond the time needed to produce their maintenance wage arises from the fact that they control the means of subsistence. This is the social relationship that makes profit possible. The impact of the accumulation of capital on the rate of profit is in turn a key dynamic element in the self-destruction of capitalism.

Capital has a normative dimension

By connecting capital accumulation to national prosperity, and by finding the source of capital to be parsimonious behavior, Smith ratifies the virtue of thrift. He compares spending capital for consumption to perverting the 'the revenues of some pious foundation to profane purpose' (1937: 322). In a similar vein Joan Robinson (1956: 33) writes, 'The distinction between capital and income is rooted in moral ideas.' She argues that the existence of a special category of objects that must not be consumed, lest survival be endangered, comes to us from our peasant ancestors.

> The morality of the peasant, who gathers his crops according to the rhythm of the seasons, is to put back into the soil what he takes out of it, and to set aside seed from each harvest, so as to preserve productive capacity for the future, not only for his lifetime, or his children's lifetime, but for the future as such ...
>
> (1956: 34)

This peasant morality manifests itself in the modern *rentier*, who feels free to spend his income, but experiences guilt if he spends his capital (1956: 35). The entrepreneur is imbued with this morality in extreme form, since he sees the purpose of income as being the expansion of his business, and he feels guilty about consuming any income (1956: 39–40). The moral compulsion to preserve capital could be viewed as underpinning the permanent capital of Clark and Knight.

As a determinant of income distribution capital is part of the discussion of whether income is distributed justly in a market system. Moral judgments may be viewed as applications of moral principles to presumed sets of facts. This implies that there are always two questions involved with a specific moral judgment. The 'normative' question concerns what is morally desirable. The 'positive' question is whether one has a grasp of the facts of the case. At least since the time of John Locke, economists have been trying to figure out exactly why interest is paid. Without such an understanding, moral judgments concerning interest are merely expressions of broad moral principles, such as 'exploitation is wrong.' The factual question is whether earning interest necessarily involves exploitation.

Both Böhm-Bawerk and Clark wanted to show that workers were not exploited in a capitalist system. More specifically both argued that workers are paid exactly what they produce. Böhm-Bawerk claimed that workers are paid the full present value of their output. Clark asserted that workers receive their marginal product. In arguing this way both economists appealed to a Lockean labor justification of acquisition.

Capital accumulation results from saving. If the moral significance of labor is in its disutility, then refraining from consumption, or abstinence, might be viewed as the unpleasant duty performed by the capitalist that corresponds to labor. Nassau Senior (1836: 87–95) advanced this theory. Senior's idea drew the scorn of socialist critics.

> Interest is the 'wage of renunciation'! Felicitous word, priceless word! Your European millionaires are ascetics. Like Indian penitents they stand, like stylites on one foot atop a pillar, and pale of mien they lean over to stretch out an arm to the populace, holding forth a plate to receive the wage of their renunciation! In their midst, and towering high above their fellow penitents, playing its role of chief penitent and leading renouncer, behold the house of Rothschild! So this is how society is organized! And to think I've been blind to it all this time![19]

While generally avoiding the question of the moral status of interest, modern economists commonly treat interest as the opportunity cost of investing. Whether this suffices to justify interest is very similar to the medieval question of whether to accept *lucrum cessans* as a justification for receiving interest on a loan.

Capital is property. The phenomenon of capitalists receiving interest is intimately bound up with the institutions of capitalism, such as private property rights and enforcement of contracts. Apart from whether capital owners are entitled to interest because of some sort of suffering involved in the accumulation or use of capital, there are positive and normative issues concerning these institutions.

Whether an object is capital or not is determined subjectively by the capitalist

Smith's (1937: 262) conception of capital is that part of a person's total wealth from which he 'endeavours' to derive a revenue. This is distinct from the part of wealth that is 'reserved' for his immediate consumption. This suggests that what is to be capital depends crucially on the intentions of the owner. This subjectivity was recognized explicitly by John Stuart Mill (1965: 56) who said, 'The distinction between Capital and Not-capital, does not lie in the kind of commodities, but in the mind of the capitalist – in his will to employ them for one purpose rather than another.'

Böhm-Bawerk (1889: 22–3) thought the economics profession was 'struck by a second confusion of tongues' when it came to defining capital. He devoted a chapter of the second edition of *The Positive Theory of Capital* (1959, Chapter 3) to a survey of capital conceptions that had found their way into the economic literature. If one studies this array with Mill's assertion in mind, it seems that there are not so many different conceptions of capital as there are different decisions as to which items to classify as capital. Marshall (1920: 648) wrote, 'things relating to man's actions can never be classified with precision on any scientific principle.' While it is possible to construct lists based on some classification scheme, for example, to guide policemen or customs inspectors, 'such lists are frankly artificial'. Marshall (1920: 60) does offer factories, raw materials, food, clothing, and shelter held by employers for the use of employees as 'conspicuous elements' of capital, but this listing is for the purpose of *illustrating* rather than defining the concept.

It is somewhat surprising that Böhm-Bawerk should have tried to objectify capital. Böhm-Bawerk generally followed Carl Menger's lead in value theory. Menger's value theory begins with a subjective notion of goods. Menger's (1976: 52) concept of a 'good' depends on people having a desire and the knowledge that the characteristics of an object allow it to be part of a plan for the fulfillment of that desire. There is no reason for a capital good to be different. This implies that the concept of capital, especially one focusing on capital goods, is inseparable from individuals' plans.[20] An important part of what makes a good capital is that an individual regards it as such, as Mill had already recognized.

A reason for Böhm-Bawerk's (1889: 65–6) elaborate attempt to list, under seven categories, all the things that are included in capital would be to do a detailed empirical study. There is no sign that Böhm-Bawerk had any such project in mind. While one might have expected Böhm-Bawerk to develop an Austrian capital theory, his objectification of capital could be called the antithesis of Austrian theory. What he presented was in fact the Classical theory with a peculiar variation – the average period of production as a measure of the capital intensity of a process.

The debates about capital

Böhm-Bawerk felt it necessary to establish a single concept of capital that would be universally embraced by the economics profession. J. B. Clark could not abide this because universal adoption of Böhm-Bawerk's capital would rule out Clark's capital. This led to a twenty year debate between Böhm-Bawerk and Clark[21] which covered topics such as the role of time in explaining interest, the use of the period of production to represent the quantity of capital, and the advance versus synchronization views of the relationship between production and consumption. The underlying issue was the concept of capital. Clark (1899, Chapter X) insisted that a distinction must be made between 'pure' capital and capital goods, and that both concepts belonged in economic analysis. Pure capital is permanent. Capital goods have finite lives. It is the function of capital goods to be used up and destroyed in production. Pure capital is perfectly mobile. The capital that used to be invested in the New England whale industry is now embodied in the textile mills. Böhm-Bawerk (1895a: 127, 130) called Clark's pure capital a 'mystical conception' and an 'elegant abstraction'.

Whatever the shortcomings of Clark's conception, he did at least recognize that there is more than one aspect to capital, and that to limit capital theory to one of these would unduly narrow the scope of the theory. In the 1930s Frank Knight debated Friedrich von Hayek, Nicholas Kaldor, Fritz Machlup, and Kenneth Boulding.[22] The issues were much the same, but now Knight was trying to establish hegemony for Clark's concept of capital. Fritz Machlup (1935: 578) complained, 'Professor Knight has proposed to discard as worthless some tools of economic analysis which I consider indispensable for successful handling of certain problems.' This remark should have been taken more seriously. That it was not was probably due to another factor that was operating.

Clark's *Distribution of Wealth* is, among other things, a record of someone discovering the pleasures of static equilibrium analysis. Clark is a non-mathematician making mathematical discoveries. Perhaps for this reason there is a certain confusion. Whatever the defensibility of the permanence of pure capital as a 'stylized fact', Clark needs some way of locking out changes in capital in order to locate his equilibria. Rather than using Marshall's device of a time frame in which changes are assumed not to occur, Clark builds this freedom from change into his definition of capital.[23] More than this concept, it is Clark's analysis of static equilibria, and the rudimentary production function that he used to do this, that carried the day.

The formally represented production function requires that capital be reduced to a scalar magnitude. Nicholas Kaldor's (1937: 231–2) statement that, 'The purpose of the "investment period" is to reduce the production function to two variables,' indicates that by the 1930s the debate had been reduced to the issue of which particular quantity to reduce it to. Joan Robinson's (1953) complaint that economists lack a unit with which to represent capital in production functions reminded economists that this issue had never been resolved, and started the Cambridge Controversies.[24] The inability to come up with a suitable unit led to capital becoming a generic input.

The production function does very little except to represent the idea that marginal products of inputs are positive and usually diminishing. This has some significance in the Neo-classical structure since diminishing marginal products provide the underlying reason for supply curves having positive slope and demand for labor curves having negative slope.[25] Apart from the question of whether diminishing returns is a very good explanation for these, the other thing to notice is that they are integrated in a structure of equilibrium relations. The quest for generality and rigor has taken the path of focusing almost entirely on equilibria. One cannot help but suspect that this has something to do with the fact that it is relatively easy to locate equilibria with mathematical tools.

Why is equilibrium so important?

The substantive reason for bothering with equilibria is that they are the outcome of arbitrage processes. Microeconomics makes no sense unless one understands that virtually all the equilibria are generated by arbitrage. A broad definition of arbitrage is: a process wherein the existence of an opportunity for a net gain results in behavior that causes that opportunity to disappear. *Equilibrium* is part of the description of an arbitrage process. A complete description would include: (1) agents and their behavioral rules; (2) an environment that, along with the agents propensities, defines the opportunities; (3) negative feedback – the impact of the agents' actions on the opportunities; and (4) equilibrium – a situation in which there is no more gain to be had by further actions by the agents.

The attractiveness of equilibria as objects of study comes from the persuasiveness of arbitrage as an explanation for certain patterns, and from the relative ease with which certain equilibria can be deductively located mathematically. By itself this ease would not be sufficient reason for investigating equilibria, except perhaps to mathematicians. The significance of equilibria to economists is derived from the power of arbitrage to help explain certain things. For example, arbitrage can explain why one usually does not find a really short checkout line at the supermarket. People leave the longer lines to join the shorter ones, thus shortening the long lines and lengthening the shorter ones. When all the lines are equal there is no reason to change lines. This is a compelling account of a frequently observed phenomenon. Its persuasiveness results from introspection (don't you want to minimize time spent waiting in line?); from logic (what happens if everyone acts the way you do?); and from observed evidence (why is there never a short line?).

Consider a related, but somewhat different case. Three lanes of high speed automobile traffic are channeled into twelve tollbooths. Even though the drivers presumably want to minimize their time waiting in line, and thus the logic of the supermarket lines applies, the tollbooth lines can often be seen to be noticeably unequal. The obvious explanation is that a decision must be made quickly based on scant information, and it is risky to change lines once a commitment is made. So the arbitrage explanation that works well in the supermarket case is not as powerful here. Information constraints and risk act as barriers to arbitrage. Even so, arbitrage and equilibrium are not entirely irrelevant. Knowing what logically should happen can lead one to look for the factors that are causing the expected outcome not to occur. In *The Theory of Economic Development*, Schumpeter takes this approach. Starting with a Walrasian style model of general equilibrium, Schumpeter argues that in equilibrium the interest rate should logically be zero. How then to account for the fact that interest rates are normally positive? Interest is paid out of profits, and profits are the result of economic development, which is to say factors that disrupt equilibrium.

As long as economists find arbitrage to be useful in explaining things, it is hard to see how the concept of equilibrium could be dispensed with. What can be argued is whether particular economic processes more closely resemble the supermarket checkout lines or the tollbooth lines; or whether arbitrage is even applicable. Because capital imposes restrictions it would seem to be a factor that interferes with the attainment of equilibrium, unless the equilibrium is defined within the context of a particular capital structure as in Marshall's short period. Lachmann's theory looks at entrepreneurs acting under constraints imposed by capital structures in a world in which unanticipated changes can happen. In Schumpeter's theory new combinations of resources, which include new capital combinations, are a factor that disrupts existing equilibria. While Schumpeter might be called a 'disequilibrium' theorist, he still uses equilibrium as a reference point as in the tollbooth line case. Marx seemed content with Smithian arbitrage as a description of the market process within the capitalist epoch. However, the accumulation of capital that results from normal market operations becomes a disruptive factor in the story. While Marx's historical process does converge to a determinate state – communism – this does not occur as a result of arbitrage. Thorstein Veblen's open-ended institutional evolution is another example of a process to which arbitrage is irrelevant.

Arbitrage generated equilibria occur in a context. The human actions leading to equilibrium take place in an environment defined by parameters. The top management of the supermarket might decide to build bigger stores or to introduce electronic scanners. This will alter the environment, possibly changing the equilibrium checkout line length for any given amount of traffic. The various attempts in the last century at an evolutionary approach to economics might be seen as attempts to understand the process by which the context changes.

So what?

The obvious concern is that limiting the concept of capital to what can be represented and analyzed by means of a particular set of tools has the effect of declaring certain topics off-limits to economists. Will this situation prevail?

Paul Krugman (1999) describes how Albert Hirschman, in *The Strategy of Economic Development* rejected rigorous modeling, because the inability of 1950s techniques to handle increasing returns to scale did not allow him to express his ideas formally. Choosing his ideas over formal techniques, Hirschman led his followers into a wilderness from which they never returned. Development economics stagnated and became one of lower status fields (along with history of economic thought). The tragedy, according to Krugman, is that Hirschman's ideas turned out to be good ones after all. This was discovered in the 1980s and 1990s as techniques emerged that did allow increasing returns to be used in formal models.

In accounting for this tragedy, Krugman points out that early maps of Africa, while inaccurate about distances and the shapes of coastlines, contained a wealth of information about the interior of the continent based on reports from explorers and travelers. As mapmaking techniques improved, accuracy about distances and shapes got better. The new techniques were first applied to the coasts; and since the new techniques raised the standard of what was deemed acceptable, maps of Africa went through a period in which coastlines were represented with detailed precision while the interiors were blank. In time, further exploration of Africa resulted in the interior being mapped to the same standard as the coast. By analogy Hirschman's ideas were like maps that described a river as being located six days walk from the end of the desert. Economics was temporarily denied the content of Hirschman's thinking until it could be expressed in a manner acceptable by modern standards.

Maybe capital theory has been like the rich interior of Africa at a time when all we know how to do is map the shoreline. In the future we might view today's economics as a development phase, perhaps the adolescence of economics.[26] What will economics grow into? *The Journal of Evolutionary Economics* (*J.E.E*), co-founded by

Mark Perlman, emphasizes dynamics and changing structures.[27] The sort of research encouraged by this journal holds at least the possibility for a revitalization of capital theory. I do not think it will happen using traditional mathematical tools. Whether or not it does happens successfully will depend on the emergence of relatively easy to use means of representing complex dynamic phenomena. There is hope for this, thanks to cheap powerful computers. Uri Wilensky at the Center for Connected Learning and Computer-Based Modeling at Tufts University (http://www.ccl.tufts.edu/cm/index.html) offers numerous examples of complex dynamic phenomena (some economic) that can be represented rather simply using object oriented programming environments such as StarLogo.

Hayek (1988: 9) notes that when he began working on his particular brand of evolutionary social theory he felt that he was nearly alone. He further notes that since that time there has been an enormous growth of research that Hayek considers to be related to his work: 'autopoiesis, cybernetics, homeostatis, spontaneous order, self-organization, synergetics, systems theory and so on.' Both the *J.E.E.* and Wilensky's Center[28] appear to be part of this growing movement about which Hayek writes. It will be interesting to see if capital theory makes a comeback as part of this.

Notes

1 Robert Solow (1991: 31) in a response to McCloskey's (1991: 6–16) claim that economists have absorbed the values of the math department, asserts that rigor is truth (or more precisely that non-rigor is falseness). The question being posed here is, what if narrowing the content in order to attain tautological certainty, which is the sort of truth that one can most confidently claim to arrive at through mathematical rigor, results in errors of omission? Is a misleading conclusion arrived at through lack of rigor worse than a misleading conclusion reached by eliminating vital elements from the story?

2 The reader may find this assessment a bit harsh. There have been some standouts in this losing effort. Irving Fisher (1896: 514) used the stock/flow distinction in delineating the difference between what is capital and what is not. This distinction has been widely embraced as a general sorting out device, though the use that Fisher made of it for conceptualizing capital has not fared as well. Fisher's (1906: 57–8) discussion implies that traditional price theory is a special case of capitalized value. This is an important element for integrating value theory into a temporal framework. The largely ignored Frank A. Fetter (1977) stressed the conventional and legal aspects of capital. Capital is not a Platonic universal with an essence to be discovered. It emerged in the context of a specific institutional setting. Fetter's approach may get renewed appreciation in light of the difficulties encountered by the former communist nations. Joseph Schumpeter (1954: 631–7) insisted that capital is a structure, that is to say, it 'is neither homogeneous nor an amorphous heap'. Schumpeter's remark found a receptive audience in Ludwig Lachmann (1978). If there has been significant progress in twentieth century capital theory it is in Lachmann's mostly neglected work.

3 For a view contrary to this see Avanish Dixit (1977). Dixit argues that Christopher Bliss's *Capital Theory and the Distribution of Income* (1975) provides a framework that can integrate the diverse monologues that have characterized capital theory. I would be prepared to agree with Dixit, were I willing to accept the view of the editors of *The New Palgrave* that capital theory is simply price theory 'in an economy in which some of the means of production are reproducible' (Eatwell, Milgate and Newman 1990: xi). One is reminded here of Joan Robinson's complaint that the Neoclassicals had abandoned the great questions of

growth, development, distribution and accumulation, after Marshall put them to work analyzing the price of a cup of tea. Defining capital theory as the *Palgrave* editors do would seem to vindicate Robinson.

4 If there exists an 'everybody knows what capital is' sort of definition it would probably be something like 'tools'. The 'everybody' in this case is people who have taken economics classes. An objection to this usage is that it wastes a term. If 'capital' is merely a fifty-cent way of saying 'tools', then is capitalism a system organized around tools?

5 An anonymous Reader points out that 'the value of capital, as a revenue-producing asset, in a business cannot be calculated by summation, for that depends both on the way that capital is structured, and also on the orientation of that structure.' But accountants do this all the time. Capital = Assets − Liabilities is a fundamental bookkeeping identity. Summation *per se* is not such a great problem as are the method of arriving at the values entered into the sum, and how to interpret such a sum. In a forward-looking assessment, such as current market value, the values of particular objects depend on expectations involving planned uses of the objects. These depend on structure and orientation, and potential profitability of those uses. This does not imply that one cannot add them together. It does mean that if plans or expectations change the value of 'capital' changes, even if the collection of physical assets remains the same. (See Kirzner [1996: 94–120] for a very detailed account of this problem.) The accountant's notion of capital is important, if for no other reason than that it was the original inspiration for the economist's concept.

Perhaps the Reader is concerned with the use made of a capital value arrived at by summation. This might be especially pernicious were it to be extended to allow calculation of 'social capital'. Yet I would guess that even the stoutest methodological individualist believes, at least in unguarded moments, that the US has more capital per head than Mexico and that this 'fact' is significant in explaining differences in the standard of living between the two nations. (See Kirzner 1996: 106). To learn otherwise would constitute a major change in economists' thinking. That we may have reason to revise our thinking is suggested by Mancur Olson (1996), and by the failures of 'capital fundamentalism' as a development policy. Perhaps having a large measure of capital per person is a symptom of a system of institutions and incentives that facilitate capitalistic behavior.

6 The foregoing discussion of the early history of the capital concept is based on Fetter (1977: 143–6, 154–8).

7 In a somewhat different vein, plans are an integral part of J. R. Hicks' treatment of production taking place in time in *Value and Capital* (1946).

8 See Edith Penrose's (1959) *The Theory of the Growth of the Firm* for an account of the manufacturing firm that comes very close to viewing it as a human capital structure.

9 See *Reflections on the Formation and the Distribution of Riches*, 3–17; 42–73. The assessment of Turgot as the originator of modern capital theory is made by Taussig (1897: 127–8) and Schumpeter (1954: 332).

10 That is to say as Schumpeter defines the entrepreneur in *The Theory of Economic Development*, Chapter II, Section III.

11 Charles Ganilh quoted in Taussig (1897: 130).

12 See Knight (1934: 258).

13 To be more precise, Stigler called this a 'regrettable failure'.

14 Taussig called this notion of capital 'goods in the pipeline'.

15 Taussig (1897, II) surveyed the works of the Classical economists and thought it difficult to find any explicit statement of the simple wages fund theory.

16 See Mill (1909, Appendix O).

17 G. L. S. Shackle (1968, Chapter VI) presents a much more elaborate and formal version of the 'time-structure of production'.

18 Schumpeter, Hayek, and Veblen are notable exceptions.

19 Ferdinand Lassalle quoted in Böhm-Bawerk (1884: 183).

20 Kirzner (1966: 37–9) points out that unless one is willing to consider human plans it is impossible to see anything in an oven but joined pieces of metal.

21 Böhm-Bawerk (1895a,b; 1907a,b); Clark (1893; 1895a,b; 1907) For a detailed account of this debate see Perlman (1996).
22 Knight (1934; 1935; 1936a,b; 1938), Kaldor (1937), Hayek (1936), Machlup (1935) and Boulding (1936a,b).
23 Hence he is in no position to argue that time preference has nothing to do with interest. In his model this possibility is ruled out by definition.
24 See Harcourt (1969; 1972) for an account of these debates. Harcourt (1995) provides his appraisal of the impact the Cambridge Controversies have had on economic thought after the passage of a quarter century.
25 The continuity running from Ricardo's diminishing returns to Clark's marginal product to modern convex production functions is one way in which Neo-classical economics is truly 'neo-classical'.
26 Deirdre McCloskey (1996: 13) locates economists at an earlier stage: boys playing in a sandbox.
27 See the article by Cantner and Hanusch in this volume.
28 See also the *Principia Cybernetica* website at http://pespmc1.vub.ac.be/CYBSWHAT.html.

References

Böhm-Bawerk, E. von. 1959 (1884) *Capital and Interest*, trans. George D. Huncke and Hans Sennholz, Libertarian Press.
—— 1891 (1889) *The Positive Theory of Capital*, trans. William Smart, G. E. Stechert & Co.
—— (1895a) 'The positive theory of capital and its critics', *The Quarterly Journal of Economics* 9: 113–31.
—— (1895b) 'The origin of interest', *The Quarterly Journal of Economics* 9: 380–7.
—— (1906) 'Capital and interest once more: I. capital vs. capital goods', *The Quarterly Journal of Economics* 21: 1–21.
—— (1907a) 'Capital and interest once more: II. a relapse to productivity theory', *The Quarterly Journal of Economics* 21: 247–82.
—— (1907b) 'The nature of capital: a rejoinder', *The Quarterly Journal of Economics* 22: 28–47.
Boulding, K. (1936a) 'Time and investment', *Economica* N. S. 3, 10: 196–220.
—— (1936b) 'Professor Knight's capital theory: a note in reply', *The Quarterly Journal of Economics* 50(3): 524–31.
Clark, J. B. 1965 (1899) *The Distribution of Wealth*, Augustus M. Kelley, Bookseller.*
—— (1893) 'The genesis of capital', *Yale Review* 2: 302–15.
—— (1895a) 'The origin of interest', *The Quarterly Journal of Economics* 9: 257–8.
—— (1895b) 'Real issues concerning interest', *The Quarterly Journal of Economics* 10: 98–102.
—— (1907) 'Concerning the nature of capital: a reply', *The Quarterly Journal of Economics* 21: 351–70.
Dixit, A. (1977) 'The accumulation of capital theory', *Oxford Economic Papers* N. S. 29: 1–29.
Eatwell, J. Milgate, M. and Newman, P. 1990 *The New Palgrave: Capital Theory*. W. W. Norton & Company.
Fetter, F. A. (1977) *Capital, Interest and Rent*, Murray Rothbard (ed). Sheed, *Andrews* and McNeel.
Fisher, I. 1965 (1906) *The Nature of Capital and Interest*, Augustus M. Kelley.
—— (1954) (1930) *The Theory of Interest*, Kelley and Millman, Inc.
—— (1896) 'What is capital?' *The Economic Journal* 6: 509–34.
Harcourt, G. C. (1969) 'Some Cambridge controversies in the theory of capital', *Journal of Economic Literature* 7: 369–405.

Harcourt, G. C. (1972) *Some Cambridge Controversies in the Theory of Capital*, Cambridge University Press.

—— (1995) 'The capital theory controversies', *Capitalism, Socialism, and Post-Keynesianism: Selected Essays of G. C. Harcourt*, 41–46. Edward Elgar.

—— (1936) 'The Mythology of Capital', *The Quarterly Journal of Economics* 50: 199–228.

Hayek, F. A. (1988) *The Fatal Conceit*, University of Chicago Press.

Hicks, J. R. (1946) *Value and Capital* (2nd edn), Oxford University Press.

Kaldor, N (1937) 'Annual survey of economic theory: the recent controversy on the theory of capital', *Econometrica* 5: 201–33.

Kirzner, Israel (1966) *An Essay on Capital*, Augustus M. Kelley.∗

Knight, Frank (1934) 'Capital, time and the interest rate', *Economica* N.S.1: 257–86.

—— (1935) 'The Ricardian theory of production and distribution', *Canadian Journal of Economics and Political Science* 1: 3–25.

—— (1936a) 'The quantity of capital and the rate of interest', Part I, *Journal of Political Economy* 44: 433–63.

—— (1936b) 'The quantity of capital and the rate of interest', Part II, *Journal of Political Economy* 44: 612–39.

—— (1938) 'On the theory of capital: in reply to Mr. Kaldor', *Econometrica* 6: 63–82.

Krugman, P. (1999) 'The fall and rise of development economics', http//web.mit.edu/krugman/www/dishpan.html

Lachmann L. (May 1947) 'Complementarity and substitution in the theory of capital', *Economica* 108–119.

—— 1978 (1956) *Capital and its Structure*, Sheed, Andrews and MacNeel.

Machlup, F. (1935) 'Professor Knight and the period of production'. *Journal of Political Economy* 43: 577–624.

—— (1991) *Economic Semantics*, Transaction Publishers.

Marshall, Alfred 1982 (1920) *Principles of Economics* 8th ed, Porcupine Press.

Marx, K. 1977 *Capital* Vol I, trans. Ben Fowkes, Vintage Books.

—— 1977 (1849) 'Wage-labour and capital', *Selected Writings* David McLellan (ed.) Oxford University Press.

McCloskey, D. 1991 'Economics science: a search through the hyperspace of assumptions?' *Methodus* 3(1): 6–16.

Menger, C. 1976 (1871) *Principles of Economics* trans. James Dingwall and Bert F. Hoselitz, New York University Press.

Mill, J. S. 1961 (1909) *Principles of Political Economy*, W. J. Ashley (ed.) Augustus M. Kelley.

O'Brien, G. 1967 (1920) *An Essay on Medieval Economic Teaching*, Augustus M. Kelley.

Penrose, E. 1995 (1959) *The Theory of the Growth of the Firm*, Oxford University Press.

Ricardo, D. 1951 (1817) *Principles of Political Economy and Taxation*, Piero Sraffa with M. H. Dobb, (ed.) Cambridge University Press.

Robinson, J. 1980 (1953) 'The production function and the theory of capital', *Collected Economic Papers* 2: 114–131, M.I.T. Press.

—— 1956 *The Accumulation of Capital*, Macmillan.

Schumpeter, J. A . 1961 (1934) *The Theory of Economic Development*, Harvard University Press.

—— 1954. *History of Economic Analysis*, Oxford University Press.

Senior, N. W. 1965 (1836) *An Outline of the Science of Political Economy*, Augustus M. Kelley.

Smith, A. 1937 (1776) *The Wealth of Nations*, Edwin Cannan (ed.) The Modern Library.

Solow, R. M. 1991 'Discussion Notes on 'Formalization', *Methodus* 3(1): 30–31.

Solow, R. M. 1964 *Capital Theory and the Rate of Return*, Rand McNally.

Taussig, F. W. 1897 *Wages and Capital*, D. Appleton and Co.

Turgot, A. R. J. 1963 (1970) *Reflections on the Formation and the Distribution of Riches*, Augustus M. Kelley.

Wicksell, K. 1934 (1901–1906) *Lectures on Political Economy*, Vol. 1, trans. E. Classen, Nogami Publishing Co.

—— 1970 (1893) *Value, Capital and Rent*, Augustus M. Kelley.

11 Evolutionary economics, its basic concepts and methods

A tribute to Mark Perlman, Editor of the *Journal of Evolutionary Economics*, 1991–96

Uwe Cantner and Horst Hanusch

Prologue

Although the roots of Evolutionary Economics can be traced quite far back, only since the beginning of this century and more intensely since about the 1960s, has it begun to constitute a comprehensive body of research. Undisputed milestones were set by Joseph Alois Schumpeter (1912; 1942) and Thorstein Veblen (1898), the famous note in Alfred Marshall (1890), the approaches of Almen Alchian (1950), Kenneth Boulding (1981) and Jack Hirshleifer (1982) and, last but not the least, the contribution of Richard Nelson and Sidney Winter (1982). These two last named have induced the setting up of a broad research agenda which still continues to provide many fields of investigation. Obviously, any new theoretical approach or paradigm requires an adequate forum for discussion and publication and for this purpose specialized niches within established economic societies and well-reputed journals have come into being. But in order to improve the recognition and reputation of the entire line of research in the consciousness of all economists elaborating on and contributing to evolutionary concepts, several further initiatives enabled an institutional framework to be created, namely, the *International Joseph A. Schumpeter Society* (ISS), and the *European Association for Evolutionary Political Economics* (EAEPE), on the one hand, and publications such as the *Journal of Evolutionary Economics*, the *Journal of New Technology and Innovation*, *Structural Change and Economic Dynamics*, and *Industrial and Corporate Change*, to name only the most important, on the other.

Mark Perlman was one of the most prominent among the group of economists engaged in this development. He was a founding member of the ISS and founding Co-Editor of the *Journal of Evolutionary Economics* (JEE). Especially in the latter function, his creativity and instinct launched a conception of the JEE as having a broad scope combined with critical and controversial topics which embraced empirical, theoretical, historical and political dimensions. With his editorial colleagues of the JEE, Mark Perlman was always ambitious to produce well-balanced issues and volumes, to give readers comfortable access to a variety of problems and questions, to methods and approaches applied, and to controversial discussions. The contents of the volumes since the Journal's founding in 1991 are a convincing index of this variety and openness.

After his resignation in 1997, Mark Perlman fortunately remained on board as Senior Advisory Editor and thus, his influence for a balanced strategy during the years 1991–7 will prevail in the future.

In the following we attempt to briefly sketch the main lines and approaches within an evolutionary approach towards economic phenomena; as we cannot cover all aspects of evolutionary economics, we will focus on the phenomena of innovations in particular and technological change in general. Our plan is accomplished by a critical comparison between the present mainstream approach of neoclassical economics and a characterization of evolutionary economics, as well as a 'tour de horizon' in the field of alternative methodological approaches. For discussion we naturally cite the core and original body of literature in evolutionary economics. In addition, the work published in the JEE (typed in capitals) is referred to in order to demonstrate the broad scope and balanced selection of issues covered by the JEE.

Introduction

About 2,500 years ago Heraklit from Ephesus (540–475 B.C) founded a school of thought which is of importance even today. '*We bathe in the same rivers, and yet we do not; we are the same persons, and yet, we are not.*' Stressing a dynamic principle of individual and social life, this philosophy later became well-known as *panta rhei*, and is considered to be an early antecedent of a school which puts change and development at the centre of scientific interest. From an empirical view point, it is only recently that men have experienced several suddenly emerging and then lasting new circumstances during their lifetimes: if we look at the period of the last 250 years, we find in the time after the industrial revolution, and even accelerated after World War II, processes of sometimes drastic change which affect nearly all fields of social and political as well as economic life.[1]

Today it is redundant to say that technological progress is considered to be the major driving force behind these developments. Economic historians (e.g. Freeman and Perez 1988; Mokyr 1990) attempt to demonstrate and to analyse why and how long-term *development processes* in various economies and at different times have been induced by certain far-reaching technologies (so-called *key technologies*): They are generated in a certain firm or in a specific branch of a firm, then start to spillover into other sectors and spread over the whole economy, developing a lasting influence on the structure of development of nearly all industrial sectors and economies. Several of these major technological pushes can be identified, beginning with mechanization in the nineteenth century and, in our day, extending to computers and telecommunication.[2] As is well known, each of these breakthroughs caused important, persistent, and powerful changes, not only in the originating sector, but also far away from the place where it began.[3] These historical observations as well as a rich literature on other empirical facts related to technological progress impressively suggest, perhaps even force economists to consider economies as a bundle of dynamic phenomena.

Doing this and referring to the empirical evidence, it is the *development perspective* which appears to be appropriate for any analysis in this field. By 'development perspective' we mean the explicit consideration of the generation and diffusion of novelty. (For the following – as already mentioned – we restrict this novelty to the phenomena of technological change and innovations – well aware of the fact that also the analysis of the generation of institutions, cultural change or the development of law could be analysed in a similar fashion (Nelson 1995) or even as a phenomenon of co-evolution.)

In retrospect, such a dynamic and especially such a long-term *development perspective* which puts emphasis on the emergence of something new has been largely neglected by economists for a long time. Since the turn of the century, and still up to our day, the neoclassical paradigm has dominated our discipline. Following *classic mechanics* or *dynamics*, this school is characterized by equilibrium thinking focusing on the persistence of economic relationships, which has the consequence of a presumed high degree of predictability of results. Consequently, research endeavours of this kind of analysis are mainly restricted to the proof of stability and optimality conditions of certain equilibrium states or equilibrium dynamics. And, following the logic of the neoclassical approach strictly, disequilibrating processes induced from within the economic system itself are not covered and cannot be treated adequately. Instead, research is concentrated on the analysis of the mechanisms which allow an economy or individuals to adapt to an optimal equilibrium state or path which, once it is reached, will neither be left due to reasons within the system nor due to any individual's will.

The dominant shield of neoclassical economics nevertheless left some room or niches for alternative approaches based on a totally different conception. Here we refer to some early apolegets.[4] Already in 1898 Veblen raised the question '*Why is economics not an evolutionary science?*' And some years later, in 1912 and in 1942, Schumpeter[5] never became tired of emphasising the crucial importance of the *development perspective* to an understanding of economic dynamics which he characterises as the endogenous creation of innovations accompanied by often destructive changes in the whole economy.[6] But for a long time these voices remained more or less unheard in academia, unable to attract lasting attention. Why was this so?

In principle, we can find a number of answers to this question. First of all, the neoclassical research programme has been extraordinarily successful in formalizing economic theory, although this has often been necessarily accompanied by a high degree of abstraction and often crude reduction and oversimplification of economic reality. Nevertheless the results achieved so far have been impressive and for a long time there seemed to be no reason to oppose such a success story. In addition, in those days the mathematical tools for dealing with more realistic and thus more complex and dynamic development processes were at a stage which did not allow the neoclassical approach to be confronted with anything equal or comparable.

The group of economists who feel uncomfortable with this development of economic science, and especially with the neglect of a *development perspective* in a Schumpeterian sense, is growing rapidly. These economists belong to different schools; among the most prominent at the moment are the *Neo-Schumpeterian* group (e.g. Nelson and Winter 1982), the *Institutionalist camp*[7] (e.g. Hodgson 1988; 1989; 1993; Dopfer 1986), and also some *Marxist* scholars (e.g. Goodwin 1986[8]), and, last but not least, the *Austrian school* (e.g. Faber and Proobs 1990). They all share a

critical assessment of neoclassical lines of reasoning and follow an alternative paradigm, namely *evolutionary economics*. Whenever it was the ability to put an argument
in formal mathematical terms which enabled neoclassical economics to dominate,
nowadays this obstacle for alternative approaches has been removed. Pathbreaking
improvements in mathematics, especially in non-linear dynamics, as well as the
nearly infinite availability of computing capacity nowadays, do allow us in economics to tackle questions and to solve problems which have been omitted or analysed
poorly in the past. And recently, evolutionary economics has used these new analytical methods and opportunities intensely in both theoretical and empirical work.[9]

As the name indicates, evolutionary economics deals with development processes
in a special way: it analyses their origins, intensities, structures and qualities. The first
evolutionary theories can be traced back to biology, in particular to Jean-Baptiste
Lamarck and Charles Darwin. The basic constituents of their approaches are the
emerging, i.e. *mutation*, and spreading, i.e. *selection* of novelties. So, evolutionary
economics attempts to transfer this line of reasoning to economic processes:
Mutations are then mainly associated with technical and organizational innovations,
which then, by the way of a selection process, either diffuse or disappear. However,
it should be mentioned here that we do not by any means postulate a *one-to-one
correspondence* between biological and economic concepts.[10] Economics rather has to
develop its own independent theory of evolution (Witt 1987; Foster 1997) and test
it against reality.

After these introductory remarks, we proceed as follows: First, we attempt to
elaborate more deeply the basic criticism with which the neoclassical paradigm is
confronted by an evolutionary point of view. Based on this, the second step derives
the basic concepts of modern evolutionary economics. Finally, some important new
analytical methods which are able to satisfy the main requirements of an evolutionary approach are introduced and briefly explained.

Neoclassical economics from an evolutionary point of view

The increasing dissatisfaction with the way neoclassical economics deals with economic development can be traced back to at least four critical features: (a) the already
mentioned equilibrium orientation of the concept, (b) the rationality assumption
represented by the conception of the *homo oeconomicus*, (c) the restriction to several
symmetric or one representative agent, and (d) the neglect of historical time in order
to describe dynamic processes. We start with the first two points.

Equilibrium, the market mechanism and innovative activities

In order to analyse and explain economic phenomena, neoclassical theory applies the
methodology and mathematics of classical mechanics, which go back to Isaac
Newton and his concept of equilibrium as a state of rest. In economics such equilibria can be characterized by an overall fit of individually optimal plans, based on
utility or profit maximization, and the stability of the state achieved, that is, the
agents have no incentive to deviate from where they are. The mechanism which

provides that all individual plans fit and will not be changed in equilibrium, is found in the working of market forces, i.e. the price mechanism. Thus, the market is seen as a co-ordinating device, allowing all market participants to achieve the best results within the framework of current and future constraints.

By this, an understanding of dynamic phenomena in the sense of our development perspective is excluded *a priori*. What the theory can offer at best is, on the one hand, the notion of a sequence of equilibrium states being the result of certain exogenous disturbances and the following adaptation to a new equilibrium state. On the other hand, endogenous change also becomes possible as a consequence of a process optimizing a deterministic or quasi-deterministic relationship of *ex-ante* known opportunities and leading to steady-state equilibrium paths into an infinite future.

Hence, because in the neoclassical world of equilibrium economic agents lack incentives to change their behaviour, the only sources of disequilibrium and thus of unexpected results must have their origin outside the economic realm. Already at the beginning of this century Schumpeter (1912) fiercely attacked this methodological position. On his understanding of our discipline, the central task for economics is to search for and to analyse the endogenous sources of economic development and change (see Louca 1997). By this, Schumpeter had no doubt about the evolutionary and never *ex-ante* optimal nature of these processes: as the driving force, he identifies the emergence and the dissemination of technological novelties – named by him as *new combinations*. Thus, development in the sense of Schumpeter includes both endogenous sources of change (Schumpeter 1912) and 'creative destruction' of equilibria (Schumpeter 1942) triggered by innovation and imitation activities.

Of course, such changes must also have been observed by neoclassical economists. But they consider them to be the results of optimal decisions of individuals, at most accompanied by some transitory dynamics. In order to achieve these optimal results, neoclassical economics – and extensively the new industrial economics – has to draw on extreme heroic assumptions concerning the cognitive abilities of the agents modelled, so-called *hyper-rationality*. To stay in a static or dynamic equilibrium, or to reach a new one after an exogenous shock, these actors – assumed to behave as *homines oeconomici* – need to know all alternatives and the respective consequences of their actions, today and in the future. This consequently leaves no room for *intrinsic* or *strong uncertainty* in the sense of Knight (1921) and Keynes (1973). Because of this, in neoclassical theory individuals neither discover new forms of behaviour, nor do any kind of experiments, nor test them in a learning process by trial-and-error.[11] The introduction of success or failure probabilities, presumed to cover those cases, only allows insurable risks to be covered and is by no means adequate to reflect the strong uncertainty characterizing innovation processes.[12]

In interpreting this neoclassical approach we could even go a step further and argue that in such a framework innovations in a genuine sense neither exist nor can be developed. Neoclassical actors always optimally choose among given and certain alternatives, due to the assumed form of rationality. And, in doing so, true innovations are never introduced. Following this reasoning, it becomes clear that there is no room in traditional neoclassical economics for a truly Schumpeterian entrepreneur, characterised as a *daredevil*. His economically motivated innovative actions are based on the willingness and also eagerness to undertake new tasks which deviate from the known, which instead of adapting to given constraints aim at removing and breaking constraints, and this may include the danger of incalculable and often severe losses.

Representative agents, homogeneous structures and reversible time

As another consequence, deducible from the assumptions of hyper-rationality and maximizing behaviour, neoclassical economics leaves no room for differences in the individual behaviour of agents. In fact, it leads to a conception which either deals with a structureless economy or allows for certain market structures – monopoly, oligopoly, polypoly – with homogeneous agents. By doing so, it is able to restrict the analysis to a representative agent or to several identical actors. Any kind of heterogeneity, though empirically observable, is either taken as being of only a transitory character or is interpreted as the result of optimization.

The representative agent is considered a well-suited construct to represent the average optimal behaviour with respect to the neoclassical kind of novelty and change; and so it allows a convenient method of aggregating from the micro to the macro level. However, the consideration of the average provides only restricted insight. Focusing on the individual innovator, it is not the average but the extreme which turns out to be the driving force of development and change. So again, the neoclassical framework of hyper-rationality and full information provides no room for a Schumpeterian kind of entrepreneur whose behaviour is guided by vision or some alleged ingenious ideas and thus, by being different from the average. This structural aspect, which is based on heterogeneous actors and due to differences in innovative engagement and success, is quite often neglected in the neoclassical approaches especially those of the new industrial economics.

Finally, from an evolutionary perspective, the analogy which draws on classical mechanics provides an additional weak point of neoclassical theory. In a static or even comparative static analysis of equilibrium, time as a problem on its own is not consid-ered. It is modelled as an unadjusted vector or, in the words of Georgescou-Roegen (1971), '*it can follow the same course phase by phase in the reverse order.*' Real time, in the sense of historical time, however, is absent from neoclassical theory, where all processes, in principle, are of a reversible nature. In reality it is the *adjusted vector of time* (Prigogine and Stengers 1993) on which agents move on by learning, accumulating know-how and experiencing successes and failures; thus, the state of a system at time $t+1$ is dependent on the state of the system at time t.[13] Again, a Schumpeterian entre-preneur is not conceivable in a world without history because the motivation of his endeavours is to reap profits by irreversibly influencing and designing his environment.

These critical points show the incompatibility or, at best, low compatibility of the *development perspective*, driven by endogenous disequilibrating economic forces, with the paradigm of neoclassical economics.[14] In it, the assumptions made and the analy-sis performed

(a) do not allow for innovation in a genuine sense, but only give a place for a choice among weakly uncertain events, and

(b) they do this by permitting global optimal actions of hyper-rational agents.

These two perspectives, to be sure, provide for a relatively easy and elegant analysis but they also exclude much of reality from their models, and here especially, prevent both the analysis of active search processes aiming at genuine novelty and the investigation of disequilibrium situations. The states of the world described by neoclassical analysis then have to be considered as *ex-ante* co-ordination equilibria lacking any surprises and unexpected events. Thus, it is more a world of order and fully anticipated change, and not of innovative change, which is in the centre of neo-classical thinking.

Criticism, even if it appears to be justified, is only one side of the coin. To build on it and to establish a theoretical counter concept is the other.[15] So we discuss next how evolutionary economics proceeds to surmount the problems of traditional theory mentioned above and what its conception looks like.

The concept of evolutionary economics

During recent years, numerous publications have appeared, emphasizing one or the other of the critical points mentioned above and suggesting evolutionary economics as an alternative paradigm[16] for analysing economic matters (e.g. Nelson and Winter 1982; Witt 1987; DeBresson 1987; Clark and Juma 1987; Hodgson 1988; 1989; 1993; Faber and Proobs 1990). Common to all this work is the claim that economic research should focus on the *development perspective*. They come to the conclusion that general evolutionary theories, attempting to explain the emergence and spread of novelties, and containing processes of change from within, are also well adapted for economics. By out-of-equilibrium dynamics,[17] economic development is associated with endogenous and disequilibrating change, which includes not only adaptation after exogenous disturbances in the relevant environment. But also refers to and focuses on the behaviour of economic agents who actively attempt to influence and manipulate their environment.

In general, any kind of evolutionary theory is characterized by the following basic features (see e.g. Witt 1987):

  (i) it deals with development in the course of time, that is, it is dynamic;
 (ii) it draws on the concept of irreversible historical time,[18] that is, it relies on the adjusted vector of time;
(iii) it explains the endogenous emergence of novelties and their implications; and
(iv) finally, heterogeneity is considered an important source of and necessary condition for evolutionary developments. On the one hand, heterogeneity concerns the behaviour of agents (e.g. applying different strategies), on the other, it also affects the technological side of firms and economies (e.g. different technological assets, different development levels etc.).

Now, how does the idea of technological progress, pushed forward by individuals or firms, fit into an evolutionary frame of analysis as characterised above?

In the economic sphere the most important components of novelties are techno-logical innovations. These innovations are no longer, or at least not only, the result of optimal *exploitation* of an already known *ex-ante* opportunity space. They derive much more from the *exploration* of new opportunities as a consequence of human creativity and entrepreneurship (criterion iii). Thus, one specific task of evolutionary theory is the explanation of the endogenous emergence of novelty in its genuine sense, and of its prerequisites. Because agents are assumed to be endowed differently with imperfect abilities and incomplete foresight, time- and resource-using experimental and learning processes (criterion i) are of foremost analytical interest. The individual here is seen in its historical and social context.[19]

The heterogeneity of actors (criterion iv) – which is not seen here as a transitory phenomenon – contains the seed for some specific dynamics: First, different actors compete against each other, with competition as the selective device and survival as the main objective pursued. Second, different actors, and thus different experiences and different know-how, allow for amalgamation effects leading to the exploration of new opportunities.[20] Then, in some respects, development is also characterized by collective invention.

Thus, heterogeneous structures characterized by different behaviour and know-how induce learning and experimental activities which feed back on behaviour and incentives, and thus on the structures. By that, cumulative developments characterized by structural change and path dependencies are to be expected – historical time enters the analysis (criterion ii).

Before we discuss these aspects in more detail, a fundamental problem has to be dealt with: Analysing the conditions of the emergence of novelties necessarily leads to the question of how to handle them without drawing on the heroic assumptions made by neoclassical theory. Does not turning away from the postulate of rationality, perfect foresight and equilibrium orientation seem to go hand in hand with

(a) accepting that the emergence of something genuinely new is not analytically tractable and

(b) allowing for an increase in complexity which is – at least – detrimental to analytical tractability? Or does evolutionary economics offer appropriate concepts and approaches?

In the following we demonstrate that alternatives allowing for an analysis in a *development perspective* are available. With respect to dealing with the genuine new, concepts are borrowed from behavioural analyses in cognitive psychology,[21] and new developments in the natural sciences allow us to tackle rather complex systems and dynamics. The latter especially allow us to break with the traditional mechanical analogy and to pursue an evolutionary conception. But, let us start with the individual and his/her behavioural foundations.

Homo creativus, the emergence of novelty and the persistence of innovative behavioural traits

Before we can discuss the emergence of novelty, naturally an important objection against any attempt to predict the results of innovation processes must be put forward. Unfortunately, hand in hand with the limits of rationality and foresight mentioned above, we find a serious restriction of the power of theories which deal with the generation of innovations. The openness of future development is responsible for an *epistemic reservation*. Innovations cannot be forecast, otherwise they would no longer be genuine innovations. Therefore, direct treatment is impossible.[22] Evolutionary economics takes this reservation seriously, although it restricts its analytical power. However, what can be offered, nevertheless, is the derivation of the *qualitative prerequisites* for change and the structure of processes going hand in hand with it.

In the preceding section we emphasized that an essential criticism of evolutionary economics concerns the neoclassical assumption of *homo oeconomicus*. The notion on which evolutionary economics draws may be described as *homo creativus* (see Foster 1987; Cantner and Hanusch 1997). Here, we explicitly have in mind the Schumpeterian entrepreneur with all his efforts to change things, combined with entrepreneurial daring. An individual characterized in this way often feels dissatisfied with prevailing circumstances and conditions. He considers present restrictions not as unchangeable but as points of departure for creativity. Of course, in this context we cannot assume perfect rationality guides behaviour. What we may permit at best is *bounded rationality* (Simon 1976) because innovative agents face strong uncertainty. By this conception we refer not only to contingencies of novelties, subsumed under the heading of *substantial uncertainty*, which limit the rationality of decision-making, we also emphasize another source of constraints which concern the *cognitive abilities* of economic agents, and which are the core of the concept of *procedural uncertainty* (DOSI and EGIDI 1991).

Allowing for these two kinds of uncertainty, is it nevertheless possible to analyse and to identify regular and stable traits of behaviour? Or do we have to accept that agents behave in a stochastic and therefore in an unpredictable manner? To be able to give a positive answer to the first question a hint concerning some results derived in cognitive psychology are relevant.

There, a number of experiments found that although empirically full rationality is an implausible conception, human beings nevertheless exhibit stable structures of behaviour, which, of course, differ between agents. Kahneman and Tversky find, for instance, a strong context dependency of individual decisions (so-called *framing effects*) and dependencies of behaviour with respect to past experience (so-called *representativeness effects*) (see Kahneman and Tversky 1979; 1986).

Applying these results to the analysis of innovative behaviour, individuals will no longer achieve only or foremost global optimization. Instead, we observe a process of learning and experimenting which – necessarily – includes the possibility of unforeseeable results. The competencies and the respective know-how required to innovate successfully and, by this, to cope with an uncertain future, have to be built up and developed by learning and the experience of both success and failure or mistakes.[23]

This behaviour shows considerable stability, implying that neither success nor failure will lead to changes at once. In this context obviously it is to the credit of Winter (1971) and Nelson and Winter (1982)[24] to have introduced the concept of *routines*. Routines are behavioural patterns which are more or less stable at least for some period of time and which are interpreted as reflecting the cumulative past experience and thus, the past individual learning of the agent. We come back to this issue of path dependency below. Routines allow actors to cope with strong uncertainty. By this, they are related to internal and external institutions which leads to another point worth mentioning here. The perception of routinized behaviour in situations of uncertainty has also shed new light on the theory of the firm. Instead of arguing using transaction costs (and a contractual perspective), we may now interpret the firm as a collective of several competencies[25] and capacities which in a specially organized manner work together in order to cope with an uncertain future. And, without going into further detail, the trade-off relationship to be considered concerns organizational stability versus strategic flexibility, an aspect which quite recently has gained importance in the revised discussion of the Neo-Schumpeterian hypotheses.[26] Thus, a firm is considered as a repository of knowledge which is embodied in its set of routines and skills. Putting this in a dynamic perspective, individual learning processes are extended here to organizational or collective learning as a major determinant of firm behaviour.[27]

Following this line of reasoning, the problem innovative actors or firms have to solve does not concern marginal returns on invested R&D budgets in order to derive an optimal amount of R&D investment. Instead, much simpler and more operational rules are looked for (see e.g. Heiner 1988). Sometimes simple *rules of thumb*, which reflect cumulated past experience, are applied, like '*invest x per cent of your return to sales in R&D*'. To provide some anecdotal evidence, we refer to an interview with the director of R&D of the Japanese firm 'Canon', published in the *Financial Times* some years ago.[28] The director reported that his firm some time before had raised its R&D/turnover-ratio from 11 to 11.5 per cent. This appeared to have been beneficial to the firm, so that the directors were now debating again whether they should raise it cautiously a little further. This example shows that routinized behaviour will only be changed very modestly, as long as the respective results match the firms' aspiration levels.

Heterogeneous structures and their development: innovation, competitive selection and imitation

Having discussed the behavioural foundations of individual or firm actions we may ask next how these shape the development and evolution of an industry in an either intra-industrial or an inter-industrial context. Innovative activities are obviously a first candidate to be analysed and although we would never deny that for the pre-innovation phase accidental effects are often of overwhelming importance, our discussion above shows that some regularity is to be expected. Of course, whenever an innovation has occurred, for the so-called post-innovation phase, less uncertain statements about further development in competitive success, imitation and diffusion can be made. We discuss these aspects in more detail and raise the question on the reasons for structural development.

Because of incomplete abilities and unavoidable uncertainty, economic agents are only able to recognize possible alternatives and technological possibilities on the basis of their own accumulated experience and knowledge, that is to say, in a highly selective way. Thus, heterogeneity is a normal phenomenon. Whereas in neoclassical approaches this heterogeneity more often than not is assumed analytically uninterest-ing, in evolutionary economics the role of heterogeneity – above all technological het-erogeneity – among firms is emphasized as an important propelling device for the abil-ity of the economy to introduce and diffuse innovations. Therefore, differences in behaviour (as well as in technologies) are explicitly permitted because the analytical interest of evolutionary economics is particularly aimed at the dynamics of this het-erogeneity. Doing this, the *population perspective*[29] is a basic feature of analysis. Through this, however, evolutionary economics is forced to face a considerable ana-lytical problem, the aggregation from the micro level of heterogeneous agents to the macro level. A sound solution has as yet not been found so that evolutionary macro models are quite rare.[30]

What does structural development based on a population perspective mean? We distinguish an increase of heterogeneity due to further innovations and a decrease of heterogeneity either due to selective competition or due to imitation or diffusion.[31] To explain these developments of emergence and spreading of novelty, in evolution-ary economics the basic mechanisms of innovation and competition are assumed to work as do their counterparts in biological theories of evolution: mutation and selec-tion.[32] A representative firm, such as that proposed by neoclassical theory, cannot be maintained in this perspective because, on the one hand, heterogeneity in specific features is a necessary requirement for selection. On the other hand, heterogeneous and thus – at least statically – non-optimal structures become the inevitable conse-quence of economic and technological evolution.

Evolutionary processes now take place within populations whose members are either firms or technologies, endowed with different characteristics. Due to muta-tions, the specific features always change, leading to increasing heterogeneity in the system. What are the determinants of these mutations?

The most important forces causing innovation are found in the (most often path-dependent) R&D endeavours of firms. In addition, however, heterogeneity among agents is explicitly considered as an additional source of novelty. This is expressed well in the role which *external knowledge sources* play and in the emphasis put on *cross-fertilization effects*.[33] Contrary to biological evolution, nearly all innovations in cul-tural evolution originate from a synthesis of, up to this time, independent and uncon-nected knowledge elements, which often can be traced back to different fields of knowledge. While in biological evolution, due to the sexual reproduction, the recom-bination of genes of different species is not possible, in cultural evolution different fields of knowledge can be combined. Thereby, often completely new technological opportunities are opened up (see e.g. DeBresson 1987). Instead of cross-fertilization, some authors (Kodama 1992) use the notion of *technology-fusion*. This idea is best explained by drawing on two recent impressive examples: First, the combination of optics and electronics has opened up the field of opto-electronics, which in turn is the seed of fibre-technologies in data-transfer. Also, the amalgamation of machinery engi-neering and electronics has led some authors to write of a new technology, mecha-tronics.

With these two sources of novelty, individual research and collective invention, eco-nomic evolution clearly distinguishes itself from biological evolution. Whereas in the latter mutations are completely random, in economic evolution *intentions* of agents and thus, intentional behaviour, are important as well as the collective effects of those intentions. In this sense, as Nelson and Winter (1982) emphasize, cultural evolution is rather *Lamarckian* because the building up of knowledge and information transfer is guided by *intentions* of the agents. In biological evolution, following a *Darwinian* pattern, the dynamics in contrast depends on randomly heritable genetic traits.

Having discussed some elements of the pre-innovation phase, we switch now to the post-innovation phase and ask what competition among the new and the old or among several new alternatives may look like.

With heterogeneous populations, selection processes are at work, determining the shares of specific features (technology or market shares). In this context, it is the *fitness* of a specific characteristic on which selection forces work. Fitness gives an idea of the ability of a specific characteristic to spread out in a time interval. Such fitness could refer, for example, to unit production cost, product quality, organizational capability, etc.[34] Competitive selection processes[35] determine which of the different technologies or firms will survive and perhaps grow, and which have to shrink and finally to disappear. And, in this respect it is the market which is considered as performing the task of selection. Whereas neoclassical economics emphasizes the coordinating function of the market, in evolutionary economics we focus on its selective functioning.

However, competitive selection processes need not necessarily end in ex-post optimal solutions. For example, in the context of the diffusion of technologies, Arthur (1989) and David (1985) show that it is not always the ex-post technologically superior solution which survives selection. Random events as well as high sensitivity with respect to initial conditions exert an important influence on the final outcome. Often cited examples in this respect are the final dominance of the technologically inferior VHS standard over Betamax in video cassette recorders, or the QWERTY typewriter in office equipment.

Finally, the post-innovation phase is not only characterized by competitive selection dynamics but also by learning processes which are so important for the diffusion of novelty. Heterogeneity of actors does not only imply that they pursue different individual tasks but also that some of them pursue the same task with a different degree of efficiency and success. This kind of heterogeneous structure – which is often called a gap structure – opens up the opportunity for the poorer performing actors to learn from the better ones. Thus, learning is also imitation of an issue which gains importance in intra-industry analyses of firm behaviour and especially in the discussion of the sources and effects of international competitiveness of firms, sectors and countries.[36]

Characteristic dynamic patterns and sources of persistency: structural and dynamic stability

Does evolutionary dynamics as described by the interacting forces of innovation, competitive selection and imitation show any regularity and stability? Or do we have to expect an irregular and therefore always unstable development? Any answer to this difficult question should distinguish between two conceptions which in reality might be intimately interrelated.

First, there seems to be some kind of an ever revolving pattern of development, the life cycle of a product, a technology or an industry. This life cycle conception is based on an ontological perception[37] of an evolutionary process implying that a number of characteristic stages will be passed through by any novelty from its 'birth' until its 'death'. A prominent field of this discussion is industrial organization, focusing mainly on the conditions for such patterns to emerge, for example, the intensity and direction of R&D activities of firms, the entry and survival of new firms.[38]

Second, the phenomenon of path-dependency is considered to be responsible for the fact that certain directions of development, whenever taken, are less and less likely to be changed. From the preceding it has already become clear that development processes which are influenced by their own history, and are thus irreversible,[39] show this feature of *path-dependency*. This applies especially to innovative processes. The necessary search endeavours of actors and firms in order to innovate or imitate, at least in the short run, are *local* in the sense that they are based on already practised technologies. Consequently, choice is guided by some generally accepted principles quite narrowly restricted to technologies and production processes applied in the past – a principle which is also the basis of the well-known paradigm/trajectory approach by Dosi (1982).[40] A *self-reinforcing cumulative* development driven by *positive feedback* is established, leading to strong *non-linearities* in technological and economic relationships.

What these dynamics result in are some stable points of orientation and some stable relationships. These range from stable behavioural traits and habits[41] of individuals or firms (see above) and certain stable strategies to the influence of specific institutions,[42] standards and conventions. They all are seen as the result of path-dependent dynamics which lead to lock-in effects[43] and which at least for some period of time provide for a stable structure or regular and focused structural development. Research efforts in this field concentrate on the mechanism of the dynamics leading to these lock-in situations (Arthur 1989; David 1985)[44] and on the stability of those situations as, for example, in evolutionary game theory.[45] However, a number of studies show that cycles and fluctuations may also be the result of path-dependencies.[46]

In this respect, non-linearities are responsible for the coexistence of *equilibrating* and *disequilibrating* forces. Consequently, attractors, temporarily emerging in the dynamic processes, are not stable situations in the long run. They will be left again and again for reasons of endogeneity, and the respective system is then confronted with *phase-transitions*[47] and *bifurcations* through which ex-ante totally unanticipated new directions of development can be revealed. Here, we also see the irreversible character of economic evolution. For example, the behaviour of agents obviously is influenced by phase-transitions – the old paths are no longer reachable. Therefore decisions made in the past and already realized changes cannot simply be withdrawn; time is pictured in its *historical dimension*. Thus, *lock-in-effects* and also cycles and fluctuations, are not (only) a consequence of exogenous shocks, but are an unavoidable consequence of mutually interdependent heterogeneous agents in a collectively driven development process (see e.g. Kirman 1992).

Methods in evolutionary economics

Economic analysis which applies the paradigm of evolutionary economics also demands new requirements for formal modelling. Nelson and Winter (1982) introduced the distinction between an appreciative (or explaining) and a formal way to analyse economic development. While the appreciative method restricts itself to a verbal and descriptive discussion of relevant phenomena, formal analysis is concerned with theoretical model building. However, due to the rich complexity of the object under investigation, a clear distinction between the methods does not seem to be possible. Instead, we suggest an integrative approach, because for the foundation of theoretical relationships we often have to rely on plausible relationships and stylized facts offered by descriptive investigations. This combination of theoretical as well as empirical work follows from the basic conception of evolutionary economics and has led recently to modelling called 'history friendly' (Malerba, Nelson, Orsenigo and Winter 1997). The models are designed more descriptively than analytically and, therefore, they focus on the description of processes instead on the solutions to analytical problems.

From an analytical point of view, the consideration of heterogeneous agents, bounded rationality and disequilibrating processes is accompanied by an increasing complexity of possible relationships and causalities. Consequently, the analytical tractability of the respective models is usually not possible. Already Edgeworth, who wrote in the early 1880s, had suggested that – although the assumption of symmetric economic agents simplifies analysis considerably – it would be desirable to model each agent as slightly different from the others. Unfortunately, this would lead to a much more difficult analytical treatment of the models and, in many cases, even this would not be possible (see Shubik 1996).

Additionally, considering disequilibrating processes requires reference to non-linear functional relationships which again are detrimental to analytical treatment. In such situations, we are often forced to base the analysis on – at first sight less elegant – *numerical methods*. This is why many of the formal approaches applied in evolutionary economics use numerical procedures, i.e. computer simulations. LANE (1993a,b) summarizes these different methods under the heading *artificial worlds* and gives an optimistic account of future possibilities and developments with respect to reliability and validity of computer simulations.

Another point worth mentioning is a shifting of the modeller's perspective. In a simulation model it becomes possible to differentiate between the modelled world and the researcher who designs the model's architecture. By doing so, especially with respect to the emergence of novelties, the method has certain advantages. In simulations it is possible to program stochastic processes, for which the respective statistical descriptions are not known to the agents in the model. So, the agents are confronted with real surprises, on which they could not have built subjective expectations.

In the following we sub-divide the different methods and approaches used in evolutionary economics into four groups:
- The first group are so-called *microsimulations* which, in a way, most likely could be compared with traditional models;
- the second group is composed of procedures and algorithms which model *self-organization* processes;
- the third group best may be summarized under the heading of *natural-analogous processes* and
- the fourth group covers evolutionary games.

First, let us consider microsimulations. These models are mainly based on traditional economic models. Using them to investigate dynamic processes and complex structures and applying numerical methods, there exist in general no restrictions with respect to the choice of functional relationships, numbers of actors, etc. *Although [the researcher] can analyse a highly simplified form of that model with more conventional techniques, simulation is dictated by the unwillingness to bear the costs of such oversimplification* (Nelson and Winter 1982: 207).

This *realistic approach* of evolutionary modelling (see Silverberg and Verspagen 1994a: 203) originated mainly from the seminal work of Nelson and Winter (1982), who modelled different simulation programs, based on Markov chains in order to analyse evolutionary processes in the technological development of firms and economies.[48] Work in this tradition models endogenous technical change in artificial worlds, drawing back on macroeconomic approaches of the New Growth Theory, as well as on models of Industrial Economics, in order to enrich them with evolutionary phenomena.

The second group of new approaches is composed of methods for describing *self-organization* processes,[49] especially so-called *stochastic differential equations*, and is wide spread in the German-speaking area. With the help of *synergetic methods*,[50] among others for instance, Weidlich and Haag (1983) describe processes of habit formation and migration, Erdmann (1993) models the emergence of technological paradigms, and Cantner and Pyka (1998) picture the evolution of technologies. This method, originally developed in theoretical physics (see e.g. Haken 1977), allows a description of behaviour of all members of a certain population (firms, technologies), which, on the one hand, is subject to stochastic processes at the micro-level and, on the other hand, is influenced by the development of the macro-level. The feed-back effects between the micro- and the macro-level are responsible for the emergence of unforeseen events, often leading to drastic changes in systemic behaviour. In an evolutionary interpretation such phase transitions are considered as formal equivalents of an uncertain and principally open future. The investigation of such bifurcations is often not tractable with analytical methods and, therefore, they have to be analysed by using numerical simulation.

Under the heading *natural-analogous simulation methods*, the third group, different approaches, such as neuronal nets, genetic algorithms,[51] classifier systems, etc. are summarized, all of which are characterized by one common feature: they attempt to apply specific natural processes to new problems in the socio-economic realm. Genetic algorithms, originally developed by Holland (1975) are well adapted to model learning processes. They are often used in connection with technological development (e.g. Silverberg 1991), or for the determination of mark-ups in oligopoly settings (e.g. Dosi, Valente and Marengo 1996). They also allow for the modelling of specific evolutionary processes, such as generating variety via recombination or the selection of local optima in a population perspective.

Neuronal nets are also used for modelling learning processes. However, they are not analogous to biological strategies of evolution, but directly follow the processes in human brains. In evolutionary economics this formalism is mainly transferred to learning processes in populations, e.g. investors on capital markets (see Hanusch and

Sommer 1998), or innovating firms (see Metcalfe and Calderini 1997). Here, the relevant learning processes are modelled by improvements in the weighting of information with respect to its impact in the past, thereby meliorating the performance of decision rules in the course of time.

Finally, the fourth group contains the approach of *evolutionary game theory* (Maynard Smith and Price 1973). Here, it is investigated how certain strategies become dominant and are not successfully competed away by any mutant strategy. Relying on the concept of evolutionary stable strategies, this approach can then be used to show why norms and institutions are stable over some period of time.[52]

Epilogue: promises and problems

The diversity of methods and theoretical sources is a good example of the intense dynamics and critical discussions which evolutionary economics is experiencing at the moment. Witt (1992) rightly speaks of a *new heterodoxy* in economic thinking. On the one hand, the abundance of problems and unexploited opportunities as well as the pluralistic approach can be seen as an advantage for the future development of evolutionary economics. Thus, it seems to be appropriate that evolutionary economics should be evolutionary in its methods and in its subject matter. On the other hand, severe problems arise out of this heterodoxy: As yet, evolutionary economics has not been able to develop a general and coherent theoretical and analytical framework.

In addition to this aspect of positive economics, it is the normative analysis which has as yet not been much developed in evolutionary economics. Whereas in the mechanical world of neoclassical economics the *optimum optimorum* always serves as a yardstick and any deviation from this calls for political intervention, in evolutionary economics such kind of a benchmarking is missing – and so, a comparable rationale for any intervention.[53] Any discussion of these issues in an evolutionary context will be forced to abandon the state as a large 'repair shop' and replace it by a conception related to the notion of behaviour under strong uncertainty.

As we see, the approach is faced with serious reservations when attempting to find acceptance in traditional economics, particularly in the well-developed neoclassical school of thought. However, an increasing number of publications, and also the foundation of international societies and specific journals, already show that evolutionary economics may be well on its way to becoming a broadly accepted methodological alternative of reasoning and thinking in our discipline.

Acknowledgements

We are very grateful to G. C. Harcourt for comments and suggestions as well as English editing. We also acknowledge the valuable comments of two readers. The usual caveats naturally apply.

Notes

1 Easterlin (1995) compares the industrial with the mortality revolution and their respective developments.

2 On long-wave theory and its relation to technological innovation, see DEBRESSON (1991).

3 The case of information technology is analysed in Antonelli (1995).

4 On evolutionary elements in the writings of Malthus, see V. TUNZELMANN (1991).

5 On Schumpeter, see TSURU (1993) comparing the Schumpeter bibliographies by R. L. Allen and by R. Swedberg; SWEDBERG (1992) providing an investigation into Schumpeter' 'Theory of Economic Development'; HEERTJE (1996; 1997) discussing the Schumpeter bibliography by W. F Stolper and comparing J. Stiglitz's "Whither Socialism?" with Schumpeter's 'Capitalism, Socialism and Democracy'.

6 On whether Schumpeter really was an evolutionary economist, see the controversy between KELM (1997) and HODGSON (1997).

7 On the relationship between evolutionary versus institutional economics exemplified for the land use systems and property rights, see HESSE (1992).

8 For a paper from the well-known Goodwin tradition, see GOODWIN (1991). An application is found in LORDON (1997).

9 See also DOSI (1991: 7).

10 For this argument see also DOSI and NELSON (1994: 155).

11 On the issue how uninformed actors can learn rational expectations, see SACCO (1994). For a discussion of theoretical human agents that behave like human agents, and how this can be used in neoclassical economics, see ARTHUR (1993). LAFFOND and LESOURNE (1992) show how unfounded beliefs can induce erratic evolution.

12 For a brief sketch of this argument, see also SILVERBERG and VERSPAGEN (1994b: 208).

13 For some further remarks on this, see LESOURNE (1991: 25).

14 The limitations imposed by the represenatitive agent and reversible time extend also to the impossibility of any substantial theory of capital, see the chapter by Samuel C. Weston in this volume.

15 In order to acknowledge how far we can get with the neoclassical approach, taking into account some core elements of the evolutionary approach, see STADLER (1991) for dealing with the product life cycle and the trajectory paradigm approach; KATSOULACOS (1991) for investigating technical change and disequilibrium strategies; DOCKNER, FEICHTINGER and MEHLMANN (1993) for analysing dynamic R&D competition with memory; FAN (1995) for discussing the issue of endogenous cycles; GREINER and HANUSCH (1994), and WIRL (1997) for pointing to endogenously generated transitory and persistent oscillations in economic variables; WIED-NEBBELING (1993) on unemployment in the presence of innovations; SEMMLER (1994) on the role of optimizing and non-optimizing agents in innovation processes. The issue of compatibility of some evolutionary concepts and neo-classical economics is discussed in AYRES and MARTINAS (1996). For an endogenous growth model dealing with Schumpeter's trustified capitalism, see THOMPSON (1996).

16 For a comprehensive discussion of evolutionary theories in economics, see DOSI and NELSON (1994). For some critical remarks referring also to the dangers of an evolutionary perspective, see DOSI (1991). For evolutionary economics as part of the larger evolutionary process of the universe in space and time, see BOULDING (1991).

17 In this respect IWAI (1991) discusses disequilibrium as a long-run phenomenon.

18 Again, see LESOURNE (1991) but also O'CONNOR (1993) who discusses this issue with respect to ecological changes.

19 This challenge to the neoclassical treatment of an abstract individual in historical and social isolation is also a feature of communitarianism, see the chapters by Charles McCann and Ewald Nowotny in this volume.

20 For those cross-fertilization effects as the result of a collective learning see SILVERBERG and VERSPAGEN (1994b); the effects of local interactions are analysed and discussed in DALLE (1997); local externalities and societal adoption are analysed in AN and KIEFER (1995).

21 For a discussion of constructionism within the cognitive research programme, see TAMBORINI (1997).

22 This is what the neoclassical treatment of innovative behaviour does not consider – decision making under strong uncertainty. Consequently, the respective neoclassical approaches are rather investment analyses under at most weak uncertainty.

23 LANE, MALERBA, MAXFIELD, and ORSENIGO (1996) contains a discussion of this, also in the context of innovative behaviour.

24 Work closely related to the seminal work of Nelson and Winter is NIGHTINGALE (1997) looking at Jack Downie as a precedessor of Nelson and Winter; SCHUETTE (1994) focussing on interindustry variation of vintage equipment replacement; KWASNICKI (1996) analysing the interdependency between entry and market structure under different innovation regimes; MEYER, VOGT and VOSSKAMP (1996) introducing a model of heterogeneous oligopoly allowing for new results on the R&D-concentration relationship, WAKELEY (1998) on the welfare effects and possible intervention in a Schumpeterian context.

25 On this distinction and for a good overview, see FOSS (1993). For a discussion of the relationship of a firm seen in a competence perspective to the industry, we refer to ELIASSON (1996).

26 On this, see also GRANSTRAND and ALÄNGE (1995) who on the empirical basis of corporate entrepreneurship in Sweden question whether Schumpeter was wrong. The evolution of the institution of the firm and its relation to economic growth is discussed in BORLAND and YANG (1995).

27 MARENGO (1992) investigates this phenomenon by the help of a computational model. For a discussion of this aspect of knowledge accumulation and its consequences and implications for transaction cost theory, see NOOTEBOOM (1992). An ecological approach to the theory of the firm is found in Gallagher (1993).

28 See also SILVERBERG and VERSPAGEN (1994b).

29 For a discussion of this issue and the resulting dynamics, see METCALFE (1994).

30 An example of an evolutionary macro model is found in ENGLMANN (1992), a Schumpeterian one in ENGLMAN (1994), or in the multi-country context of SILVERBERG and VERSPAGEN (1995); evolutionary von Neuman models are discussed in BURLEY (1992); synergetic interactions and their relationship to economic growth are dealt with in KLEIN (1991).

31 An empirical investigation of the development of technological diversity among rival firms is provided by MAITAL, GRUPP, FRENKEL and KOSCHATZKY (1994).

32 On more general selection processes in economics, see GOWDY (1992).

33 The discussion of this aspect is in CARLSSON and STANKIEWICZ (1991) focusing on technology systems; ANDERSEN (1991) discussing user-producer systems; SILVERBERG and VERSPAGEN (1994b) raising the issue of collective learning; ANTONELLI (1996) dealing with percolation processes in information networks; GRUPP (1996) provides an empirical analysis of the spillover effects between technological sectors.

34 For the basic principles, see METCALFE (1994); an explicit application is found in the simulation model of SAVIOTTI and MANI (1995).

35 For altruism to have positive selection value, see HANSSON and STUART (1992).

36 On the dynamics of trade structures in a technology gap model, see MAGGI (1993). The chances for NIC countries in such a context is discussed from a theoretical point of view by MAINWARING (1993). In an empirical study ARCHIBUGI and PIANTA (1994) show how catching-up processes have a lasting influence on the sectoral specialization of innovative activities. The role of foreign multinational enterprises as modes for technology transfer to domestic firms is analysed by PEREZ (1997).

   A special issue edited by DOPFER (1995) contains a collection of papers on this issue: ADELMAN (1995) and KINDLEBERGER (1995) present a historical analysis; the former looking at the stylized history of linkages between developed and less developed countries since 1820, the latter exploring the creative linkages between European countries up to 1850. An overview on the relationship between catch-up and growth is found in FAGERBERG (1995); a theoretical model on this issue is presented by SKONHOFT (1995); and a respective empirical investigation with respect to small and least developed countries is performed by FUKUCHI (1995). Normative issues which are relevant in this context are discussed in DALY (1995) focussing on the free trade argument; in TSURU (1995) questioning the concept of GNP growth; and in TINBERGEN (1995) considering the consequences of development policy.

37 The role of heterochrony in industry life cycle is discussed in WIJNBERG (1996).

38 For a discussion of post-entry performance of firms and the effect on industry evolution, see AUDRETSCH and MAHMOOD (1994).

39 For the notion of irreversibility and its relation to evolutionary economics, see LESOURNE (1991).

40 An introduction and overview to this conception is found in CIMOLI and DOSI (1995).

41 On the formation of habits, see FEICHTINGER, PRSKAWETZ, HEROLD and ZINNER (1995).

42 On institutional inertia and change, see VEGA-REDONDO (1993).

43 The appearance of these lock-ins is also discussed in a simulation model by SCHNABL (1991), dealing with communication structures in the diffusion process of innovations.

44 A discussion of the application of generalized urn schemes for explaining lock-ins and other dynamics is found in DOSI and KANIOVSKY (1994). AMABLE (1992) investigates the competition of new technologies in the presence of increasing returns to scale. An empirical analysis of the appearance of *de facto* standards in the PC-spreadsheet market is provided by SHURMER and SWANN (1995). On the generation and selection of innovative activities in a path-dependent fashion, see VEGA-REDONDO (1994).

45 On the evolution of conventions and their stability, see BERNINGHAUS and SCHWALBE (1996) BOYER and ORLEAN (1992). For the evolutionary stability of Cournot and Bertrand equilibria see QIN and STUART (1997); on conceptions of evolutionary stability, see JOOSTEN (1996).

46 On the possibility of a cycling of strategy profits, see POSCH (1997).

47 Phase transition models and their ability to model interaction are discussed in HORS and LORDON (1997).

48 See SILVERBERG and VERSPAGEN 1994a, b; Kwasnicki 1994; 1996; CACCOMO 1996. A similar modelling philosophy is found in BALLOT and TAYMAZ (1997).

49 The role of self-organization and dissipative structures as well as their relationship to Schumpeterian processes of creative destruction are discussed in JENNER (1994).

50 On the relationship between economic evolution and the science of synergetics, see FOSTER and WILD (1996). A synergetic model based on the Master-equation approach is presented in WEIDLICH and BRAUN (1992), WOECKENER (1993), BRUCKNER, EBELING, JIMINEZ MONTANO and SCHARNHORST (1996). Similar issues are discussed in models of deterministic chaos, as in HOLYST, HAGEL, HAAG and WEIDLICH (1996) and KOPEL (1997).

51 An application of genetic algorithms to learning issues is provided by DAWID (1996); MARKS (1992) deals with the breeding of hybrid strategies in an oligopoly; CURZON PRICE (1997) analyses strategic behaviour in markets. A general discussion of genetic algorithms within economic modelling is found in BIRCHENHALL, KASTRINOS and METCALFE (1997); an application to game theory is presented by ÖZYILDIRIM (1997).

52 For a discussion of evolutionary game theory, see FRIEDMAN (1998), WALLISER (1998), AMIR and BERNINGHAUS (1998), POSCH (1997), JOOSTEN (1996).

53 For a discussion of a 'Schumpeterian economic policy', see STOLPER (1991); issues of regulation are discussed in LEE (1991); deregulation is one of the topics in ELIASSON (1991); FORAY and LLERENA (1996) deal with information structures and coordination in technology policy. Further issues concerning the state in an evolutionary or Schumpeterian context are found in MUSGRAVE (1992), discussing Schumpeter's crisis of the tax state; GREEN (1993) deals with the development from the 'tax state' to the 'debt state'; the relationship of innovation and taxes is discussed in SCOTT (1995). Related issues deal with an evolutionary discussion of the transition problems of formerly socialist countries, as in PELIKAN (1992) and MENSHIKOV (1994).

References

Adelman, I. (1995) 'The long term impact of economic development in developed countries on developing countries since 1820', *J Evol Econ* 5(3): 189–208.

Alchian, R. (1950) Uncertainty, Evolution, and Economic Theory, *Journal of Political Economy* 58(3), 211–21.

Amable, B. (1992) Competition among techniques in the presence of increasing returns to scale, *J Evol Econ* 2(2): 147–58.

Amir, M. and Berninghaus, S. (1998) 'Scale functions in equilibrium selection games', *J Evol Econ* 8(1): 1–13.

An, M. Y. and Kiefer, N. M. (1995) 'Local externalities and societal adoption of technologies', *J Evol Econ* 5(2): 103–17.

Andersen, E. S. (1991) 'Techno-economic paradigms as typical interfaces between producers and users', *J Evol Econ* 1(2): 119–44.

Antonelli, C. (1995) 'The diffusion of new information technologies and productivity growth', *J Evol Econ* 5(1): 1–17.

—— (1996) 'Localized knowledge percolation processes and information networks', *J Evol Econ* 6(3): 281–95.

Archibugi, D. and Pianta, M. (1994) 'Aggregate convergence and sectoral specialization in innovation', *J Evol Econ* 4(1): 17–33.

Arthur, W. B. (1989) 'Competing technologies, increasing returns and lock-in by historical events', *Economic Journal* 99: 116–131.

—— (1993) 'On designing economic agents that behave like human agents', *J Evol Econ* 3(1): 1–22.

Audretsch, D. B. and Mahmood, T. (1994) 'Firm selection and industry evolution: the post-entry performance of new firms', *J Evol Econ* 4(3): 243–60.

Ayres, R. U. and Martinas, K. (1996) 'Wealth accumulation and economic progress', *J Evol Econ* 6(4): 347–59.

Ballot, G. and Taymaz, E. (1997) 'The dynamics of firms in a micro-to-macro model: the role of training, learning and innovation', *J Evol Econ* 7(4): 435–57.

Berninghaus, S. K. and Schwalbe, U. (1996) 'Conventions, local interaction, and automata networks', *J Evol Econ* 6(3): 297–312.

Birchenhall, C., Kastrinos, N. and Metcalfe, J. S. (1997) 'Genetic algorithms in evolutionary modelling', *J Evol Econ* 7(4): 375–94.

Borland, J. and Yang, X. (1995) 'Specialization, product development, evolution of the institution of the firm, and economic growth', *J Evol Econ* 5(1): 19–42.

Boulding, K. E. (1991) 'What is evolutionary economics?', *J Evol Econ* 1(1): 9–17.

Boulding, K. (1981) *Evolutionary Economics*, Beverly Hills: Sage Publications.

Boyer, R. and Orléan, A. (1992) 'How do conventions evolve?', *J Evol Econ* 2(3): 165–77.

Bruckner, E., Ebeling, W., Jiminez Montano, M. A. and Scharnhorst, A. (1996) 'Nonlinear stochastic effects of substitution – an evolutionary approach', *J Evol Econ* 6(1): 1–30.

Burley, P. (1992) 'Evolutionary von Neumann models', *J Evol Econ* 2(4): 269–80.

Caccomo, J. -L. (1996) 'Technological evolution and economic instability: theoretical simulations', *J Evol Econ* 6(2): 141–55.

Cantner, U. and Hanusch, H. (1997) 'Evolutorische ökonomik – konzeption und analytik', *WiSu* 8–9(97): 776–85.

Cantner, U. and Pyka, A. (1998) 'Technological evolution – An analysis within the knowledge-based approach', *Structural Change and Economic Dynamics* 9(1): 85–108.

Carlsson B. and Stankiewicz, R. (1991) 'On the nature, function and composition of technological systems', *J Evol Econ* 1(2): 93–118.

Cimoli, M. and Dosi, G. (1995) 'Technological paradigms, patterns of learning and development: an introductory roadmap', *J Evol Econ* 5(3): 243–68.

Clark, N. and Juma, C. (1987) *Long run economics – an evolutionary approach to economic growth*, London: Pinter Publishers.

Curzon Price, T. (1997) 'Using co-evolutionary programming to simulate strategic behaviour in markets', *J Evol Econ* 7(3): 219–54.

Dalle, J. -M. (1997) 'Heterogeneity vs. externalities in technological competition: a tale of possible technological landscapes', *J Evol Econ* 7(4): 395–414.

Daly, H. E. (1995) 'Against free trade: neoclassical and steady-state perspectives', *J Evol Econ* 5(3): 313–26.

David, P. (1985) 'Clio and the Economics of QWERTY', *Am Eco Rev* 75: 332–7.

Dawid, H. (1996) 'Learning of cycles and sunspot equilibria by genetic algorithms', *J Evol Econ* 6(4): 361–73.

DeBresson, C. (1987) 'The evolutionary paradigm and the economics of technical change', *J Eco Issues* 21: 751–62.

—— (1991) 'Technological innovation and long wave theory: two pieces of the puzzle', *J Evol Econ* 1(4): 241–72.

Dockner, E. J., Feichtinger, G. and Mehlmann A. (1993) 'Dynamic R&D competition with memory', *J Evol Econ* 3(2): 145–52.

Dopfer, K. (1986) 'Causility and consciousness in economics: concepts of change in orthodox and heterodox economy', *J Eco Issues* (20): 509–23.

—— (1995) 'Editorial introduction to special issue 'Global economic evolution: knowledge variety and diffusion in economic growth and development', *J Evol Econ* 5(3): 181–7.

Dosi, G. (1982) 'Technological paradigms and technological trajectories: a suggested interpretation of the determinants and directions of technical change', *Res Pol* 2(3): 147–62.

—— (1991) 'Some thoughts on the promises, challenges and dangers of an 'evolutionary perspective' in economics', *J Evol Econ* 1(1): 5–7.

Dosi, G. and Egidi, M. (1991) 'Substantive and procedural rationality: an exploration of economic behaviour under uncertainty', *J Evol Econ* 1(2): 145–68.

Dosi, G. and Kaniovski, Y. (1994) 'On 'badly behaved' dynamics. Some applications of generalized urn schemes to technological and economic change', *J Evol Econ* 4(2): 93–123.

Dosi, G. and Nelson, R. R. (1994) 'An introduction to evolutionary theories in economics', *J Evol Econ* 4(3): 153–72.

Dosi, G. Valente, M. and Marengo, L. (1996) 'Norms as emergent properties of adaptive learning. The case of economic routines', paper presented at the workshop Complex modelling for socio-economic systems at the Institute for Advanced Studies, Vienna, March, 21–3.

Easter lin, R. A. (1995) 'Industrial revolution and mortality revolution: two of a kind?', *J Evol Econ* 5(4): 393–408.

Eliasson, G. (1991) 'Deregulation, innovative entry and structural diversity as a source of stable and rapid economic growth', *J Evol Econ* 1(1): 49–63.

—— (1996) 'Spillovers, integrated production and the theory of the firm', *J Evol Econ* 6(2): 125–40.

Englmann, F. C. (1992) 'Innovation diffusion, employment and wage policy', *J Evol Econ* 2(3): 179–93.

—— (1994) 'A Schumpeterian model of endogenous innovation and growth', *J Evol Econ* 4(3): 227–41.

Erdmann, G. (1993) 'Elemente einer evolutorischen Innovationstheorie'. Tübingen: J. C. B. Mohr.

Faber, M. and Proobs, J. L. R. (1990) *Evolution, time, and the environment*. Berlin: Springer.

Fagerberg, J. (1995) 'Convergence or divergence? The impact of technology on 'why growth rates differ'?', *J Evol Econ* 5(3): 269–84.

Fan, J. (1995) 'Endogenous technical progress, R&D periods and durations of business cycles', *J Evol Econ* 5(4): 341–68.

Feichtinger, G., Prskawetz, A., Herold, W. and Zinner, P. (1995) 'Habit formation with threshold adjustment: addiction may imply complex dynamics', *J Evol Econ* 5(2): 157–72.

Foray, D. and Llerena, P. (1996) 'Information structure and coordination in technology policy. A theoretical model and two case studies', *J Evol Econ* 6(2): 157–73.

Foss, N. J. (1993) 'Theories of the firm: contractual and competence perspectives', *J Evol Econ* 3(2): 127–44.

——(1987) *Evolutionary macroeconomics*. London: Alien & Unwin.

——(1997) 'The analytical foundations of evolutionary economics, from biology analogy to economic self-organization', *Struct Change and Econ Dynamics* 8: 227–452.

Foster, J. and Wild, P. (1996) 'Economic evolution and the science of synergetics', *J Evol Econ* 6(3): 239–60.

Freeman C. and Perez, C. (1988) 'Structural crisis of adjustment: business cycles and investment behaviour', in: G. Dosi *et al.* (eds) *Technical change and economic theory*, London: Pinter Publishers.

Friedman, D. (1998) 'On economic applications of evolutionary game theory', *J Evol Econ* 8(1): 15–43.

Fukuchi, T. (1995) 'Technological retard in small least developed countries – small is beautiful but fragile?', *J Evol Econ* 5(3): 297–312.

Gallagher, M. (1993) 'Niche overlap and limiting similarity: an ecological approach to the theory of the firm', *J Evol Econ* 3(1): 63–77.

Georgescu-Roegen, N. (1971) *The entropy law and the economic process*, Cambridge: Cambridge University Press.

Goodwin, R. M. (1986) 'The M-K-S-System: The functioning and evolution of capitalism', in: H. Wagner *et al.* (eds) *The economic law of motion of modern society*, Cambridge: Cambridge University Press.

——(1991) 'Schumpeter, Keynes and the theory of economic evolution', *J Evol Econ* 1(1): 29–47.

Gowdy, J. M. (1992) 'Higher selection processes in evolutionary economic change', *J Evol Econ* 2(1): 1–16.

Granstrand, O. and Alänge, S. (1995) The evolution of corporate entrepreneurship in Swedish industry – was Schumpeter wrong?, *J Evol Econ* 5(2): 133–56.

Green, C. (1993) 'From 'tax state' to 'debt state'', *J Evol Econ* 3(1): 23–42.

Greiner, A. and Hanusch, H. (1994) 'Schumpeter's circular flow, learning by doing and cyclical growth', *J Evol Econ* 4(3): 261–71.

Grupp, H. (1996) 'Spillover effects and the science base of innovations reconsidered: an empirical approach', *J Evol Econ* 6(2): 175–97.

Haken, H. (1977) *Synergetics*, Berlin: Springer, 1977.

Hansson, I and Stuart, C. (1992) 'Socialization and altruism', *J Evol Econ* 2(4): 301–12.

Hanusch, H. and Sommer, J. (1998) *A neural net model of portfolio choice*, mimeo.

Heertje, A. (1996) 'Stolper on Schumpeter', *J Evol Econ* 6(4): 339–45.

——(1997) 'From Schumpeter to Stiglitz', *J Evol Econ* 7(3): 255–67.

Heiner, R. A. (1988) 'Imperfect decisions and routinized production: implications for evolutionary modelling and inertial technical change', in: G. Dosi *et al.* (eds) *Technical change and economic theory*, London: Pinter Publishers.

Hesse, G. (1992) 'Land use systems and property rights – evolutionary versus new institutional economics', *J Evol Econ* 2(3): 195–210.

Hirshleifer J. (1982) 'Evolutionary Models in economics and law', *Res Law Econ* 4: 1–60.

Hodgson, G. M. (1988) *Economics and Institutions*, Philadelphia: University of Philadelphia Press.

—— (1989) Institutional economic theory: the old versus the new', *Rev Pol Econ* 1(3): 249–69.

Hodgson, G. M. (1993) *Economics and evolution: bringing life back into economics*, Cambridge K: Polity Press.

—— (1997) 'The evolutionary and non-Darwinian economics of Joseph Schumpeter', *J Evol Econ* 7(2): 131–45.

Holland, J. (1975) *Adaption in natural and artificial systems: an introductory analysis with applications in biology, control and artificial intelligence*, Ann Arbor: Michigan University Press.

Holyst, J. A., Hagel, T., Haag, G. and Weidlich, W. (1996) 'How to control a chaotic economy?', *J Evol Econ* 6(1): 31–42.

Hors, I. and Lordon, F. (1997) 'About some formalisms of interaction. Phase transition models in economics?', *J Evol Econ* 7(4): 355–74.

Iwai, K. (1991) 'Towards a disequilibrium theory of long-run profits', *J Evol Econ* 1: 19–21.

Jenner, R. A. (1994) 'Schumpeterian growth, chaos, and the formation of dissipative structures', *J Evol Econ* 4(2): 125–39.

Joosten, R. (1996) 'Deterministic evolutionary dynamics: a unifying approach', *J Evol Econ* 6(3): 313–24.

Kahneman, D. and Tversky, A. (1979) 'Prospect theory', *Econometrica* 47: 263–91.

—— (1986) 'Rational choices and the framing of decisions', in: R. M. Hogarth, M. W. Reder (eds) *Rational choice, the contrast between economics and psychology*, Chicago: The University of Chicago Press.

Katsoulacos, Y. (1991) 'Technical change and employment under imperfect competition with perfect and imperfect information', *J Evol Econ* 1(3): 207–18.

Kelm, M. (1997) Schumpeter's theory of economic evolution: a Darwinian interpretation, *J Evol Econ* 7(2): 97–130.

Keynes J. M. (1973) *The general theory and after, part II: Defence and development. collected writings of John Maynard Keynes, vol. 4*, London: Macmillan.

Kindleberger, C. P. (1995) 'Technological diffusion: European experience to 1850', *J Evol Econ* 5(3): 229–42.

Kirman, A. (1992) 'Whom or what does the representative individual represent?', *J Econ Persp* 6: 117–36.

Klein, B. H. (1991) 'The role of positive-sum games in economic growth', *J Evol Econ* 1(3): 173–88.

Knight, F. H. (1921) *Risk, uncertainty and profit*. Chicago.

—— (1921) *Risk, uncertainty and profit*, New York: Houghton Mifflin.

Kodama, F. (1992) 'Technology fusion and the new R&D', *Harvard Business Review*, July–August, 70–8.

Kopel, M. (1997) 'Improving the performance of an economic system: controlling chaos', *J Evol Econ* 7(3): 269–89.

Kwasnicki, W. (1994) *Knowledge, innovation and economy. An evolutionary explanation*, Wroclaw: Oficyna Wydawnicza Politechniki Wrocslawskiej.

—— (1996) 'Innovation regimes, entry and market structure', *J Evol Econ* 6(4): 375–410.

Laffond, G. and Lesourne, J. (1992) 'The genesis of expectations and of sunspot equilibria', *J Evol Econ* 2(3): 211–31.

Lane, D. A. (1993a) 'Artificial worlds and economics, Part 1', *J Evol Econ* 3(2): 89–108.

—— (1993b) 'Artificial worlds and economics, Part 2', *J Evol Econ* 3(3): 177–97.

Lane, D. A. Malerba, F., Maxfield, R. and Orsenigo, L. (1996) 'Choice and action', *J Evol Econ* 6(1): 43–76.

Lee, L. W. (1991) 'Entrepreneurship and regulation: dynamics and political economy', *J Evol Econ* 1(3): 219–35.

Lesourne, J. (1991) 'From market dynamics to evolutionary economics', *J Evol Econ* 1(1): 23–7.

Lordon, F. (1997) 'Endogenous structural change and crisis in a multiple time-scales growth model', *J Evol Econ* 7(1): 1–21.

Louca, F. (1997) *Turbulence in economics*, Cheltenham: Edward Elgar.

Maggi, G. (1993) 'Technology gap and international trade: an evolutionary model', *J Evol Econ* 3(2): 109–26.

Mainwaring, L. (1993) 'Endogenous NIC-formation in a North–South framework', *J Evol Econ* 3(4): 317–35.

Maital S., Grupp, H., Frenkel, A. and Koschatzky, K. (1994) 'The relation between the average complexity of high-tech products and their diversity: an empirical test of evolutionary models', *J Evol Econ* 4(4): 273–88.

Malerba, F., Nelson, R. R., Orsenigo, L. and Winter, S. G. (1997) History Friendly modelling: The case of the computer industry, mimeo, Milan: Bocconi University.

Marengo, L. (1992) 'Coordination and organizational learning in the firm', *J Evol Econ* 2(4): 313–26.

Marks, R. E. (1992) 'Breeding hybrid strategies: optimal behaviour for oligopolists', *J Evol Econ* 2(1): 17–38.

Marshall, A. (1890) *Principles of economics*, London: MacMillan.

Maynard S. J. and Price G. R. (1973) 'The Logic of Animal Conflict', *Nature* 246: 15–18.

Menshikov, S. (1994) 'The role of state enterprises in the transition from command to market economies', *J Evol Econ* 4(4): 289–325.

Metcalfe, J. S. (1994) Competition, Fisher's principle and increasing returns in the selection process, *J Evol Econ* 4(4): 327–46.

Metcalfe, J. S. and Calderini, M., (1997) 'Compound learning, neural nets and the competitive process', Paper presented at the workshop Economic evolution, learning and complexity, in Augsburg, May 23–25.

Meyer, B., Vogt, C. and Vosskamp, R. (1996) 'Schumpeterian competition in heterogeneous oligopolies', *J Evol Econ* 6(4): 411–23.

Mokyr, J. (1990) *The lever of riches*, New York: Oxford University Press.

Musgrave, R. A. (1992) 'Schumpeter's crisis of the tax state: an essay in fiscal sociology', *J Evol Econ* 2(2): 89–113.

Nelson, R. R. and Winter, S. G. (1982) *An evolutionary theory of economic change*, Cambridge, Mass.: Cambridge University Press.

Nelson, R. R. (1995) 'Recent evolutionary theorizing about economic change', *J Econ Lit* 33: 48–90.

Nightingale, J. (1997) 'Anticipating Nelson and Winter: Jack Downie's theory of evolutionary economic change', *J Evol Econ* 7(2): 147–67.

Nooteboom, B. (1992) 'Towards a dynamic theory of transactions', *J Evol Econ* 2(4): 281–99.

O'Connor, M. (1993) 'Entropic irreversibility and uncontrolled technological change in economy and environment', *J Evol Econ* 3(4): 285–315.

Özyildirim S, (1997) 'Computing open-loop noncooperative solution in discrete dynamic games', *J Evol Econ* 7(1): 23–40.

Pelikan, P. (1992) 'The dynamics of economic systems, or how to transform a failed socialist economy', *J Evol Econ* 2(1): 39–63.

Perez, T. (1997) 'Multinational enterprises and technological spillovers: an evolutionary model', *J Evol Econ* 7(2): 169–92.

Posch, M. (1997) 'Cycling in a stochastic learning algorithm for normal form games', *J Evol Econ* 7(2): 193–207.

Prigogine, I. and Stengers, I. (1993) *Das Paradox der Zeit. Zeit, Chaos und Quanten*, München: Piper.

Qin, C. Z. and Stuart, C. (1997) 'Are Cournot and Bertrand equilibria evolutionary stable strategies?', *J Evol Econ* 7(1): 41–7.

Sacco, P. L. (1994) 'Can people learn rational expectations? An "ecological" approach', *J Evol Econ* 4(1): 35–43.

Saviotti, P. P. and Mani, G. S. (1995) 'Competition, variety and technological evolution: a replicator dynamics model', *J Evol Econ* 5(4): 369–92.

Scott, J. T. (1995) 'The Damoclean tax and innovation', *J Evol Econ* 5(1): 71–89.

Schnabl, H. (1991) 'Agenda-diffusion and innovation. A simulation model', *J Evol Econ* 1(1): 65–85.

Schuette, H. L. (1994) 'Vintage capital, market structure and productivity in an evolutionary model of industry growth', *J Evol Econ* 4(3): 173–84.

Schumpeter, J. A. (1912) *Theorie der wirtschaftlichen Entwicklung*, Berlin: Duncker & Humblot, 8. Aufl.

—— (1994b) 'Collective learning, innovation and growth in a boundedly rational, evolutionary world', *J Evol Econ* 4(3): 207–26.

—— (1995) 'An evolutionary model of long term cyclical variations of catching up and falling behind', *J Evol Econ* 5(3): 209–27.

—— (1942) *Capitalism, socialism and democracy*, London: Unwin.

Semmler, W. (1994) 'Information, innovation and diffusion of technology', *J Evol Econ* 4(1): 45–58.

Shubik, M. (1996) 'Simulations, models and simplicity', *Complexity* 2: 60.

Shurmer, M. and Swann, P. (1995) 'An analysis of the process generating de facto standards in the PC spreadsheet software market', *J Evol Econ* 5(2): 119–32.

Silverberg, G. (1991) 'Selforganization, technical change and evolution', in W. Ebeling *et al.* (ed.) *Models of selforganization in complex systems*, Berlin.

Silverberg, G. and Verspagen, B. (1994a) 'Learning, innovation and economic growth: A long-run model of industrial dynamics', *Industrial and Corporate Change* 3: 199–223.

Simon, H. A. (1976) 'From substantive to procedural rationality', in S. J. Latsis (ed.) *Method and appraisal in economics*, Cambridge, London *et al.*

Skonhoft, A. (1995) 'Catching up and falling behind, a vintage model approach', *J Evol Econ* 5(3): 285–95.

Stadler, M. (1991) 'R & D dynamics in the product life cycle', *J Evol Econ* 1(4): 293–305.

Stolper, W. F. (1991) 'The theoretical bases of economic policy: the Schumpeterian perspective', *J Evol Econ* 1(3): 189–205.

Swedberg, R. (1992) 'Schumpeter's early work', *J Evol Econ* 2(1): 65–82.

Tamborini, R. (1997) 'Knowledge and economic behaviour. A constructivist approach', *J Evol Econ* 7(1): 49–72.

Thompson, P. (1996) 'Technological opportunity and the growth of knowledge: a Schumpeterian approach to measurement', *J Evol Econ* 6(1): 77–97.

Tinbergen, J. (1995) 'The duration of development', *J Evol Econ* 5(3): 333–9.

Tsuru, S. (1993) 'Two studies of Schumpeter's life: A review essay', *J Evol Econ* 3(4): 263–8.

—— (1995) 'A positive vision for the forerunner economies in the present global context', *J Evol Econ* 5(3): 327–32.

Veblen, T. B. (1898) 'Why is economics not an evolutionary science?', *Q J Econ* 12: 371–97.

Vega-Redondo, F. (1993) 'Technological change and institutional inertia: a game-theoretic approach', *J Evol Econ* 3(3): 199–224.

—— (1994) 'Technological change and path dependence: a co-evolutionary model on a directed graph', *J Evol Econ* 4(1): 59–80.

von Tunzelmann, G. N. (1991) 'Malthus's evolutionary model, expectations, and innovation', *J Evol Econ* 1(4): 273–91.

Wakeley, T. M. (1998) 'Schumpeterian process competition, welfare and laissez-faire: an experiment in artificial economic evolution', *J Evol Econ* 8(1): 45–66.

Walliser, B. (1998) 'A spectrum of equilibration processes in game theory', *J Evol Econ* 8(1): 67–87.

Weidlich, W. and Braun, M. (1992) 'The Master equation approach to nonlinear economics', *J Evol Econ* 2(3): 233–65.

Weidlich, W. and Haag, G. (1983) *Concepts and models of a quantitative sociology*, Berlin: Springer.

Wied-Nebbeling, S. (1993) 'Technical change and market structure. Effects on employment', *J Evol Econ* 3(1): 43–61.

Wijnberg, N. M. (1996) 'Heterochrony, industrial evolution and international trade', *J Evol Econ* 6(1): 99–113.

Winter, S. G. (1971) 'Satisfying, selection and the innovating remnant', *Q J Econ* 85: 237–61.

Wirl, F. (1997) 'Stability and limit cycles in one-dimensional dynamic optimizations of competitive agents with a market externality', *J Evol Econ* 7(1): 73–89.

Witt, U. (1987) *Individualistische Grundlagen der evolutorischen Ökonomik*, Tübingen: J. C. B. Mohr Siebeck.

—— (1992) 'Üerlegungen zum gegenwärtigen Stand der evolutorischen Ökonomik', in B. Bievert (ed.) *Evolutorische ökonomik: Neuerungen, Normen und Institutionen*, Frankfurt a.M.: Campus.

Woeckener, B. (1993) 'Innovation, externalities, and the state: A synergetic approach', *J Evol Econ* 3(3): 225–48.

12 Growth and social welfare with interdependent utility functions*

John Komlos and Peter Salamon

Mark Perlman's distinguished scholarly career encompasses several phases, with one aspect becoming increasingly important over time, namely open skepticism toward mainstream economics (Perlman 1995). Along with McCann's and Nowotny's contributions in this volume, we view conventional assumptions pertaining to the utility maximizing behavior of individual economic agents – fundamental to almost all microeconomic theory – as overly simplified. As they point out, conventional theory abstracts from society and social interaction, and conceptualizes the individual as practically independent of social constraints and forces. Human beings are said to act independently, practically without being imbedded in a social nexus. They are individuals in their consumption decision. Yet, as Perlman, and McCann and Nowotny argue, the economy and the society is more than the sum of individual consuming units. Culture, like institutions, influences utility functions, and hence consumption. In short, human beings in our view are socially defined.

In this essay, presented in Mark's honor, we explore the implications of economic growth for welfare in the presence of interdependent utility functions with negative externalities in consumption, that is, envy. In conventional theory, the utility function of a 'typical' economic agent is generally assumed to be independent of the consumption of others; hence more consumption invariably '… leads to more happiness' not only of the individual, but in the aggregate as well. According to the common wisdom, economic growth leads invariably to an increase in welfare (Layard and Walters 1978: 5). Mark, we are certain, would doubt the validity of this textbook supposition and rightfully so, for experimental evidence refutes the notion that people invariably feel better off with increased consumption (Easterlin 1974; Abramovitz 1979: 9).[1]

Mark would almost certainly fault us for the absence of institutions in our model, and he would probably not be impressed by the mathematics either, but he would be pleased by its linkages to the tradition of two economists whom he greatly admires, Josef Schumpeter and Harvey Leibenstein (Perlman 1990; 1996). Our paper is linked to some extent to their thinking by being concerned with economic growth, by emphasizing that economic and social processes are inextricably intertwined, and by

*The authors are indebted to Kai Konrad, and Hans-Werner Sinn for their helpful suggestions on an earlier version of this paper, without implicating them in any way in its conclusions.

not reducing rationality of economic agents to the simple maximization of their own welfare. That consumption in our model is a social activity implies that '... the individual does not think and act in the same way irrespective of whether he is or is not a member of a group' (Weisskopf 1971: 161; Katona 1975: 49; Leibenstein 1950; Frank 1985; McCracken 1988: xi; Konrad 1992). 'Reference groups' are important for providing standards for the subjective evaluation of one's own well-being, and in formulating expectations and aspirations on which satisfaction frequently depends.[2] Thus, '... people's standards of wealth are determined by comparisons with kin, peers, etc., and thus if they all rise together [over time] the relative difference disappears, and so as people get wealthier over time they do not become any more happy' (Furnham and Lewis 1986: 109).

To be sure, Mark's skepticism toward the received wisdom is shared by others (Sen 1977; Hammond 1989; Konrad and Lommerud 1992); interdependent utility functions have been formulated ever since the publication of Veblen's seminal theory of conspicuous consumption[3] (1899; Mishan 1961; Frank March 1985; Bagwell and Bernheim 1996; Postlewaite 1998). Duesenberry '... specifie[d] utility of an individual as a function of his own income and that of the income of the other members of the society'[4] (Duesenberry 1949: 97). Admittedly, consumption can also have positive externalities, for example, a wife's utility can enter the utility function of her spouse altruistically (Becker 1981).

Empirical and theoretical investigations of the social nature of utility functions are important for several reasons: the 'neglect of interdependence of welfare functions may substantially bias policy conclusions' (Kapteyn and Herwaarden 1980: 395); it also has major implications for progressive taxation (Feldstein 1976: 81; Ng 1987), for income redistribution, for the formulation of growth policy, as well as for the justification of the existence of the welfare state in general (Freshtman, Murphy and Weiss 1996; Hammond 1991).[5] We proceed in this vein, and explore some implications of economic growth for welfare in the presence of interdependent utility functions following Feldstein's formulation.[6] We demonstrate that, contrary to standard theory, growth need not raise aggregate welfare, if its benefits accrue unevenly, and if the utility functions of the economic agents are interdependent (Konrad 1992). Mark, we believe, would find that conclusion intuitively plausible.

The model

We begin with a model in which the society is assumed to be composed of two individuals A and B with interdependent Cobb–Douglas utility functions with one good, x (i.e., income).[7]

$$U_\mathrm{A} = \frac{(x_\mathrm{A}^{\alpha_a})}{(x_\mathrm{B}^{\beta_a})} \quad ; \quad U_\mathrm{B} = \frac{(x_\mathrm{B}^{\alpha_b})}{(x_\mathrm{A}^{\beta_b})}. \tag{1}$$

where the α's and β's are constants. The social welfare function is assumed to be additive and democratic:

$$U_\mathrm{T} = U_\mathrm{A} + U_\mathrm{B}. \tag{2}$$

Suppose that national income increases exogenously, for example, through the discovery of new resources. Assume that the increment in x accrues only to A. The question is under what circumstances, if any, might economic growth lead to a decline in total welfare, contrary to standard analysis (McAdams 1992).

Noting that

$$\frac{\partial U_T}{\partial x_A} = \alpha_a \frac{U_A}{x_A} - \beta_b \frac{U_B}{x_A}, \tag{3}$$

we obtain that the aggregate utility of the society decreases if and only if

$$U_A/U_B < \beta_b/\alpha_a. \tag{4}$$

The outcome depends on the relative magnitudes of the terms on the two sides of this inequality. The right-hand side is an index of the degree of interdependence of the utility functions, while the left-hand side measures the inequality in the initial distribution of utility. The initial income distribution determines U_A/U_B, and hence whether it is smaller than β_b/α_a. The stronger is the interdependence, that is, the larger is the value of β_b/α_a, the larger is the range of utility values for which inequality (4) holds.

The ratio β_b/α_a, indicates the extent to which the consumption of x by A decreases B's utility as compared with the extent that it increases A's own utility. The size of the ratio is indicative of the degree to which members of society may be characterized as 'envious' (β) relative to being self-sufficient (α). The larger is the ratio, the stronger is the interdependence. Without interdependence $\beta = 0$ and the ratio on the right-hand side is zero, making it impossible for inequality (4) to ever hold, since the left hand side is always positive. In an altruistic society $\beta < 0$, and again the inequality becomes impossible. Consequently, in these two cases we have the standard conclusion that growth always increases total welfare. If $\beta > 0$, however, the inequality can hold provided the ratio of utility levels is less than β_b/α_a. The case $\beta_b/\alpha_a > 1$ corresponds to the unrealistic case of a society in which enviousness dominates over self-centeredness.[8] Hence, we assume that $0 < \beta_b/\alpha_a < 1$.

In this parameter range, growth can lead to a diminution in total social welfare in the two-person case, provided the gain accrues to the individual whose utility is initially lower by a sufficient ratio. This result becomes understandable by noting that in this model a part of the utility of the 'wealthier' person, B, is derived from his relative wealth. If he is sufficiently envious, his utility can decrease more than the increase in A's utility.[9]

The main conclusion from the above example is that there exists a region of parameter space where an exogenous increase in income which changes the distribution of income, decreases total welfare in a democratic aggregate utility function. One should note that this conclusion is dependent on the assumed form of the utility function. In particular, if we repeat the analysis with $U' = \ln U$, where U is as in Equation 1, the conclusion changes and welfare increases in response to growth with any income distribution provided only that $\beta_b < \alpha_a$, as expected. On the other hand, replacing the Cobb–Douglas utility functions (Eq. 1) with Stone-Geary, or, in fact, with separable utility functions of the form

$$U_A = \frac{\widehat{U_A}}{\widehat{U_B}^{\delta_a}} \; ; \quad U_B = \frac{\widehat{U_B}}{\widehat{U_A}^{\delta_b}} \tag{5}$$

where $\widehat{U}$ indicates the utility of a consumer at some fixed level of utility for the other consumer,[10] we obtain that total welfare can decrease provided[11]

$$\frac{U_A}{U_B} < \delta_b. \tag{6}$$

The parameter δ_b now plays the role of β_b/α_a.

Conclusion

The above model explores the welfare implications of economic growth in a society composed of individuals with interdependent utility functions with negative externalities in consumption. We demonstrate that there do exist specifications of utility functions with regions of parameter space in which the welfare consequences of a rise in per-capita income are ambiguous, if the gains are distributed unequally. Hence, economic growth might bring about an increase as well as a decrease in aggregate social welfare depending on the relationship between the two indices in Equation (4). One index measures the extent of envy in the society and the other the degree of income inequality as measured by the initial ratio of utilities. Total welfare is more likely to decrease if (a) the gains from growth accrue disproportionately to the individual with the lower level of utility, (b) the more envious is the individual who does not benefit from growth, (c) the less selfish is the individual who gains from growth, and (d) the more unequally income is distributed initially.[12]

These considerations are important, insofar as economic growth has been frequently associated with the skewing of the income distribution in favor of the upper income brackets. In a historical context, Simon Kuznets recognized this pattern for the early phases of modern economic growth (Kuznets 1966: 212; Williamson and Lindert 1980: 62, 67; Lindert 1991: 216; Williamson 1985: 18; Williamson 1991: 15),[13] and recent evidence confirms the increase in the Gini coefficient in Eastern Europe and the successor states of the Soviet Union during the recent transition to a market economy (Milanovic 1996: 133). In many of these countries the Gini coefficient increased from 0.25 to 0.30 in just five years (United Nations Development 1993: 17). In the United Kingdom a 2.1 per cent growth rate in per capita GNP between 1965 and 1993 has been accompanied by a rise in the Gini coefficient from 0.25 to 0.32. (The World Bank, 1993). In most countries of the world a wide divide separates the poor from the rich. In the United States, for instance, the richest 20 per cent of the population earns nine times as much as the poorest 20 per cent.[14] Hence, insofar as the benefits of economic growth often accrue unevenly, our theoretical considerations have practical policy implications.

Clearly, we analyzed a special case, and therefore, the result ought not be assumed to pertain generally. Nonetheless, our derivation does have far-reaching policy implications. One issue to explore is the extent to which the utility functions of economic agents are interdependent. We have demonstrated that with gains of economic growth accruing unevenly, circumstances do exist such that a society could be better off either by choosing to forgo the opportunities for growth, or by government policy affecting the distribution of gains. Thus, there is room for government intervention: as Nowotny points out in Chapter 5, p. 64 under the general heading of distributional objectives, 'it is legitimate in a democratic state to influence income distribution if the order which results from free interaction of market forces is regarded as unjust by the majority of the people.' The reason for the existence of the welfare state is not only the amelioration of market failure, or the provision of comprehensive security, but also because of the existence of externalities in consumption – envy – imply that individual utility maximization does not automatically bring about utility maximization for the society. The society could be not only happier, but also more stable politically, with a more even distribution of the gains from growth, and a diminution in envy (Hammond 1995). Our conclusion vividly redirects our focus from growth *per se* to its distributional consequences for aggregate welfare.[15] In sum, the interdependent nature of a society's utility function should not be neglected in the formulation of economic policy, particularly with regard to such key issues as progressive taxation, redistribution of income, and the enactment of growth-inducing policy measures.[16]

Notes

1 Admittedly, in the short run '… one might feel happier by a recent increase in the standard of living, [but] one soon adapts to this and the positive relationship disappears.' Hence, over time '… no strong positive relationship [has been found] either cross-sectionally or longitudinally between money [income] and happiness' (Furnham and Lewis 1986: 109). We are not substantially happier than our ancestors even though we consume much more than they did (Scitovsky 1976).

2 As Duesenberry pointed out a generation ago, 'the utility derived from one's own house or car depends on a friend's house or car' (1949: 27).

3 Its main insight fits well the post-World War II U.S. private consumption experience (Bassman, Molina and Slottje 1988).

4 Furthermore, the price of the consumed good can be included in the utility function, thus generating a 'snob appeal' effect (Basmann, Molina and Slottje 1983; Haavelmo 1970; Fisher 1977; Spiegel and Templeman 1985; Frank 1987).

5 For instance, Spiegel and Templeman have shown '… that a 'compulsory bundle' which a group … accepts as binding upon all its members might be superior to any other consumption pattern from the point of view of each and every member of the group' (1985: 315). Moreover, employees care about relative income within a firm, not only about their own absolute salaries (Frank 1984).

6 In Feldstein's analysis initially $U_A = U_B$, and $\alpha = \beta$ (notation as in Equation 1). He finds that an increment accruing unequally between two members of a society raises social welfare.

7 The presence of additional goods complicates the notation while leaving the analysis and conclusions unchanged.

8 If the distribution of income is egalitarian to begin with (i.e. $U_B = U_A$), then social welfare is likely to increase. This follows, since in this case inequality (4) holds only if $\beta_b/\alpha_a > 1$.

9 We can extend the analysis of the model in Equation (1) to n individuals. We treat only the simplest case of a society with two types of individuals A and B. We assume that all type A (or type B) individuals have identical utility functions and are at identical levels of utility. If there are n_A individuals of type A and n_B individuals of type B, then the total democratic welfare function becomes $U_T = n_A U_A + n_B U_B$. The constants n_A and n_B are carried through the derivation, yielding a modified form of inequality (4): $n_A U_A / n_B U_B < \beta_b / \alpha_a$. The larger is the number of individuals who do not partake in the benefits of growth relative to the number of individuals who do benefit, the smaller β_b / α_a can be and still allow the last inequality to be satisfied, implying a decline in welfare as a consequence of growth.

Note that similar inequalities also follow for non-democratic welfare functions if one reinterprets the coefficients n_A and n_B as the degrees to which society values the utility that accrues to A and B. The n person case also follows if the coefficients are again reinterpreted as the number of individuals times the degree to which the utility of such individuals is valued. Again, if the total initial welfare of the subgroup to which the gain accrues is sufficiently small as compared with the total welfare of the subgroup not enjoying gains, the total combined welfare of the two subgroups will decrease. Thus, there exist ways to apportion additional income to a population so as to decrease its total welfare.

10 We require that the indifference curves of each consumer be unaffected by the consumption of the other.

11 Once again, using a democratic welfare function and assuming that the gains accrue entirely to A as an increase in x_A, we have

$$U_T = \frac{\widehat{U_A}}{\widehat{U_B}^{\delta_a}} + \frac{\widehat{U_B}}{\widehat{U_A}^{\delta_b}}$$

and

$$\frac{\partial U_T}{\partial x_A} = \frac{\partial \widehat{U_A}}{\partial x_A} \left(\frac{1}{\widehat{U_B}^{\delta_a}} - \delta_b \frac{\widehat{U_B}}{\widehat{U_A}^{\delta_b+1}} \right)$$

which is negative provided $(\widehat{U_A})^{\delta_b+1}/(\widehat{U_B})^{\delta_a+1} < \delta_b$. If we note that $U_A / U_B = (\widehat{U_A})^{\delta_b+1}/(\widehat{U_B})^{\delta_a+1}$ the inequality reduces to $U_A / U_B < \delta_b$.

12 In the n person case the outcome depends also on the number of people who benefit from the gains from growth relative to the number who do not.

13 This is the case partly because economic growth is never a Pareto-optimal process: technological change depresses the market value of some skills and capital.

14 The comparable figure for Brazil is 32 (United Nations Development 1993: 17).

15 In addition, envy can have an influence on the growth process itself (Cole *et al.* 1992).

16 'If growth is less important for welfare than we have so far supposed, other goals would rise in the scale of social priorities' (Abramovitz 1979: 20).

References

Abramovitz, M. (1979) 'Economic growth and its discontents', in Michael J. Boskin (ed.) *Economics and Human Welfare. Essays in Honor of Tibor Scitovsky* New York: Academic Press, pp. 3–22.

Bagwell, L. S. and Bernheim, B. D. (1996) 'Veblen effects in a theory of conspicuous consumption', *American Economic Review* 86(3): 349–73.

Basmann, R. L., Molina, D. J. and Daniel, J. S. (1983) 'Budget constraint prices as preference changing parameters of generalized Fechner–Thurstone direct utility functions', *American Economic Review* 73: 411–13.

Basmann, R. L., Molina, D. J. and Slottje, D. J. (1988) 'A Note on measuring Veblen's theory of conspicuous consumption', *Review of Economics and Statistics* 70: 531–5.

Becker, G. S. (1981) 'Altruism in the family and selfishness in the market place', *Economica*, new ser 48: 1–15.

Cole, H. L., Maliath, G. J. and Postelwaite, A. (1992) 'Social norms, saving behavior, and growth', *Journal of Political Economy* 100(6): 1092–125.

Duesenberry, J. S. (1967) *Income, Saving, and the Theory of Consumer Behavior.* New York: Oxford University Press. First published in 1949.

Easterlin, R. A. (1974) 'Does economic growth improve the human lot?', in P. A. David and M. W. Reder (eds) *Nations and Households in Economic Growth* (New York: Academic Press, pp. 89–125.

Feldstein, M. (1976) 'On the theory of tax reform', *Journal of Public Economics* 6: 77–104.

Fershtman Chaim, Murphy Kevin, M. and Yoram Weiss (1996) 'Social status, education, and growth', *Journal of Political Economy* 104: 108–32.

Fisher, F. M. (1977) 'On donor sovereignty and united charities,' *American Economic Review* 67: 632–8.

Frank, R. H. (Sept. 1987) 'If homo economicus could choose his own utility function. Would he want one with a conscience?', *American Economic Review* 77(4): 593–604.

—— (1985) *Choosing the Right Pond. Human Behavior and the Quest for Status*, New York: Oxford University Press.

—— (1985) 'Demand for unobservable and other nonpositional goods', *American Economic Review* 75: 101–16.

—— (1984) 'Interdependent preferences and the competitive wage structure', *Rand Journal of Economics* 15: 510–20.

Furnham, A. and Lewis, A. (1986) *The Economic Mind. The Social Psychology of Economic Behavior*, New York: St Martins Press.

Haavelmo, T. (1970) 'Some observations on welfare and economic growth', in W. A. Eltis, M. FG. Scott, and J. N. Wolfe (eds) *Induction, Growth and Trade: Essays in Honour of Sir Roy Harrod*, Oxford: Clarendon Press, pp. 65–75.

Hammond, P. J. (1989) 'Some assumptions of contemporary neoclassical economic theology', in G. R. Feiwel, (ed.) *Joan Robinson and Modern Economic Theory.* New York: New York University Press; distributed by Columbia University Press, pp. 186–257.

—— (1991) 'Interpersonal comparisons of utility: why and how they are and should be made', in Jon Elster and John E. Roemer (eds) *Interpersonal comparisons of well-being. Studies in Rationality and Social Change*, Cambridge; New York and Melbourne: Cambridge University Press in collaboration with Maison des Sciences de l'Homme, pp. 200–54.

—— (1995) 'Altruism', in Stefano Zamagni, (ed.) *The Economics of Altruism*, Elgar Reference Collection. International Library of Critical Writings in Economics, vol. 48. Aldershot, UK, pp. 165–67.

Kapteyn, A. and Van Herwaarden, Floor G. (1980) 'Interdependent welfare functions and optimal income distribution', *Journal of Public Economics* 14: 375–97.

Katona, G. (1975) *Pycological Economics*, New York: Elsevier Scientific Publishing Co., Inc.

Konrad, K. (1990) 'Statuspräferenzen: soziobiologische ursachen, statuswettrüsten und seine besteuerung', *Kyklos* 43: 249–70.

—— (1992) 'Wealth seeking reconsidered', *Journal of Economic Behaviour and Organization* 18: 215–27.

Konrad, K. and Lommerud K. E. (1992) 'Relative standing comparisons, risk taking, and safety regulations', *Journal of Public Economics* 48.

Kuznets, S. (1966) *Modern Economic Growth: Rate, Structure, and Spread*, New Haven: Yale University Press.

Layard, P. R. G. and Walters, A. A. (1978) *Microeconomic Theory*, New York: McGraw Hill Book C.

Leibenstein, H. (May 1950) 'Bandwagon, snob, and Veblen effects in the theory of consumers' demand.' *Quarterly Journal of Economics* 64(2): 183–207.

Lindert, P. (1991) 'Toward a comparative history of income and wealth inequality', in Y. S. Brenner, H. Kaelble, and M. Thomas (eds) *Income Distribution in Historical Perspective*, Cambridge: Cambridge University Press, pp. 212–231.

McAdams, R. H. (1992) 'Relative Preferences', *The Yale Law Review* 102: 1–104.

McCracken, G. (1988) *Culture and Consumption. New Approaches to the Symbolic Character of Consumer Goods and Activities*, Bloomington: Indiana Univ. Press.

Milanovic, B. (1996) 'Income, inequality and poverty during the transition: a survey of the evidence', *MOCT-MOST Economic Policy in Transitional Economies* 6(1): 131–47.

Mishan, E. J. (1961) 'Theories of consumer's behaviour: a cynical view', *Economica*, new ser., 27: 1–11.

Ng, Y. K. (March 1987) 'Diamonds are a government's best friend: burden-free taxes on goods valued for their values', *American Economic Review* 77(1): 186–91.

Perlman, M. (1995) 'What makes my mind tick', *American Economist* 39(2): 6–27.

—— (1996) *The Character of Economic Thought, Economic Characters, and Economic Institutions: Selected Essays of Mark Perlman*, Ann Arbor: University of Michigan Press.

Postlewaite, A. (1998) 'The social basis of interdependent preferences', *European Economic Review*, 42: 779–800.

Scitovsky, T. (1976) *The Joyless Economy*, New York: Oxford University Press.

Sen, A. (1977) 'Rational fools: a critique of the behavioral foundations of economic theory', *Philosophy and Public Affairs* 6: 317–44.

Spiegel, U. and Templeman, J. (1985) 'Interdependent utility and cooperative behaviour.' *Journal of Comparative Economics* 9: 314–28.

United Nations Development Programme (1993) *Human Development Report 1993*, New York: Oxford University Press.

Veblen, T. (1899) *The Theory of the Leisure Class*, New York: Macmillan.

Weiermair, K. and Perlman, M. (eds) (1990) *Studies in Economic Rationality: X-efficiency Examined and Extolled: Essays Written in the Tradition of and to Honor Harvey Leibenstein*, Ann Arbor: University of Michigan Press.

Weisskopf, W. A. (1971) *Alienation and Economics*, New York: E. P. Dutton and Co., Inc.

Williamson, J. (1985) *Did British capitalism breed inequality?*, London: Allen & Unwin.

—— (1991) *Inequality, Poverty, and History. The Kuznets Memorial Lectures of the Economic Growth Center, Yale University*, Oxford: Basil Blackwell.

Williamson, J. and Peter Lindert (1980) *American Inequality: A Macroeconomic History*, New York: Academic Press.

The World Bank (1993) *World Development Report 1993. Investing in Health*, New York: Oxford University Press.

13 New perspectives on the role of the state

Joseph E. Stiglitz

It is an honor for me to contribute to this *Festschrift* for Mark Perlman. Both through his writings and service to the economics profession as the long-time editor of the *Journal of Economic Literature*, Mark has had a lasting impact. He sought to break out of the mold of the standard neoclassical paradigm that had come to dominate the economics profession during the second half of this century, and equally importantly, he encouraged others to do the same. His broad historical background not only made clear the limitations of that approach, but also gave him a broader perspective to look at these current fashions – he knew that they too would someday pass.

This essay is also dedicated to the memory of Professor Recktenwald. An earlier and shorter version of the paper was presented on the occasion of my receiving the second biennial Rechtenwald Prize, at Nuremberg, on February 4, 1998.[1] The topic of the essay reflects Professor Rechtenwald's lifelong interests in the subject of public economics, as well as Professor Perlman's lifelong skepticism of the neoclassical paradigm and his emphasis on the role of collective action. It puts forward a view of the role of the state which explicitly takes into account the deficiencies of the market, yet recognizes the key limitations of the state.

Those of us who have devoted so much of our interest to the study of public finance and public economics more generally, do so based on three premises:

1　Collective action is important,
2　There is scope for improving the efficiency and responsiveness of government,
3　Rational, scientific analyses combined with careful historical research can shed light on how this can be most effectively done.

My experience over the past five years in the White House and at the World Bank, has reinforced my conviction on each of these counts – and my belief that there is much that the public sector can do both to improve its performance and to improve the lives of the people whom it is supposed to serve.

I want now to describe how theory, experience, and history have changed our perspectives on the answers to four key issues:

1　What government should do,
2　At what level of government should various activities be conducted,

3   How government should do what it does,
4   How government relates to its citizens.

First, on the question of what government should do. The question most often posed is whether government is too large. But this is not really the central issue. The key question *should* be, is the government doing the right thing?

Our thinking about this has developed through several stages in recent decades. Adam Smith, who is often interpreted to have provided the rationale for why markets are better than government in addressing economic needs, actually imparted a more nuanced message. He recognized the importance of collectively provided goods, the role of the government in providing certain goods such as education. Over the succeeding 150 years, this perspective became refined into what is now called the 'market failures' approach. The market provides too much of some goods – like pollution – and too little of other goods – like research. About a decade ago, my research with Bruce Greenwald showed that the scope for market failure was much greater than had previously been realized. We showed that in the presence of incomplete markets and imperfect information, the market equilibrium would not even be constrained Pareto optimal.[2]

In the meanwhile, a counterattack, attempting to delimit the scope for government, was launched. It had three arguments: that government is harmful, that it is ineffective, and that it is unnecessary. The extreme versions of these statements may be a peculiarly American preoccupation, but the general ideas have spread across the globe and are used in almost every discussion of policy.

The first proposition, that government is necessarily harmful to growth and development, can be easily refuted by pointing to East Asia's progress over the past few decades.[3] Marked government intervention did not seem to impede the rates of growth in Korea, Thailand, Singapore or the other high-performing East Asian economies. In contrast, I would argue that the governments' intervention has actually had an enormous effect in *promoting* this unprecedented rapid economic growth, growth which the recent crises, despite their severity, has not erased. This is not the place to discuss the causes of those crises, but let me simply note that in many ways it was the consequence of the state doing too little in some areas, e.g. pursuing rapid financial liberalization without strengthening regulation or supervision.

A glance at the history of the United States' (US) development demonstrates that the idea of selective state activism is not new. The US government provided the initial information and expertise for several key sectors which have contributed strongly to US' growth. The federal government basically founded the telecommunications industry, for example, when it financed the first telegraph line between Baltimore and Washington in 1842. The state withdrew as soon as it had demonstrated the viability of the new technology, allowing subsequent development to come from the private sector. The state's catalytic role remains quite clear. More recently, the Internet was developed by the Federal Government for a very small cost in relation to the huge effect it has had on the way modern business – and increasingly modern life – is conducted.

I could easily give other examples of successful state activism over the past few centuries. Most people believe, for example, that the enormous increase in productivity of agriculture in the US in the nineteenth century can be traced back to the establishment of the Land Grant colleges in the Agricultural Extension Services that began in 1863 by the Morrell Act. More broadly, the role of the Federal Government in education in the US actually began in 1785, even before the US Constitution was ratified.

Although it is unambiguously clear that governments do make mistakes, the previous examples show that it is far from clear that governments are harmful. On balance, the impressive list of government achievements – stimulating economic growth, attacking inequality, and providing safety nets, to provide just a few examples – shows that the state can be a beneficial partner in growth and development, and in raising living standards more broadly.

Anecdotes of success or failure are, perhaps, not as convincing as the argument put forward by critics of a large governmental role, who contend that governments necessarily have adverse effects. They look for behaviors that are inherent in the political process, identifying discrepancies between incentives of politicians and those of the people they are supposed to serve.[4] Such 'agency' problems are important, but of course they arise in the private sector as much as they do in the public; and they are more important in those lines of activity where performance in general (and individual output in particular) is hard to assess.[5]

The discussion below shows how today governments, like businesses, can work to mitigate these problems. The more general point is that the presence of such problems is a factor which determines what government should do or how it should do it; but there are still key roles which government needs to perform, as discussed further below.

Among these, one of the more widely accepted is that of stabilization. But critics of government action (like Milton Friedman) have even argued that in this realm government has failed. But these criticisms of government's macro-economic performance is not substantiated by detailed empirical analysis. In Stiglitz (1997) I show that since World War II economic downturns have been shorter while expansions longer than prior to World War I, and that, while in the earlier period, downturns were predictable (and thus, presumably, could have been avoided by timely government actions), since World War II, they have not been. I interpret this to suggest that government has taken actions to offset any anticipatable downturn; it is only 'unexpected' events – like the oil price shock – that give rise to downturns. By contrast, in the earlier period, recoveries were random; since World War II, the longer is the downturn, the more likely is the recovery in the following period. Again, I interpret this to imply that activist government policies limit the duration and severity of recessions.

The evidence from the US and East Asia also addresses the second critique of the state: the statement that anything the Government does will be undone by the private sector.[6] This second argument about the state's ineffectiveness is used most often in the debate about monetary policy, but even this narrow argument contains flaws. The theorems developed by new classical macroeconomics that demonstrate government's inability to affect the economy's expansion and contraction, for example, rely on very special assumptions that account neither for the asymmetries of information, the lags in responses, nor for the government's inability to change the relative prices faced by firms and households. A closer look at the literature and the world shows that, in fact, private sector reactions generally do not undo the actions of the Government.

The final critique of the state is in some sense the deepest question: 'Why do we have a Government in the first place instead of just voluntary organizations, firms, households, and collectivities?'[7] I would answer that question by invoking the well-developed theory of collective goods. Although recognition of the scope for voluntary organizations and collective action taken by voluntary organizations has grown over recent years, few would argue that public goods such as national defense could be privately provided without a real problem with free riding.[8] Most societies have recognized this and allowed the state, the only organization with universal membership and certain powers of compulsion, to intervene and alleviate this free riding problem.[9] Everyone in a particular area must be a citizen of the relevant state, and this citizenship includes both obligations and benefits.

The limitations of the state

Despite its unique powers, however, certain constraints prevent the state from competing effectively with the private sector. The first set of constraints are prudential restrictions created by citizens. Most societies have recognized that the same characteristics that enable the state to promote the collective good can and have been used for damaging ends. Legal frameworks of due process, mandatory provisions for equal treatment, and extensive regulation of the civil service are some of the most common examples of the ways that these dangers have been addressed. Although prudential, these constraints also mean that the Government cannot function as effectively as the private sector. A public sector supervisor, unlike a private manager, cannot simply hire the person he or she believes to be the best for the job and pay him or her accordingly. On the one hand, these kinds of regulations make sense as safeguards against corruption and cronyism in the government. They prevent the taxpayers from having to pay unjustly high salaries to people whose skills have been mistakenly overvalued. On the other hand, civil service codes can make it difficult for the government to attract good workers.

The second set of constraints has to do with the nature of the government and its inherent lack of ability to make binding commitments. The Government enforces the commitments of the private sector, but it cannot make commitments *of the same kind*. To be sure, courts can ensure that legislation complies with the Constitution and that the government fulfills its contracts with private citizens. But ultimately, the only device the government as a whole can use to enforce its commitments is to create transaction costs, the cost of revising or reneging on its agreements. These range from very low in the case of a politician's campaign pledge to very high in the case of constitutional provisions. Nevertheless, the state can basically break almost any commitment if it is willing to undertake those transaction costs.

In summary, the state has both powers and limitations which set it apart distinctly from other forms of organization in our society. There are different ways in which societies can engage in collective actions, each with their strengths and weaknesses; and different extents to which collective and private actions can be used to address societal needs. We should focus our attention on determining what blends of public and private action are most effective, for example, in addressing the market failures and distribution issues that motivate the need to go beyond pure market solutions. And the answer will depend on the circumstances of each country; while market failures may be more significant in less developed countries, so too the ability of government to address them may be more limited. Thus, there is not even an *a priori* view about the appropriate 'scale' of government in the process of development.

Evolution of thought about the role of the state

Thought about the appropriate role of the state has evolved through three main stages over the past 50 years.

We accepted and in fact encouraged a large role for the state in the years just after World War II. Russia's success in growing from a less developed state to what seemed, at the time, to be a modern economy, was considered by some to be an inspirational model. There was an emphasis on planning and many countries went so far as to establish planning commissions. The planning mentality influenced the way people thought about politics as well; some textbooks written around that period agonized about a trade-off between democracy and economic growth. Within the World Bank, my predecessor Hollis Chenery contributed many interesting ideas as well as some very sophisticated planning models to the debate.

Nevertheless, a growing number of economists believed that these models left out incentives, institutions, and other key factors that make economies work. The belief in the value of the large planning state began to erode in the 1970s and Chenery's later work demonstrates his growing understanding of the limitations of the planning approach. The intellectual basis for central planning came under strong attack on the grounds that one simply could not have the level of information required to run a modern, complex economy in any centralized place. Given these limitations it is not surprising that their success was short-lived. People in the highly interventionist countries sacrificed economic opportunities as well as democracy and freedom.

We should remember, however, the origins of the planning-interventionist strategies: markets by themselves seemed to have failed to generate development. The market failures approach, to which I alluded earlier, provided a theoretical structure which helped explain why markets could not be relied upon. But the problems were even deeper: they concerned inadequacies in entrepreneurship and innovation, topics which the traditional economics paradigm gave short shrift, though they had been at the center of some of the earlier discussions of development, for example, Schumpeter (1942, 1986; 1946). As the limitations of the central planning in the Soviet system became apparent, many sought to combine the allocative efficiency of free-market prices with socialism to create market socialism. Nevertheless, I would argue that the idea of market socialism really failed to understand what makes market economies work. In *Whither Socialism* I attributed this flaw in market socialism to misguided notions within neoclassical economics.[10] Market socialists believed strongly in the power of the price system partly because neoclassical economics claimed that prices were the core mechanism that makes a market economy work. We now realize, however, that this neoclassical paradigm leaves out entrepreneurship, innovation, and other important dimensions that are central to the market economy's success. Market socialist economies may have been a bit more successful than the command-and-control economies, but they still did not capture the whole flavor of the market economy and clearly did not achieve anything like what those who advocated this approach had hoped.

A general consensus that planning and state intervention was not likely to deliver economic progress formed by the end of the 1980s. Nearly all economists recognized that the government could not run everything and many went further to argue that government was the problem rather than the solution.[11] The prevailing line of thought gave markets a primary place and assigned the very limited role of correcting market failures to the government. Market failures were narrowly defined as well, leaving government to focus on maintaining income stability, providing public goods, and correcting major externalities, like those associated with the environment.

Dissatisfaction with this particular perspective grew as many countries followed these policies without achieving much higher growth. In contrast, we witnessed the experience of the East Asian countries who achieved rapid growth without following many of the prescriptions, especially the ones pertaining to liberalization and deregulation.

States as a complement to markets

This led to the third view, which places markets at the center, but recognizes that governments play an important role in making markets work well. It sees the role of the state not just to implement Pigouvian taxation to correct externalities but to complement markets by helping provide the information and institutional, human and physical infrastructure required for markets to exist and function well.

The working of the financial sector illustrates the complementarity between the state and the market. We all recognize the importance of the financial sector, for example. In the wake of the Mexican crisis in 1995 and the more recent crises in East Asia, the topic is getting a lot more resonance than usual, but even before that there was widespread recognition of the importance of a healthy financial sector because of its role in mobilizing and allocating past and present savings. We *should* all recognize the role of the state in this sector: virtually every country that has an effective financial system has a large regulatory role for the government and a strong legal system that protects the rights of minority shareholders.

The Czech experiment in developing capital markets highlights the importance of these legal foundations for capital markets. A weak legal structure and the absence of a securities and exchange commission has allowed companies to, in effect, steal from the minority shareholders. People have no confidence in a securities market where these kinds of events can occur.[12]

Government action in the financial sector can be seen as illustrating the complementarity between the state and private sector. When the government performs its regulatory role well, the private sector can also perform its role well, with competition among the financial institutions for gathering funds and performing efficient financial intermediation.

The evolution of the technology in telecommunications and electricity sectors demonstrates the need for flexibility in determining the extent of state involvement. We used to think of electricity and telephone services as natural monopolies where one could have either a state enterprise or a single firm and a strong regulator to prevent abuse of monopoly power. Economics departments taught this approach and countries throughout the world practiced it. Changes in technology, however, have forced us to alter our views. We were slow to recognize the developments which reduced the scope for natural monopoly and made some forms of competition quite viable, but we now realize, for example, that we can have competition in the generation of electricity. Long-line transmission may still be a natural monopoly, but several countries including the US and Britain have moved to an open-access system where anybody can link their generating plants to the transmission grid. These countries now have effective competition and less state involvement in electricity generation.

Telecommunications policy has evolved in a similar fashion and, while local service remains highly concentrated, long-distance service has become quite competitive. The role of the state in these sectors has had to be redefined along the way. Regulatory concerns in these sectors have changed, for now regulators must watch to make sure that particular elements of natural monopoly are not leveraged to get monopoly control over other potentially competitive sections of the industry.

The meat-packing industry offers a mundane, but illustrative, example of need for flexible, evolving, government action in the face of changing technology. Government regulation of the meat-packing industry began as a confidence-inspiring measure to assure citizens that the meat they bought was safe. After Upton Sinclair's *The Jungle* graphically exposed the unsanitary conditions in Chicago stockyards, meat-packing companies themselves pushed for more stringent state regulation. The government complemented the private sector by establishing a credible system for visual inspection. With the discovery of nearly-invisible disease-causing microbes and advances in microbiology, however, the government has had to adapt its inspection strategy. As the government has switched to more sophisticated risk analysis systems, it has had to overcome opposition from the meat inspectors. With the advent of meat irradiation, it has also had to prove the safety, rather than just the efficacy, of its techniques. There has clearly been a constant role for the government in ensuring meat safety, but how it performs this duty has changed significantly over the years.

Although we can still create a long generic list of the core elements that the government must provide to complement the private sector, we have become increasingly aware the ideal role of the state in each country is more difficult to determine. The role of the state in providing the institutional infrastructure of an economy has become more apparent. We recognize that this may be one of the most important ingredients in differentiating between the economies that have been successful in economic growth and development and those that have not.

Indeed, it is increasingly recognized that the failure of so many of the countries in the former Soviet Union to make an effective transition to a market economy was precisely because they failed to provide the institutional infrastructure (e.g. the legal underpinnings) for a market economy.

What the government should do will clearly change with the changes in technology and the changing circumstances of each country – with changes in the market and the institutional capacity of government. But while there is no simple formula, no single recipe, the analysis of this section should have made clear that what is required is 'balance': more than a minimalist role, but less than an all-encompassing role, a role in which the government *focuses* on areas of relative strength, where there are well identified lacuna in the market. But the market complementarity view goes beyond the simplistic approach which says that certain areas (like defense) should be the domain of the public sector, while others (like making steel) should be the domain of the private. The public and private sectors often need to work in tandem as 'partners' within the same arena, as we noted in the context of financial markets.

At what level should the state act?

Throughout the world, there is increasing emphasis on devolution and decentralization, on the notion that more of the responsibilities of government should be conducted at the local level. The motivations for these changes are complex – involving matters of politics as well as principles. I do not have time here to review all the relevant considerations, but I do want to target a theme which I stressed in the previous section: that changes in the world necessitate rethinking the appropriate balance.

From the normative perspective, there are two simple principles: The first principle states that decisions, the impact of which is local, should be made locally: local public goods (public goods, the benefits of which are received by those in a particular locality) should be provided by local communities. To enhance the likelihood of congruence between marginal (social) benefits and costs, those who benefit (the local community) should also be made to pay, as federal subsidies tied to the provision of particular local public goods may lead to distorted resource allocations.

But devolution of decision-making and finance is not without its costs: there may be limits in the extent of redistribution. Localities cannot impose taxes on mobile factors (such as capital), since they respond by moving to a locale with lower taxes. Localities may have difficulties in imposing taxes on higher income individuals, because they too are mobile. Redistribution thus must occur at the level of the nation-state – though even this is becoming more problematic as increasing globalization renders many high-income factors highly mobile across nation-states.

Thus, in the US, there was a great deal of concern that delegating more responsibility for welfare to the states (and providing them with lump sum funds) would result in a 'race to the bottom.' By lowering benefits, each state could not only reduce its tax burden directly (thereby making itself more attractive to high productivity mobile factors), but the lower welfare payments would induce emigration of welfare recipients, reducing the burden on taxpayers further. The empirical evidence in support of this 'race to the bottom' seems weaker than theory might have predicted.

More broadly, while globalization has restricted the scope of actions of the nation state, the stress on devolution has taken away other responsibilities, leaving the national state potentially far weaker.

The debate about devolution/decentralization involves several other elements: participation and voice (the importance of which is stressed in the discussion below) may be more effective at the local level; decentralization enables decisions to be made that more accurately reflect the preferences of the citizens and that employ their local information; decentralization may enhance 'democratic accountability.' Finally, the devolution of decision making may allow for more experimentation.

But there are factors (beyond the limitations on redistribution) which militate against decentralization. There is, in particular, concern that the capacities (for decision making/governance/administration) at the local level may, in some places at least, be weak.

Perhaps the strongest drive for – and the greatest reservations concerning – devolution are associated with politics. Many advocates of devolution of welfare believed, for instance, that support at the state level for welfare would be weaker than at the national level. Devolution was thus a strategy for cutting back welfare. And these concerns were precisely what motivated welfare advocates to oppose devolution. There is not a well developed theory to explain why the constellation of political forces that play out at the local/state level should differ from those at the national level, but there is evidence that there is indeed a difference.

How should the state act? Market-like mechanisms and participation

Until recently, the preoccupation with shrinking the size of the state led many economists to neglect the vital task of understanding how to improve the state. In the last few years, both through the observation of the private sector and of successful governments, we have developed a much better idea of how the government can function better.

An important component is the use of *market-like* mechanisms. One lesson from successful states is that they use market-like mechanisms to improve their efficiency. These include:

(i) Using auctions both for procuring goods and services and for allocating public resources
(ii) Contracting out large portions of government activity
(iii) Using performance contracting, even in those cases where contracting out does not seem feasible or desirable
(iv) Designing arrangements to make use of market information. For instance, it can rely on market judgments of qualities for its procurement (off-the-shelf procurement policies); it can use information from interest rates paid to, say, subordinated bank debt to ascertain appropriate risk premiums for deposit insurance.

Another lesson governments can learn from businesses is to be more responsive to citizens. This is well-illustrated by the US' 'Reinventing Government' initiative. Based on observing the private sector, our first step was to ask each department in the government for a statement of purpose and suggestions for improving the ways in which their actions contributed to this purpose. This participatory exercise helped set an agenda for where the reforms would go. In some areas we could combine the two main innovations, client responsiveness and performance measures. We found that surveys were very helpful performance measures which improved our client responsiveness. The success of strategy was particularly evident in Social Security. We found that just by changing the vocabulary and treating citizens as 'clients,' we made progress in changing the attitudes of public agencies.

Although government has much to learn from business, there are important differences between the two. In most of its core areas, government has a dominant position if not a monopoly. That is why the participation, 'voice' to use Hirschman's term,[13] is so important, to determine not just what the government does but also how it does it. This not only makes governments serve the interests of its citizens rather than its own interests, but also can help it implement policies more effectively. Michael Bruno, for instance, emphasized the importance of consensus building in ending inflation.[14] The reason for this should be obvious: if workers believe that they are not being fairly treated, they may impose inflationary wage and other demands, making the resolution of the inflationary pressures all but impossible.

At the microeconomic level, government aid agencies and non-governmental organizations have been experimenting with ways of providing decentralized support and encouraging community participation in the selection, design and implementation of projects. Recent research provides preliminary support for this approach: one study found the success rate for rural water projects that involved participation was substantially higher than the success rate for those that did not.[15] It is not just that localized information is brought to bear in a more effective way; but the commitment to the project leads to the long-term support (or 'ownership' in the popular vernacular) required for sustainability.

Both in the public and in the private sector there are important agency problems, where the interests of 'managers' (politicians, bureaucrats) differ from those that they are supposed to serve. There will never be a perfect congruence of interests, a complete resolution of agency problems, especially in areas where appropriate performance criteria are hard to define and performance is hard to measure. But openness in government and the encouragement of greater participation may reduce the magnitude of these agency problems in the public sector, and at the same time dispel some of the distrust between government and those that it is supposed to serve.[16]

Concluding remarks

I began this lecture with the observation that collective action is important. What the government should do and how it should do it needs to evolve, with changes in the world (including changes in technology) and with our changing understanding of that world. Research in the economics of the public sector has, I believe, enhanced our ability to redefine the role of the state, and provided us with insights into how to make the government both more efficient and more responsive. The challenge is to translate these understandings into practice: to create a modern public sector, more able to provide effectively those collective goods which are so essential to the well-being of all of us.

Notes

1 On that occasion, Professor Neumann presented an excellent account of my contributions to the economics of information, for which I am greatly indebted.
2 See Greenwald and Stiglitz (1986).
3 For a review, see World Bank (1993) or Stiglitz (1996). Among the most ardent advocates of the view that governments have had adverse economic impacts has been Milton Friedman. See for instance Friedman (1996; 1962). While he persuasively identifies several important instances in which governments have had negative impacts, a full account must balance these failures with the successes; and while there have been isolated cases of strong growth with a very limited role of government (e.g. Hong Kong – but even there government played a much larger role, e.g. in housing and infrastructure, and financial market regulation – than advocates of free market doctrines typically recognize), these are the exception. The major success stories, from the United States, to Japan, to the other Asian tigers, all involved governments assuming key roles.
4 See, e.g. Buchanan (1986).
5 See Edlin and Stiglitz (1995).
6 This idea has been most closely associated with Lucas (1976).
7 See, e.g. Coase (1960).
8 Even in the case of externalities when information about impacts on different individuals is imperfect and costly to obtain, voluntary solutions may not work well. See, e.g. Farrell (1987). Transaction costs, too, may be far higher for voluntary solutions.
9 For a more extensive discussion of these perspectives, see Stiglitz (1989).
10 The pendulum seemingly swung from one extreme to another: from a very strong role of Government, in the planning models, to the opposite extreme that stressed a 'minimalist' role for government and emphasized government failures (such as those that resulted from rent-seeking) rather than market failures.
11 See, for example, Krueger (1986; 1990).
12 See Levine (1999).
13 Hirschman (1970).
14 Bruno (1986).
15 See Narayan-Parker (1995).
16 See Stiglitz (1999) for a discussion of the eviscerating role of secrecy, even in modern democracies such as the United States.

References

Bruno, M. (1986) *Crisis, Stabilization, and Economic Reform: Therapy by Consensus*. Clarendon Lectures in Economics. Oxford University Press.

Buchanan, J. (1986) *Liberty, Market, and State, Political Economics in the 1980s*, New York University: New York Press.

Coase, R. (1960) 'On the problem of social cost', *Journal of Law and Economics* 3: 1–44.

Edlin, A. and Stiglitz, J. E. (1995) 'Discouraging rivals: managerial rent-seeking and economic inefficiencies', *American Economic Review* 85(5): 1301–12.

Farrell, M. J. (1970) 'Information and the Coase theorem', *Journal of Economic Perspectives* 1: 113–29.

Friedman, M. 1996 (1962). 'The role of government in a free society', in Peretz,-Paul, Armonk, N. Y. (eds) *The Politics of American Economic Policy Making.*

Greenwald, B. and Stiglitz, J. E. (1986) 'Externalities in economics with imperfect information and incomplete markets', *Quarterly Journal of Economics* 229–64.

—— (1993) 'Monetary policy and the theory of the risk-averse bank', Paper given at Macroeconomic Stabilization Policy: Lessons for the Future, CEPR, Stanford University and the Federal Reserve Bank of San Francisco.

Hirschman, A. O. (1970) *Exit, Voice, and Loyalty,* Cambridge: Harvard University Press.

Krueger, A. (1986) 'Changing perspectives on development economics and World Bank research.' *Development Policy Review* 4: 195–210.

—— (1990) 'Government failures in development', *Journal of Economic Perspectives* 4: 9–23.

Levine, R. (1999) 'Law, finance and economic growth', *Journal of Financial Intermediation*

Lucas, R. E. (1976) 'Econometric policy evaluation: a critique', *Carnegie-Rochester Conference Series on Policy* 1: 19–46.

Narayan-Parker, D. (1995) 'The contribution of people's participation: evidence from 121 rural water supply projects', World Bank Environmentally Sustainable Development Occasional Paper Series; No.1. Washington, D.C.: World Bank.

Schumpter, J. (1942) *Socialism, Capitalism, and Democracy,* New York: Harper.

—— 1986 (1946) *The Dynamics of Market Economies,* New York: McGraw-Hill.

Stiglitz, J. E. (1996) 'Some Lessons from the East Asian Miracle', *World Bank Research Observer* 11(2): 151–77.

—— (1997) 'The Long Boom? Business Cycles in the 1980s and 1990s', Paper presented to Stanford University Center for Economic Policy Research.

—— (1999) On Liberty, the Right to Know, and Public Discourse: The Role of Transparency in Public Life. Given as Annual Amnesty International Lecture, Oxford.

World Bank (1993) *The East Asia Miracle,* World Bank Policy Research Report.

Part VI

Applied economics

14 Germany and Europe since 1947[1]

Herbert Giersch

The debate at Mont Pelerin

After having read the minutes of the 1947 Mont Pelerin debate on the future of Germany the following points came to my mind.

The participants seem to have been mainly concerned with the current situation and the immediate future – rather than the longer run.

- Karl Brandt, an expert in agriculture, stressed the food shortage and the danger of starvation; this was imminent as I can personally testify.
- Lionel Robbins – from an English perspective – emphasized the need for maintaining the rationing system.
- Walter Eucken and Milton Friedman gave priority to monetary reform and the removal of controls. They were absolutely right in their opinion about positive supply responses as Ludwig Erhard, an MPS-member, demonstrated in June 1948, when he courageously lifted price controls to complete the currency reform.
- Wilhelm Röpke from Geneva was almost the only participant to stress the international dimension when he said: 'The problem of Europe is Germany. The problem of the World is Europe'.

Foreign help was considered indispensible, not only in the short run for preventing starvation, but also in the medium run for investment to close a capital gap. However, none of the participants anticipated the export boom that West Germany would experience in the process of multilateral trade liberalization. Obviously, trade was just not yet on the public agenda – as if Bretton Woods and Havannah (GATT) had not yet happened. This neglect may also mirror the historical fact that the world economy had broken down long before, that is, before the Second World War and even before Hitler's ascent to power. Let me, therefore, try to concentrate on the relevance of the international dimension for Germany's and Europe's recovery.

The Ordoliberals' emphasis on competition policy

The underestimation of the international dimension had already been somewhat characteristic of Eucken's and the Ordoliberals' view of competition policy. This view stems largely from the German experience since Bismarck's turn towards protectionism. In 1897, the German Supreme Court explicitly legitimized the formation of cartels which soon began to prosper behind the tariff walls. Later on, after the First World War, the weak governments of the Weimar Republic (1918–33) tried to broaden their appeal by bending to sectional interests so that the state fell prey to the thriving private interest groups and their lobbying for restraints on competition. Such corporatism surely facilitated the subsequent concentration of all power in the hands of the totalitarian Nazis.

Having this fatal experience in mind, the Ordoliberals attached fundamental importance to safeguarding individual freedom against intrusions by private agents, especially monopolies, cartels and organizations of vested interests. Distrusting unrestrained evolutionary processes, including competition from abroad or from new technologies, they called for a powerful state agency to pursue an active anti-cartel and antitrust policy. The anti-cartel law of 1957 and the anti-monopoly provisions in the Treaty of Rome met their demands to a considerable extent. Nevertheless, I fear that German corporatism would have dominated the scene much more, had there not been increasing competitive pressures from abroad thanks to the liberalization of trade in goods and services and the removal of controls on international capital movements. Openness was essential.

Trade as a form of aid

When the Federal Republic of Germany was founded in late 1949, Intra-European trade was just as constrained as West Germany's internal economy before the 1948 currency reform and Erhard's simultaneous abolition of price controls. Although these internal reforms turned out to be a great success, the West German authorities did not yet dare to focus on a sweeping external liberalization. A shock treatment would have implied a thorough devaluation (analogous to the currency reform) and a far-reaching removal of import quotas and tariffs (as a counterpart to the decontrol of the internal economy). Four objections were apparently decisive:

   (i) the apprehension that a sufficiently large devaluation would make socially sensitive food imports from the US more expensive;

  (ii) the fear that this would induce an inflationary wage-price spiral just after the post-currency-reform inflation had run out;

 (iii) the desire to increase productivity by exposing firms – via an overvalued exchange rate – to fierce external competition; and

 (iv) the trade policy argument that one's own import barriers should be used as a weapon to prise foreign markets open.

Contrary to widespread beliefs, the Marshall Plan receipts were not a major cause of Germany's growth spurt after the 1948 reforms. In fact, the first large shipments did not arrive until early 1949, that is, at a time when the economy had already started to cool down again. Sure enough, Marshall aid – and the food aid of the previous three years – significantly alleviated West Germany's balance-of-payments constraint well until 1950. Yet, with less Allied red tape for exporters, with a devaluation of the D Mark, and with an easy access to short-term credits (to cushion the J-curve effect), West Germany should not have needed any aid to pay for its food imports.

Early import liberalization

In late 1949, the OEEC Council of Ministers decided to abolish quantitative restrictions on 50 per cent of intra-OEEC trade within six weeks. This liberalization requirement was raised to 60 per cent one year later and to 75 per cent in February 1951. In early 1955 the quota was finally set at 90 per cent.

Early in this process, Germany experienced its balance-of-payments crisis (1950). It was due to an inflationary demand-pull and provided the last serious challenge to West Germany's liberal economic order. In early 1951, the conservative Chancellor, Konrad Adenauer and the Allies urged Ludwig Erhard, the Economics Minister, to return to a central administration of major raw materials. Erhard courageously stuck to his optimism, insisting that the trouble would soon disappear. He was right thanks to the adjustment flexibility of the market economy that turned out to be far greater than expected by his opponents. As with the currency reform, Erhard was courageous and right.

The export miracle

West Germany became a pioneer of European liberalization. From 1953 onwards, it took unilateral steps ahead, usually in times of cyclical upswings. In mid 1958, ten years after the currency reform, 94 per cent of West German private imports (equal to 82.6 per cent of its overall imports) from the OEEC area were free of quantitative restrictions.

In response to the swelling influx of foreign exchange reserves, West Germany used unilateral tariff cuts and the relaxation of administrative controls as a substitute for a revaluation of its currency.

Erhard secured five major rounds of unilateral tariff reductions between 1955 and 1957. But, as in the case of quantitative import restrictions, organized interest groups were able to shape the sectoral profile of protection. Contrary to the wishes of Erhard and the Social Democrats, who had advocated linear tariff reductions affecting all imports alike, the actual measures passed by parliament were highly differentiated.

In contrast to Olson's celebrated hypothesis, the comparatively successful liberalization of West Germany's external economy in the 1950s cannot be explained by a general weakness of organized interest groups due to the disruptions of war, occupation and the division of the country.

The Federation of Industry's resistance to Erhard's unilateral steps was mitigated by pressure from abroad. From 1953 onwards, the OEEC and the GATT repeatedly asked West Germany for a unilateral liberalization to reduce the growing current account surpluses, sometimes backing their demands with unveiled threats of retaliation.

The long way to full convertibility

From April 1954 onwards, the D Mark became freely convertible for residents of more and more non-dollar countries. West Germany under Erhard went one step further; it removed most of the remaining restrictions on capital flows in late 1958 and early 1959. Nevertheless, I find it deplorable that Western Europe, including West Germany, did not take the short road to multilateral trade and currency convertibility via exchange rate adjustment.

There was reluctance on both sides of the Atlantic to revalue the dollar or to devalue European currencies. It retarded the removal of barriers to payments (and trade) for more than a decade. The shortest way to currency convertibility, that is, the option of genuinely flexible or at least readily adjustable exchange rates, was still tabu. Milton Friedman's 'Case for Flexible Exchange Rates', presented in a memorandum in late 1950, had not yet convinced policy-makers and fellow economists.

Instead of realigning exchange rates sufficiently, Europe opted to wait for its special post-war import needs to abate before it dared to liberalize imports from the technologically more advanced North America.

The US administration exerted pressure – and used payments – to promote Intra-European integration. It thus helped to integrate West Germany into the European economy, but also alleviated fears of import competition in the US.

Ironically, the major recipients of the Marshall Plan aid, namely the United Kingdom and France, became the two countries that happened to face recurrent balance-of-payments crises in the 1950s, whereas West Germany which actually suffered a net outflow of resources (if war reparations and costs of military occupation are deducted from the Marshall Plan payments and the other foreign assistance) experienced an unprecedented export boom and outstandingly high rates of economic growth. Although it started from a much lower base, the standard of living in West Germany eventually surpassed the levels reached in the United Kingdom and France.

To sum up: less inflation than almost everywhere else in Europe and a traditional strength in high-quality goods enabled West Germany to accumulate huge balance-of-trade surpluses. A relatively far-reaching and rapid liberalization of imports and a faster growth of productivity than in most other EPU countries permitted West Germany to outpace its OEEC partners in terms of export and import growth and to gain market shares overseas. Most importantly, West Germany increased its share of the North American market more rapidly than the rest of the OEEC.

Thus, having started as an impoverished country with an overvalued currency and tight controls on cross-border transactions, West Germany benefited from good luck (high demand for German capital goods) and a conservative policy (less inflation than abroad). It attempted to fend off an imported inflation by unilateral liberalization at fixed exchange rates. This process tended to feed on itself. It raised the degree of internal competition and hence the elasticity of domestic supply. Thus it contributed to an export-led growth and to what has become known as an economic miracle.

The European Economic Community

At the beginning of 1958, West Germany and five other countries in Western Europe formed the European Economic Community (EEC). The differences voiced in the discussion mirrored a fundamental conflict between two concepts of integration best described by the terms 'liberal' and 'authoritarian'. The liberal position was based on two tenets:

(i) progress towards global free trade is more important than the establishment of any narrow regional scheme and
(ii) government interference with economic affairs should be reduced anyhow.

The authoritarian position assumed that free competition between different countries would not produce desirable results unless there were common institutions to harmonize micro- and macro-policies as a prerequisite to the abolition of internal barriers to trade. Hence, the integration effort ought to be limited to those states that would be ready to cede sovereignty to a supra-national body.

While Ludwig Erhard and Wilhelm Röpke presented the liberal position rather vocally, the more pragmatic Advisory Council to the German Federal Minister of Economics pleaded for a mixture of authoritarian and liberal elements. Both Röpke and the Advisory Council, however, agreed

(i) that a process of regional integration in Europe should not be confined to the ECSC six,
(ii) that the introduction of currency convertibility was the key to all further liberalization efforts, and
(iii) that the maintenance of currency convertibility at fixed exchange rates presupposed a coordination of policies in the member countries.

In Röpke's eyes, the European (and worldwide) economic disintegration had been a direct consequence of the turning away from liberalism after the liquidity crisis of 1931 and once again in the aftermath of the Second World War – often in the name of macroeconomic stabilization. If countries like France carried out liberal reforms, no EEC was needed; if they did not, the establishment of an EEC would cause a further disintegration of markets in Europe. A centralization of wage bargaining and a harmonization of social policy would result in community-wide inflationary pressures, with inflation being the main obstacle to currency convertibility and trade liberalization. Therefore, the idea of a 'little Europe' should be abandoned in the absence of a free-trade agreement between the six and the other OEEC members.

Röpke clearly equated trade diversion with disintegration. Although this is correct from a static point of view, it neglects the dynamic aspect. Distortions to the detriment of outsiders might well provide an impetus to join the club, or at least to consent to a mutual abolition of those trade barriers which they would otherwise not have been ready to reduce.

Neither trade unions nor industry in Germany favoured the 'little Europe' which finally materialized. Both supported freeish trade, at least within the OEEC area. Thus, arguments of political economy alone cannot explain why Germany finally consented to the 'little European' solution. Politics played a decisive role.

The abolition of the intra-EEC barriers to trade was the most notable achievement in the following decade. But the introduction of a common external tariff meant that West Germany could no longer use unilateral liberalization as a means to fend off imported inflation and to enhance the opportunities for a continuation of rapid and spontaneous growth.

For most industrialized countries, the 1960s and early 1970s were a golden age. For West Germany, the period looks more like a time of transition from the economic miracle of the 1950s to normal international standards and to the secular growth slack of later years.

A deteriorating supply side: labor, energy, and government

During the late 1960s and early 1970s West Germany suffered from imported demand pull inflation due to an undervalued currency in a fixed exchange-rate system. Towards the end of this period, however, the economy lost much of its former supply elasticity. Three major reasons stand out: (i) a drastic increase in labour costs; (ii) a virtual explosion of energy prices; and (iii) a fast growth of the government sector. I shall briefly review each of them.

Labor cost (The revolt of labor)

When the grand coalition of Social and Christian Democrats replaced the Erhard government in 1966, the general spirit of social partnership was high. It called for a temporary suppression of rank-and-file instincts by union leaders. Unions found themselves under persistent moral pressure to moderate money-wage demands so as to make an active contribution in the corporatist fight against price inflation.

For some time, unions took their assigned active role as a corporatist guardian of stability seriously enough to keep money-wage increases in check. Economically, the moderation provided the non-pecuniary rewards that are characteristic of a seller's labour market: employers voluntarily shouldered the costs of mobility and search, and immigrants took inferior jobs at the contractual minimum wage so that German employees gained the chance of moving to better-paid and more respected positions. In this sense, the wage drift which prevailed during the 1960s had its positive side.

The spirit of money-wage moderation came to an abrupt end in autumn 1969, when a first wave of wild-cat strikes swept over West Germany, as an immediate reaction to the soaring wage drift and the profit explosion that was supported by the government's refusal to upvalue the DM-exchange rate. The strike wave initiated a dramatic increase in money-wages: for the first time since 1950, nominal wages rose at an annual rate of more than 15 per cent, and contractual minimum wages at a rate of 13 per cent. In the following years, the wage pressure hardly abated, and so there was a fundamental upward shift of real unit labour costs. This sudden switch of union behaviour is unique in West German economic history. The outcome of the public-sector wage round of 1974, even damaged the authority of the social demo-cratic Chancellor; it thus contributed to Willy Brandt's resignation over the so-called Guillaume affair. The radical posture was quite popular among workers: between 1969 and 1974, the unions gained one million members; and the unionization rate rose from 35 to about 39 per cent.

But let us remember that the unions turned much more militant in virtually all European industrialized countries by the late 1960s, following a general resurgence of radical left-wing and Marxist ideas, after the wave of student revolts in spring 1968.

Energy

The first oil price shock and the rise of raw material prices resulted in a dramatic worsening of West Germany's terms of trade (by almost 14 per cent from 1972 to 1974). Instead of absorbing it in lower money wage increases for the sake of full employment, organized labor defended its position in the struggle over the distribu-tion of income – at the expense of profits and employment.

The government sector

The growth of government can be seen from major macroeconomic indicators: As a percentage of GNP, total public spending went up from 32.0 per cent in 1960 to 42.1 per cent in 1973; if social security expenditures are excluded, the numbers are 23.7 per cent in 1960 and 29.2 per cent in 1973.

The tax burden increased markedly: in 1960, taxes and social security contribu-tions made up 35.9 per cent of GNP, and in 1973 43.3 per cent; taxes alone covered 25.8 per cent of GNP in 1960, and 29.0 per cent in 1973. Not surprisingly, it was in these years – to be precise in 1971 – that, for the first time in West German post-war history, a federal Minister of Finance (Karl Schiller) resigned from office as he felt unable to take responsibility for the fiscal stance of the government.

What are the reasons behind government growth? After the economic reconstruc-tion of the 1950s had lifted West German living standards (up to or even above the level of most other industrialized countries), a general consensus emerged that political and economic priorities ought to shift away from mere material progress to raising the quality of life and to achieving more social justice, whatever that meant in detail.

Until 1966, this had little effect on government growth. After all, Ludwig Erhard – Chancellor since 1963 – had no zeal for pushing anything that could smack of wel-farism. If he had any particular social concern apart from his vague vision of the *Formierte Gesellschaft*, it was the promotion of a kind of 'people's capitalism', that is, spreading the country's ownership of productive resources to as many hands as pos-sible and thus turning workers and private households into responsible shareholders.

In the first four years of the centre–left coalition, most sectors of the welfare state were enlarged. A pension reform law was passed in 1972 which, more or less guaranteed a minimum living standard independently of prior contributions to the system; other branches of social security (especially health insurance) benefits were substantially raised and usually extended in application. The result was a considerable financial burden, since the expansion of the welfare state has ratchet effects, but not the character of a social investment which promises future tax returns.

All in all, by the mid 1970s, supply-side conditions had drastically worsened because of a wage revolution, an oil-price hike and a creeping but sustained government growth.

In the EEC, the 'Luxemburg compromise' of early 1966 reinstated the unanimity requirement for all major decisions in the EEC Council of Ministers and thus helped the authoritarian approach to gain the upper hand. While the customs union was completed on 1 July 1968, that is, eighteen months ahead of schedule, further attempts to liberalize trade in services and capital movements remained largely unsuccessful. In addition, the EC Commission began to develop a common structural policy, a regional policy and an industrial policy which were neither necessary for an integration of markets nor explicitly mentioned in the Treaty of Rome.

The erosion of the Bretton Woods system

The appropriate external value of the D Mark and the optimal exchange-rate regime were major issues in West Germany's external economic policy throughout the 1960s and early 1970s.

Already in 1957 and 1958, its authorities came under pressure to revalue. They escaped the storm thanks to two devaluations of the French franc and the cyclical downturn of 1958. To counter the inflow of short-term capital, interest payments on foreign deposits were prohibited in June 1960. In early March 1961, the accelerating inflation finally convinced the government to agree to a 5 per cent revaluation (from 4.20 to 4.00 D Marks per dollar). Rumour says that Adenauer would have prevented it had he not been in need to divert public attention from an embarrassing ruling of the constitutional Court on one of his internal pet projects.

But the rate of revaluation turned out to be insufficient, though West Germany prematurely repaid several (3.1) billion D Marks of its foreign debt and, in March 1964, started to subsidize capital exports (by offering favourable terms for hedging against exchange-rate risks for West German buyers of US treasury bills). One month later, the authorities announced that interest payments on foreign time deposits in West Germany were prohibited and that foreign holders of German bonds had to pay a 25 per cent 'coupon tax' on interest payments (the coupon tax went into force in March 1965).

The undervaluation of the D Mark had emerged gradually; it gave an artificial boost to the level of exports and jeopardized internal price stability. The main obstacle to setting up a watertight stabilization framework was rigid fixed exchange rates. This system began to disintegrate – despite a D M revaluation (by 8.5 per cent) *vis à vis* the dollar in October 1969 and a period of floating the D Mark in 1971 – and finally died in spring 1973.

The slowdown after 1973

After 1973 West Germany gradually turned into a laggard in the international growth race, with the lowest real GDP growth of the six largest industrialized countries. Though the unemployment record remained better than in most other economies of Western Europe, the shift from a general labour shortage in the 1960s and early 1970s to a chronic labour surplus thereafter was very disquieting.

In several respects, the two cyclical downturns of 1974/5 and of 1981/2 had a similar macroeconomic genesis: a deliberate and sharp U-turn of monetary policy towards restriction, a worldwide oil-price hike and a concomitant worsening of the terms of trade. As Brandt in 1974, Schmidt lost office as chancellor in 1982. In 1982, the centre–left government was replaced by a centre–right one under Chancellor Helmut Kohl who in early elections in spring 1983 gained a comfortable majority and could thus cut public expenditures straight away. By the mid 1980s, the government deficit was reduced to 1–2 per cent of GNP, about the level of the late 1960s and early 1970s. Both the Bundesbank and the government followed a wholly undramatic steady course with only very modest counter-cyclical elements.

Demand management virtually disappeared from the policy agenda. After the bad experience with the Keynesian programme of the Schmidt era, both the government and the Bundesbank stuck to their course. While they paid lip-service to the idea of internationally coordinating macroeconomic policies, their actual policy stance remained fairly steady and reliable.

West German unemployment calls for a structural explanation, but the sudden bursts of unemployment in the mid 1970s and early 1980s must no doubt be attributed to the cyclical downturns.

The structural explanation is a lack of wage flexibility. This flexibility which allowed a rapid expansion of employment in the US was and is not a feature of Germany's labour market. As a consequence, Germany missed the fast service-sector expansion that the US experienced. As a corollary, labour productivity growth throughout the economy slowed down much more in the US than in West Germany.

Any labour market reform would require a major overhauling of Germany's tightly knit social net. At present, unemployment support amounts to 60 per cent of the last net wage (67 per cent if the person has at least one child); it is paid on an insurance basis for a limited period, (mostly 6–12 months, depending on age and other factors). Thereafter, means-tested unemployment aid of 53 per cent or 57 per cent is paid indefinitely out of taxpayers money. Traditionally, West German law gives an unemployed person the right to decline a job offer (without losing his claim to benefit) if the job would significantly worsen his long-term chances as happens in the case of many low-wage offers. Hence, once mass unemployment was there, a generous social minimum standard has become the ultimate obstacle to an adjustment of the wage structure.

By international standards, the West German labour market has always been heavily regulated. The main constraint is the protection against dismissal. By passing the Employment Promotion Act (*Beschäftigungsförderungsgesetz*) in 1985, the legislator made a first move towards liberalization: *inter alia*, the period for which fixed-term contracts are generally permitted was extended from 6 to 18 months (and in special cases to 24 months). The law has been a success, albeit not a spectacular one. This is no wonder: the core of the employment protection laws has been left untouched. As these laws apply most forcefully to the fringe groups (which are also hit hardest by long-term unemployment) they figure as a persistent impediment to employment growth.

Capital formation

Since the early 1970s, the profitability of investment in West Germany has been much lower than in earlier periods. Three points need to be made to understand the investment weakness:

- First, it took a prolonged period of wage moderation until the increase of labour costs in the early 1970s was finally reversed.
- Second, real interest rates rose in the 1980s when inflationary expectations were successively driven down as a by-product of stabilization.
- Third, after 1983, a fundamental upward movement of the natural rate of interest in the market took place as a worldwide phenomenon. It can be explained by the American 'Tax Reform Act' of 1981, which temporarily caused a sharp rise of the US budget deficit, a US current account deficit, a surge of interest rates and also – temporarily – a drastic appreciation of the US dollar. In West Germany (and also in continental Europe in general), no comparable changes in the tax legislation took place, so that firms there could not escape the pressure of capital costs. Note that, on this view, the US budget deficit by itself was not harmful. The main reason for the crowding out of investment in Europe lies in a 'transatlantic tax-reform gap' which – at a given interest rate – raised the profitability of investment in the US, but not in Europe.

Industrial relations

Most observers of the West German economic scene diagnose a fading away of the general spirit of constructive cooperation between labour and capital which had its heyday in the 1960s. In the later 1970s and the 1980s, the country may still have appeared to be an island of labour tranquility, but its appeal as a model of social peace was gradually lost through a deep-seated sociological and economic transformation. After long political deliberations, going back to the early 1970s, a new co-determination law was passed in 1976. It enforced labour participation on the board of directors of all larger firms outside heavy industry. In principle, the law provided for a parity of capital and labour representation; however, as one member of the labour side was required to be a white-collar managerial employee who could well be expected to identify more with the interests of capital owners than with those of blue-collar workers, a slight but decisive dominance of capital was preserved.

Nevertheless, the employers' associations went to the Supreme Court. For the unions, this suit gave a signal to take a tougher stand on some major issues, partly as a substitute for wage demands. Their focus shifted to the introduction of new technologies and the shortening of the working week. In 1978, for example, the printers' union demanded severe restrictions on the use of new electronic printing. After six weeks of bitter strikes a compromise was struck which provided quasi-job guarantees to the printers at firm level. More important was the economy-wide psychological effect: for the first time a union had deliberately blocked an obviously profitable labour-saving innovation. West Germany – once a pacemaker in the modernization of capital equipment – suddenly looked set to become a laggard. As in the 1920s, the unions rejected the argument of economists that labour-saving investments and a low labour-intensity of production were themselves a direct consequence of the wage pressure of earlier times.

The main thrust of anti-technology feeling came from outside the unions, namely from the rapidly growing ecological movement. A similar technological scepticism arose in other parts of Europe – notably the Protestant northern belt from the Netherlands to Sweden. But in West Germany, the whole movement had a particularly emotional and quasi-religious flavour which signalled the revival of the seemingly forgotten traditions of German romanticism.

The main new issue of collective bargaining became the shortening of working time, as a measure against unemployment. The steel workers' strike in winter 1978–9 and the metal worker's strike in 1984 were basically fought over moves towards this end, roughly meaning a reduction of working hours without a corresponding reduction of gross income per worker.

Industrial policy

Public subsidization of economic activity had always been a significant feature of the West German economy, yet it took on a new qualitative dimension in the 1970s and 1980s. The bulk of public support is falling on structurally weak sectors such as agriculture, mining, shipbuilding and, after the recession of 1981–2, iron and steel. Only one modern industry – the aircraft industry – enjoyed a higher degree of subsidization than the average for the whole economy. Most subsidy programmes are based on very poor welfare-theoretic reasoning, and many were originally designed as a strictly temporary measure. Due to the successful lobbying of industry pressure groups and unions, however, most of them have become permanent. The persistence of subsidization not only involved heavy static welfare losses but, even more importantly, reduced the growth dynamics of the West German economy: capital and labour were channelled into sectors of economic activity which, in the long run, could not stand the competition from newly industrialized and less developed countries.

Sclerosis

The second large array of impediments to structural change lies in the regulation of large areas of the West German economy. As long as West Germany could rely on its industrial export machine as the main engine of growth, the high level of regulation may have been just a nuisance, but since the early 1970s, the need for changing towards services has become more pressing. While other countries – notably the US, the United Kingdom and the Netherlands – made courageous attempts at deregulating services Germany lagged far behind. The almost trivial matter of liberalizing the rigid West German shopping hours can be taken as a paradigmatic example of Teutonic inflexibility.

There are three reasons to believe that, despite chronic unemployment, there are supply-side constraints to economic growth from the labour side. First, a shortage of skilled labour in expanding sectors and regions became visible. Second, from 1973 onwards, the influx of foreign workers came to a virtual halt. Third, the system of income and payroll taxation is likely to have had a noticeable disincentive effect on work effort. Let me add a few comments.

After 1983, the centre–right government put much effort into lowering the marginal tax burden. A tax reform provided for tax reductions in three successive steps to take place in 1986, 1988 and 1990. But only the last step was to lead to a substantial reduction of marginal income-tax rates for the vast majority of taxpayers. The top marginal rate was only slightly reduced from 56 to 53 per cent. Compared to tax reforms in the United Kingdom and the US, the achievement looked modest indeed. As to payroll taxes, they have risen from 8–10 per cent of GNP in the 1950s and 10–12 per cent in the 1960s to more than 17 per cent throughout the 1980s, largely because of the rise of unemployment, because of a worsening of the age structure, and because of the soaring costs of medical treatment.

Trend productivity growth was much slower after than before the first oil-price shock. Until the early 1970s, the driving force of West German economic growth was certainly its manufacturing industry. A technological gap with the US was gradually closed. By the early 1970s, this catching-up process had finally run its course. West Germany's 'natural' productivity growth fell to the levels which had long been common in the US. The less export-orientated service sector had to become the growth locomotive. Although, in the 1980s, labour productivity grew somewhat faster in services than in manufacturing, it never reached the dimensions of industrial productivity growth before. With something like full computerization being reached by the late 1980s, there is reason to hope that this transition period is soon coming to an end.

Summary

The quarter-century 1948–73 was a golden age for West Germany's tradable goods sector. The rewards of a rapidly intensifying international division of labour were huge, while the pains of adjustment hardly mattered at all. The high rates of growth ensured that structural change implied no significant threat of medium- or long-term unemployment, as people laid off in declining industries had good prospects of finding new and ultimately even better-paid jobs elsewhere. And the undervaluation of the D Mark since the late 1950s contributed to the emergence of a somewhat oversized manufacturing sector. The golden age came to an end in the early 1970s. Wage hikes, oil-price increases, a sharp revaluation of the D Mark and a deterioration of the general macroeconomic climate in most industrial countries brought Germany's structural adjustment problems to the fore. Instead of being a challenger to technologically more advanced countries like the US, West Germany had to cope with challenges from below, namely the rise of Japan and the newly industrializing countries.

Between 1973 and the early 1980s, employment went down in almost every branch of West German manufacturing as well as in mining and agriculture. Given the macro-economic slack and high unemployment – to which the microeconomic rigidities contributed significantly – it is remarkable that policy-makers did at least prevent the outbreak of severe international trade conflicts. The overall level of industrial protection did not get out of hand, thanks to the umbrella organizations of employers and workers, namely the Federation of German Industry (BDI) and the German Federation of Trade Unions (DGB). They mitigated protectionist demands from particular industries and special interest group by broader considerations of national welfare within the corporatist set-up.

The drop in oil prices and the slowdown of the US economy in the mid 1980s gave rise to new demands for fiscal expansion on the part of West Germany (and Japan). In spite of their fundamental differences on the vices and virtues of coordination, neo-Keynesians and supply-side orientated economists sometimes joined forces in these years. While Keynesians urged the West German government to cut direct taxes mainly as a means of raising domestic demand, supply oriented advisors proposed them as steps towards an improvement of the incentives to work and invest. 'Two-handed approaches' urged a combination of macro-expansion and micro-deregulation to enhance the responsiveness of aggregate production to demand stimuli. Yet the West German authorities stuck to their cautious position. The Government timidly rejected the repeated calls for bolder measures, notably for carrying the 1988 and 1990 tax cuts forward in time.

West and east

Before the war, those regions of East-Central Germany that were to become the Soviet zone of occupation (1945–9) and subsequently the Soviet satellite state called the German Democratic Republic (1949–90), had been roughly on par with the Western parts of the German Reich in terms of per capita GDP and the level of industrial development. East Germany started to fall behind the West from 1948 onwards. The reason for this is strikingly simple: West Germany linked the currency reform to a return to a market economy; in East Germany an absurdly controlled economic system (which all occupying powers had maintained in the first post-war years) remained intact; it was gradually transformed into a Soviet-type command economy by successive waves of expropriations and some modifications in the planning mechanism. Until the collapse of communism, the East German economy was no special case in communist East-Central Europe. In terms of most socio-economic indicators, it was roughly comparable to the Czech part of Czechoslovakia.

In 1990, however, East Germany became a place apart. It could import the proven political stability of the Federal Republic, so as to

- make the regime switch absolutely credible and irreversible,
- gain access to a highly developed social security system and
- expect huge transfers from the West.

Most domestic financial assets and liabilities were converted at a rate of 2 East Mark = 1 D Mark. Savings were revalued at the preferential rate of 1 : 1. On average, a rate of 1.8 : 1 applied to monetary assets. More importantly, however, recurrent payments such as rents and wages were converted at the rate of 1 : 1.

Remembering the West German reforms of 1948, many people hoped that East Germany would experience a speedy upswing. Political stability, generous social security provisions, unrestricted access to the world capital market and the transfer of administrative know-how initially made the privatization process in East Germany look much easier than elsewhere in East-Central Europe. However, in spite of these apparent advantages and the massive subsidies to firms, the decline of production in East Germany was much more pronounced. The short-term fall in output was more than double that observed in Poland. The 1 : 1 conversion rate for current payments brought a dramatic overvaluation of East German economic output. Furthermore, fostered by the political promise to narrow the gap in living standards between the two parts of Germany, East German nominal wages rose by more than one-third over the course of 1990, while at the same time production collapsed.

Whereas Poland had levied punitive taxes on real wage increases in state-owned firms, there were no constraints on collective agreements in East Germany. Wage increases were in most cases granted by managers of state firms who had no strong incentive to care about the profitability of their firm. At the beginning of 1991, those East German workers who were still fully employed earned roughly eight times as much as their Czechoslovakian counterparts and six times as much as Polish workers. Much industrial capacity became economically obsolete, and the cost hike prevented much investment to improve productivity.

As early as March 1990, the government of the German Democratic Republic had established a holding company of virtually all East German state-owned enterprises, the '*Treuhandanstalt*', which was to become the decisive agent in the subsequent process of privatization. It started its work after German political unification on 3 October 1990 when it was assigned three major tasks, namely the restructuring, the privatization and the de-monopolization of existing firms.

The privatization of small firms and shops in the service sector was nearly completed by the end of 1991. From the stock of roughly 13,000 larger firms about 58 per cent had been privatized by late 1993. For large parts of industry this privatization could only come about because the Bonn government gave the '*Treuhand*' the financial leeway to sell existing plants even if their market value was actually negative; in fact, a considerable part of the eastern German industrial capacity was privatized with a 'golden handshake'. It is highly unlikely that, in the end, the process of privatization will have generated a positive fiscal balance.

In no other post-communist economy of central and eastern Europe has the institutional break with the past been so complete and the building-up of new institutions so rapid as in eastern Germany. In this respect, German unification was certainly successful. However, whether this fast transformation was successful in the broader sense of supplying the basis for a sustained future growth remains an open question.

It is still impossible to make any firm conjecture on whether German economic unification may some day be called a success or not. Three major points should be recognized.

- First, the eastern German economy has gone through a process of de-industrialization which may be historically unique both in its extent and its depth; by early 1992, output and employment in manufacturing had contracted to roughly one-third of its level in the first half of 1990.

- Second, the structure of this industrial base has a marked bias towards non-traded goods because the shock of price liberalization in the wake of German economic unification led to the most pronounced worsening of market conditions in those branches of manufacturing that happened to be most thoroughly exposed to international competition. Along with the chemical industry, which also suffered badly, these investment goods branches correspond exactly to those parts of the West German economy that had been the traditional backbone of its international competitiveness and the driving motor of the spectacular export-led growth in the 1950s. They had also been the pride of the GDR-economy providing its main export products.

- Third, the process of de-industrialization has left deep traces in the eastern German labour market; by 1992, the official unemployment rate had risen to about 15 per cent, and the degree of effective underemployment came close to 30 per cent. Notably the sharp rise of eastern wages made the eastern German economy shrink to a competitive core which is small by all standards. This capital gap will only close if eastern Germany can attract substantial direct investment. There have been vast public investments to improve the physical infrastructure; and there has been a long array of different investment subsidy schemes that lower the cost of investing in eastern Germany by about 20–30 per cent. While one may wonder whether such a heavy subsidization does not put future growth onto a too capital-intensive track – thus creating too few jobs per unit of investment outlay – the measures do certainly contribute to a re-industrialization of eastern Germany.

The most likely prospect for eastern Germany may well be to have something like a dual economy. On the one side, there will be a growing modern latest-vintage capital stock which allows a part of the active labour force to reach or even surpass western labour productivity levels. On the other side, there will be a high degree of underemployment, which may well remain higher than in those regions of the West that experienced the most severe industrial crisis in the 1970s and the 1980s.

German unification is likely to have quite profound long-run consequences for the institutions of collective bargaining. Pressures of outsider competition in the labour market may become more virulent and may induce ever more firms to leave employers' associations and to put together a workforce at subcontractual conditions. Thus there may be more and more elements of flexibility injected into the traditionally rigid wage structure, and this may well spill over to the western parts of the country. In the end, the labour market in united Germany may increasingly resemble that of the US. This may finally turn out to be the most sustained impact of German unification on corporatism in the 'social market economy'.

Some lessons from German experience

The German experience since 1947 may be summarized as follows.

After three dismal years of central administration by the Allied authorities, the West German economy was subjected to a shock therapy: Ludwig Erhard completed the currency reform by radical price liberalization. It unleashed supply-side forces and allowed for a very fast reconstruction and a thorough structural adjustment of the economy's productive potential within about two years. An initial surge of price inflation could be kept at bay.

In the 1950s, the early momentum of reconstruction gave rise to something like a growth miracle. Given the ample supply of highly mobile and well-trained surplus labour, the only temporary impediment to high growth and the reduction of unemployment was the shortage of capital. It could be overcome in a rather short time, mainly through high business profits which were heavily favoured by tax exemptions. Foreign aid was only of minor importance, although it raised private investors' confidence in political stability and facilitated the reintegration of West Germany into the world economy.

In the 1950s several major factors helped to initiate a virtuous growth circle.

- The Korea boom gave an unexpected head start for a viable process of export-led expansion, above all of investment goods industries.
- After just one short-lived balance-of-payments crisis, West Germany ran a persistent current account surplus; it piled up currency reserves and thus became a pacemaker of trade liberalization.
- Monetary and fiscal policy refrained from any cyclical activism. Any sign of cyclical overheating could be taken as a strong case for further steps towards import liberalization.
- As the speed of productivity advance was persistently underestimated, unions turned out to be relatively moderate in their money-wage demands so that the scope for supply-side growth was not diminished through an undue rise in labour costs.

By the 1960s, the rapid integration into the world economy continued, albeit with a pronounced bias towards intra-EEC trade and with heavy protectionism in agriculture and mining. The undervaluation of the West German currency led to a state of persistent overemployment and a growing influx of foreign labour. The increasing employment of foreign workers reduced the frictions of structural change and thus made for an exceptionally peaceful industrial climate, with the unions being quite cooperative in the fight against inflation and the macro-economic policy efforts to overcome the 1966–7 recession. On the negative side, the currency undervaluation prevented an early structural change away from industry to the modern service sector.

In the early 1970s, the exchange rate was adjusted; supply-side conditions worsened because of a drastic rise of labour and energy costs. The Bundesbank prevented an accelerating price inflation. As a consequence, the West German economy stumbled first into a severe recession and then into a vicious situation of slow growth and high unemployment.

After 1973, three sets of factors contributed to a slowdown of capital formation.

- A sharp rise in labour costs, two oil price hikes and a drastic increase of real interest rates by the early 1980s depressed the rate of return on capital which remained chronically low, lower than in earlier periods.
- Sharply rising competitive pressures emanating from newly industrialized countries forced major traditional industries – such as textiles, clothing, shipbuilding and iron and steel – into painful adjustments to a new international division of labour.
- A cluster of diverse institutional characteristics reduced the scope for promising investments: a deterioration of industrial relations, the heavy subsidization of ailing industries, undue regulation of the service sector, and a fairly rigid labour market which hindered the reintegration of the umemployed into the labour force. West Germany lagged well behind the Anglo-American world in its efforts to give its economy a more supply-friendly incentive structure through tax reform and a less stifling system of regulations.

Thus the persistent surplus on current account became an indicator of unattractiveness for foreign capital in the second half of the 1980s. West Germany had become just another part of Europe, with its fair share in all positive and negative characteristics of the old continent. In terms of growth dynamics, it had become a laggard. But there were still reasons for growth optimism.

By the late 1980s, supply-side conditions had – after all – markedly improved. The rate of return on capital had finally climbed back to levels not reached since the late 1960s, thanks to a sharp decline in imported raw material prices by 1986 and the sustained reduction of real unit labour costs. In addition, the last step of the tax reform coming into effect in 1990 brought the first sizeable reduction of marginal income tax rates since the mid-1950s. The years 1988–90 brought an average real GDP growth of 3.9 per cent p.a., a rate not known since the late 1970s, with price inflation far less of a threat than at that time. In these three years, employment increased by a respectable total of 1.4 million jobs; it led to a reduction of the unemployment rate by almost two percentage points.

Another reason for optimism arose from the European Community's 'Project 1992'. In late 1985, the EC had set itself the task that all elements of hidden protectionism in product norms, service regulations, public procurement, and border formalities, etc., were to disappear. Although the project has not been completed, an EC-wide growth push could be expected. For West Germany, the 1992-project offered a unique opportunity to expose its heavily regulated service sector to a new wave of competitive pressures. A fair amount of overall liberalization in the service sector had been achieved by the early 1990s.

Growth optimism was finally inspired by dramatic events of central and eastern Europe from 1989 onwards. Even now, however, it is still not entirely clear whether all member countries of the former Soviet bloc will be able to transform their mismanaged command systems into genuine market economies in a reasonable period of time. Some of them face much more difficulties than West Germany at the threshold of its liberal reforms in 1948. Once they are successful they will add important elements of dynamics to economic growth in Europe just as EC integration did two decades earlier. Germany should be well placed to take full advantage of this growth spurt. Fast-growing export markets may become open for its manufacturing, most of all its investment goods industries.

A deeper structural adjustment crisis seems to be arising from near competitive pressures on the import side and in traditional export markets. With central and eastern European economies improving their export mixes and raising the technological standards of their products, there is evidence that a new phase of shrinking gains from technological leadership was on the horizon. What had been the great advantage of countries like Sweden, Switzerland and Germany for over four decades, notably the excellent reputation of their engineering workforces, seemed to be devalued most dramatically by the onslaught of foreign competition. The adjustment to these new pressures is fully underway in:

- new forms of work organization;
- a genuine attempt to make working conditions more flexible on the plant level; and
- a temporary moderation of wage demands in collective bargaining.

As to the long run, there is reason to remain basically optimistic. In a global perspective, worldwide growth, including growth in China and India, will open up new opportunities for beneficial trade and investment for Germany as well as Europe, though the process of adjustment may lead to a further rise of unemployment which may dominate the public discussion well into the first years of the new century.

Finally, the German economy will gradually cope with the fiscal burden of unification, namely (i) a higher level of taxation, (ii) a higher level of social security contributions, and (iii) a higher level of public debt.

The disincentive effects are enormous; even in the medium run, they call for drastic reforms. In the long run, the drawbacks of unification are likely to be outweighed by the supply potential that will be created through public and private investment in the eastern part of the country. Institutional competition for mobile investment capital and jobs can be expected to speed up the reform of the tax and welfare state that currently is in preparation. The Netherlands may serve as an example to follow.

Note

1 This is a paper presented to the Special Gathering of the Mont Pelerin Society (50th Anniversary) at Mont Pelerin, Switzerland, April 9–12, 1997. It draws heavily on passages in Giersch, Paqué, Schmieding, *The Fading Miracle – Four decades of market economy in Germany*, Cambridge University Press, first published 1992, revised and updated paperback edition 1994. The book was published in the Cambridge Surveys in Economic Policies and Institutions series, edited by Mark Perlman. I appreciate his encouragement and owe him great thanks for a long friendship.

15 Free and open trade in the Asia Pacific

A new economic regionalism

Hank Lim

Introduction

Ideas for Pacific economic cooperation were initiated in the mid 1960s. Four distinct periods can be identified. The first period, from mid-1960s to around 1967, is a period marked by efforts made exclusively by Japan to initiate and develop Pacific economic cooperation ideas and schemes. The second period, from 1968 to 1977, witnessed the 'internationalization' of the idea. The third period, starting in 1978, was marked by serious attempts to translate ideas into reality. The last stage saw increased involvement by governments. Concurrently this last stage saw the emergence of regional consensus primarily through the work and process of the Pacific Economic Cooperation Council (PECC), the Pacific Business Council (PBEC) and the Pacific Trade and Development (PAFTAD) and the emergence of inter-governmental Asia-Pacific Economic Cooperation (APEC).

In the first period, three different developments of the idea of Asia-Pacific regional cooperation can be identified in Japan. The first involved a concept of cooperation to promote regional cohesion, an idea that originated with Morinosuke Kajima, a businessman and LDP politician. Kajima's proposal was based on the idea of pan-Asianism rather than on a pan-Pacific concept. The proposal was motivated by Japan's broader regional interests. The second idea was developed independently of Kajima's proposal and was manifested in a series of studies and in research on regional economic cooperation undertaken by leading Japanese economists such as Saburo Okita and Kiyoshi Kojima. The underlying concept was the promotion of regional economic integration which started to develop in the early 1960s. While Kajima's proposals seem to have no major subsequent impact, the works by Okita and Kojima have contributed significantly to the further development of the concept of Pacific economic cooperation.

The third development was the establishment of the Japan Economic Research Center (JERC) which provided an institutional mechanism in Japan for studies on Pacific economic cooperation by leading Japanese economists. The Center's first report entitled 'Economic Cooperation in The Pacific Area' proposed that annual meetings be held among representatives from the five developed Pacific countries, namely, Australia, Canada, Japan, New Zealand and the United States, to discuss issues of common interest in the fields of economic relations, transportation and communication as well as cultural exchanges.

In November 1965, at the first international conference of the Japan Economic Research Center first international, the idea of a Pacific Free Trade Area (PAFTA) was proposed. In their proposal, Kojima and Kurimoto argued that a PAFTA, comprising the five developed Pacific countries, had the necessary conditions for effective regional integration. Ultimately, these series of academic initiatives for regional economic cooperation led to endorsement for the idea of regional consultation at an official level. With Prime Minister Sato's encouragement, Foreign Minister Miki formally endorsed the notion of an 'Asia-Pacific Policy' for Japan. This foreign policy initiative could be seen as the first attempt by Japan to play a greater role in Asia in the postwar period.

In addition to this initiative, Japan and Australia implemented other important regional initiatives in subsequent periods. Japan and Australia each sought to encourage closer economic relations with their major Pacific trading partners and to pursue a commercial policy designed to counter the effects of European protectionism by developing an alignment of interests within the Pacific community. Japan and Australia have brought the Pacific regionalization concept onto the agenda of national and international discourse.

The second period of development of the Pacific Economic Cooperation concept was marked by externalization of the concept, largely in academic circles. Outside Japan, studies on the idea of Pacific Economic Cooperation were undertaken in the United States at the Brookings Institution, the Asia Society, the Pacific Forum and other research centres. In addition, the end of this period saw the beginning of a series of international meetings and conferences that were specifically convened to examine the concept of Pacific Economic Cooperation. These meetings brought about greater awareness of the idea on the part of policy-makers in the region.

The Pacific Community Seminar held in Canberra in September 1980 was a crucial next step in the development of cooperative institutions in the Asia-Pacific. This seminar was directly sponsored by the Australian government and closely supported by the Japanese Prime Minister, Masayoshi Ohira. Discussions focussed on the forces promoting the Pacific Community idea, the issues for substantive cooperation and the concrete next steps that might be taken. The Seminar recommended the establishment of a Standing Committee and the Pacific Cooperation Committee with the task of coordinating an expanded information exchange within the region and setting up task forces to undertake major studies of issues for regional cooperation.

The Pacific Seminar indicated that while there was increasing support for the idea of Pacific Economic Cooperation, there was still no consensus on the concrete actions that should be followed. However, the Seminar started a gradual emergence of regional consensus on the principles of cooperation, the direction of its development and a gradual involvement of governments in the process. This culmination of consensus provided the impetus for the establishment of a tripartite regional organization known as the Pacific Economics Cooperation Conference (PECC). PECC was renamed the Pacific Economic Cooperation Council in 1972.

In November 1989 Asia-Pacific regional economic cooperation was considerably strengthened by the formation of the Ministerial-level inter-governmental forum called Asia-Pacific Economic Cooperation (APEC). The basic objectives of APEC are to encourage economic development through consultation and cooperation based on equality, openness and gradual evolution, and the promotion of free and open trade in the region and the world. Since its formation, APEC has emerged as the leading regional policy-making group to accelerate the pace and to change the character of Asia-Pacific Economic Cooperation.

The development of Asia-Pacific regional cooperation and the APEC process in particular, have been guided by the wisdom that processes are more important than structures. This implies that institutional structures should be dictated by what is required by processes.

The genesis of the new Pacific regionalism started with the emergence of regional economic interdependence resulting from rapid sustainable economic development in East Asia for the last thirty years. Increased trade and investments flows in the region and the weakening of multilateralism and the non-discriminatory principle of international trade have contributed to the emergence of Asia-Pacific economic regionalism.

At the APEC Ministerial Meeting in Seattle in November 1993, the APEC Eminent Persons Group (EPG) submitted a recommendation for the progressive development of a community of Asia-Pacific economies with free and open trade and investment. Furthermore, APEC Heads of Government at their Informal Economic Summit following the APEC Ministerial Meeting issued their Economic Vision Statement which 'welcome the challenge presented to us in the report of the APEC Eminent Persons Group to achieve free trade in the Asia Pacific, advance global trade liberalization and launch concrete programs to move us towards these long-term goals'.[1]

At the second Informal APEC Heads of Government Meeting in Bogor, Indonesia, in November 1994, the 'Bogor Declaration' was issued; it set out a target date for achieving free and open trade in the Asia-Pacific by the year 2020. (Tables 15.1, 15.2 and 15.3.)

Table 15.1 Forecast of real economic growth and increase of consumer prices of 19 economies, 1998–2000 (*Per cent*)

	Real GDP/GNP			CPI		
	1998	*1999*	*2000*	*1998*	*1999*	*2000*
Australia	4.7	2.8	3.5	0.9	2.0	2.7
Canada	3.0	3.1	3.2	1.0	0.9	1.1
Chile	3.4	3.0	5.5	4.7	4.3	3.0
China	7.8	7.4	8.0	−0.8	1.0	1.5
Colombia	0.2	1.4	3.4	16.7	15.9	12.0
Hong Kong, China	−5.1	−0.5	2.7	2.8	−1.7	2.2
Indonesia	−13.1	−2.5	3.7	78.0	21.5	18.2
Japan	−2.9	0	2.0	0.6	0	0.4
Korea	−5.8	3.5	4.4	7.5	1.6	3.5
Malaysia	−6.7	2.0	4.0	5.3	4.8	5.0
Mexico	4.8	2.5	3.6	18.6	14.4	12.6

Table 15.1 Continued

	Real GDP/GNP			CPI		
	1998	1999	2000	1998	1999	2000
New Zealand	−0.3	2.2	3.7	1.3	0	4.0
Peru	0.7	3.2	4.0	6.0	7.0	7.2
Philippines	−0.5	2.2	3.4	9.7	8.8	7.5
Singapore	1.5	1.5	2.0	−0.5	−1.0	0.5
Chinese Taipei	4.8	5.0	5.5	1.7	2.0	2.5
Thailand	−7.8	0.9	2.5	8.2	3.0	4.0
United States	3.9	3.5	1.6	1.6	1.9	2.4
Vietnam	5.8	4.0	3.5	9.2	12.5	9.5
Weighted Average (1994–6)	0.9	2.6	2.9	3.8	2.2	2.8
Wt. Ave. Excl. US and Japan	0	2.7	4.0	6.1	2.9	3.7
Wt. Ave. Excl. Latin America	0.8	2.6	2.9	3.3	1.6	2.4

The weighted average is based on the respective economies' exports during the period indicated.

Source: 1999–2000 Pacific Economic Outlook.

Table 15.2 Forecast of real export and import growth of PECC economies, 1998–2000 (*Per cent*)

	Export growth			Import growth		
	1998	1999	2000	1998	1999	2000
Australia	−0.9	5.5	9.5	5.3	3.0	5.5
Canada	8.1	8.5	6.3	6.4	6.2	5.6
Chile	6.0	7.0	4.5	2.1	−0.5	5.0
China	−0.5	2.0	8.0	−1.5	3.0	10.0
Colombia	−6.0	2.5	5.0	−4.8	−4.7	0
Hong Kong, China	−3.9	−4.9	5.4	−6.9	−2.2	6.5
Indonesia	−20.9	0.2	0.6	−28.2	2.8	−0.9
Japan	−1.5	1.8	3.2	−7.5	−0.6	2.2
Korea	15.0	0.8	4.0	−23.0	16.8	17.0
Malaysia	22.5	0.2	1.9	−2.6	8.4	13.3
Mexico	6.4	7.8	8.4	14.1	5.0	8.9
New Zealand	0.1	2.1	4.7	2.1	5.9	5.6
Peru	−16.0	14.0	7.2	−4.1	0.7	4.4
Philippines	16.9	15.6	15.0	−17.5	14.6	17.1
Singapore	−0.8	1.5	3.5	−12.0	1.8	3.0
Chinese Taipei	−9.4	3.5	3.7	−8.5	2.7	4.5
Thailand	10.0	4.8	5.5	−30.0	8.0	9.0
United States	1.5	4.8	5.8	10.6	9.1	8.9
Vietnam	1.2	0	0	−1.2	0	0
Weighted Average (1994–6)	2.1	3.4	5.3	−0.7	5.6	7.5
Wt. Ave. Excl. US and Japan	3.3	2.9	5.6	−6.3	4.8	7.9
Wt. Ave. Excl. Latin America	2.0	3.1	5.3	−1.2	5.7	7.5

The weighted average is based on the respective economies' exports during the period indicated.

Source: 1999–2000 Pacific Economic Outlook.

Table 15.3 1998–2000 Forecast of current account balance of payments (US$ Billions and % of GNP)

	1998	% of GNP	1999	% of GNP	2000	% of GNP
Australia	−18.7	−5.1	−17.8	−4.5	−17.5	−4.1
Canada	−12.4	−2.1	−12.3	−2.0	−10.0	−1.6
Chile	−4.5	−6.3	−3.7	−4.9	−4.1	−4.0
China	27.0	2.8	25.0	2.4	29.0	2.6
Colombia	−6.0	−6.8	−5.3	−5.9	NA	−5.2
Hong Kong, China	0.5	−0.1	−0.6	−0.1	−3.1	−0.2
Indonesia	3.5	6.3	2.0	3.1	1.0	1.1
Japan	97.2	2.6	152.1	3.3	157.4	3.7
Korea	40.0	13.5	20.0	6.0	8.5	2.0
Malaysia	9.5	13.8	6.6	9.5	0.8	1.1
Mexico	−15.8	−3.8	−12.2	−2.9	−13.6	−3.0
New Zealand	−3.2	−6.0	−3.3	−6.1	−2.7	−4.8
Peru	−3.8	−6.0	−3.3	−5.5	−3.4	−5.9
Philippines	7.9	1.0*	4.4	0.6	−3.7	−0.4
Singapore	16.4	19.1	11.6	13.5	11.2	12.6
Chinese Taipei	3.5	1.6	8.0	3.2	7.4	2.7
Thailand	15.6	13.3	15.2	10.7	15.0	10.0
United States	−214.0	−2.5	−261.0	−2.9	−306.0	−3.3
Vietnam	−1.0	−8.1	−0.9	−7.6	−0.9	−7.2
Total	−58.3		−75.5		−134.7	
Total excluding US and Japan	70.5		33.4		13.9	
Total excluding Latin America	−28.2		−51.0		−113.6	
Weighted Average (1994–6)		1.7		0.9		0.2
Wt. Ave. Excl. US and Japan		4.3		2.7		1.7
Wt. Ave. Excl. Latin America		2.1		1.1		0.4

The weighted average is based on the respective economies exports from 1994 to 1996.

NA: not available

*January–September 1998.

Source: 1999–2000 Pacific Economic Outlook.

Economic regionalism

Since the end of the Second World War the fundamental basis of the world trading system has been the Most Favoured Nation (MFN) clause that underlies all General Agreement on Tariffs and Trade (GATT)-negotiated reductions in tariffs. Through the MFN clause, non-discrimination established a global trading order for almost half a century. Enormous progress towards global free trade has been made under this non-discriminatory approach to tariff reductions. For example, in 1987 just before the start of the Uruguay Round, the average nominal tariff for the United States was 4.9 per cent, for the European Community it was 6 per cent, and for Japan it was 5.4 per cent.

This progressive trade liberalization process witnessed two distinct periods of active regionalization manifestation. During the 1960s, under the impetus of the European Common Market, regionalism spread throughout Africa, Latin America and other parts of the developing world. Due to the fact that the United States was a strong supporter of multilateralism and because of the economic hegemony of the time, regionalism did not survive beyond the 1970s.

The second wave of regionalism started in the middle of the 1980s. Following the negotiation of bilateral free trade areas with Israel and Canada, the United States launched a proposal for a hemispheric free trade area under the framework of the Enterprise for the American Initiative (EAI). In 1993, the United States concluded the North America Free Trade Area (NAFTA) with Canada and Mexico. At the same time, European integration spread with Southern and Northern enlargements. A Single Market was formed in Europe in 1992.

Likewise, throughout Africa, Asia, Latin America and the Middle East, old arrangements were being revived and new ones created. By its nature, regionalism is discriminatory because it extends preference to members. At the same time regionalism could be interpreted as a move towards freer trade among members which could be a complement to global free trade. This issue whether regionalism is a building or stumbling block to multilateralism and non-discriminatory global trade and investment is currently hotly debated by economists and policy makers.

What is the major factor contributing to the revival of regionalism around the world? Jagdish Bhagwati argues that the single most important reason why regionalism is making a comeback is the conversion of the United States. The first manifestation of regionalism failed basically because the United States was firmly committed to the multilateral approach and did not endorse the regional approach, except in the case of the European Community. Empirical evidence indicated that an organized Western Europe under the aegis of the European Community facilitated the GATT-led multilateral negotiations.

In recent years, because of lack of progress at the GATT negotiations, continued balance of payments problems and the end of ideological conflict with the former Soviet Union, the United States has switched course from a multilateral to a unilateral, bilateral and regional approach. Having concluded first the Canada–US Free Trade Agreement (CUSTA) and subsequently North American Free-Trade Agreement (NAFTA), the United States has also announced its intention to negotiate free-trade agreements with groups of other Latin American countries under the EAI (Enterprise for the American Initiative). The European Community has also continued to widen and deepen its integration.

These developments have, in turn, led other countries to reconsider the regional option. East Asia, in particular, is beginning to fear that Europe and the Americas are turning inwards and protectionist.

A key reason for the United States' conversion to inward-looking regionalism was initially due to the slow progress of the GATT. Paul Krugman offers four reasons:[2]

1   the number of players participating in the process has grown large which makes negotiations difficult and the free-rider problem difficult to handle;
2   the character of protection has changed. Present voluntary export restraints, anti-dumping mechanisms and protection makes negotiation much more complicated than in the past;

3   the decline of United States dominance has made it more difficult to run the multilateral system; and
4   institutional differences among major countries make negotiations more complicated.

Whether regionalization is a positive or negative force for the promotion of global trade is the most controversial current trade issue. However, there is general agreement that complete free trade in the world is the most desirable goal. But in getting to there from here, there are alternatives, and the disagreements among economists over these possibilities are pronounced.

The issue has two broad aspects. First, the static impact question focuses on whether the immediate effect of regional integration on world welfare is positive or negative; second, a dynamic time-path question asks whether, regardless of the impact, regionalism will lead to multilateral free trade by merging regional blocs into a single world bloc.

The theoretical literature on the economics of trading blocks is still in its infancy. Some innovative models have been developed, but their applicability to the real world is limited. More important than the static impact question is the dynamic time-path question. Very little is known about the issue. The ultimate issue is whether, over time, a few large trading blocs will lead to free world trade faster, and with greater certainty than the multilateral process. As with the static impact question, the answer is not clear cut. There is no clear presumption on whether blocs will lead to free trade faster and with greater certainty than the multilateral process.

To some extent, the question of whether regionalisation and trading blocs are good or bad is a moot one. Regionalism is likely to continue. Therefore, a more constructive approach is to ask whether a mechanism can be devised through which to turn the stumbling blocks into the building blocks of global trading system. In particular, how can we design regional arrangements in such a way that regionalism complements, rather than substitues for multilateralism.

Three suggestions have been made. First, Article XXIV could be modified to rule out FTAs and allow only customs unions. A customs union requires a common external tariff and, given GATT bindings on most tariffs, ensures that all tariffs come down to the lowest level prevailing in the union at the time of its formation. A common external tariff can also generate some important side benefits. For one thing, it eliminates the need for rules of origin, which often become instruments of protection. Second, Article VI on anti-dumping and Article XIX on voluntary export restraints (VERs) must be reformed.

The liberalization of tariffs by the GATT over the years has been accompanied by the erection of alternative trade barriers in the form of anti-dumping actions and VERs. A customs union will intensify competition among partners, which, in turn, will increase pressure for anti-dumping action and VERs against countries outside the union. To reduce this possibility, Articles VI and XIX must be strengthened.

Third, countries should be encouraged to adopt liberal rules of entry when designing regional arrangements. Such schemes are equivalent to conditional MFNs, where an existing regional arrangement is open to any nation willing to abide by its rules and responsibilities. Rule-writing in the GATT/World Trade Organization (WTO) alone is insufficient. A strong and effective enforcement regime is required. In the past, regional arrangements have violated the articles of the GATT/WTO but the former GATT had formally declared only four arrangements to be compatible with its articles. Yet it never censured a single agreement as being incompatible with its requirements?

Asia-Pacific Economic Cooperation (APEC) and Pacific Economic Cooperation Council (PECC) have endorsed the concept of open regionalism in the Asia-Pacific region. In the next section, we examine and analyse its nature, structure and compatibility with the GATT/WTO multilateral and non-discriminatory trade regime.

Free and open trade: the Asia-Pacific model

For the last thirty years East Asia has achieved sustained rapid economic growth, and the region has become the most dynamic component of the world economy. The East Asia 'economic miracle' has been made possible by internal and external factors. Externally, rapid economic growth was made possible through open and trade-oriented economic policy. Its share of world output and trade has risen remarkably throughout this period. Based on various reliable projections and certain assumptions, it is likely that the Asia-Pacific economies would resume their rapid expansion path well into the next century, after recovering from the present economic crisis.

One of the distinguishing characteristics of the region is the fact that despite its rapid economic growth it has not developed institutional organizations to support its dynamism. There are three basic explanations for this apparent paradox. One is the central role of market forces in driving the region's dynamic growth performance. Economic interdependence in the region has resulted from initiatives and activities of the private sector, strongly supported by pro-business regional governments.

The experience of the region contrasts markedly with that of other regions, especially the European Community, where the process of market integration was initiated primarily through a series of intergovernmental agreements.

The second explanation for the lack of formal institutions in the region is the great diversity of countries and economies in the region. Economic, cultural and political systems differ markedly. Recently, the region also witnessed increasing trade conflicts notably between the United States and Japan.

The third explanation is to be found in the effectiveness of the global economic institutions. During this crucial period of East Asia economic take-off, the GATT created a relatively open trade regime that permitted successful realization of the market-driven strategies of outward orientation that characterized the successful economic transformation of the East Asian economies.

Major events after the end of the Cold War have threatened the favourable environment that had facilitated the rapid economic development of the region for the last three decades.

First, the global trading system is shifting increasingly toward inward-oriented regionalism and protectionism among major trading countries and blocs. The United States has resorted to arbitrary trade actions while widespread perceptions of restricted market access in Japan have produced serious bilateral trade disputes between the two major trading partners.

Secondly, the threat of inward-looking regionalism is emerging throughout the world. The Single European Market is now the single largest economic entity in the world and is expanding its membership and geographical scope. Due to its massive preoccupation with its internal economic problems, there are increasing signs that the European Union is turning inward and tends to discriminate against non-members.

There is a close relationship between the weakening of the multilateralism and the growth of regionalism. The spurt for regional initiatives represents, to an important degree, a hedge against further weakening of global multilateralism.

The third development that calls for a new vision of economic regionalism in the Asia-Pacific is the increasing number of trade disputes among key players in the region such as the United States, Japan and People's Republic of China (PRC). If this continues or worsens, the dynamism of the regional economy could be seriously threatened.

For these reasons the APEC Eminent Persons Group (EPG) in its first submission to APEC Ministers in Seattle in November 1993 recommended the creation of an Asia-Pacific economic community through an open regionalism. The central issue is what constitutes the concept of open regionalism?

There are various interpretations of the concept of a New Pacific economic community. The broadest definition is given by Noordin Sopiee (1994), Chairman of Malaysia's Institute of Strategic and International Studies (ISIS), based on the following eight principles:[3]

1   the principle of free trade and investments;
2   the principle of international cooperation;
3   the principle of regional solidarity;
4   the principle of mutual benefits;
5   the principle of mutual respect and egalitarianism;
6   the principle of pragmatism;
7   the principle of decision-making on the basis of consensus; and
8   the principle of open regionalism which ensures the region's commitments to the maintenance and strengthening of the international community.

These principles are contained and further elaborated in the second submission of the Eminent Persons Group Report submitted to the APEC Ministers in Jakarta, in November 1994. Basically, the concept of free and open trade as the basis of the Asia-Pacific economic community has the following economic characteristics.

Unilateral liberalization

A number of economies in the region have unilaterally reduced their barriers to both trade and investment to a significant degree over the past decade. Such initiatives have been a major element in expanding trade, investment and growth in the region. It is inherently extended to all trading partners on an unconditional MFN basis, avoiding any problems of discrimination. Naturally, the pace of progress towards free and open trade in the region can be accelerated by going beyond unilateral liberalization.

Open regionalism

One of APEC's primary purposes is to promote trade liberalization on a global basis. This implies that APEC members are committed to continue reducing barriers to non-member countries while APEC liberalizes internally on an MFN basis. Such a commitment would go considerably beyond the requirement of Article XXIV of GATT that countries engaged in creating regional free trade avoid increases in barriers to countries outside the region. The extent and pace of APEC liberalization towards non-members would not, of course, have to be identical to its internal actions. Implicitly, this would mean that the region could move ahead further and faster than the world as a whole.

Open Economic Association

Open Economic Association is based on the guiding principles of openness, equality, mutual respect and evolution which have characterized the successful emergence of economic cooperation in the Asia-Pacific region during the past twenty five years. The evolution of an open economic association will build on the region's broad-ranging unilateral measures in recent years to deregulate and open their economies to global competition in the interest of economic efficiency. This economic integration has been driven by the private sector rather than formal inter-governmental institutions. Market-driven integration is rapidly transcending political boundaries. An effective voluntary association is compatible with the promotion of market-driven economic integration of the region far more than the highly structured, regulation-driven model developed in Europe. An open economic association will have the flexibility to cope with the enormous changes in the evolving patterns of comparative advantage in the dynamic economies of the Asia-Pacific.

Dismantling impediments to international transactions

- Improving communication to reduce physical impediments to trade has already proven to be a pragmatic approach to regional and global cooperation. Specifically, efforts must be undertaken to reduce bottlenecks in transport and telecommunications;
- Reducing uncertainties have considerable scope in promoting economic transactions in the region. In the longer term, the most effective means of reducing uncertainties of regional trade and investment will be to encourage greater frequency and coverage of policy-oriented consultations among officials and private sector representatives;
- The adoption of a non-binding set of investment principles to reduce the risks and uncertainties of international investment in the region. The code must be based explicitly on GATT's guiding principles of transparency, non-discrimination and national treatment;
- As Asia-Pacific economies interact more intensively, trade and investment disputes are expected to increase. A lack of coherent understanding about how

trade policy conflicts are resolved increases unilateral actions and uncertainty affecting economic transactions in the region;

- Competitive policy is becoming increasingly important in international economic relations. High priority should be given to developing competition policy and anti-dumping, with a view to developing a pragmatic initial set of non-binding guiding principles. In the longer term, deeper integration of Asia Pacific economies will also lead to pressure from the private sector for increasing transparency and gradually greater consistency of domestic legislation as well as of standards of accounting and auditing;
- Initial work has started in moving towards mutual recognition of products standards. Relevant international conventions, including those developed by the United Nations Commission on Trade Law (UNCITRA), are being examined for reference.

Technical cooperation

The development of the Asia-Pacific region has been primarily market-driven, and is expected to continue with this approach. However, at this stage of its developments, it critically requires massive investment in infra-structural facilities such as public roads, ports, telecommunications and other public-goods projects.

At the same time the developing economies of the region urgently need the development of their domestic technologies and small and medium enterprises.

In this respect, regional governments must play an important catalytic and facilitating role. All such efforts would seek to accelerate economic interaction and thus growth in the region. Projects of common interest throughout the region could be in three important areas such as human resources, telecommunications, transportation, and energy development. See Appendix.

Asia-Pacific towards 2020 – a new economic regionalism

At the conclusion of the Second APEC Economic leaders meeting in Bogor in November 1994, they issued the 'Bogor Declaration'. A decision at that meeting was to set a long-term goal of free trade in the Asia-Pacific regions by 2020. It should be clearly understood that the 'Bogor Declaration' does not envisage the creation of a Free Trade Area in the Asia-Pacific by 2020. Rather, APEC members aim for the creation of free trade through the strengthening of the multilateral trading system, expanding regional and global trade, and improving investment rules and procedures in a GATT – consistent manner through open and free trade in the region.

However, the approach and strategy toward achieving free trade in the Asia Pacific region create a controversy and different conclusions. On the relationship between global and regional trade liberalization, the EPG argued that there is no need to choose between regional and global liberalization since they are mutually reinforcing. On the second question of how APEC should treat non-members, the EPG recommended that reciprocity should be applied in order to increase incentives for non-members to liberalize. APEC members are not required to have a common policy toward non-members.

The best possible outcome of the Bogar meeting was based on the four parts outlined by Ross Garnaut. They represent the basic view of a large number of developing APEC members:[4]

1   a commitment to liberalisation to open and free trade in the region;
2   a target date for achieving open and free trade in the region;
3   consistency with WTO/GATT rules and principles; and
4   details to be worked out by APEC Ministers.

Under GATT, in order to justify discrimination in favour of APEC members, APEC would need a binding agreement to establish free trade in substantially all products traded between all APEC members according to a clear schedule of transition to free trade within a specified period. However, an unbinding commitment to move toward free trade, rather than an agreement to achieve free trade by a specified date, is the best that is realistically possible. This group argued that such a commitment would reflect the fact that APEC is built on an understanding that economic process would be gradual, informal and by consensus.

A strong endorsement of APEC liberalization should be based on and designed to strengthen the role of the WTO and the new international rules. APEC members made a start in 1995 toward achieving the commitments made in Bogor, building on the implementation of their Uruguay Round obligations and developing an agreed approach to monitor progress toward the year 2010 and 2020 targets for free and open trade and investment in the Asia Pacific.

The pragmatic and most beneficial way forward for APEC continues to be in line with the concept of open regionalism: to dismantle all impediments to all international transactions in the region without seeking to divert trade and investment from the rest of the world. There are three broad alternatives for APEC governments to achieve GATT/WTO consistent liberalization of trade in goods.

1   through independent, unilateral trade liberalization by APEC members;
2   through coordinated non-discriminatory trade liberalisation; and
3   through the negotiation of an APEC-wide preferential trading arrangement.

The first two are consistent with Article I of GATT, with all liberalization taking place on an MFN basis. The third option would discriminate against non-members and could be pursued only if all APEC members negotiated a formal discriminatory trading arrangement consistent with Article XXIV.

On trade-in services, there is a framework of guiding principles for bringing trade-in services under the WTO rules. APEC governments have an important and strategic opportunity to initiate vital codes and regulations in priority areas of concern such as transport and communications.

To achieve free and open trade in the Asia Pacific in 2020, the region would require trade and investment liberalization through unilateral and common efforts but also trade and investment facilitations, and technical cooperation. These three fundamental measures are not sequential but are manually re-inforcing for a sustained and effective implementation of free and open trade and investment in the Asia Pacific region.

Summary and conclusions

Economic regionalism in the Asia Pacific is the product of internal and external factors governing economic transactions in the region. Internally, correct and conducive economic fundamentals operating in East Asia have produced sustained rapid economic growth resulting from allocative efficiency and an outward-oriented economic structure. For thirty years the East Asian economies have experienced unprecedentedly rapid economic growth and major structural transformations.

Starting with Japan in the early sixties, economic dynamism soon spread widely to the newly industrializing economies of Korea, Taiwan, Hongkong and Singapore. Subsequently, ASEAN economies also achieved rapid economic growth. Since its open-door policy in 1979 China's economy has been growing very fast. Lately, Vietnam and other Indo-China countries are opening their economies in order to reap the economic dynamism of the region.

Externally, since the end of the Cold War in 1990, protectionism and inward-looking regionalism have gained currency worldwide due to the emergence of The Single European Market and more importantly because the United States has become a proponent of regionalism and often resorted to arbitrary unilateral economic actions against its major trading partners.

Conceptually, regionalism has emerged because major trading nations or blocs have declining faith in the efficacy of the time-tested GATT's multilateral and non-discriminatory trading regime. Alternatively, regionalism thrives because trading countries are insuring themselves against inward-looking and protectionistic trading blocs.

For the last thirty years, East Asia economies have experienced the most rapid economic growth in the world. Their dynamism is dependent on the existence of a multilateral and non-discriminatory trade regime. Without a favourable and conducive global economic environment, further growth would be very much hindered. Moreover, the region is characterized by economic, social, cultural and political heterogeneity. For these two basic reasons regionalism in the Asia Pacific must be based on free and open trade. Since the formation of APEC in 1989, the region has taken new and concrete initiatives in promoting the concept of open regionalism. This concept has come to be interpreted as a regional process based on a free and open trading regime. APEC members have not agreed to form a free trade area by the vision of the Asia Pacific 2020.

Instead they have agreed based on the 'Bogor Declaration', to achieve free trade in the region of 2020. The exact mechanism and modality on how to get to the goal of free trade in 2020 are yet to be defined.

One possibility is to proceed by trade liberalization on MFN basis. The benefits of regional trade liberalization would be extended to non-members. Starting trade liberalization on an MFN basis will give APEC members initiative in setting the WTO agenda aimed at global liberalization of comparable scope and extent. If non-members, in particular the EU respond positively, APEC will offer to undertake liberalization of comparable scope in the context of global negotiations. But if non-members fail to respond accordingly, APEC would be able to limit the scope, and the extent of any gains to non-members accordingly. Such a trade strategy in essence is an open economic association modality in achieving free and open trade in the Asia Pacific in 2020.

If APEC resorts to the principle of reciprocity and preferential trade liberalization, the process and modality of achieving free trade must be negotiated in detail in accordance with the Article XXIV of GATT. Based on the EPG Second Report, it proposed the creation of a three-stage free-trade area; the first stage is a free-trade area among APEC industrial economies to be completed in 2010; the second stage is expanding the members to include APEC NIEs to be completed in 2015; and the third and final stage to be realized in 2020 to include all APEC developing economies. Throughout this process, until its completion in 2020, trade discrimination will be applied among APEC member. At any point in time the APEC liberalization will be extended to non-members on the basis of reciprocity. If APEC trade liberalization is not through a free trade area (approval of Article XXIV is not required), it should also not require exemption from Article I of GATT (non-discrimination).

It seems quite clear that non-discriminatory trade liberalization offers considerable advantages in terms of flexibility which allows APEC members to pursue a gradual, voluntary approach to liberalization, consistent with the evolutionary nature of Asia Pacific economic cooperation. Furthermore, members can set their own priorities and timetable for achieving the agreed goal of open and free trade in the Asia Pacific.

Consistent with the concept of voluntary association, economic cooperation in the region has been based on consensus. This suggests that APEC governments can implement the Bogor commitments as a voluntary open economic association of Asia-Pacific economies. Shared principles for policy-making or to set targets for specific action are interpreted as APEC common policy codes or goals. Consequently, realization of policy decisions based on joint resolutions will be made by individual APEC members in accordance with their domestic policy constraint.

To be a viable and effective policy option in the Asia-Pacific, free and open trade must be accompanied by effective trade and investment facilitation and development of cooperation among APEC members. Unilateral and non-discriminatory trade liberalization is a necessary but not a sufficient condition for the realization of the Asia-Pacific free and open trade vision in 2020.

In the final analysis, whether regionalism would become a building or stumbling block to global multilateral trade regime hinges on whether there is a strong and effective multilateral framework to monitor international economic transactions and to enforce agreed codes and regulation in cases of trade conflicts and disputes among trading countries. In turn, such an eventuality hinges on what modality and forms of regionalism are taking shape in the radically changing and rapidly expanding Asia-Pacific economies.

Notes

1 APEC Heads of Government Meeting, 'Vision Statement' Blake Island, Vancouver, 19 November 1993.
2 In Jagdish Bhagwati. 'Regionalism and multilateralism: an overview' in De Melo and Panagariya (eds) *New Dimensions in Regional Integration*, Cambridge University Press, 1993: 22–46.

3 Hadi Soesastro, *ASEAN and The New Pacific Economic Community*. ASEAN-ISIS, Colloquium, Singapore, September 1994: 1.
4 Center for Strategic and International Studies (CSIS). *APEC-Where Do We Go From Here?* Proceedings of an Open Forum, Jakarta, 14 November 1994: 11–20.

References

APEC Eminent Persons Group (EPG), First Report (October 1993) 'A vision for APEC – towards an Asia-Pacific economic community'.

APEC Eminent Persons Group (EPG), Second Report. 'Achieving the APEC vision-free and open trade in the Asia-Pacific.'

APEC. Report of The Pacific Business Forum (October 1994) A Business Blueprint for APEC.

Bergsten, C. F. 'APEC – The Bogorl declaration and the path ahead', Institute For International Economics 95: 1.

Kojima, K. (1980) *Economic Cooperation In a Pacific Community*, Tokyo: Japan Institute of International Affairs.

Lloyd, P. J. (1992) *Regionalization and World Trade, OECD Economic Studies*, 18:

De Melo and Panagariya (eds) (1993) *Indonesian Perspectives on APEC and Regional Integration*, Cambridge University Press.

Soesastro, H. (ed) *Indonesian Perspectives on APEC and Regional Cooperation in Asia Pacific.*

Young, S. (September 1992) Globalism and Regionalism: Complements or Competition? Korea Development Institute.

World Bank Policy Research. Bulletin, Vol. 3, Number 3, May–June 1992.

Appendix

Table 15.A1 Share of exports and imports with PECC economies (As a % of Total)

	Exports to PECC economies				Imports from PECC economies			
	*1970**	*1995*	*1996*	*1997*	*1970**	*1995*	*1996*	*1997*
World	33.0	45.3	45.7	46.2	36.2	47.3	47.2	48.7
PECC	57.0	74.5	73.4	74.0	62.0	71.6	71.7	70.4
Australia	61.1	77.2	74.7	74.7	50.0	67.1	67.4	67.3
Brunei Darussalam	99.5	85.5	76.5	72.2	85.5	78.6	61.2	67.8
Canada	71.0	90.6	91.3	91.6	76.1	83.3	82.9	83.1
Chile	28.6	52.9	54.5	55.9	46.0	49.6	49.5	47.1
China	55.3	77.0	77.2	76.7	51.8	74.9	75.9	75.1
Colombia	44.7	49.9	54.7	50.8	60.2	58.1	57.2	57.3
Hong Kong, China	61.1	76.3	76.7	77.2	68.5	84.5	84.3	84.4
Indonesia	80.5	77.0	75.7	75.8	66.7	69.8	66.5	69.0
Japan	62.6	75.0	75.4	74.5	60.6	69.5	69.6	69.1
Korea	85.5	71.4	70.2	69.3	81.8	70.4	67.7	65.8
Malaysia	68.8	77.4	78.3	77.3	65.2	78.6	79.2	79.4
Mexico	66.8	89.2	89.8	90.8	69.5	87.4	87.9	87.4
New Zealand	43.5	71.9	70.4	71.5	51.1	71.5	72.8	72.7
Papua New Guinea	NA	67.7	67.8	61.4	NA	92.5	92.3	93.6
Peru	50.7	53.1	52.6	53.8	55.7	59.9	59.9	58.9
Philippines	89.8	79.4	77.6	78.1	75.0	74.3	71.3	72.6
Russia	NA	19.9	20.0	17.3	NA	13.1	14.9	16.7
Singapore	59.9	77.3	77.5	76.8	69.2	75.9	73.4	74.0
Chinese Taipei	77.0	80.0	78.2	78.1	81.9	78.8	78.3	77.6
Thailand	67.7	68.4	70.8	71.4	64.4	68.2	68.4	68.8
United States	46.1	63.7	64.1	63.7	56.7	69.2	68.1	67.2
Vietnam	NA	60.5	59.4	57.0	NA	77.4	73.7	75

NA: Not available

Source: Direction of Trade Statistics Yearbook 1998, International Monetary Fund.

*Compiled by the East-West Center (Honolulu), 1970.

Table 15.A2 Direct investment from and into PECC economies (Millions of US dollars)

		1992	1993	1994	1995	1996	1997
Australia	Outflow	5,033	2,500	2,473	3,842	5,838	5,722
	Inflow	5,184	4,031	4,578	12,802	5,429	9,151
Canada	Outflow	3,547	5,711	9,303	11,565	11,632	14,044
	Inflow	4,777	4,749	8,224	9,208	6,826	7,132
Chile	Outflow	398	434	911	757	1,163	1,950
	Inflow	935	1,034	2,583	2,978	4,724	5,417
China	Outflow	4,000	4,400	2,000	2,000	2,114	2,563
	Inflow	11,156	27,515	33,787	35,849	40,180	44,236
Colombia	Outflow	50	240	152	284	68	791
	Inflow	729	959	1,652	2,227	3,276	5,982
Indonesia	Outflow	*	356	609	603	600	178
	Inflow	1,777	2,004	2,109	4,346	6,194	4,673
Japan	Outflow	17,390	13,830	18,090	22,510	23,440	26,060
	Inflow	2,760	120	910	40	200	3,200
Korea	Outflow	1,162	1,340	2,461	3,552	4,671	4,449
	Inflow	728	589	810	1,776	2,326	2,844
Malaysia	Outflow	*	*	*	*	2,035	738
	Inflow	5,183	5,006	4,342	4,178	5,078	2,002
Mexico	Outflow	NA	NA	NA	NA	NA	NA
	Inflow	4,393	4,389	10,973	9,526	9,185	12,477
New Zealand	Outflow	−805	1,281	1,700	−356	−998	−201
	Inflow	2,095	2,401	2,451	3,536	1,577	933
Peru	Outflow	NA	NA	NA	−48	−16	NA
	Inflow	136	670	3,084	2,000	3,226	2,030
Philippines	Outflow	*	374	302	399	182	136
	Inflow	228	1,238	1,591	1,478	1,517	1,222
Russia	Outflow	NA	NA	101	357	770	2,617
	Inflow	NA	NA	638	2,016	2,478	6,241
Singapore	Outflow	1,317	2,152	4,008	4,437	4,146	3,970
	Inflow	2,204	4,686	8,368	7,386	7,444	8,631
Chinese Taipei	Outflow	1,967	2,611	2,640	2,983	3,843	5,222
	Inflow	879	917	1,375	1,559	1,864	2,248
Thailand	Outflow	147	233	493	886	931	401
	Inflow	2,113	1,804	1,366	2,068	2,336	3,745
United States	Outflow	42,660	77,950	75,210	96,650	81,070	121,840
	Inflow	17,940	48,990	44,590	57,650	77,620	93,450
Vietnam	Outflow	450	800	1,200	1,800	2,500	NA
	Inflow	1,939	2,928	3,574	5,480	7,860	NA
Total	Outflow	77,316	114,212	121,653	152,221	143,989	190,480
	Inflow	65,156	114,030	137,005	166,103	189,340	215,614

*Indicates less than US$1 M

NA: Not available

Hong Kong does not provide figures for direct investment.

Sources: International Financial Statistics, February 1999, International Monetary Fund; Balance of Payments Quarterly, August 1998, The Central Bank of China.

Table 15.A3 Human resources

	Labor force growth rate 1980–96 96 (%)	Population growth rate 1980–96 96 (%)	Total fertility rate*		Life expectancy at birth 1996		Aged 60 and above as % of total population 1996
			1980	1996	Male	Female	
Australia	1.8	1.4	1.9	1.8	75	81	15.6
Canada	1.5	1.2	1.7	1.7	76	82	16.2
Chile	2.3	1.6	2.8	2.3	72	78	9.7
China	1.7	1.3	2.5	1.9	68	71	9.8
Colombia	3.2	1.8	3.8	2.7	67	73	7.8
Hong Kong, China	1.6	1.4	2.0	1.2	76	81	14.1
Indonesia	2.6	1.8	4.3	2.6	63	67	6.7
Japan	0.9	0.5	1.8	1.4	77	83	21.0
Korea	2.1	1.1	2.6	1.7	69	76	9.2
Malaysia	2.6	2.5	4.2	3.4	70	74	6.0
Mexico	3.0	2.1	4.5	2.9	69	75	6.2
New Zealand	1.7	1.0	2.0	2.0	73	79	15.4
Peru	2.9	2.1	4.5	3.1	66	71	6.7
Philippines	2.7	2.5	4.8	3.6	64	68	5.4
Russia	0.1	0.4	1.9	1.3	60	73	17.1
Singapore	2.0	1.8	1.7	1.7	74	79	9.5
Chinese Taipei	2.1	1.2	2.3	1.5	72	78	11.4
Thailand	2.1	1.6	3.5	1.8	67	72	7.8
United States	1.2	1.0	1.8	2.1	74	80	16.4
Vietnam	2.3	2.1	5.0	3.0	66	70	7.2

*Births per woman

Sources: World Development Indicators 1998, The World Bank; Taiwan Institute of Economic Research.

Table 15.A4 Financial markets

Country (Stock Index)	Short-term Interest rates		Long-term Interest rates		Stock index (year end)			Exchange rates (local currency per US dollar)		
	1997	1998	1997	1998	1997	1998	% Change	1996	1997	1998
Australia (All Ordinaries)	5.1	4.8	6.1	5.0	2,616.50	2,813.40	8	1.3	1.5	1.6
Canada (Composite)	4.3	5.1	6.4	5.1	6,699.40	6,485.94	−3	1.4	1.4	1.5
Chile (IGPA Gen)	12.0	10.8	15.7	15.7	4,794.41	3,594.75	−25	425.0	440.0	474.0
China (Shenzhen B-shares)	5.7	3.8	8.6	6.4	98.97	53.58	−46	8.3	8.3	8.3
Colombia (IBB)	23.8	38.1*	34.2	45.9	1,431.67	1,109.20	−23	1,005.3	1,293.6	1,507.5
Hong Kong, China (Hang Seng)	4.5	5.5	9.5	9.0	10,722.76	10,048.58	−6	7.7	7.7	7.7
Indonesia (Composite)	27.8	74.2*	21.8	34.9*	401.71	398.04	−1	2,383.0	4,650.0	8,025.0
Japan (Nikkei)	0.5	0.4*	1.7	0.9*	15,258.74	13,842.17	−9	116.0	130.0	115.6
Korea (Composite)	13.2	10.2*	11.7	11.9*	375.15	562.46	50	844.2	1,695.0	1,204.0
Malaysia (Composite)	7.3	5.5	7.8	6.7	594.44	586.13	−1	2.5	4.0	3.8
Mexico (IPC)	21.9	36.7	20.0	NA	5,206.44	3,959.66	−24	7.9	8.1	9.9
New Zealand (NZSE-40)	7.3	6.5*	11.4	11.1*	2,314.91	2,065.28	−11	1.4	1.7	1.9
Peru (Lima Gen)	15.0	16.2	30	29.9*	1,794.19	1,355.88	−24	2.6	2.7	3.2
Philipines (Composite)	10.2	10.7*	16.3	15.3	1,869.23	1,968.78	5	26.3	40.0	39.1
Russia (RTS)	21.0	27.8	32.0	46.8*	396.86	58.93	−85	5,574.0	5,997.5	20,900.0
Singapore (Strait Times)	4.4	2.3	6.3	7.7*	1,529.84	1,392.73	−9	1.4	1.7	1.7
Chinese Taipei (Weighted Index)	6.8	6.5	6.0	6.5	8187.27	6,418.43	−22	27.5	32.6	32.2
Thailand (SET)	14.6	2.63	10.8	10.8	372.69	355.81	−5	25.6	47.2	36.7
United States (Dow Jones Indust.)	5.6	5.0	6.4	4.7	7,908.25	9,181.43	16	86.1(c)	93.9(c)	96.5(c)
Vietnam	10.8	13.8	14.4	12.36	0	0	0	11,150.0	12,500.0	13,880.0

*Third-quarter rate

(c) Multilateral weighted real value of the US dollar (March 1973 = 100).

NA: Not available

Sources: Financial Times Dec. 31, 1998 and Jan. 4, 1999; US Economic Report of the President, February 1999; International Financial Statistics, February 1999, IMF; Financial Statistics Taiwan District, August 1998, The Central Bank of China; Taiwan Institute of Economic Research; PEO forecasters; Classic 164 Currency Converter; WWW.

16 East Asia through a glass darkly

Disparate lenses on the road to Damascus[1]

James W. Dean

Preface

The most recent of many memorable meals I have shared over the years with Mark and Naomi Perlman was January 1998 in Chicago. The occasion was to have been a brief chat with Louis Uchitelle of the *New York Times* about the East Asian economies, which were then deteriorating daily. But our conversation soon evolved into a philosophical discussion on the merits of Asian capitalism, then capitalism in general, and finally the human condition.

Mark's presence was not incidental to this development. What had begun as a 'just the facts, ma'am' interview between Uchitelle and me on the frailties of Asia's capital accounts blossomed under Mark's Talmudic tutelage into a wide-ranging discourse on the frailties of humanity since its exodus from the Garden of Eden. That evening typified what I have always enjoyed most about Mark: his gift for painting narrow economic concerns on the grand canvas of history and historical thought. He is an artist among economists.

This essay in no sense captures the quality of our Chicago conversation, but it touches on some of the same concerns.

Introduction

Since the humiliation of Asia, economists may or may not be on the road to Damascus, but as yet, no divine revelation has yet come their way. On the contrary, they see at best 'through a glass darkly.'[2] Worse, they see the Asian crisis through disparate lenses. Some see that Asian 'crony' capitalism has dramatically failed, and interpret the past two years' financial chaos as a final vindication of the West. But others see the very same events through a radically different lens, with Western market capitalism the villain and Asian capitalism the victim. In short, where some see a failure of Asian capitalism, others see a failure of Western capitalism.

The collapse in currency values suffered by half-a-dozen Asian economies between July and December 1997 was unprecedented in modern history. It was preceded by collapses in other asset values – notably equities and real estate in Japan – that were almost as dramatic. None of these events was even remotely anticipated by the world's leading financial analysts (Irvine 1997). Such lack of precedence, drama and surprise all call into question the carefully crafted theories of efficient markets that dominate our profession.

The existence of efficient markets in Asia is easy to dismiss, given the murkiness of information and absence of arms-length dealing that seems to characterize the region. The existence of efficient international capital markets is also easy to dismiss. But the murkiness and arms-on-dealing was more or less known in advance, and thus we would have expected financial markets that were rational and forward-looking – in other words, that incorporated rational expectations – to have reacted smoothly and gradually as new information was revealed. As I have suggested elsewhere (Dean 1998a,b), there was no obvious external trigger for the events that followed collapse of the Thai baht in mid-1997. Asian currency and equity markets seemed simply to collapse of their own accord. But as Krugman (1997) has acknowledged, even the most recent theoretical literature on self-sustaining currency crises does not do the job.

Conventional analysis based on open-economy macroeconomics more or less did do the job for the Mexican crisis of 1995–6. When Cline (1995: 13) stated that '[t]he Mexican mixture of the sheer scale of the current-account imbalance, the short-term nature of the debt, and quasi-fixed exchange rate was unique', he was correct in that none of the Asian crisis economies exhibited these factors in combination on quite the scale as did Mexico. Indeed, in a speech delivered in Mexico City in 1994, Krugman, alone among his peers, actually predicted a Mexican crisis unless the exchange rate was unpegged. But neither Krugman nor Cline nor anyone else predicated the Asian crisis. Cline, in fact, went so far as to assert that '[t]he surprise factor of the [Mexican] peso crisis as the first jolt to the post-Brady capital market cannot, by its very occurrence, be repeated' (Cline 1995: 13).

In late 1997 and early 1998, Krugman (1997; 1998a,b) was the first to articulate a revision of the conventional view, which could be characterized as the Asian-failure view, and which I will characterize later in this essay more generally as the *government-failure* view. Krugman suggested that the missing piece in our *ex ante* analysis of the Asian economies was their internal financial intermediation. Asian banking systems, as the world now belatedly knows, are rife with insider lending and government quasi-guarantees – far rifer than their far-from-pure Western counterparts – and this led to extreme moral hazard and adverse selection. These factors prompted 'Panglossian' valuations of asset values, until, that is, the funds for government subsidization and bailouts simply ran out. At that point the dynamics that had led to overvaluation went into reverse. It is perhaps safe to say that by late 1998, Krugman's lens for viewing the Asian crisis was widely enough shared among professional economists, at least in the West, that his version of events had become neo-conventional.

By early 1998, a radically different view of the Asian crisis was also being articulated, notably (though by no means exclusively) by Wade (1998) and Wade and Veneroso (1998). The view holds to a model of Asian development that starts from extraordinarily high household savings and relies heavily on intermediation through the banking system. This system, they claim, necessarily led to debt–equity ratios in the real sector that far exceed Western norms. Such a mode of finance was too vulnerable to be left to the vagaries of arms-length capitalism. It had to be complemented by a set of triangular, mutually supportive and symbiotic relationships between government, banking and industry – what neo-conventional commentators now call 'crony capitalism.' Subscribers to this view argue further that unrestricted inflows of foreign capital upset this symbiotic system and caused it to come unstuck. This could be characterized as the Western-failure or *market-failure* lens, through which the Asian crisis is seen by a growing minority.

This paper begins, with a stylized series of events that might be used to organize thought about the 'causes' of the crisis. While greatly simplified and shorn of detail, none of these assertions is, by itself, remarkably deviant from the conventional wisdom that prevailed before the crisis. But conventional wisdom did not predict the crisis because these components were not synthesized into a coherent, semi-chronological story. Although this chronology itself necessarily embodies a point of view, I have attempted to cast widely and neutrally enough that it is broadly consistent with both the Asian-failure and Western-failure versions of events.

The paper then proceeds to assess the above chronology twice, first through an Asian- or government-failure lens, and then through a Western- or market-failure lens. The next part addresses a critical policy quandary – whether or not to re-regulate capital flows – that arises directly from the two conflicting views, and goes onto report the fragile consensus, such as it is, that is now emerging about what national and international policies might avert crises in future. The last part concludes.

A stylized chronology of events leading to the Asian crisis

High domestic saving rates

High domestic saving rates led to rapid physical and human capital formation and high growth. It is probably safe to surmise that by the late 1990s, conventional wisdom among informed economists no longer held to the 'myth of the Asian miracle,' if it ever had. Extravagant popular projections such as John Niasbitt's *Megatrends Asia* (1996), and equally extravagant claims for a neo-Confucian productivity advantage, had been put to rest rather decisively by Paul Krugman's (1994) widely-read article entitled 'The Myth of Asia's Miracle'. Based on empirical work by Alwyn Young (1992; 1994a,b), Krugman argued that the Asian tigers' growth rates could be accounted for almost entirely by growth in inputs of physical and human capital, and thus that rumours of a mysterious unexplained Asian 'residual' were false. Put another way, Young and Krugman purported to document that Asian growth had involved no appreciable increases in total factor productivity. Superior technology, innovation, organizational or managerial methods, cultural kinship – none of these seemed to have played a role. Naturally, this message – that growth had been achieved by 'perspiration, not inspiration' – was unpopular in Asia. But it made sense to most Western-trained economists. Hence economists, led by Krugman, at least had it half right based on conventional theory and empirical technique. Asian growth was no miracle and would ultimately slow down because it would be subject to diminishing returns.

Nevertheless, Asian growth was an achievement unparalleled in human history. Neither Britain nor America nor any newly industrialized country had in the past grown so rapidly. What Japan followed by the 'tigers' achieved in decades or less took Britain and America half a century or more. The combination of very high saving rates, long hours of hard work, and a strong emphasis on education (at least in the Chinese and Japanese communities) translated into high rates of investment in physical and human capital. In fact to deny that this mobilization of capital was aided and abetted by culture, organization and the like is to deny credit where credit is due. The lasting legacy of the Young and Krugman message is not that nothing remarkable happened, but rather that no endogenous productivity enhancement was evident once all inputs had been measured. In fact in some cases, notably Singapore, when the very high investment rates were compared with real GDP growth, the productivity of capital appeared to be very low by the standards of developed economies. This suggested that capital might be both misallocated and over-invested, a theme that is expanded below.

Asia's growth, based as it was on capital accumulation, might have slowed down naturally and gradually in the early 1990s as the large but nevertheless limited supply of domestic savings confronted diminishing returns to capital. Interest rates might have risen and marginal returns to investment projects fallen until the rate of investment equilibrated at a lower rate than it actually did. But this did not happen. Interest rates did not rise to choke off investment because foreign capital was readily available. And expected returns to investment did not fall because of a perception – by both domestic and foreign lenders – that they would be bailed out by domestic governments, and if not, by the IMF. In the 1990s, capital inflows accelerated in part because of widespread *deregulation of capital accounts*. Perceptions of domestic bailouts were an intrinsic part of what I will call *Asian capitalism*. The next three sections deal with these topics.

Capital account liberalization

Capital account liberalization added to high growth encouraged rapid capital inflows.[3] Deregulation of capital flows to and from developed countries – notably Western Europe and to a lesser extent Japan – was complete by the early 1980s, after a post-World War II legacy of exchange rate inconvertibility and capital movement restrictions that took more than four decades to dismantle. Similar liberalization came to Eastern Europe and the former Soviet Union after the fall of the Berlin Wall in 1989.

The spread of liberalization to *developing* countries was sporadic and often serendipitous. Small island economies were frequently induced to open up their external and financial sectors by the twin carrots of membership in free trade agreements and potential for offshore banking (Dean 1993; Dean and Felmingham 1998). Others were prodded or even panicked into liberalization by balance of payments crises (Haggard and Maxfield 1996). In the 1990s, increased opportunities for cheap foreign money and high domestic returns prompted both borrowers and lenders to push for deregulation.

On the surface, rapid and early deregulation by certain developing countries is puzzling, as it proceeded further than in most developed countries at the time, and in retrospect was often premature. For example, Argentina, Chile and Uruguay all liberalized during the late 1970s, and later suffered dire consequences (Edwards and van Wijnbergen 1986; Corbo and de Melo 1985). More recently, in late 1994 and early 1995, Mexico's liberalization seemed premature to some. Although the appropriate sequencing of economic de-control may even then have been clear to those with common sense and no self-interest in the outcome, and although the lessons for sequencing are by now well documented (e.g. McKinnon 1991; Sachs, Tornell and Velasco 1996), deregulation in practice is subject to pressure from the forces of *realpolitik*.

Of course *realpolitik* often operates in opposing directions. Freeing up capital flows stands to harm private sector lenders and dealers in black market foreign exchange whose rents would be eroded by foreign competition (Grosse 1994). Governments often have even more to lose, benefiting as they do under capital controls from the ability to run fiscal deficits financed by monetary creation without discipline from international lenders. Governments also stand to lose powers of patronage toward sectors of the economy they may, for good reasons or bad, care to favour.

On the other hand as liberalization in the developed world proceeds, with the consequent increase in global economic integration, the balance of *realpolitik* begins to shift. The opportunity cost of controls on the private sector increases, as do opportunities for evading such controls. Increased external trade leads to greater incentives and occasions for under- and over-invoicing. Banks in their turn see opportunities for tapping international sources of savings, and are tempted to open branches or subsidiaries abroad, particularly in New York and in the London Eurocurrency market. Over the last decade, Korean banks, for example, have engaged in this process with a passion. Governments find such operations increasingly difficult to monitor. Witness the South Korean government's apparently honest confusion, in October and November of 1997, over the external liabilities of overseas branches of Korean commercial banks. These monitoring difficulties are exacerbated by enhanced communications and travel possibilities. Indeed cheap air travel alone has made the enforcement of capital controls on individuals almost impossible. Finally, foreign firms and financial institutions see opportunities for profit in markets that are as yet relatively closed, and begin to lobby for looser controls on entry.

Although these trends might ultimately lead to liberalization in and of themselves, their force has typically been strengthened by a *balance of payments crisis*. This might seem paradoxical, since a crisis should surely prompt government to tighten capital controls rather than loosen them. Yet between 1985 and 1990, when much of the developing world was mired in sovereign debt crisis, developing countries consistently and increasingly liberalized their capital accounts: the number of liberalizing measures increased from twenty-two in 1985 to a peak of sixty-two in 1988 before falling off to forty-nine in 1990 (Haggard and Maxfield 1996). To be sure, in some cases (e.g. in Argentina, Mexico and Venezuela) the initial response to the debt crisis in 1982–3 was to tighten controls against capital flight, but these responses were soon reversed.

Why should a balance of payments crisis prompt loosening, rather than tightening, of capital controls? The answer is that the political position of those interests that favour liberalization is suddenly strengthened. Such interests include holders of foreign exchange, exporters, foreign creditors and investors, foreign financial intermediaries, and the international financial institutions (IFIs): in short, the owners, earners and potential lenders of foreign exchange. Only if the capital account is liberalized will foreign exchange holders desist from (illegal) capital flight, exporters desist from false invoicing, and potential creditors be prepared to resume lending.

The extended balance-of-payments-cum-debt crisis of the 1980s was resolved by the Brady Plan, under which from 1989 to 95, creditor commercial banks essentially wrote off about one-third of the $211 bn long-term debt of some twenty-four severely indebted middle income countries, mostly but not exclusively in Latin America.[4] The Brady Plan triggered an abrupt end to the prolonged international debt crisis in the sense that by 1990 capital flows to Latin America had resumed with a vengeance. And the inflow to East and Southeast Asia was already well underway.

Lenders were motivated by the alluring triple prospects of high returns, sharply lowered country and exchange rate risks, and deregulated and privatized domestic environments. Borrowers for their part chose foreign over domestic sources of funds because on the margin (and the margin was large), foreign funds carried substantially lower interest rates. Where capital account liberalization was not complete, particularly in Asia, such prospects for profit motivated both lenders and borrowers to push for closure, with strong encouragement from the IFIs. As Wade (1998: 9) puts it, '… (in East and Southeast Asia during the 1990s) firms and banks, both national and international, pressured governments to undertake financial deregulation, their pressure converging with that of the IMF and the World Bank.'

Why was foreign capital so cheap? Two factors were paramount. First, contrary to conventional opinion, which focuses solely on low inflation, monetary policy in the developed world has been rather expansionary. In Japan and Europe this has reflected largely unsuccessful attempts to revive lagging growth; in the US it has reflected Alan Greenspan's concern to keep the good times rolling. With slow real growth and low inflation in Japan and Europe, excess funds flowed into financial assets around the world: into the fabled US stock market, of course, but also into Asia. The bulk of foreign bank claims on the crisis Asian economies are from Japan and Western Europe, not the US. But from the US, where nominal growth throughout its sustained boom has rarely exceeded 4%, broad money growth of 10% and above has flowed substantially into asset markets, including Asia's. Of course lenders ignored default risk, for reasons that we will attend to shortly.

The second reason that foreign capital was so cheap in Asia is that borrowers ignored foreign exchange risk. As any beginning student of international finance knows, interest rates on yen- or dollar-denominated loans can only be different from those denominated in domestic currency if expected changes in exchange rates are ignored. Otherwise, if international capital markets are deregulated and otherwise unencumbered, perfectly mobile capital will ensure that expected (risk adjusted) interest rates equalize internationally (uncovered interest parity), or that actual (risk adjusted) forward-hedged interest rates equalize (covered interest parity). *Asian borrowers in effect assumed that exchange rates would not be devalued.*

Fixed exchange rates

Fixed exchange rates added to rapid capital inflows, led to rapid monetary growth. Most East and Southeast Asian countries (with the notable exception of Japan) pegged their currencies to the US dollar, or to a basket of currencies dominated by the US dollar. This had two consequences. First, net capital inflows (unless 'sterilized', a losing proposition in the long run[5]) were automatically added to foreign exchange reserves, and thence monetized – turned into domestic currency. In short, rapid capital inflows led to rapid monetary growth. The second consequence followed from the first. Monetary growth in excess of real output growth was translated into inflation. Hence *real* exchange rates rose even though nominal exchange rates were pegged. Overvalued real exchange rates then led to widening trade deficits. Added to growing debt service on accumulating foreign debt, this meant widening current account deficits, financed of course by ever-larger capital inflows: that is, ever-larger capital account surpluses. This process proceeded much further in Thailand, Indonesia and Malaysia than it did in South Korea, although it was underway there too.

Conventional wisdom *c.* 1996, at the end of the Mexican crisis, was that this circumstance alone – fixed exchange rates and easy money – was necessary but not sufficient to precipitate an exchange rate crisis. Conventional wisdom was right in principle, but wrong in practice. The implicit assumption behind the comfort accorded countries like Thailand, Indonesia, Malaysia and Korea was that, unlike most of their Latin American counterparts, these were economies that invested rather than consumed borrowed funds, and furthermore that invested funds wisely and productively. Hence current account deficits of the order of 8 per cent of Gross Domestic Product (GDP) were sustainable since GDP would continue to grow and debt-to-GDP ratios would stabilize or decline. In practice this assumption was at least half-wrong. To be sure, these were economies that invested heavily; but in retrospect they over-invested. Worse, they misallocated their investment: a large part of it proved unproductive. The reasons for both over-investment and misallocation are intimately related to imperfect financial intermediation.

Imperfect financial intermediation

Imperfect financial intermediation – adverse selection and moral hazard – added to rapid monetary growth, led to both misallocation and over-investment of capital.[6] Financial intermediation is necessary because some direct financial markets are imperfect, even in the most advanced economies. Were direct financial markets universally efficient, intermediation would be unnecessary to transfer funds from savers to borrowers: equity and bond markets would suffice. But given that intermediation is often necessary, *its* efficiency can in principle be improved via judicious supervisory and regulatory systems. Yet in practice no economy has yet devised, let alone implemented, banking or other intermediation systems that align the incentives of lenders and borrowers as closely as do the world's major and more efficient equity and bond markets.

We begin this section by reviewing very briefly the reasons that all monetary economies employ financial intermediation, and the reasons that it is by nature imperfect. We then examine the nature of financial intermediation in the Asian crisis economies. Finally, we draw the connection between imperfect financial intermediation, capital inflows, and misallocation and over-investment of capital in these economies.

Why all economies employ financial intermediation

Financial intermediation is a response to asymmetric information. Borrowers usually know more about the risks and returns associated with the projects in which they wish to invest than do savers. Banks and other intermediaries capitalize on economies of scale to pool risks as well as investigate and monitor both risks and returns. Banks thus act as agents for depositors. Hence all economies employ financial intermediation in order to reduce the costs of asymmetric information below what they would be were the task of matching savers and borrowers left solely to direct financial markets. But however diligent bankers may be in pooling, investigating and monitoring risks, they are never in practice completely successful in eliminating two consequences of asymmetric information: adverse selection and moral hazard.

Why financial intermediation is imperfect

Adverse selection (Stiglitz and Weiss 1981) refers to the fact that riskier borrowers self-select themselves. Banks and other financial intermediaries attempt to limit adverse selection *ex ante* by discriminating among borrowers and pricing loans accordingly (Diamond 1984). But even with the best *ex ante* discrimination in the world, enough asymmetric information remains that banks are unable to set interest rates on bank loans that fully discriminate according to risk. Hence, among bank borrowers, inferior investment projects are over-represented, and superior projects under-represented. Lower risk borrowers disproportionately choose to obtain direct finance, or finance themselves, because bank loans are overpriced from their point of view. All this derives from asymmetric information between borrowers and savers.

A second consequence of asymmetric information is moral hazard. This refers to the fact that *ex post*, after a contract is in effect, the insured have incentives to act against the interests of the insurer. In order to attract savers, borrowers must offer them some compensation for risk. In an ideal world of symmetric information, savers know as much about investment projects as do borrowers and thus they are able to price risk accurately by charging riskier borrowers appropriate risk premiums.

As we have seen, in our less than ideal world of asymmetric information, banks and other financial intermediaries are able to add value over and above direct financial markets because they are better able to act as agents for savers. They do this *ex ante* by discriminating among borrowers, charging them appropriate risk premiums, and passing these risk premiums on to depositors (savers) as higher interest rates. They also act as agents *ex post* by monitoring and influencing borrowers' behaviour (Stiglitz and Weiss 1983). Hence they are able to combat moral hazard as well as adverse selection. Nevertheless, in the real world, banks' ability to monitor is limited. In practice, moral hazard remains because borrowers know more about projects than banks.

Government

Notably, we have yet to mention government. In a nutshell, current conventional wisdom has made government indulgence of banking the primary scapegoat for Asia's crisis. Conventional wisdom would have it that Asian governments greatly exacerbated adverse selection by underwriting foreign-exchange-risk-free interest rates, and moral hazard by implicitly assuring banks and bank depositors of bailouts.[7] It is hard to dispute this view, either on factual or theoretical grounds. Yet it may be a half-truth: all governments indulge commercial banking and for good reason. Ideally, governments should intervene so as to reduce rather than exacerbate the adverse selection and moral hazard inherent in financial intermediation. Unfortunately this is not necessarily the case, even in the arms-length Anglo-American systems that have come so much into vogue in the 1990s, when continental Europe and now Asia demonstrably under-performed America. The reason that government intervention in banking faces a dilemma is that banks not only play the role of reducing information asymmetries between savers and borrowers, they also provide the economy's money supply.

Commercial banks supply economies with highly liquid deposits. Thus added to the value that commercial banks add to economies by reducing information asymmetries is the value that they add by providing liquidity. The reason that commercial banking attracts government assurance is that this liquidity acts as the economy's means of payment, and is thus a public good. Governments are mandated to ensure the economy's supply of public goods.

The supply of bank deposits is vulnerable because deposits are contractually redeemable at par whereas their value derives largely from assets that at short notice can be cashed only at a discount. Hence a bank's contract with depositors is good only as long as net withdrawals of deposits do not exceed its liquid assets. As long as net withdrawals proceed within statistically-predictable boundaries, bank deposits can be backed up by a statistically-predictable quantity of liquid assets. But if there is a shock to depositors' confidence, and withdrawals accelerate beyond those boundaries, and if depositors are denied cash, it becomes rational for any and all individual depositors to try to withdraw as well. Thus the initial shock develops into a run – and not only a run on the original bank but a run on other banks that might otherwise have been sound.

A useful abstraction is to consider that before the run, deposits retained value because each individual depositor was able to *free ride* on the willingness of other depositors to refrain from withdrawing. Conversely, after the run, deposits lose value because free rider behaviour goes into reverse. This phenomenon has of course been long understood, although the modern literature has analysed it in new frameworks with new names.[8]

The supply of bank deposits is thus not only a public good – in fact a market economy's most fundamental and valuable public good – but a public good that is vulnerable to disruption. Thus governments in all developed economies underwrite commercial banks: implicitly by proffering lender of last resort facilities from a central bank, and sometimes by limiting competition, and often explicitly as well, by providing deposit insurance. However, such comfort from government is a double-edged sword. While on the one hand it is designed to preserve the economy's liquidity, on the other hand it increases banks' susceptibility to adverse selection and moral hazard, the former by suppressing risk premiums on interest rates, and the latter by interfering with banks' role as agents who transmit the true riskiness of loans to depositors. As a consequence, governments' assurances to banks typically lead them to over-allocate funds to risky projects; it may lead them to over-investment in the aggregate as well.

Our argument thus far has run as follows. The Asian 'miracle' economies translated high saving rates into high investment rates and high growth. This was complemented in the late 1980s and early 1990s by rapid liberalization of their external capital accounts, which led in turn to rapid capital inflows. Throughout this period, these Asian economies by and large ran fixed exchange rate regimes; thus capital inflows were mostly translated into monetary growth. This monetary growth had two negative consequences. First, it was intermediated (from savers to borrowers) imperfectly; adverse selection and moral hazard led to misallocation of capital as well as over-investment in the aggregate. Secondly, moral hazard in conjunction with rapid growth in credit led to asset inflation, as will now be explained.

Ceilings on price inflation

Ceilings on price inflation on flows of goods and services, added to rapid monetary growth and moral hazard, leads to asset inflation. Consistent with the above remarks, Krugman (1998b) tells a tale of misallocation and over-investment under conditions of rapid capital inflows that confront adverse selection and moral hazard once they are intermediated through the banking system. His tale assumes that the supply of capital goods is perfectly elastic. Krugman then continues his story by reversing this assumption and replacing it with one of complete price inelasticity in the supply of assets. Assets in this context refer not only to capital goods in quasi-fixed supply but also to financial instruments such as equity shares, real estate, works of art and any other assets that readily attract investment and are in fixed supply for significant periods of time. The assumption of price inelasticity, in conjunction of course with the unrealistic 'Panglossian' assessments of returns that are induced by moral hazard – what Krugman calls 'Panglossian' expectations – adds price-inflation in fixed assets to quantity-inflation in reproducible assets. In short, it leads to asset price bubbles.

Asset price inflation can be thought of as produced by an inelastic supply of assets in conjunction with an elastic supply of money. Only if money and credit expands readily to the Panglossian demand for investment can the latter be translated into asset bubbles. Why wasn't the supply of money checked? We have already given part of the answer: unrestricted capital inflows together with a credibly pegged exchange rate lead to rapid monetary growth. But why didn't the Asian economies check their monetary growth? A partial answer is that they tried but failed. Sterilization efforts were largely abandoned by 1995 because of their quasi-fiscal costs (Dean 1996).

But a deeper answer is that there seemed no need. Inflation in goods and services prices was low – at least under 10 per cent – and well within 'Washington consensus' limits. Central banks have learned to target product inflation but not asset inflation. Moreover Asian central banks faced the dilemma that under fixed exchange rate regimes, tightening credit and raising domestic interest rates would have drawn in more foreign capital and imposed quasi-fiscal costs of sterilization. The second dilemma that they faced was that raising rates would have risked bringing down financial institutions and also pricking the stock-price bubble, as Thailand was already discovering to its dismay by early 1997. Hence monetary growth and asset inflation proceeded more or less unchecked.[9]

Fiscal limits on bank bailouts

Fiscal limits on bank bailouts turns asset inflation into asset deflation. The next step of Krugman's argument is crucial. Asset inflation proceeds only so long as banks maintain their Panglossian views. As the likelihood of bailouts declines, so too do asset prices. This outcome is fairly obvious if the change in the bailout regime is assumed to be exogenous: the election of a new government that no longer tolerates 'crony capitalism', or intervention by the IMF. The outcome is less obvious when change is endogenous. Krugman (1998b) models this by assuming that implicit guarantees continue only until they turn out to be too expensive. In the context of a simple three period model, this is tantamount to the proposition that creditors of financial intermediaries will be bailed out only once. If asset returns are 'bad' (less than Panglossian) in period 2, bank depositors will have to be bailed out, and future depositors can no longer expect the same. Hence the banks will collapse immediately, in period 2, because the book value of their assets now exceeds its market value, and they will be able to attract new depositors only up to market value.

If, however, asset returns in period 2 are 'good' (that is, Panglossian hopes are indeed realized), the one-time bailout option will not be exercised, implicit government assurance will continue, as will inflated land values and the ability of banks to attract deposits up to these values. Banks will not fail.

The most interesting possibility is that despite good returns in period 2, depositors' expectations about bailouts change: they no longer expect future bailouts in case of less-than-Panglossian realized asset values. In that case banks will no longer be able to attract funds beyond the assets' actual market values, and thus they will fail. This outcome is what Krugman characterizes as 'self-fulfilling' and uses it as the basis for a story about self-fulfilling financial crises. It is an important story because it differs fundamentally from previous stories about self-fulfilling financial crises based on self-fulfilling currency crises (reviewed in Krugman 1997 and 1998a). This is, by contrast, a story that is based on self-fulfilling asset crises that result from diminished expectations about bailouts.

As Krugman points out, the story nicely addresses several puzzles associated with the Asian crisis: the absence of macroeconomic or external-account indicators of unsustainable currency pegs; the boom-bust cycles in asset prices that preceded the crises (particularly in Thailand); the absence of sharp external (or internal) shocks; and apparent contagion to countries not strongly linked through trade or capital flows. That the crisis hit several economies almost simultaneously with neither a common external shock nor contagion is consistent, Krugman argues, with the view that they were already 'in a sort of "metastable" state ... highly vulnerable to self-fulfilling pessimism.' (1998b: 9).

High debt ratios

High debt ratios added to asset deflation leads to debt servicing difficulties and exacerbates currency crises. The story that burst asset bubbles and collapsed financial institutions leads to currency crises is missing a link. The link is high ratios of external debt, and debt service obligations, to export earnings. If the asset and investment boom was sustained in part by an inflow of foreign capital that was mostly borrowed by domestic banks, which have now failed, the inflow will slow down or perhaps turn into an outflow. If in addition the inflow had been sustained for some time, it would have resulted in a considerable accumulation of external debt, with associated debt service obligations. Thus the likelihood that an inflow turns into an outflow is enhanced.

The depth of the affected countries' currency crises should be related to their debt ratios, both internal and external, including, crucially, the debt-equity ratios of private firms, especially large conglomerates. Moreover, such countries are vulnerable to a dilemma: if interest rates are raised to stem capital outflow, they will simultaneously increase the debt service burden. But if interest rates are not raised, currency values will drop and the debt service burden will increase in local currency terms.

Our stylized 'explanation' of Asia's crisis is now complete. The essence of the story is that Asian capitalism and unrestricted capital flows did not mix well. In fact they proved to be an extremely volatile combination, much more volatile than anyone had suspected. A basic issue not yet addressed is whether it is Asian capitalism that must go, or unrestricted capital flows. This issue has, over the past year, become a litmus test that rather reliably divides 'salt water' from 'fresh water' economists.[10] But before addressing it, let me attempt to classify economists' perceptions of East Asia more fundamentally: according to whether they perceive the tale I have just told through a lens of *government failure*, or one of *market failure*.

Government failure or market failure?

Government failure

Those who attribute the crisis to *government failure* see unwarranted intervention by the state at every stage of the logical chronicle just recounted.

Saving rates were too high in Asian countries because of extra-market government policies that encouraged or even forced saving. In fact Singapore's 'Provident Fund' and its counterpart in Malaysia not only forced saving (for retirement), it also forced government investment of the proceeds. This phenomenon was often cited to rationalize Alwyn Young's (1992) findings that Singapore's average growth rate was no higher than Hong Kong's, even though the latter has had substantially lower rates of saving and investment. Hong Kong's higher returns on investment are rationalized as the result of its heavier reliance on mobilization and allocation of saving by the private sector.

Rapid capital inflows were the product of easy money in the developed world combined with government guarantees of investment outcomes in the developing world. Although developed-world inflation rates have been low throughout the 1990s, so have interest rates. This has prompted an exodus of investment funds to emerging markets. Attractive nominal rates of return in emerging markets partly reflected attractive real and risk-adjusted returns, but were partly illusory because they failed to take account of both exchange rate and default risk. Both types of risk were masked by implicit but widely-credited government guarantees: guarantees of exchange rate pegs, and guarantees to financial intermediaries.

Imperfect financial intermediation was the result of government interference with banking at every level. Ultimate borrowers, typically large conglomerates, were prompted and implicitly underwritten by national industrial strategies. The banks through which they borrowed were comforted by assurances of government bailouts, or at least lax supervision and regulation. This led to moral hazard and its classic consequences. One consequence was over-investment in the aggregate, since down-side risks were discounted. A second was misallocation of investment, since funds were directed by government plan or, worse, by 'cronyism' between borrowers and banks. Both over-investment and misallocated investment meant that risk-adjusted rates of return were bound to be sub-normal.

Asset inflation was the combined product of rapid capital inflows, government's failure to sterilize the impact of those inflows on domestic money supplies, and implicit government assurances of bailouts. Rapid monetary and credit growth, combined with Panglossian expectations, resulted not only in high rates of expenditure on reproducible capital, but also in speculative spending on fixed and quasi-fixed assets such as real estate and equity shares. The result was overvalued real estate and stock markets: bubbles that were set to burst at the first sign the river of money was about to dry up. This phenomenon, not incidentally, had already manifested itself in Japan in the late 1980s, but in that case as a result of easy money that was domestically generated rather than the product of capital inflows from abroad.

Asset deflation was the result of government's unwillingness, and ultimately inability, to bail out banks and borrowers under on-going regimes of misallocation and over-investment, combined with inflated asset prices. The trigger for the Asian crisis was Thailand, where asset prices began to sag once the first financial intermediaries failed, or even before, when borrowers in default were first held to account and easy credit ceased.

Currency collapse, in the view of those who ascribe Asia's crisis to government, was a culmination of the above factors, and was triggered by the banks' inability to meet their foreign currency obligations. Borrowing banks' illiquid assets and short-term liabilities combined with lending banks' reverse free rider behaviour turned what might have been temporary illiquidity into virtual bank insolvencies. Short-term lines of credit from foreign lenders were simply not rolled over. As the net flow of foreign funds into East Asian economies turned increasingly negative, currency values plummeted below any conceivable long-term equilibria.

Finally, *IMF intervention*, in this view, has exacerbated the crisis and sowed the seeds for yet more moral hazard in future by bailing out both delinquent borrowers and imprudent lenders.

Market failure

Those who see the Asian crisis through the lens of *market failure* rather than government failure see these phenomena quite differently.

Saving rates are seen as endogenous, cultural phenomena rather than the result of exogenous government dictate. Government schemes to encourage household saving were expressions of a popular consensus, a consensus that individual free choice is properly subordinated to the national interest. Indeed, East Asia's extraordinary saving and investment rates translated for several decades into a 'growth miracle' that was the envy of the Western world. When properly managed, as in Singapore and Taiwan, domestic saving eventually exceeded domestic investment, leading to net capital outflows rather than inflows, and thus relative immunity from the current crisis.

Rapid capital inflows are seen as an unfortunate by-product of premature capital account liberalization: that is, too little government intervention rather than too much. In the 1980s, external liberalization was often adopted under duress by developing countries when they were under the knife of balance of payments crises. Both then and in the 1990s, liberalization was encouraged by advice and pressure from the International Financial Institutions, particularly the IMF. As well, indirect pressure came from such underwriters and bastions of free market capitalism as the US Treasury and Wall Street investment banks: what has been described by some as the 'IMF-[US] Treasury-Wall Street' complex.

The alleged market failure that is encouraged by rapid capital inflow could be classified into two types. What might be defined as first-order failure refers to misallocation and over-investment. On the demand side this results from the inability of underdeveloped, under-regulated and under-supervised financial intermediaries to absorb and allocate funds efficiently or even honestly. On the supply side it results from the blindness of foreign investors to the fact that borrowing banks cannot allocate funds efficiently, as well as the tendency of such investors toward herd behaviour. Second-order failure could be defined as vulnerability to capital outflows. It too results from tendencies toward herd behaviour and related 'inefficient' market phenomena.

Imperfect financial intermediation is seen as a given that invites government intervention, rather than the other way around. This stems from the view that even in advanced economies, financial markets are subject to failure because borrowers and lenders have asymmetric information, leading to adverse selection of borrowers *ex ante* as well as moral hazard *ex post*. Compounding this is the risk of a systemic deposit run on the banking system, a risk that almost inevitably prompts government to provide guarantees on bank assets or bank deposits or both, thereby adding to moral hazard.

Financial market imperfections are typically so endemic in emerging markets that they turn to hands-on intermediation between lenders and borrowers through the banking system rather than the impersonality of direct financial markets, which operate by trading claims and contracts such as stocks and bonds. But relying on banks does not magically generate the necessary infrastructure of supervision and regulation; nor does it magically generate qualified human capital. In practice the failure of financial markets in Asia has led to a call for more government intervention rather than less, and not just from those who were previously suspicious of markets. The call for stronger bank supervision and regulation is particularly widespread. Interestingly, the private sector in Asia is also calling for advice and intervention and advice from government, think tanks and academia, since the need for analytical skills in risk management and the like, notably absent from the banking sector, is more available in the better-educated public sector.

Countering the conventional wisdom on Asian 'crony capitalism': financial intermediation in Asia

A view of the need for government intervention in emerging market financial systems that is at once more radical and specific to Asia is that there, economic success is derived directly from a symbiotic system that worked well until it was ruptured with the liberalization of its external and internal financial markets.

Financial intermediation in the Asian crisis economies differs from that in Anglo-American economies in two important respects. First, there is far more of it, relative to GDP. And second, both the relationships between government and banks, and those between banks and industry, are far more intimate. Since the onset of the Asian crisis, it has become fashionable to refer pejoratively to the Asian system as 'crony capitalism,' and to bask in the glory of our 'arms-length' financial markets. It is easy to forget that this recently-reviled system is one that produced, or at very least was consistent with, a decade of high and sustained real growth such as Western capitalism has never seen. Indeed, it is possible to paint the Asian financial system in a positive light by considering it as a set of reinforcing components.

Wade and Veneroso (1998: 6) have succinctly described these components as '[h]igh household savings, plus high corporate debt-equity ratios, plus bank-firm-state collaboration, plus national industrial strategy, plus investment incentives conditional on international competitiveness...[that add up to] the "development state".' Their analysis[11] begins with the observation that saving rates in Asia are much higher than in western economies: one-third of GDP or more in Asia, versus 15 or 20 per cent in the west. Moreover the bulk of this saving is done by households and held in bank deposits, rather than in bonds or equities.[12] Since neither households nor governments are major net borrowers, most of this household saving is channelled, through banks, to firms. This, in combination with relatively undeveloped equity markets, means that firms in East and Southeast Asia have very high debt-equity ratios, especially in Japan and Korea, where the ratios are often two to one or more (in contrast to a norm of less than one in the West).

High ratios of financial intermediation (bank deposits and loans) relative to GDP, as well as high debt-equity ratios, make the entire financial system very vulnerable to shocks: for example, reductions in rollovers of bank deposits or increases in interest rates. Until the 1990s, Asian financial systems insulated themselves against such shocks by imposing external and internal controls: externally, restrictions on inflows and outflows of portfolio capital, and internally, ceilings on interest rates. For further insulation, Asian systems enveloped close cooperation between banks and firms, and between both and government. Borrowing from abroad was restricted or at least orchestrated by government, but as a *quid pro quo* government bailed out banks and firms whose costs or revenues were buffeted by systemic but temporary shocks.

Government's intimacy with finance and industry also had a long-term dimension: national industrial strategy. Thus Japan's famous MITI, and to some extent their counterparts in Korea and elsewhere, guided the growth or decline of entire industrial sectors, particularly with an eye to export performance.

According to Wade (1998), this system began to unravel when the soon-to-be-crisis-economies rushed to liberalize their external capital accounts in the early 1990s. Wade suggests that blame falls equally on national governments and international organizations. As suggested earlier, a myriad of domestic interest groups stand to gain from liberalization. So do foreign banks and other lenders: in fact Wade and Veneroso (1998: 8) state baldly that 'In Korea key people were bribed by Japanese and western financial institutions … to do something that was counter to the whole thrust of Korean development policy for decades past.' The Korean government, eager to join the OECD club of industrialized countries, abolished the Economic Planning Board, which had been the main body for making economic strategy since the 1960s.

Once the system of control and coordination was liberalized – or unravelled if one accepts the Wade and Veneroso interpretation – the Korean *chaebol* and corporate and bank borrowers elsewhere, discovered that they could borrow abroad much more cheaply than at home. This was possible, of course, only so far as potential devaluation of domestic currencies was kept out of the calculation: i.e. the perception of cheapness depended on an assumption that exchange rates were truly fixed. Most of the debt incurred was short term – perhaps because of a lingering suspicion that exchange rates just *might* fall in the long run – and most of it was private. For example, Korea ran up its foreign debt from $39 bn in 1989 to over $160 bn by late 1997.

Should capital flows be re-regulated?

Those who argue for what Emmerson (1998) calls (but does not fully endorse) 'Americanizing Asia', suggest that the intimacy between finance, industry and government characterizing Asian capitalism must be replaced by Anglo-American arms-length relationships. But the intimacy of Asian capitalism worked for decades in Japan, and more recently in the 'tigers', to produce the most rapid sustained growth in human history. According to analysts such as Wade and Veneroso, this intimacy was comprised of symbiotic relationships which worked on balance to produce rather than inhibit growth: not, perhaps with ideal allocative efficiency, or a maximum of individual liberty (to save or not to save, for example), but compensated by high investment rates.

In this view, the cozy success of Asian capitalism was rudely interrupted by capital liberalization. First-order benefits from foreign capital inflows were minor at best since they were not necessary to finance investment, given the Asian economies' very high domestic saving rates. In fact on balance any benefits turned into net costs due to over-investment and misallocation due to moral hazard. In addition, capital inflows engendered second-order costs given the recipient economies' vulnerability to sudden reversals.

This cannot be a universally compelling argument, since some economies are more vulnerable than others. Few, and not Wade and Veneroso I suspect, would argue that the US should restrict capital inflows, or that Japan should restrict capital outflows. Indeed, not all East Asian economies do have dangerously high debt-equity ratios: Taiwan's, for example, is well below 100 per cent and, not incidentally, Taiwan has weathered the Asian crisis better than any economy in the region. The more fundamental basis for Wade and Veneroso's argument is that the highly debt-leveraged *keiretsu, chaebol,* and *konglomerat* of Japan, Korea and Indonesia are far more vulnerable than the less leveraged firms of America and Western Europe. In the case of Japan, which is a net exporter of capital, this vulnerability has been buffered by indulgent domestic banks backed by passive domestic depositors, but in the cases of Korea and Indonesia, which are capital importers, the vulnerability was quite naked. This line of reasoning leads Wade and Veneroso to endorse Jagdish Bhagwati's recent (1998) call for a halt to capital liberalization, at least in Asia. Notably, his prescription for India, which remains relatively closed at least to portfolio capital inflows and outflows, is to keep it closed. Similar reasoning, as well as the simple observation that China has thus far weathered the storm that has engulfed its neighbours, is persuading other Western observers to endorse China's longstanding policy of restricting capital flows and currency conversion.

Bhagwati's position is startling as he is a highly respected mainstream economist, who endorses free trade. His argument, as well as that of another eminent international economist, Dani Rodrick (1998), is that the logic for free trade in goods and services does not carry over to free flows of capital. The logic for free trade rests on the gains that ensue from specialization in lines of production coincident with comparative advantages. The logic for free capital flows rests on gains that ensue from moving capital to projects and regions with higher than average rates of return.

Although neither Bhagwati nor Rodrick spell it out, the argument against free capital flows in the light of Krugman's story is presumably that *ex post* these returns may turn out to be lower than expected because of the misallocation and over-investment biases introduced by asymmetric information. *Ex ante*, domestic borrowers and lenders expect higher rates of return than are actually realized because they expect private 'Panglossian' returns rather than the true returns that net out either the costs of publicly-funded bailouts for as long as they continue, or the costs of higher interest rates or bankruptcy once they cease. Foreign lenders expect rates of return that are higher *ex ante* than *ex post* because they too expect bailouts, whether from the governments that they presume will stand behind domestic borrowers, or from international institutions like the IMF. It may also be that foreign lenders are less well informed about the creditworthiness of domestic borrowers than are domestic lenders.

To this view may be added the Krugman argument that unrestricted access to foreign capital greatly compounded the Asian financial system's potential for moral hazard, and led to Panglossian over-investment in reproducible capital and over-valuation of fixed assets. But this does not necessarily lead to the Bhagwati/Rodrick/Wade conclusion that capital inflows should be restricted; rather, it leads more readily to the conclusion that cozy, comfortable relationships between government, financial intermediaries and industrial conglomerates should be ruptured. To do so strikes at the heart of Asian capitalism, since the extraordinary debt-equity ratios would be unsustainable were government quasi-guarantees to be withdrawn.

In fact, whether or not to restrict capital flows into countries where liberalization is a done deal may well be moot, since capital liberalization may be irreversible. Once the river of foreign funds has begun to flow, those with an interest in keeping it flowing – not least, those who have borrowed heavily and contracted high debt loads – will strongly resist re-regulation. Moreover, capital inflows are likely ultimately to force the dismantling of non-arms-length financial relationships. If capital liberalization so severely exacerbates adverse selection and moral hazard that financial crisis ensues, reform is almost inevitable. Cold-eyed capitalism will prevail.

Hence the Asian economies that did enthusiastically liberalize portfolio flows in the 1990s – Indonesia, Thailand and, to some extent South Korea – are those most likely to continue the course, both because they are now reliant on continued inflows, and because the damage to their financial intermediaries, and to the government fiscal accounts dedicated to supporting them, has been so profound that reversion to the *ancien regime* is unthinkable. Should the idea even be mooted, it is probable that IMF, World Bank and other official emergency lending would be cut off; more importantly, so would private capital inflows. Malaysia, which has thus far avoided (or at least postponed) submission to an IMF programme as well as bank and corporate restructuring, is also likely to retain its liberalized regime in the long run, despite its imposition of short-term capital controls in September 1998.

In contrast to the crisis economies, Japan postponed full liberalization until the late 1990s, with its 'big bang' (which will, *inter alia*, allow unrestricted access to foreign financial institutions) just now underway. Yet Japan pioneered the Asian financial crisis with its asset bubble that burst in 1989. Throughout the period both before and after the bubble burst, Japan was a capital exporter, not importer; hence it was not the free availability of foreign capital that exacerbated moral hazard and led to the bubble and burst. This suggests that capital account liberalization was *not* the root cause of Asia's crisis, but rather that it was cozy 'crony' capitalism. Capital from domestic saving was available in sufficient abundance to swamp the system with misallocated capital without help from abroad. Non-performing loans at Japanese banks are of the same order of magnitude as those in the crisis economies. That Japan avoided banking and currency crises for nine years after its asset bubble burst was due to its prolonged ability as an extremely affluent nation to subsidize bleeding banks and the like, as well as its decision (at least *de facto*) to let the yen float and thus fall gradually. Indeed, the yen has depreciated by over 40 per cent since 1995, more than the net depreciation of all but Indonesia of the 'crisis' economies since July 1997; but 40 per cent over four years rather than a few months does not constitute a currency crisis or precipitate a banking crisis.

Although it is unlikely that the Asian economies which liberalized will revert to closed capital accounts, those which did not are equally unlikely to liberalize in the near future. Neither India nor China has yet moved to fully convertible currencies or to unrestricted capital accounts, nor, in practice, has Taiwan. While China, dramatically for some decades now, and India more tentatively and more recently, have welcomed and received foreign direct investment, they have not opened themselves to the volatility of unrestricted portfolio flows. It is likely that the lesson they will learn from the Asian crisis is to postpone liberalization for the foreseeable future. Whereas the IMF, as part of its efforts to promote capital account liberalization under its newly amended Articles of Agreement, might have pressured them in the recent past, its official stance is now, in the words of its First Deputy Managing Director, Stanley Fischer at the September, 1997 annual IMF/World Bank meetings, '... to phase capital account liberalization appropriately – which means retaining some capital controls in the process'.

It should be apparent from this discussion of capital liberalization that the pure and polar visions which divide economists on *a priori* ideological grounds – government failure versus market failure – become much less pure, polar and divisive in the *a fortiori* world of practice. Indeed, in offering practical advice about what should have been done then, and especially, what should be done now, economists on both sides of the ideological divide have proved uncharacteristically confused. They seem to see through a glass darkly, with their previous ideological clarity badly blurred.

Despite no vision on the road to Damascus, has a fragile consensus emerged?

What should have been done before disaster struck

Hindsight is cheap wisdom; nevertheless the Asian crisis has probably clarified the minds of many analysts about what should have been done well before disaster struck. Although there is no complete consensus, more economists than before agree that far better domestic financial disclosure, supervision and regulation should have been put in place in the borrowing countries. The reasons this did not happen had much to do with interest group obstacles in the context of win/win high-growth economies. But it also had to do with the prevailing ideology of de-regulation, an ideology that overarched itself when it came to the banking sector.

One might suppose also that consensus has moved further toward the merits of *flexible exchange rates* for borrowing countries that, like the Asian crisis economies, had their inflation rates well under control and therefore had no need for the monetary discipline that fixed rates provide. After all, since an exchange rate crisis is, almost by definition, the involuntary relinquishment of a fixed exchange rate, flexible rates should preclude such crises.

However, the extreme volatility in the baht, won, rupiah and ringhit since they were floated – amounting in the case of the rupiah to a virtual free-fall throughout the second half of 1997 and first half of 1998 – has led some to call for a return to fixed rates, hardened, perhaps, by currency boards. Dornbusch (1998) calls for currency boards in Indonesia and Russia, and more recently in Brazil; but others (see Roubini 1998) warn of the 'myths' surrounding such an arrangement. If there is any consensus, it is that 'automaticity' – pure flexibility or a strict currency board – is preferably to a managed-rate or even fixed-rate system that is prone to government intervention.

It is probably safe to say that economists have become more sensitive to safe sequencing of deregulation: *cautious* phasing out of capital controls seems to be the order of the day, even at the IMF, implying that liberalization may have been too rapid or too wholesale in the past. In fact economists who never did so before have begun to talk about *taxes on international capital flows*: the debate about foreign exchange turnover taxes like the Tobin tax has been revived, and attention has turned to Chile's reserve requirement on short-term foreign deposits. Nevertheless throwing sand into the wheels of international finance remains intensely controversial; undoubtedly, there is much less consensus surrounding this measure than the other three.

What was done wrong when the crisis broke

There is less consensus about how the crisis was managed. Criticism has focused on the IMF. At least two eminent economists have called for its abolition (Schultz 1998; Schwartz 1998), primarily on the grounds that it generates moral hazard among both developing-country borrowers and developed-country lenders. Less extreme judgments are that the IMF acts well beyond its mandate by imposing surrogate government on independent countries (Feldstein 1998), or that it relies too readily in crisis on restrictive monetary and fiscal measures, in particular high interest rates, to arrest currency decline (Sachs 1997; Stiglitz 1998). Others, notably representatives of the IMF itself, defend its past and present roles and call urgently for renewed funding from its shareholders (Fischer 1998).

These disparate views of the IMF's role are manifestation of the disparate lenses through which equally eminent economists view international financial markets.

What should be done now[13]

If the emerging consensus about what went wrong and what was done wrong is fragile, any consensus about what should be done now is even more so. To be sure, most policy-makers at both domestic and international levels agree that financial disclosure, supervision and regulation should be enhanced – indeed, standing committees of the BIS, IMF and G-10 have been studying such measures since the Halifax G-7 summit of 1995, and in June, 1998, Canada took a proposal for international 'peer supervision' to the G-22 meetings – but both the political and practical impediments to achieving financial reforms remain profound.

As for exchange regimes, the 'Washington consensus' that developing countries should adhere to fixed rates had about run its course at the IMF well before the crisis broke, but it remains to be seen what new conventional wisdom will emerge should inflation pose a problem in Asian countries where currencies have depreciated sharply. Jeffrey Sachs, perhaps the world's the most prominent critic of the IMF's part in this (and previous) crises, advocates fully flexible rates (Sachs 1998b). At the other extreme, Rudiger Dornbusch, equally eminent and Sach's former mentor, one high profile economist advocates currency boards for Indonesia, Russia and Brazil. However, it was abundantly clear that the IMF would not condone a currency board for Indonesia when President Suharto flirted with the idea in early 1998, shortly before his political demise; as of early 1999, Russia is out of the question, given its lack of reserves, pariah status with both private and official lenders, and de-capitalized banks; Brazil is perhaps a better candidate, but it currently lacks sufficient reserves to back its monetary base. Moreover, none of the other crisis countries seems remotely interested in, or indeed positioned, even to peg their exchange rates given continued turbulence in exchange markets as well as their depleted reserves. On the other hand the economies that have held their pegs – Hong Kong, China and Taiwan, – are well aware that to be forced to devalue would invite loss of control – currency crises – that could infect the banking and then real sectors and escalate into full-blown financial and economic crises. And so far, these three economies have avoided crisis.

What about capital controls, or at least 'sand in the gears of international finance'? Prominent economists such as Dani Rodrick and Jagdish Bhagwati have questioned the merits of free capital flows. It is likely that skepticism from them and other reputable quarters will lend moral support to countries that have yet to liberalize their capital accounts and are not so inclined – notably India and China. It is also likely that such skepticism in professional quarters will slow down the IMF's campaign to liberalize capital flows under an extension of its Articles of Agreement. Countries that have already liberalized are studying techniques for throwing sand in the wheels, and Malaysia has already implemented such measures.

On balance, it is unlikely that any country will eschew capital inflows on a blanket basis. Distinctions will be drawn between direct and portfolio investment, and between long term and short-term flows. China, for example, has thrived for two decades on massive inflows of direct investment (mostly as joint ventures, and more recently as 'Build Operate Transfer' and similar arrangements), despite severe restrictions on both the inflow and outflow of portfolio capital and without even a convertible currency. Similarly, no country in its right mind would advocate restrictions on short-term trade capital.

Conclusion

In short, there is a consensus about Motherhood measures, but no consensus about most measures. Economists still see Asia's convulsions through a glass darkly, and no divine revelation has descended upon them. What follows is a summary of prevailing opinion, in declining order of broad consensus.

All agree on better international disclosure and supervision but the practical obstacles are formidable.

Few advocate re-regulating capital flows to the crisis economies but many now advocate slowing down de-regulation of non-crisis economies.

Some now toy with the idea of slowing down the turnover of short-term capital flows via taxes or other means of 'throwing sand in the gears'.

Many now argue that the role of the IMF should be re-examined, although opinions run the spectrum from those who would see it abolished to those who advocate both increased funding and increased powers. Among the increased powers that are being mooted are authority to disclose unfavourable information about member countries without their permission, and increased authority to mobilize private lenders to restructure debt and debt payments.

On exchange rates there is no consensus whatsoever. While some maintain that the crisis economies should keep the flexible exchange rates regimes circumstances have chosen for them, others argue for the opposite, credibly fixed-rate regimes underpinned by currency boards. Between the two extremes, proposals are now afoot to create a 'snake in the lake' for East Asia, modelled on the 'snake in the tunnel' that Western European economies engineered after the collapse of the Bretton Woods fixed-rate regime in 1971.

Most observers do agree that the non-crisis Asian economies should stick to their fixed rate regimes, if only because the potential for precipitating more regional instability, were China and/or Hong Kong to relinquish their pegs, is too horrible to contemplate.[14]

Notes

1   Acts 9 recounts how St Paul, then Saul of Tarsus, was struck to the ground by a light from heaven, leading to his conversion to Christianity. It is notable that in the process of conversion he was blinded for three days.

2   In 1 Corinthians 13, verse 12, St Paul writes, 'For now we see through a glass darkly, but then face to face…'.

3   The first half of this section draws on Dean (1999c).

4   See Dean (1992) and Dean and Bowe (1997) for extensive reviews of the 1980s debt crisis and its resolution.

5   See Dean (1996).

6   Parts of this section draw on Crockett (1997).

7   The best articulation of this view is Krugman (1998b).

8   See for example Diamond and Dybvig's (1983) analysis of bank values subject to multiple equilibria. The combination of illiquid assets, short-term liabilities and free rider behaviour that they model would be useful to analyse the Asian crisis if it were extended to an international context with countries taking the place of banks.

9   The parallel to the US economy in mid- to late-1998 is hard to ignore. See *The Economist* magazine of May 8, 1998, as well as the three previous issues.

10 Several years ago, the *New York Times* used these epithets to distinguish the non-interventionist, pure market economists, who mostly seem to hail from institutions located on fresh water, like the University of Chicago, from their less-than-pure brethren who preach and practice at places like Harvard, MIT and Stanford, on the salt water East and West coasts.

11 In addition to Wade (1998) and Wade and Veneroso (1998a) see the succint summary of their view in Wade and Veneroso (1998b).
12 The direction of cause and effect is not clear here. The absence of alternatives to bank deposits could be because (Asian) household savers are risk averse and value liquidity, or it could be that Asian savers are forced to rely on bank deposits because equity and bond markets are underdeveloped and thus excessively risky and illiquid.
13 See also Dean (1999a).
14 See also Dean (2000, 2001).

References

Bhagwati, J. (May/June 1998) 'The Capital Myth', *Foreign Affairs* 77(3): 7–13.

Cline, W. (1995) *International Debt Reexamined*, Washington, D.C.: Institute for International Economics.

Corbo, V. and Jaime M. de (1985) 'Liberalization with stabilization in the southern cone of Latin America: overview and summary' *World Development* 13: 836–66.

Crockett, A. (April 1997) 'The theory and practice of financial stability', *Essays in International Finance*, Princeton University: International Finance Section, No. 203.

Dean, J. W. (15 March 1992) 'The debt confessional', *World Competition* Vol.

—— (Autumn 1993) 'Will financial deregulation be good for Malta?' *Bank of Valletta Review* 8: 1–12.

—— (1996) 'Recent capital flows to Asia-Pacific countries: trade-offs and dilemmas', *Journal of the Asia Pacific Economy* 1(3): 287–317.

—— and Michael Bowe (November 1997) 'Has the market solved the sovereign debt crisis?', *Princeton Studies in International Finance No. 83*, 55 pages.

Dean, J. W. (March/April 1998a) 'Why fiscal conservatives and left wing academics are wrong about Asia', *Challenge* 41.

—— and Felmingham, Bruce (1998b) 'Financial deregulation and offshore banking: lessons for Malta from Australian/Asia-Pacific Experience', in (Lino Briguglio, Michael Bowe, and James W. Dean (eds) *Banking and Finance in Islands and Small States*, London: Pinter, Cassell Publishers, 35–52.

—— (1998c) 'Asia's financial crisis in historical perspective', *Journal of the Asia Pacific Economy* 3(3): 267–83.

—— (1999a) 'A role for Canada in global financial reform', in Bruce MacLean (ed.) *Canada and Global Financial Reform*, Toronto: Lorimer Press.

—— (Fall 1999b) 'Is east Asia illiquid or insolvent?', *Multinational Business Review*.

—— (1999c) 'Can financial liberalization come too soon? Jamaica in the 1990s', *Social and Economic Studies* 47(4): 47–59.

—— (2000) 'Can China's triangle of woes survive the WTO?' *Challenge* 43(4):

—— (2001) 'Why financial crisis may come to China but not Taiwan', in A. Chowdhury and I. Islam (eds) *Beyond the East Asian Crisis: The Path to Innovation and Economic Growth*, Cheltenham, UK: Edward Elgar.

Diamond, D. W. (July 1984) 'Financial intermediation and delegated monitoring', *Review of Economic Studies* 51: 393–414.

—— and Dybvig, Philip (June 1983) 'Bank runs, deposit insurance and liquidity', *Journal of Political Economy* 91: 401–19.

Donald K. E. (May/June 1998) 'Americanizing Asia? *Foreign Affairs*

Edwards, S. and van Wijnbergen, S. (February 1986) 'The welfare effects of trade and capital market liberalization' *International Economic Review* 27(1): 141–8.

Feldstein, M. (6 October 1998) 'Reforming the International Monetary Fund' *Wall Street Journal.*

Grosse, R. (1994) 'Jamaica's foreign exchange black market' *Journal of Development Studies* 31(1): 17–27.

Haggard, S. and Sylvia M. (Winter 1996) 'The political economy of financial internationalization in the developing world' *International Organization* 50(1): 35–68.

Irvine, S. (December 1997) 'Asian research: worth the paper it's printed on?', *Euromoney.*

Krugman, P. (November/December 1994) 'The myth of Asia's miracle', *Foreign Affairs* 62–78.

—— (October 1997) 'The Currency Crisis', prepared for NBER conference, http://web.mit.edu/krugman/www/crises.html.

—— (January 1998a) 'What happened to Asia?' prepared for a conference in Japan, http://web.mit.edu/people/krugman/index.html.

—— (January 1998b) 'Bubble, boom, crash: theoretical notes on Asia's crisis,' http://web.mit.edu/krugman/index.html.

McKinnon, R. (1991) *The Order of Economic Liberalization: Financial Control in the Transition to a Market Economy,* Baltimore, Md.: Johns Hopkins University Press.

Naisbitt, J. (1996) *Megatrends Asia: eight Asian megatrends that are reshaping our world,* New York: Simon & Schuster.

Roubini, N. (1998) 'The case against currency boards: debunking 10 myths about the benefits of currency boards', http://www.stern.nyu.edu/~nroubini/asia/CurrencyBoardsRoubini.html

Rodrick, D. (May 1998) 'Should the IMF pursue capital-account convertibility?' in Stanley F., Richard N. C., Rudiger D., Peter N. G., Peter B. K., Carlos M., Jacques J. P. Dani R., and Savak S. T. (eds) *Essays in International Finance,* Princeton University: International Finance Section, No. 207.

Sachs, J. D., Aaron T. and Andres V. (1996) 'Financial crises in emerging markets: the lessons from 1995', *Brookings Papers on Economic Activity* 1: 147–215.

Sachs, J. D., (11 December 1997) 'IMF is a power unto itself', *Financial Times*

—— (12 September 1998) *The Economist* 23–25.

Schwartz, A. J. (1998) 'International financial crises: myths and realities', *The Cato Journal* 17(3) http://www.cato.org/pubs/journal/cj17n3-3.html.

Stiglitz, G. and Weiss, A. (June 1981) 'Credit Rationing with Imperfect Information,' *American Economic Review* 71: 393–410.

Wade, R. (August 1998) 'The Asian debt-and-development crisis of 1997: causes and consequences', *World Development*

—— and Veneroso, F. (March-April 1998a) 'The Asian crisis: the high debt model vs. The Wall Street-Treasury-IMF complex,' *New Left Review.*

—— (7 November 1998b) 'The resources lie within,' *The Economist.*

Young, A. (1992) 'A tale of two cities: factor accumulation and technical change in Hong Kong and Singapore,' *NBER Macroeconomics Annual,* MIT Press.

—— (March 1994a) 'The tyranny of numbers: confronting the statistical realities of the east Asian growth experience,' NBER Working Paper No. 4680.

—— (May 1994b) 'Lessons from the east Asian NICS: A contrarian view,' *European Economic Review Papers and Proceedings.*

Bibliography of Mark Perlman

1951

'The Australian Arbitration System: An Analytical Description.' *Arbitration Journal* 6: 168–76. Also appeared as a University of Hawaii Occasional Paper, Honolulu: University of Hawaii, 1951.

Review of *Bonds of Organization: An Appraisal of Corporate Human Relations* by E. Wight Bakke. *Journal of Business* 24 (January): 73–74.

1952

Labor, Trade Unionism, and the Competitive Menace in Hawaii. with John B. Ferguson. Honolulu: University of Hawaii Industrial Relations Center.

'Organized Labor in Hawaii,' *Labor Law Journal* 3: 263–75.

Review of *The Australian Party System*, by Louise Overacker. *Industrial and Labor Relations Review* 6: 447–8.

1953

'An Industrial Problem – Australia's Longshoremen,' *Labor Law Journal* 4: 462–73.

Review of *Reflections of an Australian Liberal*, by Sir Frederic Eggleston. *Political Science Quarterly* 58 (September), 439–41.

'Australia' (Proceedings of the Industrial Relations Research Association), *Monthly Labor Review* 78 (June), 591–2.

Review of *Studies in Australian Labour Law and Relations* by Orwell de R. Foenander. *Industrial and Labor Relations Review* 6 (July), 609–10.

1954

Judges in Industry: A Study in Labour Arbitration in Australia, Melbourne, London, and New York: Melbourne University Press.

'Wage Regulation in Australia,' *Labor Law Journal* 5: 25–30.

'An Analytical Theory of Labor Arbitration in Australia,' *Sydney Law Review* 1: 207–12.

1955

Review of *Relation of the State to Industrial Action and Economics and Jurisprudence*, by Henry Carter Adams. With an Introductory Essay by Joseph Dorfman. *Industrial and Labor Relations Review* 8: 439–40.

Review of *The Australian Federal Labor Party, 1950–1951*, by L. F. Crisp. *Industrial and Labor Relations Review* 9: 498–9.

1956

Review of *Scientific Management and the Unions, 1900–1932: A Historical Analysis*, by Milton J. Nadworny. *Industrial and Labor Relations Review* 9: 671–2.

1957

'Economic Growth and Government Wage Regulation: The Australian Problem,' *Annals of the American Academy of Political and Social Science* 310: 123–32.
Review of *The Response to Industrialism*, by Samuel P. Hayes. *Industrial and Labor Relations Review* 11: 301–2.

1958

Review of *The Response to Industrialism, 1885–1914* by Samuel P. Hays. *Industrial and Labor Relations Review* 11 (January): 301–2.
Labor Union Theories in America: Background and Development, Evanston, IL: Rowe Peterson.

1959

Review of *The Development of Australian Trade Union Law*, by J. H. Portus. *Industrial and Labor Relations Review* 13: 132–4.

1960

'Labor Movement Theories: Past, Present, and Future.' *Industrial and Labor Relations Review* 13: 338–48.
'Sumner Huber Slichter.' *Dictionary of American Biography, 1955–1960*, 585–7. New York: C. Scribner's sons.
Review of *Studies in Income and Wealth, Vol. 24*, Princeton University Press; for the National Bureau of Economic Research. *Schweizerische Zeitschrift für Volkswirtschaft und Statistik* 98: 362–4.
'Economics of Metropolitan Medical Care,' *Public Health Reports* 77 (May): 388.

1961

The Machinists: A New Study in American Trade Unionism, Cambridge: Harvard University Press.
Review of *Industrial Conciliation and Arbitration in Australia* by Orwell de Foenander. *Industrial and Labor Relations Review* 14 (July): 621–2.

1962

Democracy in the IAM, New York: Wiley.
'Commentarios Sobre el Trabajo 'La Evaluacion del impacto economica de las actividades Sanitarias.' *Boletin de la Oficina Sanitaria Panamerica* 52: 40–45. 'Methods of Evaluation of the Contribution of Health Programs to Economic Development: Discussion of Atilio Macchiavello's Paper – 'Evaluation of the Economic Impact of Health Activities.' 30 September 1961.
Review of *The Pennsylvania Manufacturers' Association* by J. Roffe Wike. *Business History Review* 4 (June): 131–3.

1963

Human Resources in the Urban Economy (ed.). Washington: Resources for the Future.
'Economic Aspects of the Health Industry in Dynamic Societies.' *American Journal of Public Health* 53: 381–91.

'The Economics of Human Resources in the American Urban Setting: Some Concepts and Problems,' in Mark Perlman (ed.) *Human Resources in the Urban Economy*, Washington: Resources for the Future, 1–20.

1964

'Some Economic Aspects of Public Health Programs in Underdeveloped Areas.' *The Economics of Health and Medical Care*. Proceedings of the Conference on the Economics of Health and Medical Care, May 10–12, 1962. Ann Arbor: University of Michigan Press.

Review of *The Economics of Labor* by E.H. Phelps Brown. *Industrial and Labor Relations Review* 17 (January): 320–2.

1966

'Measuring the Effects of Population Control on Economic Development: Pakistan as a Case Study.' with Edgar M. Hoover. *Pakistan Development Review* 6: 168–76.

'On Health and Economic Development: Some Problems, Methods, and Conclusions reviewed in a Perusal of the Literature,' *Comparative Studies in Society and History* 8: 433–48.

1967

Health Manpower in a Developing Economy with Timothy D. Baker, M.D. Baltimore: Johns Hopkins Press.

Contemporary Economics and Selected Readings, (ed. with Reuben E. Slesinger and Asher Isaacs) Boston: Allyn and Bacon.

1968

'Labor in Eclipse,' in J. Braeman, R. H. Bremmer, and D. Brady (eds.), *Twentieth Century America*, Columbus, OH: Ohio State University Press, 103–45.

'Theories of the Labor Movement,' *New International Encyclopedia of the Social Sciences*. New York: Macmillan 8: 516–22.

Review of *Australian Labour Economics: Readings* and *Australian Labour Relations: Readings* by J.E. Isaac and G.W. Ford in *Industrial and Labor Relations Review* 21: 451–2.

1969

'Editor's Note.' *Journal of Economic Literature* 7; iii.

'Government and the Economy: How Much Intervention?' in Judd Teller (ed.) *Government and the Democratic Policy*, New York: American Histadrut Cultural Exchange, 67–74, ff.

'Rationing of Medical Resources: The Complexities of the Supply and Demand Problem,' *Sociological Studies in Economics and Administration*. Monograph 14 of the *Sociological Review* 105–19.

1970

'Cost/Benefit Ratio of Population Planning,' in Dong-A Ilbo, *Population Planning and Economic Development*, being a report on an international conference held in Pusan, Korea, February 25–28, 6–13.

1971

Carter Goodrich, Memorial. Pittsburgh: University of Pittsburgh.

'Some Comments on the American Productivity Growth Rate.' *Monetary Indicators* November 12, 1971.

'The Trend in Physician and Hospital Bills,' *Monetary Indicators* November 19, 1971.

'Union Negotiations, 1971: Whither?,' *Monetary Indicators* March 26, 1971.

Review of *Health Manpower Planning in Turkey: An International Research Case Study*, by Carl F. Taylor, Rahmi Dirican, and Kurt W. Deuschle. *Economic Development and Cultural Change* 19: 490–4.

Review of *Medical Care use in Sweden and the United States: A comparative analysis of systems and behavior*, by Ronald Andersen, Bjorn Smedby, and Odin Anderson, *Journal of Economic Literature* 9: 1224–6.

1972

'Some Reflections on Theorizing About Industrial Relations,' in Norval Morris and Mark Perlman (eds.) *Law and Crime: Essays in Honor of Sir John Barry*, New York, London, and Paris: Gordon and Breach, 181–209.

'On Health, Population Change, and Economic Development,' in Mark Perlman, Charles Levin, and Benjamin Chinitz (eds.), *Spatial, Regional, and Population Economics: Essays in Honor of Edgar M. Hoover*, New York, London, and Paris: Gordon and Breach, 293–310.

'Economics Libraries and Collections,' in *Encyclopedia of Library and Information Science* 7 (New York, NY: Marcel Dekker) 345–63.

1973

'Comments on 'Consumption Values of Trade Unions,' *Journal of Economic Issues* 7: 303–5.

'Communications, The Editor's Comment,' *Journal of Economic Literature* 11: 56–8.

'Editor's Comment: On the classification of economics materials,' *Journal of Economic Literature* 11: 898–9.

'Model for hospital micro-costing,' (with Larry J. Shuman and Harvey Wolfe) *Industrial Engineering* (July 1973), 39–43.

1974

'Introduction' and 'Economics of Health and Medical Care in Industrialized Nations,' in Mark Perlman (ed.) *Economics of Health and Medical Care*, New York: Halsted Press, xiii–xx, 21–33.

Review of *Population Change, Modernization and Welfare*, by Joseph Spengler. *Journal of Economic Literature* 22: 1372–3.

'Family Health in Urban Migrants,' National Council for International Health. *Health of the Family*. International Health Conference, October 16–18, 1974, held at Reston, VA. 51–54.

Review of *The Effects of Income on Fertility*, by J. L. Simon. *Economic Journal* 84: 1053–5.

1975

'Economics of the Family: Marriage, Children, and the Human Capital,' *Demography* 12: 549–56.

'The Editor's Comment: The 1975 Kiel Conference on Economics Bibliography,' *Journal of Economic Literature* 13: 1320–1.

'Some Economic Growth Problems and the Part Population Policy Plays.' *Quarterly Journal of Economics* 89: 247–56.

1976

'Jews and Contributions to Economics: A Bicentennial Review,' *Judaism* 25: 301–11.

'Foreword,' in Michael C. Keeley (ed.) *Population, Public Policy, and Economic Development*. New York: Praeger Publishers, vi–vii.

Review of *The Great Instauration: Science, Medicine, and Reform 1626–1660*, by Charles Webster. *Journal of Economic Literature* 14: 1289–91.

Review of *Studies in the Colonial History of Spanish America*, by Mario Góngora. *Journal of Economic Literature* 14: 898–900.

'The Changing Modes of Data in Recent [Economic] Research (with Naomi W. Perlman),' in Mark Perlman (ed.) *The Organization and Retrieval of Economic Knowledge*, New York: Halsted Press, 197–229.

'The Editing of the *Economic Record*, 1925–1975,' in J. P. Nieuwenhuysen and P. J. Drake (eds.) [Wilfred Prest]: *Australian Economic Policy.* Melbourne: Melbourne University Press, 218–30.

'Introduction,' in Mark Perlman (ed.) *The Organization and Retrieval of Economic Knowledge*, New York: Halsted Press, 1–11.

'Orthodoxy and Heterodoxy in Economics: A Retrospective View of Experiences in Britain and the U. S. A.' *Zeitschrift. für Nationalökonomie* 37: 151–64.

'Economics and Health,' *Tribuna Médica (A Weekly Newspaper Sent to All Physicians in Spain)* 16 December 1977.

1978

'Considering the Future of American Health Care Capital Funding: A Working Paper.' (with Gordon K. MacLeod) in Gordon K. MacLeod and Mark Perlman (eds.) *Health Care Capital: Competition and Control.* Proceedings of the Capital Investment Conference Sponsored by the University of Pittsburgh. Cambridge, MA: Lippincott, Ballinger, 379–97.

'Discrepancies of Supply and Demand in the Labor Market: Sectoral, Regional and Professional – Causes and Cures.' in Herbert Giersch (ed.) *Capital Shortage and Unemployment in the World Economy: Symposium*, Tübingen: Mohr (Paul Siebeck), 159–60, 329–30.

'Labor Movement,' *World Book Encyclopedia* 12: 6–17.

'Reflections on Methodology, Persuasion, and Machlup,' in Jacob S. Dreyer (ed.) [Fritz Machlup]: *Breadth and Depth in Economics.* Lexington, MA: Health, pp. 5.

Review of *The Last Great Subsistence Crisis in the Western World*, by John D. Post. *Journal of Economic Literature* 26: 120–3.

Review of *Knowledge and Ignorance in Economics*, by T.W. Hutchinson. *Journal of Economic Literature* 26: 582–5.

Review of *William Beveridge: A Biography*, by José Harris. *Journal of Economic Literature* 26: 1079–81.

Review of *Ethics and Society in England: The Revolution in the Social Sciences, 1870–1914*, by Reba N. Stoffer. *Journal of Economic Literature* 26: 1447–9.

1979

'One Man's Baedeker to Productivity Growth Discussions,' in William Fellner (ed.) *Contemporary Economic Problems, 1979*, Washington: American Enterprise Institute, 79–113.

Review of *Historical Studies of Changing Fertility*, edited by Charles Tilly. *Journal of Economic Literature* 16: 120–3.

Review of *On Revolutions and Progress in Economic Knowledge*, by T.W. Hutchinson. *Zeitschrift für Nationalökonomie* 39: 225–420.

1980

'Prices, Technological Change, and Productivity in the American Health Care Industry,' in William Fellner (ed.) *Contemporary Economic Problems, 1980*, Washington: American Enterprise Institute, 227–62.

Review of *Corn, Cash, Commerce: The Economics Policies of the Tory Governments, 1815–1830*, by Boyd Hilton; *Political Economists and the English Poor Laws: A Historical Study of the Influence of Classical Economics on the Formation of Social Welfare Policy*, by Raymond G. Cowherd. *History of Political Economy* 12: 299–302.

Review of *Worker's Control in America: Studies in the History of the World*, by David Montgomery. *Journal of Economic History* 40: 656–9.

Review of *Daniel DeLeon: The Odyssey of An American Marxist*, by L. Glen Seretan. *Journal of Economic Issues* (Sept 1980), 804–7.

Review of *Imagination and the nature of choice*, by G.L.S. Shackle. *Journal of Economic Literature* 18: 115–8.

Review of *Labour and the Law*, by Charles O. Gregory and Harold A. Katz. *Journal of Economic Literature* 28: 648–51.

Review of *Malthus*, by William Petersen and *Population Malthus: His Life and Times*, by Patricia James. *Journal of Economic Literature* 28: 1100–3.

Review of *The rise and fall of economic growth: A study in contemporary thought*, by Heinz W. Arndt. *Journal of Economic Literature* 28: 1558–9.

Review of *Research in Health Economics: A Research Annual*, by Richard M. Scheffler. *Southern Economic Journal* 47: 562–5.

1981

Health, Economics, and Health Economics, (ed. with J. van der Gaag) Amsterdam, New York, Oxford: North-Holland Press.

'Some Economic Consequences of the New Patterns of Population Growth' in William Fellner (ed.) *Essays in Contemporary Economic Problems: Demand, Productivity, and Population*, Washington: American Enterprise Institute, 247–79.

'[Valedictory] Editor's Note,' *Journal of Economic Literature* 19: 1–4.

Review article of *Population Change in Developed Countries*, by Richard A. Easterlin (ed.). *Journal of Economic Literature* 19: 74–82.

'Professor Clarifies Economic Talk,' *The Pitt News* March 25, 1981.

Review of *The Dynamics of Industrial Conflict: Lessons from Ford*, by Henry Friedman and Sander Meredeen. *Journal of Economic History* 41: 441–2.

Review of *The Ownership Theory of the Trade Union*, by Donald L. Martin. *Journal of Economic Issues* (Dec 1981), 1099–1102.

Review of *The Origins and Development of Labor Economics: A Chapter in the History of Social Thought*, by Paul J. McNulty, *Journal of Economic Literature* 19: 1083–5.

'Schumpeter as a Historian of Economic Thought,' in Helmut Frisch (ed.) *Schumpeterian Economics*, Eastbourne, East Sussex, England: Praeger, 143–61.

1982

'Opportunity in the Face of Disaster: A Review of the Economic Literature on Famine,' in Kevin M. Cahill (ed.) *Famine*, Maryknoll, NY: Orbis, 75–81.

'Patterns of Regional Decline and Growth: The Past and What Has Been Happening Lately,' in William Fellner (ed.) *A Study in Contemporary Economic Problems, 1982* (series). Washington: American Enterprise Institute, 1–56.

'Schumpeter as a Historian of Economic Thought,' [reprinted from Frisch, *Schumpeterian Economics*, Eastbourne, East Sussex, England: Praeger, 1981.

'G.L.S. Shackle as a Historian of Economic Thought,' in Warren J. Samuel (ed.) *Research in the History of Economic Thought and Methodology: A Research Annual*, volume 1. Greenwich, CT: JAI Press, 113–30 (Schumpeter) and 223–8 (Shackle).

[Also reprinted in Warren J. Samuels (ed.), item listed immediately above.]

Review of *Hospital Costs and Health Insurance*, by Martin Feldstein. *Journal of Political Economy* 90: 872–9.

Review of *The Economics of Population Growth*, by Julian Simon. *Population Studies* and *The Ultimate Resource*, by Julian Simon. *Population Studies* 36: 490–4.

1983

'Human Resources and Population Growth,' in Paul Streeten and Harry Maier (eds.) *Human Resources, Employment and Development*. Volume 2: Concepts, Measurement and Long-Run Perspective. Proceedings of the Sixth World Congress of the International Economic Association held in 1980 in Mexico City. London: Macmillan, 167–80.

'Tres Clases de economistas,' [a translation by Manuel Siquenza of 'The Tensions Between Abstraction and Generalization: The Uses of Economics] *Papeles de Economia Española*, 16: 275–8.

Review of *Population Change and Social Policy*, by Nathan Keyfitz. *Population and Development Review* 9: 727–30.

1984

'Collective Bargaining and Industrial Relations: The Past, the Present, and the Future,' in William Fellner (ed.) *Contemporary Economic Problems*, 1983–84. Washington: American Enterprise Institute, 287–322.

'Governmental Intervention and the Socioeconomic Background,' in Bela Gold *et al. Technological Progress and Industrial Leadership: The Growth of the U.S. Steel Industry, 1900–1970*. Lexington, MA: Lexington Books, 609–31.

'L'audience de Malthus aux Etats-Unis Comme Economiste,' being a translation of 'Malthus's Economics and Its Early American Reception,' in Antoinette Fauve-Chamoux, *Malthus, Hier et Aujourdhui*, Congrès international de démographie historique/CNRS mai 1980. Paris: Editions des CNRS, 1984. Being the Proceedings of a 1980 Paris Conference on the 150th anniversary of the birth of Thomas Robert Malthus, 117–25.

'Perlman on Shackle,' in Henry W. Spiegel and Warren J. Samuels (eds.) *Contemporary Economists in Perspective*, Greenwich, CT: JAI Press, 579–90.

'The Role of Population Projections for the Year 2000,' in Julian L. Simon and Herman Kahn (eds.) *The Resourceful Earth*. Oxford: Basil Blackwell, 50–66.

Review of *The Baby Boom Generation and the Economy*, by Louise B. Russell. *Journal of Economic History* 44: 224–6.

1985

'A Coming Inflection in the American Economic Policy?' in [Horst Klaus Recktenwald] *Staat und Ökonomie heute*, edited by Horst Hanusch, Karl W. Roskamp, and Jack Wiseman. Stuttgart and New York: Gustav Fischer Verlag, 135–45.

Review of *History of the Human Gamble*, by Reuven Brenner. *Journal of Economic Behavior and Organization* 6: 395–8.

1986

'Perceptions of our Discipline: Three Magisterial Treatments of the Evolution of Economic Thought,' History of Economic Society Meetings, May, 1985, George Mason University, Fairfax, VA. *Bulletin [of the History of Economics Society]*, (Winter), 9–28.

'Subjectivism and American Institutionalism,' in [Ludwig M. Lachmann], *Subjectivism, Intelligibility, and Economic Understanding: Essays in Honor of the 80th Birthday of Ludwig M. Lachmann.* Edited by Israel Kirzner. New York University Press, 268–80.

1987

'Are Five Billion [People on the Earth] Too Many?' *San Diego [California] Union* August 9, 1987. (Later syndicated).

'Concerning Winters of Discontent: Does Methodology or Rhetoric Contain the Answer to a Possible Malaise?' *International Journal of Social Economics* 14: 9–18.

'An Essay on Karl Pribram's *A History of Economic Reasoning,*' *Revue Economique* 38: 171–6.

'Political Purpose and the National Accounts,' *The Politics of Numbers*, edited by William Alonso and Paul Starr. New York: Russell Sage, 133–51.

1988

'Foreword,' Arthur F. Burns. *The Ongoing Revolution in American Banking.* Washington, D.C.: American Enterprise Institute v–x.

The Fundamental Issues in the Controversy of the [Macroeconomic] Policy Paradigms: Policies, Theories, and Underpinnings. A working paper published by the Institut für Weltwirtschaft an den Universität Kiel.

'On the Coming Senescence of American Manufacturing Competence,' in Horst Hanusch (ed.) *Evolutionary Economics: Applications of Schumpeter's Ideas*, New York: Cambridge University Press, 343–83.

1989

'Comment' on Philip T. Hoffman, 'Institutions and Agriculture in Old-Regime France,' *Journal of Institutional and Theoretical Economics* 145: 182–64.

'Comments I, 'On Stiglitz's *The Economic Role of the State,*' in Stiglitz, Joseph E. *et al. The Economic Role of the State*, Oxford: Blackwell, 89–106.

'Foreword,' in Cassing, James H. and Husted, Steven L. (eds.) *Capital, Technology, and Labour in the New Global Economy*, Washington: American Enterprise Institute.

1990

'Demographie et Fiscalite.' *[Paris] Le Figaro* June 8, 1990.

'Die Bienen-Fabel: Eine moderne Würdigung,' in Friederich A. von Hayek, Mark Perlman, and Frederick B. Kaye, *Bernard de Mandevilles Leben und Werk*, Düsseldorf/-Darmstadt (FRG): Verlag Wirtschaft und Finanzen GMBH. (Ein Unternehmen der Verlagsrupppe Handelsblatt), pp. 65–107. Being an interpretation of Bernard de Mandeville. *Fable of the Bees: Or, Public Vices Publick Benefits* [London, 1714].

'The Fabric of Economics and the Golden Threads of G.L.S. Shackle.' in Frowen, Stephen S.F. *Unknowledge and Choice in Economics.* London: Macmillan; and New York: St. Martin's, 9–19.

'Introduction,' (with Arnold Heertje) in Heertje, Arnold and Perlman, Mark (eds.) *Evolving Technology and Market Structure: Studies in Schumpeterian Economics*, Ann Arbor, Michigan University Press, 1–13.

'Preface;' 'Introduction' (with Klaus Weiermair), and 'The Evolution of Leibenstein's X-Efficiency Theory,' in Weiermair, Klaus and Perlman, Mark (eds.) *Studies in Economic*

Rationality: X-Efficiency Examined and Extolled. Essays Written in the Tradition of and to Honor Harvey Leibenstein, Ann Arbor: University of Michigan Press, 1–6, 7–26.

Review of *Breaking the Academic Mould: Economists and American Higher Learning in the Nineteenth Century*, edited by William J. Barber. *History of Political Economy* 22: 2 (Summer 1990), 406–8.

Studies in Economic Rationality: X-Efficiency Examined and Extolled, in Weiermair, Klaus and Perlman, Mark (eds.) *Essays Written in the Tradition of and to Honor Harvey Leibenstein*, Ann Arbor: University of Michigan Press.

Political Power and Social Change: The United States Faces a United Europe (ed. with Norman Ornstein) Washington, DC: American Enterprise Institute.

'Early Capital Theory in the Economics Journals: A Study of Imputed Induced Demand,' *Economic Notes*, 20: 58–88.

'On the Editing of American Economic Journals: Some Comments on the Earlier Journals and the Lessons Suggested.' *Economic Notes* 20: 159–72.

'Fraternity, Free Association, and Socio-Economic Analysis.' Being part of a Symposium on the French Revolution and the History of Economic Thought. In Samuels, Warren J. (ed.) *Research in the History of Economic Thought and Methodology: A Research Annual*, vol. 8. Greenwich, CT: JAI Press.

'Introduction' to Machlup, Fritz. *Essays in Economic Semantics*. New Brunswick, Transactions Press (2nd ed.) vii–xxi.

'Two Concurrent Explorations of the Frontiers of the Economic Science,' in *Colloque International: 'J.A. Schumpeter et J.M. Keynes'*, Paris: Centre National d'Enseignement a Distance de Vanve for the Universite de Droit, D'Economie, et de Sciences Sociales de Paris. Paris: Proc., 29–43.

Review of *The management of labor unions: Decision making with historical constraints*, by John T. Dunlop, *Journal of Economic Literature* 29: 111–12.

Horst Claus Recktenwald, A Memorial.

1992

Entrepreneurship, Technological Innovation, and Economic Growth: Studies in the Schumpeterian Tradition (ed. with Frederic M. Scherer), Ann Arbor: Michigan University Press.

Industry, Services, and Agriculture: The United States Faces a United Europe (ed. with Claude Barfield), Washington, DC: American Enterprise Institute.

'Harvey Leibenstein,' in *New Horizons in Economic Thought* by Warren Samuels (ed.) Cheltenham, Glos. (UK) Edward Elgar, 184–201.

'Agenda für die Zukunft der Mikroökonomen,' (translated into German from an article, 'Agenda for the Microeconomists' Future'), in Recktenwald, Horst-Klaus and Hanusch, Horst (eds.) *Ökonomische Wissenschaft in der Zukunft: Ansichten führender Ökonomen: (Economic Science in the Future: Perspectives by Eminent Scholars)*. Düsseldorf: Verlag Wirtschaft and Finanzen, 1992, 303–21.

'Understanding the 'Old' American Institutionalism,' *Revue d'Economie Politique*, 102 (1992), 281–295.

Review of *Essays on the Intellectual History of Economics*, by Jacob Viner. ed. by Douglas Irwin. *Journal of the History of Economic Thought*, 14: 116–18.

Review of *The Economic Problems in Biblical and Patristic Thought* by Barry Gordon in *Judaism* 161: 106–08.

1993

(with Charles McCann). 'On Thinking About George Stigler,' *Economic Journal*, 104: 1–21.

'George Lennox Shackle,' *Review of Political Economy* 5: 270–2.

Review of *The Theory of Economic Growth From Hume to the Present* by Walt Rostow. *Research in the History of Economic Thought and Methodology: A Research Annual* vol. 13, Greenwich, CT: JAI Press.

Review of *Eminent Economists* by Michael Szenberg. *Journal of the History of Economic Thought* 15: 330–3.

'Rhetoric and Normativism: An Idiosyncratic Appraisal from the Standpoint of the History of Economic Thought, A Review Essay,' being reviews of Albert O. Hirschman, *The Rhetoric of Reaction*; and Donald N. McCloskey, *If You're So Smart: The Narrative of Economic Expertise*, in *Methodus*, 5 (June): 129–39.

'Series Editor's Note' to Shigeto Tsuru, *Japan's Capitalism: Creative Defeat and Beyond*, Cambridge: Cambridge University Press, 267–70.

'Review of Roy Weintraub, *Stabilizing Dynamics: Constructing Economic Knowledge, Journal of the History and Philosophy of Science* 1993, 60: 669–71.

1994

'Introduction,' Joseph A. Schumpeter, *History of Economic Analysis*, London: Routledge, [1954] 1994, xvii–xxxix.

'Foreword,' Charles R. McCann, Jr. *Probability Foundations of Economic Theory*, London & New York: Routledge, ix–xi.

'Introduction,' (with Yuichi Shionoya) in Shionoya, Yuichi and Perlman, Mark (eds.) *Schumpeter in the History of Ideas*, Ann Arbor: University of Michigan Press, 1–3.

'Commentary,' in Shionoya, Yuichi and Perlman, Mark (eds.) *Schumpeter in the History of Ideas*, Ann Arbor: University of Michigan Press, 125–7.

'Introduction,' in (with Yuichi Shionoya) Shionoya, Yuichi and Perlman, Mark, *Innovation in Technology, Industries and Institutions: Studies in Schumpeterian Perspectives*, Ann Arbor: University of Michigan Press, 1–6.

'Remarks to the History of Economics Society Pertaining to the Reprinting of Schumpeter's *History of Economic Analysis*,' presented at the History of Economics Society meetings, June 1994, Babson Park.

1995

'The Population Summit: Reflections on the World's Leading Problem.' *Population Development Review*, 21 (June): 341–9.

Review of Laurence S. Moss and Christopher K. Ryan, (eds.) *Economic Thought in Spain: Selected Essays of Marjorie Grice-Hutchinson, Journal of the History of Economic Thought* 17: 166–7.

with Vibha Kapuria-Foreman. 'An Economic Historian's Economist: Remembering Simon Kuznets,' *Economic Journal* 105(433): 1524–47.

Review of Johannes J. Klant, *The Nature of Economic Thought: Essays in Economic Methodology*, in *European Journal of the History of Economic Thought* 2: 227–30.

'What Makes My Mind Tick,' *The American Economist*, XXXIX, Fall 1995, 6–27.

'Foreword,' Kofi Kissi Dompere and Ejaz. *The Epistemics of Development Economics: Toward a Methodological Critique and Unity*, Westport (CT): Greenwood Publishing Group, Inc., ix–xi.

Review of Walt Whitman Rostow's *Theorists of Economic Growth from David Hume to the Present; With a Perspective on the Next Century. Research in the History of Economic Thought and Methodology*, vol. 13. Greenwich, CT: JAI Press, 279–85.

Review of Wolfgang F. Stolper's *Joseph Alois Schumpeter – The Public Life of a Private Man. Zeitschrift für Nationalökonmie*, 62: 94–7.

'Preface,' G.C. Harcourt, *Capitalism, Socialism, and Post-Keynesianism: Selected Essays* of G.C. Harcourt. Economists of the Twentieth Century. Aldershot: UK; Brookfield (VT). Edward Elgar, vii–x.

1996

The Character of Economic Thought, Economic Characters, and Economic Institutions: Selected Essays by Mark Perlman. Ann Arbor: University of Michigan Press.

With Ernst Helmstädter, 'Introduction,' in *Behavioral Norms, Technological Progress and Economic Dynamics: Studies in Schumpeterian Economics,* edited by Ernst Helmstädter and Mark Perlman. Ann Arbor: University of Michigan Press.

With Enrico Colombatto, 'Introduction,' in *The Rational Foundations of Economic Behaviour,* edited by Kenneth Arrow, Enrico Colombatto, Mark Perlman and Christian Schmidt.

Proceedings of the IEA Conference held in Turin, Italy. London: Macmillan XIX–XXVI. 'Economics and social conscience: The theoretical case'

With Charles R. McCann, Jr. 'Varieties of Uncertainty' in *Uncertainty in Economic Thought,* edited by Christian Schmidt. Cheltenham, Glos. U.K.: Edward Elgar Ltd, 9–20.

Review of *Aging and Old Age* by Richard A. Posner for *Population and Development Review.*

Review of *Economic Thought Before Adam Smith: An Austrian Perspective of the History of Economic Thought,* Volume 1, and *Classical Economics: An Austrian Perspective of the History of Economic Thought,* Volume 2. By Murray N. Rothbard. *Economic Journal,* 106: 1414–48.

(With David Bloom, Dale Jorgenson, Henry Rosovsky, and Amartya Sen [Chrmn]. 'Faculty of Arts and Sciences – Memorial Minute: Harvey J. Leibenstein,' *Harvard University Gazette,* April 25.

'Assessing the Reprinting of Schumpeter's *History of Economic Analysis'.* From Laurence S. Moss (ed.) *Joseph A. Schumpeter, Historian of Economics.* Perspectives on the History of Economic Thought: Selected Papers from the History of Economics Conference, 1994. London & New York, 15–20.

1997

'Some Aspects of Our Western Heritage,' in *Ancient Economic Thought* edited by B.B. Price. London: Routledge, 63–77.

Introduction to the 1997 Edition,' in Joseph A. Schumpeter (ed.) *Ten Great Economists* with an Introduction by Mark Perlman, University of Pittsburg. London: Routledge, vii–xli.

'Economics and Social Conscience: The Harcourt Case', in [Harcourt, Geoff] *Capital Controversy Post-Keynesian Economics and the History of Economics: Essays in Honour of Geoff Harcourt.* Edited by Arestis, Philip, Gabriel Palma and Malcolm Sawyer. London & New York: Routledge, 456–65.

(With Charles R. McCann, Jr) *The Phillars of Economic Understanding: Ideas and Traditions,* Ann Arbor: University of Michigan Press.

'Hayek, the Purposes of the Economic Market, and the Institutionalist Tradition,' in Frowen, Stephen F. (ed.) *Hayek The Economist and Social Philosopher: A Critical Retrospect,* London: Macmillan, 221–35.

With James W. Dean, 'Harvey Leibenstein as a Pioneer in Our Time,' *Economic Journal,* 108: 132–52.

'Styles of Population Economics: A Review Essay,' *Population and Economic Development* 24: 846–59.

'Keynesian Economics and the Meaning of Uncertainty' with Charles R. McCann in [Tarshis, Lorie] *Keynesianism and the Keynesian Revolution in America: A Memorial Volume in Honour of Lorie Tarshis,* edited by Omar F. Hamouda and Betsey B. Price. Cheltenham, UK and Northamption, MA: Edward Elgar, 173–85.

'The opening of America Academia to Jews in the Post-World War II Period' in [Waxman, Mordecai] *Yakar Le-Mordecai: Jubilee Volume in Honor of Rabbi Mordecai Waxman.* Great Neck, NY: KTAV Publishing House, Inc., Temple Israel of Great Neck, NY, 327–41.

1999

Review of *The Rise of political Economy as a Science: Methodology and the Classical Economists* by Deborah A. Redman. *Journal of Economics/Zeitschrift für National Ökonomie.* 69: 197–201.

Review of *Some British Empiricists in the Social Sciences, 1650–1900* by Richard Stone. *Population and Economic Development,* 25: 367–74.

(with Morgan Marietta), 'Die Nobelpreise der ökonomischen Wissenschaft in den Jahren 1994 bis 1998,' in Grüske, Karl-Dieter (Hrsg.) *Die Nobeslpreisträger der ökonomischen Wissenschaft. Band IV: 1994–1998,* Düsseldorf: Verlag Wirtschaft und Finanzen, s. 21–62.

'Authority Systems and Schools of Economic thought,' in [Arnold Heertje] *Economics, Welfare Policy and the History of Economic Thought: Essays in Honour of Arnold Heertje,* Edited by Martin M. G. Fase, Walter Kanning and Donald A. Walker Cheltenham, UK: Edward Elgar, 410–27.

2000

(with Charles R. McCann, Jr.) *The Pillars of Economic Understanding: Factors and Markets.* Volume II, Ann Arbor: University of Michigan Press.

(with Francisco Louca), (eds.) *Is Economics an Evolutionary Science?* Cheltenham, Glos, UK & Northampton, MA.: Edward Elgar.

'Introduction' and 'Mind-sets,' and 'why Veblen Was Ineffectual,' in Louca and Perlman *op. cit.,* pp. 3–10, and 13–24, respectively.

(with Morgan Marietta), 'The Uses of Authority in Economics: Shared Intellectual Frameworks as the Foundation of Personal Persuasion and Schools of Economic Thought,' *American Journal of Economics & Sociology,* 59, April 2000, 151–89.

'Getting On and Off the Merry-Go-Round,' in *Exemplary Economists* edited by Roger Backhouse and Roger H. Middleton, vol. 1. Cheltenham, Glos, UK & Northampton, MA.: Edward Elgar, 74–91.

2001

Two Phases of Kuznets's Interest in Schumpeter. In [Warren Samuels' *Economics, Broadly Considered.* Edited by Steven g. Medema. London and New York: Routledge, pp. 128–41.

Schumpeter and Schools of Economic Thought, in [Frisch, Helmut] edited by Günther Chaloupek, Alois Guger, ewald Nowotny, and Gerhard Schwoediauer. *Ökonomie in theorie und Praxis: Eine Festschrift für Helmut Frisch.* Springer–Verlag, Berlin–Heidelberg New York, pp. 279–96.

2002

Career Disagreements: Simon Kuznets's Relationships with Joseph alois Schumpeter and Arthur Frank Burns, in *Studien zur Geschichte der oekonomischen Theorie XXII: Ideen, Methoden und entwicklungen der Dogmengeschichte (Schriften des vereins fuer Socialpolitik, Neue folge 115/XXII)* edited by Christian Scheer. Berlin: Buncker & Humblot.

Mark writes:

There are several more, including an essay on Kuznets and Schumpter in a *Festschrift* volume for Warren Samuels edited by Steve Medema; a piece on my father in the new *Dictionary of American Biography*; a piece on personal conflicts in recent economics, being a summary of the Kuznets-Schumpeter and the Kuznets-Arthur Frank Burns antagonisms which is to appear in the publications of the History of Economics Committee of the Verein fuer Socialpolitik.

September 2000

Index